VIRGIL'S WORKS

THE AENEID · ECLOGUES · GEORGICS

Translated by J. W. MACKAIL

With an introduction by CHARLES L. DURHAM, Ph.D.

Professor of Latin, Cornell University

THE

MODERN LIBRARY

NEW YORK

INTRODUCTION COPYRIGHT, 1934,
BY THE MODERN LIBRARY, INC.

Random House IS THE PUBLISHER OF

THE MODERN LIBRARY

BENNETT A. CERF · DONALD S. KLOPFER · ROBERT K. HAAS

Manufactured in the United States of America

Printed by Parkway Printing Company   Bound by H. Wolff

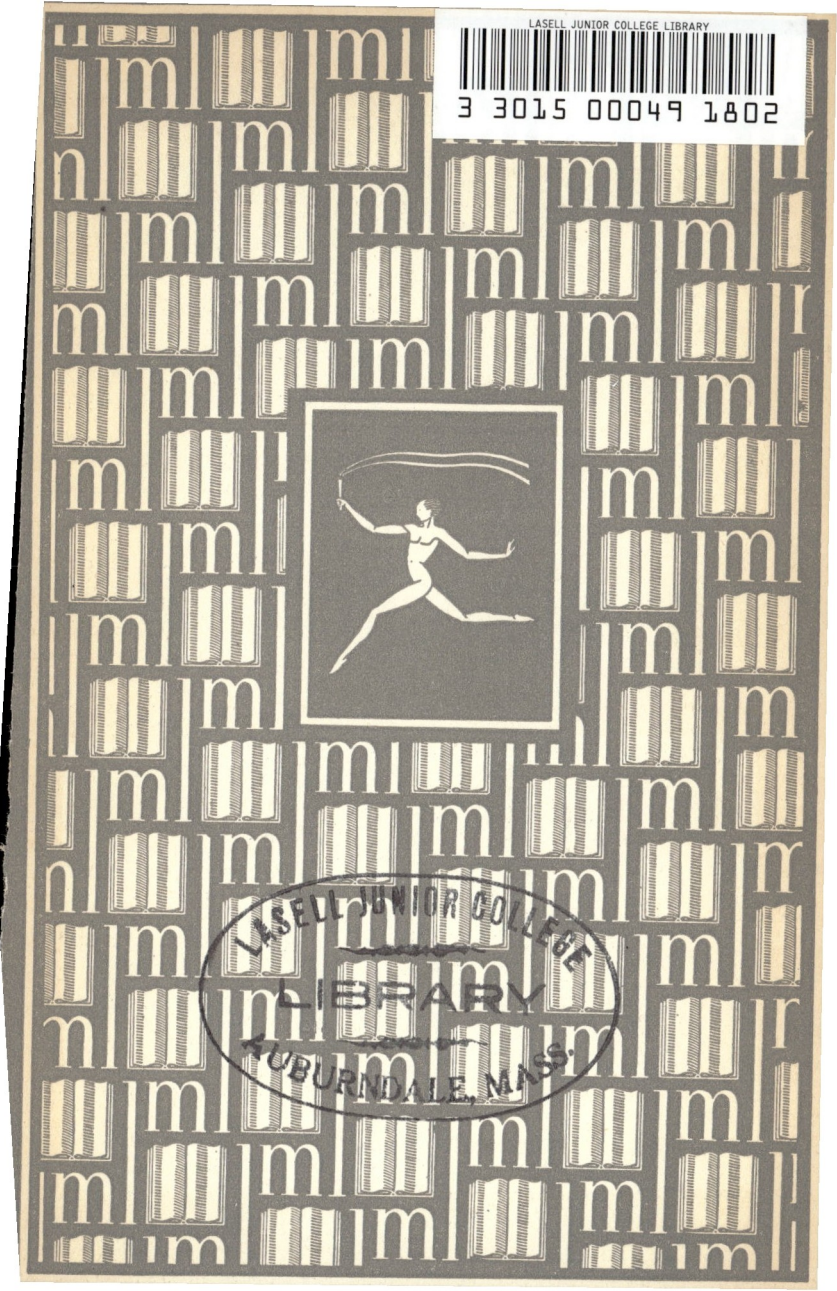

VIRGIL'S WORKS

THE MODERN LIBRARY
OF THE WORLD'S BEST BOOKS

The publishers will be pleased to send, upon request, an illustrated folder setting forth the purpose and scope of THE MODERN LIBRARY, *and listing each volume in the series. Every reader of books will find titles he has been looking for, handsomely printed, in unabridged editions, and at an unusually low price.*

CONTENTS

	PAGE
INTRODUCTION BY CHARLES L. DURHAM	ix

THE AENEID

Book First 3
   The Coming of Aeneas to Carthage
Book Second 23
   The Story of the Sack of Troy
Book Third 44
   The Story of the Seven Years' Wandering
Book Fourth 63
   The Love of Dido, and Her End
Book Fifth 82
   The Games of the Fleet
Book Sixth 104
   The Vision of the Under World
Book Seventh 128
   The Landing in Latium, and the Roll of the Armies of Italy
Book Eighth 150
   The Embassage to Evander
Book Ninth 169
   The Siege of the Trojan Camp
Book Tenth 190
   The Battle on the Beach
Book Eleventh 214
   The Council of the Latins, and the Life and Death of Camilla
Book Twelfth 237
   The Slaying of Turnus

CONTENTS

THE ECLOGUES

	PAGE
Eclogue I	265
Tityrus	
Eclogue II	268
Alexis	
Eclogue III	270
Palaemon	
Eclogue IV	274
Pollio	
Eclogue V	276
Daphnis	
Eclogue VI	279
Silenus	
Eclogue VII	282
Meliboeus	
Eclogue VIII	284
The Sorceress	
Eclogue IX	288
Moeris	
Eclogue X	290
Gallus	

THE GEORGICS

Book First	295
Book Second	309
Book Third	323
Book Fourth	338

INTRODUCTION

By Charles L. Durham

*Mantua me genuit; Calabri rapuere; tenet nunc
Parthenope. Cecini pascua, rura, duces.*[1]

So ran the epitaph which an old but surely unreliable tradition tells us that Rome's greatest poet himself composed to mark his final resting place. The inscription with the grave has disappeared, and another spot on Posilipo is pointed out to the curious traveler today as the tomb of Virgil, but posterity still knows him as the author of the three immortal works, the *Bucolics* (rura) [the *Eclogues* in the Modern Library edition], the *Georgics* (pascua), and the *Aeneid* (duces).

Born near Mantua on the fifteenth of October, 70 B.C., Publius Vergilius Maro died on September twenty-first, 19 B.C., at Brindisi, in Calabria, where after an interrupted sojourn in Greece, he had barely landed once again on the soil of his beloved Italy. His ashes were carried back to Campania, for there in Sorrento and Posilipo, his favorite spots near Naples, he had for many years lived and pursued his literary labors.

From no authentic sources or contemporary evidence do we learn, nor do we need to know, concerning Virgil all of those more intimate details of private life and of personal experience without which a poet like Catullus or Horace could not adequately be interpreted.

A lofty genius, set apart from the emotions of love and hate, from passing fancy, from the closer comradeship of those with puny talents, with few intimate friendships, he went on

---

[1] Mantua bore me; the Calabrians snatched me away; Naples now holds me. I sang of pastures, country, leaders.

his majestic and secluded way. By the brilliancy of his talents, Virgil won the favor of Maecenas and merited the recognition of Augustus. The plaudits of the Roman populace, however, on the rare occasions of his visits to the great city, were, we are told, the source of intense embarrassment to his modest and retiring spirit. To the genial Horace there was "no soul of purer white" nor one "to whom he was more deeply attached." It was "optimus Vergilius" who vouched for the lyric bard to Maecenas, the head of perhaps the most famous literary circle that the world has ever known. His younger contemporary, the elegiac poet Propertius, heralds the coming of the *Aeneid* by the author whose recognition had already been assured through the *Bucolics* (the *Eclogues*) and the *Georgics:* "Virgil now wakes to life the arms of Trojan Aeneas and the city walls he built on the Lavinian strand! Yield ye, O writers of Rome, yield ye, Greeks! Something mightier than the *Iliad* now comes to birth!"[1] Ovid—born in 43 B.C. and therefore only twenty-four years of age when Virgil died—laments in his later years of exile at Tomi, far from the imperial city and Italy, that he "had only caught a glimpse" of Virgil, but in the *Ars Amatoria* this singer of tender loves bears eloquent witness to "Exile Aeneas, the founding of lofty Rome" as the most brilliant work of the Latian land, and his famous prophecy in the *Amores* has been more than fulfilled: "Tityrus (the *Bucolics*) and the Harvest (the *Georgics*) and the Arms of Aeneas (the *Aeneid*) will be read as long as Rome is mistress of a conquered world."

The splendor of Virgil's poetic genius was thus fully recognized in his own lifetime, and through the succeeding centuries his greatness is universally attested. Silius Italicus[2] was a devoted admirer of Virgil. He possessed a famous col-

---

[1] *qui nunc Aeneas Troiani suscitat arma*
  jactaque Lavinis moenia litoribus.
 Cedite Romani scriptores, cedite Grai;
  nescio quid maius nascitur Iliade.

[2] Silius, who died in 101 A.D., was the composer of the longest poem in the Latin language, the *Punica,* an epos on the Second Punic War. His greatest literary indebtedness was to Virgil.

INTRODUCTION

lection of Virgilian busts, and annually celebrated the poet's birthday with great solemnity, visiting his tomb with as much reverence as if it had been a temple. To St. Augustine (354-430 A.D.), Virgil was *poeta ille clarissimus*, and even in the succeeding darker ages before the Renaissance the Virgilian influence persisted in manifold ways. Dante, in the first Canto of the Inferno, acknowledges Virgil as his inspiration:

> *Tu se' lo mio maestro, e il mio autore!* [1]

In the second Canto, Virgil is addressed:

> *O anima cortese Mantovana,*
> *di cui la fama ancor nel mondo dura,*
> *e durerà quanto il moto lontana!* ...

Professor Mackail [2] has finely said: "Virgil is not merely a prince of poets; he is one of the makers and founders of English poetry. He has exercised, and continues to exercise, this influence both directly and by indirect transmission. The influence has been continuous, from Bede and Cynewulf in the eighth century down to poets who are writing now. Virgil is one of the few Latin classics who were never lost sight of even in the Dark Ages. He has always been a schoolbook for youth, a treasure-house for mature appreciation, a model for artists. He is a 'lord of language,' as Tennyson truly says of him, who stands out as having shown what perfect expression is, as having achieved the utmost beauty, melody and significance of which human words seem to be capable. He has given expression, once for all, to many of our highest thoughts and most profound emotions. Nor has he, like others who in their day have been great germinal forces, become absorbed in or been replaced by his successors. For he is a consummate artist; and a work of art is substantive and permanent in its value. It is not a means to an end, but an end

---

[1] "Thou art my master and my author."
"O courteous Mantuan Spirit, whose fame still lasts in the world, and will last as long as Time!" (*Divine Comedy*—Modern Library, pp. 21, 25.)

[2] *Virgil and His Meaning to the World of Today.* Boston, 1922, p. 7.

attained. Homer, Virgil, Shakespeare remain alive after hundreds or thousands of years."

Virgil's immortal fame rests on his three "major" works, the *Bucolics*, the *Georgics*, the *Aeneid*. The earliest of these, the *Bucolics*, published when the poet was in his late twenties, shows a perfection of technique which surely must have had a background of rather extensive earlier experience in the poetic art. Within a short time after the death of the poet a group purporting to be youthful poems of Virgil was published, and by the end of the first century A.D., several additional poems, some of considerable length, were also currently attributed to the great Maro. Concerning the authenticity of these minor poems, scholarship is today sharply divided, some critics accepting as genuinely Virgilian practically all of the poems in this so-called *Appendix Vergiliana*, while others reject the whole collection. In the translation of Mackail presented in this volume, the "minor works" are not included, and properly so, for Virgil as the heritage of the literary world is the creator of the *Bucolics*, the *Georgics*, the *Aeneid*.

The Bucolics. These poems, ten in number, were composed between 42 B.C. and 39 B.C., when Virgil was approximately thirty years of age. The name "Bucolic," *i.e.* "pastoral," is appropriate for each poem in the group with the possible exception of the fourth; the term Eclogue ("selection") appears in the manuscripts for the individual poems in the group, and the name "Eclogues" is frequently applied to the group as a whole.

The *Bucolics* are formally pastoral poems in the spirit of the Idyls of the Sicilian poet Theocritus (flourished *c.* 280 B.C.). They are however far from being mere superficial reproductions of the shepherd songs with the rustic swains of Arcadia and Sicily. On this transmitted form of pastoral poetry Virgil has imprinted the mark of his own genius, and through his own poetic power the Latin "pastoral" in Virgil's hands became for all succeeding ages the classic form of this type of poetry. There has unfortunately been an effort to interpret as allegorical well nigh all of the *Bucolics*. The Fourth Eclogue in particular, the so-called Messianic Prophecy, with Virgil

INTRODUCTION

in the rôle of a pagan Isaiah, has been a center of attraction for the allegorizers of every generation.

The Georgics. In this perhaps the most perfect work of Virgil, we see a poet who has now become the truly national singer of the glories of Italy with a clearly heralded promise of the *Aeneid,* the epos of Rome's destiny as ruler of the world.

Dedicated to Maecenas and undertaken apparently at his suggestion, the introductory lines of the First Georgic give in adequate outline the subjects of the four books into which the work is divided.

The *Georgics* do not form a practical manual of husbandry, and the purpose of the work is primarily in no sense didactic. To be sure, Italian agriculture had in large measure been destroyed by generations of civil war, and the Roman world was at the time in sore need of a clarion call back to the simple life, to nature, to industry and unremitting toil, but the *Georgics* as a work of poetic art is essentially the song of the glories of Italy. No one who reads the magnificent passage in the second book (lines 136-137) can fail to be thrilled with its patriotic fervor. In no other work of Virgil do we so fully realize the perfection of the poet's craftsmanship, the felicity of his thought and word, the serene majesty and beauty of his poetic style.

After seven laborious years, Virgil completed the *Georgics* with their scarcely more than two thousand lines, and the finished work was read to Augustus on his return from the East in 29 B.C. The remainder of the poet's life was devoted to the composition of the *Aeneid,* but this great work still lacked the finishing hand when Virgil died in 19 B.C. We are informed that his last wish was that the whole poem should be suppressed, but at the behest of Augustus it was subsequently given to the world substantially as Virgil had left it.

The Aeneid. To the general lover of literature, Virgil's best-known work is unquestionably the *Aeneid.* Unfortunately, however, the average reader's familiarity with this great poem does not extend beyond the sixth of the twelve books, and he

INTRODUCTION

therefore completely fails to grasp the real spirit and full meaning of this consummate work of art.

The *Aeneid* is the epic song of Rome's imperial destiny and of the mission of the House of Julius through Augustus to direct and guide the conquered world.

The fall of Troy, the wanderings of Aeneas and his devoted band, the sojourn in Carthage and the pathetic episode of Dido's love, the landing at Cumae, all lead to that mighty scene in the Elysian Fields, where, in the sixth book, Anchises relates to Aeneas the glories of the Rome that is to be.

The concluding six books with their stirring drama are introduced by a new invocation to the Muse and a new prologue, as a mightier story is now begun. The Trojans land where the Tiber flows into the sea; the ever-mindful wrath of Juno still pursues them with her deadly hatred; the Italian hosts are marshalled to repel the sons of a Troy that would rise again. The leader of the native forces, Turnus—the most dramatic character perhaps in the whole *Aeneid*—stands out as the supreme foe of Aeneas. Innumerable brilliant and moving episodes are interspersed: that of Nisus and Euryalus; the death of the young prince Pallas; Camilla, the virgin warrior. Then comes the end with tragic climax in the closing book whose mighty force Virgil does not elsewhere equal. The hostile gods are appeased at last; Turnus falls in single combat with the hero Aeneas. The decree of heaven will be fulfilled, the imperial grandeur of Rome as mistress of the world is now assured!

No introduction to the works of Virgil would be complete without Tennyson's tribute on the occasion of the nineteenth centenary of Virgil's death:

> Roman Virgil, thou that singest
>   Ilion's lofty temples robed in fire,
> Ilion falling, Rome arising,
>   wars, and filial faith, and Dido's pyre;
>
> Landscape-lover, lord of language
>   more than he that sang the Works and Days,
> All the chosen coin of fancy
>   flashing out from many a golden phrase;

Thou that singest wheat and woodland,
	tilth and vineyard, hive and horse and herd;
All the charm of all the Muses
	often flowering in a lonely word;

Poet of the happy Tityrus
	piping underneath his beechen bowers;
Poet of the poet-satyr
	whom the laughing shepherd bound with flowers?

Chanter of the Pollio, glorying
	in the blissful years again to be,
Summers of the snakeless meadow,
	unlaborious earth and oarless sea;

Thou that seëst Universal
	Nature moved by Universal Mind;
Thou majestic in thy sadness
	at the doubtful doom of human kind;

Light among the vanish'd ages;
	star that gildest yet this phantom shore;
Golden branch amid the shadows,
	kings and realms that pass to rise no more;

Now thy Forum roars no longer,
	fallen every purple Cæsar's dome—
Tho' thine ocean-roll of rhythm
	sound for ever of Imperial Rome—

Now the Rome of slaves hath perish'd,
	and the Rome of freemen holds her place,
I, from out the Northern Island
	sunder'd once from all the human race,

I salute thee, Mantovano,
	I that loved thee since my day began,
Wielder of the stateliest measure
	ever moulded by the lips of man.

Professor Mackail regards Virgil not only as the precursor, but also as "one of the most direct, powerful and continuous sources of the whole splendid body of our poetry from the fourteenth to the twentieth century. As a master, a model, an inspiration, he has not lost and will not lose his virtue," and with this opinion I cordially agree.

As a contribution toward a more intimate knowledge of the

works of the great Mantuan, the inclusion of the Mackail translation of Virgil in the Modern Library is most welcome. The version itself is accurate and adequate, and is distinguished by that felicity of expression with which this eminent Latinist has for so many years charmed the thousands of his readers.

Cornell University,
Ithaca, New York.

THE AENEID

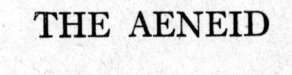

BOOK FIRST

THE COMING OF AENEAS TO CARTHAGE

I SING of arms and the man who came of old, a fated wanderer, from the coasts of Troy to Italy and the shore of Lavinium; hard driven on land and on the deep by the violence of heaven, by reason of cruel Juno's unforgetful anger, and hard bestead in war also, ere he might found a city and carry his gods into Latium; from whom is the Latin race, the lords of Alba, and high-embattled Rome.

Muse, tell me why, for what attaint of her deity, or in what vexation, did the Queen of heaven urge on a man excellent in goodness to circle through all those afflictions, to face all those toils? Is anger so fierce in celestial spirits?

There was a city of ancient days that Tyrian settlers dwelt in, Carthage, over against Italy and the Tiber mouths afar; plenteous of wealth, and most grim in the arts of war; wherein, they say, alone beyond all other lands had Juno her seat, and held Samos itself less dear. Here was her armour, here her chariot; even now, if fate permit, the goddess strives to nurture it for dominion over the nations. Nevertheless she had heard that a race was issuing of the blood of Troy, which sometime should overthrow her Tyrian fortress; from it should come a people, lord of lands and tyrannous in war, the destroyer of Libya: thus the Fates unrolled their volume. Fearful of that, the daughter of Saturn, the old war in her remembrance that she fought at Troy for her beloved Argos long ago,—nor had the springs of her anger nor that bitter pain yet gone out of mind: deep stored in her soul lies the judgment of Paris, the insult of her slighted beauty, the hated race and the dignities of ravished Ganymede; fired by these also, she drove all over ocean the Trojan remnant left of the Greek host and merciless

Achilles, and held them afar from Latium; and many a year were they wandering driven of fate around all the seas. Such work was it to found the Roman people.

Hardly out of sight of the land of Sicily did they set their sails joyously to sea, and upturned the salt foam with brazen prow, when Juno, the undying wound still deep in her heart, thus broke out alone:

'Am I then to abandon my baffled purpose, powerless to keep the Teucrian king from Italy? and because fate forbids me? Could Pallas lay the Argive fleet in ashes, and sink the Argives in the sea, for the guilt and madness of Oilean Ajax alone? Her hand darted Jove's flying fire from the clouds, scattered their ships, upturned the seas in tempest; him, his pierced breast yet breathing forth the flame, she caught in a whirlwind and impaled on a spike of rock. But I, who move queen among immortals, I sister and wife of Jove, wage warfare all these years with a single people; and is there any who still adores Juno's divinity, or will lay sacrifice with prayer on her altars?'

Such thoughts inly revolving in her fiery heart, the goddess reaches Aeolia, the home of storm-clouds, the land teeming with furious southern gales. Here in a dreary cavern Aeolus keeps under royal dominion and yokes in dungeon fetters the struggling winds and resounding storms. They with mighty moan rage indignant round their mountain barriers. In his lofty citadel Aeolus sits sceptred, assuages their temper and soothes their rage; else would they carry with them seas and lands, and the depth of heaven, and sweep them through space in their flying course. But, fearful of this, the Lord omnipotent has hidden them in caverned gloom, and laid mountains high over them, and appointed them a ruler, who under a fixed covenant should know to strain and slacken the reins at command. To him now Juno spoke thus in suppliant accents:

'Aeolus—for to thee has the father of gods and king of men given to lull and to lift the wind-blown waves—the race I hate sails the Tyrrhene sea, carrying Ilium and her conquered household-gods into Italy. Rouse thy winds to fury, and overwhelm and sink their hulls, or drive them asunder and strew ocean with their corpses. Mine are twice seven nymphs of passing loveliness, and Deïopea is most excellent in beauty of them all; her will I unite to thee in wedlock to be thine for ever; that for this thy service she may fulfil all her years at thy side, and make thee father of a beautiful race.'

Aeolus thus returned: 'Thine, O queen, the task to search out what thou wilt; for me it is right to do thy bidding. From thee I hold all this my realm, from thee my sceptre and Jove's grace; thou dost grant me to take my seat at the feasts of the gods, and makest me sovereign over clouds and storms.'

Even with these words, turning his spear, he struck the side of the hollow hill, and the winds, as in banded array, pour where passage is given them, and cover earth with eddying blasts. East wind and south wind together, and the gusty south-wester, falling prone on the sea, stir it up from its lowest chambers, and roll vast billows to the shore. Behind rises shouting of men and creaking of cordage. In a moment clouds blot sky and daylight from the Teucrians' eyes; black night broods over the deep. The heavens crash with thunder, and the air quivers with incessant flashes; all menaces them with instant death. Straightway Aeneas' frame grows unnerved and chill, and stretching either hand to heaven, he cries thus aloud: 'Ah, thrice and four times happy they who found their doom in high-embattled Troy before their fathers' faces! Ah, son of Tydeus, bravest of the Grecian race, that I could not have fallen on the Ilian plains, and gasped out this my life beneath thine hand! where under the spear of Aeacides lies fierce Hector, lies mighty Sarpedon; where Simoïs so often caught and whirled beneath his wave shields and helmets and brave bodies of men.'

As the cry leaves his lips, a gust of the shrill north strikes full on the sail and raises the waves up to heaven. The oars are snapped; the prow swings away and gives her side to the waves; down in a heap comes a broken mountain of water. These hang on the wave's ridge; to these the yawning billow shows ground amid the surge, where the tide churns with sand. Three ships the south wind catches and hurls on hidden rocks, rocks amid the waves which Italians call the Altars, a vast reef banking the sea. Three the east forces from the deep into shallows and quicksands, piteous to see, dashes on shoals and girdles with a sandbank. One, wherein loyal Orontes and his Lycians rode, before his very eys a huge sea descending strikes astern. The helmsman is dashed away and rolled forward headlong; her as she lies the billow sends spinning thrice round with it, and engulfs in the swift whirl. Scattered swimmers appear in the dreary eddy, armour of men, timbers and Trojan treasure amid the water. Ere now the stout ship of Ilioneus, ere now of brave Achates, and she wherein Abas rode, and she wherein aged Aletes, have yielded to the storm; the framework of their sides is started, and they all let in the deadly stream through gaping leaks.

Meanwhile Neptune discerned with astonishment the loud roaring of the vexed sea, the tempest let loose from prison, and the still water boiling up from its depths, and looking forth over the deep, raised his head serene above the waves. He sees Aeneas' fleet scattered all over ocean, the Trojans overwhelmed by the waves and the tempest of heaven. Juno's guile and wrath lay clear to her brother's eye; East wind and West he calls before him, and thereon speaks thus:

'Stand you then so sure in your confidence of birth? Dare you without my warrant, O winds, confound sky and earth, and raise so huge coil? you whom I— But better to still the vexed waves; for a second transgression you shall pay me another penalty. Speed your flight, and say this to your king: not to him but to me was allotted the empire of ocean and the stern trident. His fastness is on the monstrous rocks where thou and thine, East wind, dwell: there let Aeolus glory in his court and reign over the barred prison of his winds.'

Thus he speaks, and quicker than the word he soothes the swollen seas, chases away the gathered clouds, and restores the sunlight. Cymothoë and Triton together push the ships strongly off the sharp reef; himself he eases them with his trident, channels the vast quicksands, and assuages the sea, gliding on light wheels along the watery floor. Even as when oft in a throng of people strife has risen, and the base multitude rage in their minds, and now brands and stones are flying; madness lends arms; then if perchance they catch sight of one reverend for goodness and worth, they are silent and stand by with attentive ear; he with speech sways their temper and soothes their breasts; even so has fallen all the thunder of ocean, when riding with forward gaze beneath a cloudless sky the lord of the sea wheels his coursers and lets his gliding chariot fly with loosened rein.

The outworn Aeneadae hasten to run for the nearest shore, and steer for the coast of Libya. There a place lies deep withdrawn; an island forms a harbour, thrusting forth its sides, whereon all the waves break from the open sea and part into the hollows of the bay. On this side and that enormous cliffs rise threatening heaven, and twin crags beneath whose crest the sheltered water lies wide and calm; above is a background of waving forest, and a woodland overhangs dark with rustling shade. Beneath the seaward brow is a rock-hung cavern, within it fresh springs and seats in the living stone, a haunt of nymphs; here tired ships need no fetters to hold nor anchor to fasten them with crooked fang. Hither with seven sail gathered of all his company Aeneas glides in; and disembarking on the land so sorely desired the Trojans gain the chosen beach, and fling their limbs dripping with brine upon the shore. Forthwith Achates has struck a spark from the flint and caught the fire on leaves, and laying dry fuel round kindled the touchwood into flame. Then, in their weary case, they fetch out sea-soaked corn and weapons of corn-dressing, and set to parch over the fire and bruise with stones the grain that they have rescued.

Meanwhile Aeneas scales the cliff, and scans the whole view wide over ocean, if he may see aught of Antheus and his storm-tossed Phrygian galleys, aught of Capys or of the lofty hulls that bear the arms of Caïcus. Ship in sight is none; three stags he espies straying on the shore; behind whole herds follow, and graze in long train across the valleys. Stopping short, he snatched up a bow and swift arrows, the arms that trusty Achates was carrying; and first the leaders, their stately heads high with branching antlers, then the common herd he lays low, as he drives them with his shafts in a broken crowd through the leafy woods. Nor stays he till seven great victims are stretched on the sod, and the number of his ships is equalled. Thence he seeks the harbour and parts them among all his company; next the wine-casks that good Acestes had loaded on the Trinacrian beach, the hero's gift at their departure, he shares, and assuages their sorrowing hearts with speech:

'O comrades, for not ere now are we ignorant of ill, O tried by heavier fortunes, to these also God will appoint an end. The fury of Scylla and the roaring recesses of her crags you have come nigh, and known the rocks of the Cyclops. Recall your courage, put sorrow and fear away. This too sometime we shall haply remember with delight. Through chequered fortunes, through many perilous ways, we steer for Latium, where destiny points us a quiet home. There the realm of Troy may rise again unforbidden. Keep heart, and endure till prosperous fortune come.'

Such words he utters, and sick with deep distress he feigns hope on his face, and keeps his anguish hidden deep in his breast. The others set to the spoil that is to be their banquet, sever chine from ribs and lay bare the flesh; some cut it into pieces and pierce it still quivering with spits; others plant caldrons on the beach and feed them with flame. Then they repair their strength with food, and lying along the grass take their fill of old wine and fat venison. After hunger is driven away by feasting, and the board cleared, they talk with lingering regret of their lost companions, swaying between hope and fear, whether they may believe them yet alive, or now meeting the last enemy and deaf to mortal call. Most does good Aeneas inly wail the loss now of valiant Orontes, now of Amycus, the cruel doom of Lycus, of brave Gyas, and brave Cloanthus.

And now they ceased; when Jupiter looked through the height of air on the sail-winged sea and outspread lands, the shores and broad countries, and looking stood on the cope of heaven, and cast down his eyes on the realm of Libya. To him thus troubled at heart Venus, her bright eyes brimming with tears, sorrowfully speaks:

'O thou who dost sway mortal and immortal things in eternal lordship with the terror of thy thunderbolt, how can my Aeneas have transgressed so grievously against thee? how his Trojans? on whom, after so many deaths borne, all the world is barred for Italy's sake. From them sometime in the rolling years the Romans were to arise indeed; from them were to be rulers who, renewing the blood of Teucer, should hold sea and all lands in dominion. This thou didst promise: why, O father, is thy decree reversed? This was my solace for the wretched ruin of sunken Troy, doom balanced against doom. Now so many woes are spent, and the same fortune still pursues them; Lord and King, what limit dost thou set to their distresses? Antenor could elude the encircling Achaeans, could thread in safety the Illyrian bays and inmost realms of the Liburnians, could scale Timavus' source, whence through nine mouths pours the bursting tide amid dreary moans of the mountain, and covers the fields with hoarse waters. Yet here did he set Patavium town, a dwelling-place for his Teucrians, gave his name to a nation and hung up the armour of Troy; now settled in peace, he rests and is in quiet. We, thy children, we whom thou beckonest to the heights of heaven, our fleet miserably cast away for a single enemy's anger, are betrayed and severed far from the Italian coasts. Is this the reward of goodness? is it thus thou dost restore our throne?'

Smiling on her with that look which clears sky and storms, the parent of men and gods lightly kissed his daughter's lips; then answered thus:

'Spare thy fear, Cytherean; thy people's destiny abides unshaken. Thine eyes shall see the city Lavinium, their promised fortress; thou shalt exalt to the starry heaven thy noble

Aeneas; nor is my decree reversed. He whom thou lovest (for I will speak, since this care keeps torturing thee, and will unroll further the secret records of fate) shall wage a great war in Italy, and crush warrior nations; he shall appoint his people a law and a city; till the third summer see him reigning in Latium, and three winters' camps are overpast among the conquered Rutulians. But the boy Ascanius, whose surname is now Iülus—Ilus he was while the Ilian state stood sovereign—thirty great circles of rolling months shall he fulfil in government; he shall carry the kingdom from its seat in Lavinium, and make a strong fortress of Alba the Long. Here the full space of thrice an hundred years shall the kingdom endure under the race of Hector's kin, till the royal priestess Ilia from Mars' embrace shall give birth to a twin progeny. Thence shall Romulus, gay in the tawny hide of the she-wolf that nursed him, take up their line, and name them Romans after his own name. To these I ordain neither period nor boundary of empire: I have given them dominion without end. Nay, harsh Juno, who in her fear now troubles earth and sea and sky, shall change to better counsels, and with me shall cherish the lords of the world, the gowned race of Rome. Thus is it willed. A day will come in the lapse of cycles, when the house of Assaracus shall lay Phthia and famed Mycenae in bondage, and reign over conquered Argos. From the fair line of Troy a Caesar shall arise, who shall limit his empire with ocean, his glory with the firmament, Julius, inheritor of great Iülus' name. Him one day, thy care done, thou shalt welcome to heaven loaded with Eastern spoils; to him too shall vows be addressed. Then shall war cease, and the iron ages soften. Hoar Faith and Vesta, Quirinus and Remus brothers again, shall deliver statutes. The dreadful steel-clenched gates of War shall be shut fast; inhuman Fury, his hands bound behind him with an hundred rivets of brass, shall sit within on murderous weapons, shrieking with ghastly blood-stained lips.'

So speaking, he sends Maia's son down from above, that the lands and towers of Carthage, the new town, may receive the Trojans with open welcome; lest Dido, ignorant of doom, might debar them her land. Flying through the depth of air on winged oarage, the fleet messenger alights on the Libyan coasts. At once he does his bidding; at once, for a god willed it, the Phœnicians allay their haughty temper; the queen above all takes to herself grace and compassion towards the Teucrians.

But good Aeneas, nightlong revolving many and many a thing, issues forth, so soon as bountiful light is given, to explore the strange country; to what coasts the wind has borne him, who are their habitants, men or wild beasts, for all he sees is wilderness, this he resolves to search, and bring back the certainty to his comrades. The fleet he hides close in embosoming groves beneath a caverned rock, amid rustling shadow of the woodland; himself, Achates alone following, he strides forward, clenching in his hand two broad-headed spears. And amid the forest his mother crossed his way, wearing the face and raiment of a maiden, the arms of a maiden of Sparta, or like Harpalyce of Thrace when she tries her coursers and outstrips the winged speed of Hebrus in her flight. For in huntress fashion had she slung the ready bow from her shoulder, and left her blown tresses free, bared her knee, and knotted together her garments' flowing folds. 'Ho, gallants,' she begins, 'shew me if haply you have seen a sister of mine straying here girt with quiver and dappled iynx-pelt, or pressing with shouts on the track of a foaming boar.'

Thus Venus, and Venus' son answering thus began:

'Sound nor sight have I had of sister of thine, O maiden, how may I name thee? for thy face is not mortal, nor thy voice of human tone; O goddess assuredly! sister of Phoebus perchance, or one of the nymphs' blood? Be thou gracious, whoso thou art, and lighten our distress; deign to instruct us beneath what skies, on what coast of the world, we are thrown. Driven hither by wind and desolate waves, we wander in a strange land among unknown men. Many a sacrifice shall fall by our hand before thine altars.'

Then Venus: 'Nay, to no such offerings do I aspire. Tyrian

maidens are wont ever to wear the quiver, to tie the purple buskin high above their ankle. Punic is the realm thou seest, Tyrian the people, and the city of Agenor's kin; but their borders are Libyan, a race untameable in war. Dido sways the sceptre, who flying her brother set sail from the Tyrian town. Long is the tale of crime, long and intricate; but I will follow its argument in brief. Her husband was Sychaeus, wealthiest in lands of the Phoenicians, and loved of her with all-fated passion; to whom with virgin rites her father had given her maidenhood in wedlock. But the kingdom of Tyre was in her brother Pygmalion's hands, a monster of guilt unparalleled. Between these madness came; the unnatural brother, blind with lust of gold, and reckless of his sister's love, lays Sychaeus low before the altars with stealthy unsuspected weapon; and for long he hid the deed, and by many a crafty pretence cheated her love-sickness with hollow hope. But in slumber came the very ghost of her unburied husband, lifting up a face pale in wonderful wise; he exposed the cruel altars and his breast stabbed through with steel, and unwove all the blind web of household guilt. Then he counsels hasty flight and abandonment of her country, and to aid her passage discloses treasures long hidden underground, an untold mass of silver and gold. Stirred thereby, Dido gathered a company for flight. All assemble in whom hatred of the tyrant was relentless or terror keen; they seize on ships that chanced to lie ready, and load them with the gold. Pygmalion's hoarded wealth is borne overseas; a woman guides the enterprise. They came at last to the land where thou wilt descry a city now great, New Carthage, and her rising citadel, and bought ground, called thence Byrsa, as much as a bull's hide would encircle. But who, I pray, are you, or from what coasts come, or whither hold you your way?'

At her question he, sighing and drawing speech deep from his breast, thus replied:

'Ah goddess, should I go on retracing from the fountain head, were time free to hear the history of our woes, sooner will the evening star lay day asleep in the closed gates of heaven. Us, as from ancient Troy (if the name of Troy has haply passed through your ears) we sailed over distant seas, the tempest at his own wild will has driven on the Libyan coast. I am Aeneas the good, who carry in my fleet the household gods I rescued from the enemy; my fame is known high in heaven. I seek Italy my country, and my kin of Jove's supreme blood. With twenty sail did I climb the Phrygian sea; oracular tokens led me on; my goddess mother pointed the way; scarce seven survive the shattering of wave and wind. Myself unknown, destitute, driven from Europe and Asia, I wander over the Libyan wilderness.'

But staying longer complaint, Venus thus broke in on his half-told sorrows:

'Whoso thou art, not hated I think of the immortals dost thou draw the breath of life, who hast reached the Tyrian city. Only go on, and betake thee hence to the courts of the queen. For I declare to thee thy comrades are restored, thy fleet driven back into safety by the shifted northern gales, except my parents were pretenders, and unavailing the augury they taught me. Behold these twelve swans in joyous line, whom, stooping from the tract of heaven, the bird of Jove routed over the open sky; now in long train they seem either to take the ground or already to look down on the ground they took. As these again disport with clapping wings, and utter their notes as they circle the sky in company, even so do those ships and crews of thine either lie fast in harbour or glide under full sail into the harbour mouth. Only go on, and point thy steps where the pathway leads thee.'

Speaking she turned away, and her neck shone roseate, the immortal tresses on her head breathed the fragrance of deity; her raiment fell flowing down to her feet, and a very goddess was manifest in her tread. He knew her for his mother, and with this cry pursued her flight: 'Thou also merciless! why mockest thou thy son so often in feigned likeness? Why is it forbidden to clasp hand in hand, to hear and to reply in true speech?' Thus reproaching her he bends his steps towards the city. But Venus girt them in their going with dim mist, and her deity wrapped them deep in clothing of cloud, that none might descry them, none touch them, or work delay, or ask wherefore they came. Herself she speeds through the sky to Paphos, and joyfully revisits her habitation, where the temple and its hundred altars steam with Sabaean incense, and are fresh with fragrance of chaplets in her worship.

They meantime have hasted along where the pathway points, and now were climbing the hill which hangs enormous over the city, and looks down on its facing towers. Aeneas marvels at the mass of building, pastoral huts once of old, marvels at the gateways and hum of the paved streets. The Tyrians are hot at work to trace the walls, to rear the citadel, and roll up great stones by hand, or to choose a place for their dwelling and enclose it with a furrow. They ordain justice and magistrates, and the august senate. Here some are digging harbours, here others lay the deep foundations for theatres, and hew out of the cliff vast columns, the lofty ornaments of the stage to be: even as bees when summer is fresh over the flowery country ply their task beneath the sun when they lead forth their nation's grown brood, or when they press the liquid honey and strain their cells with nectarous sweets, or relieve the loaded incomers, or in banded array drive the idle herd of drones far from their folds; the hive is aswarm, and the odorous honey smells sweet of thyme. 'Happy they whose city already rises!' cries Aeneas, looking on the town roofs below. Girt in the cloud he passes amid them, wonderful to tell, and mingling with the throng is descried of none.

In the mid town was a grove deep with luxuriant shade, wherein first the Phoenicians, buffeted by wave and whirlwind, dug up the token Queen Juno had appointed, the head of a war-horse: thereby was their race to be through all ages illustrious in war and at ease in living. Here to Juno was Sidonian Dido founding a vast temple, rich with offerings and her godhead's presence: brazen steps rose on the threshold, the beams were clamped with brass, doors of brass grated on the hinge. First in this grove did a strange chance meet his steps and allay his fears; first here did Aeneas dare to hope for safety and have fairer trust in his shattered fortunes. For while he closely scans the temple that towers above him, while, awaiting the queen, he inly marvels at the fortune of the city, at her craftsmen's handiwork and labouring toil, he sees ranged in order the battles of Ilium, that war whose fame was already rumoured through all the world, the sons of Atreus, and Priam, and Achilles whom both found pitiless. He stopped and cried weeping, 'What land is left, Achates, what tract on earth that is not full of our agony? Behold Priam! Here too is the meed of honour, here are tears over fortune and mortal estate touches the soul. Dismiss thy fears; the fame of this will somehow, I deem, bring salvation.'

So speaks he, and feeds his soul with the painted show, sighing often the while, and his face wet with an abundant flood. For he saw, how warring round the Trojan citadel here the Greeks fled, the men of Troy hard upon them; here the Phrygians, plumed Achilles in his chariot pressing their flight. Not far away he knows, weeping, the snowy canvas of Rhesus' tents, which, betrayed in their first sleep, the blood-stained son of Tydeus has laid desolate in heaped slaughter, and turns the fiery steeds away to the camp ere ever they tasted Trojan fodder or drunk of Xanthus. On another panel Troïlus, his armour flung away in flight—luckless boy, ill-matched to meet Achilles!—is borne along by his horses, and thrown back entangled with his empty chariot, still clutching the reins; his neck and hair are dragged over the ground, and his reversed spear scores the dust. Meanwhile the Ilian women went with disordered tresses to unfriendly Pallas' temple, and bore the votive garment, mournfully beating their breasts with open hands: the goddess turning away held her eyes fast on the ground. Thrice had Achilles whirled Hector round the walls of Troy, and was selling the lifeless body for gold; then at last he heaves a loud and heart-deep groan, as he descried the spoils, the chariot, the very body of his friend, and Priam outstretching unarmed hands. Himself too he saw and knew joining battle with the foremost Achaeans, knew the Eastern ranks and swart Memnon's armour. Penthesilea leads her crescent-shielded Amazonian columns in furious courage with thousands around her, clasping a golden belt under her naked breast, a warrior maiden who dares the battle-shock of men.

While these marvels meet Dardanian Aeneas' eyes, while he hangs rapt in one long breathless gaze, Dido the queen entered the precinct, beautiful exceedingly, a youthful train thronging round her. Even as on Eurotas' banks or along the Cynthian ridges Diana wheels the dance, while behind her a thousand mountain nymphs crowd to left and right; she carries quiver on shoulder, and as she moves overtops all her goddesses; Latona's heart thrills with silent joy; such was Dido, so she joyously advanced amid the throng, urging on the toils of her rising empire. Then in the gates of the goddess, beneath the central vaulting of the temple, she took her seat girt with arms and high enthroned. And now she gave justice and laws to her people, and adjusted or allotted their taskwork in due portion; when suddenly Aeneas sees advancing with a great crowd about them Antheus and Sergestus and brave Cloanthus, and other of his Trojans, whom the black squall had sundered at sea and borne far away on the coast. Dizzy with the shock of joy and fear he and Achates together were on fire with eagerness to clasp their hands; but in confused uncertainty they keep hidden, and clothed in the sheltering cloud wait to espy what fortune befalls them, where they are leaving their fleet ashore, why they now come; for they advanced, chosen men from all the ships, praying for grace, and clamorously sought the temple.

After they entered in, and public speech was granted, aged Ilioneus with placid mien thus began:

'Queen, to whom Jupiter has given to found this new city, and lay the yoke of justice upon haughty tribes, we beseech thee, we wretched Trojans storm-driven over all the seas, stay the dreadful flames from our ships; spare a guiltless race, and bend a gracious regard on our fortunes. We are not come to deal slaughter through Libyan homes, or to drive plundered spoils to the coast. Such violence sits not in our mind, nor is a conquered people so insolent. There is a place Greeks name Hesperia an ancient land, mighty in arms and foison of the clod; Oenotrian men dwelt therein; now rumour is that a younger race from their captain's name have called it Italy. This was our course ... when Orion rising on us through the cloudrack with sudden surge bore us on blind shoals, and scattered us afar with his boisterous gales and whelming brine over waves and trackless reefs. To these your coasts we have floated, a scanty remnant. What race of men, what land how barbarous soever, allows such a custom for its own? We are debarred a resting-place on the beach; they rise in war, and forbid us to set foot on the brink of their land. If you slight human kinship and mortal arms, yet look for gods who mark innocence and guilt. Aeneas was our king, foremost of men in righteousness, incomparable in goodness as in warlike arms; whom if fate still preserves, if he draws the breath of heaven and lies not yet low in dispiteous gloom, fear we have none; nor mayest thou repent of challenging the contest of service. In Sicilian territory too are cities and arms, and Acestes himself is of the high Trojan blood. Grant us to draw ashore our storm-shattered fleet, to shape forest trees into planks and strip them for oars; so, if to Italy we may steer with our king and comrades found, Italy and Latium shall we glady seek; but if salvation is clean gone, if the Libyan gulf holds thee, kindest lord of thy Trojans, and Iülus our hope survives no more, seek we then at least the straits of Sicily, the homes open for us whence we sailed hither, and Acestes for our king.'

Thus Ilioneus, and all the Dardanian company murmured assent. ... Then Dido, lowering her eyes upon them, briefly speaks:

'Cheer your anxious hearts, O Teucrians; put by your care. Hard fortune in a strange realm forces me to this task, to keep watch and ward on my wide frontiers. Who can be ignorant of the race of Aeneas' people, who of Troy town and her men and deeds, or of the great war's consuming fire? Not so dull are the hearts of our Punic wearing, not so far does the sun yoke his steeds from our Tyrian town. Whether your choice be broad Hesperia, the fields of Saturn's dominion, or Eryx for your country and Acestes for your king, my escort shall speed you in safety, my arsenals supply your need. Or will you even find rest here with me and share my kingdom? The city I establish is yours; draw your ships ashore; Trojan and Tyrian shall be held by me in even balance. And would that he your king, that Aeneas were here, storm-driven to this same haven! But I will send messengers along the coast, and bid them trace Libya to its limits, if haply he strays shipwrecked in forest or town.'

Stirred by these words brave Achates and lord Aeneas both ere now burned to break through the cloud. Achates first accosts Aeneas: 'Goddess-born, what purpose now rises in thy spirit? Thou seest that all is safe, that our fleet and comrades are restored. One only is wanting, whom our eyes saw whelmed amid the waves; all else answers to thy mother's words.'

Scarce had he spoken when the encircling cloud suddenly parts and melts into clear air. Aeneas stood discovered in sheen of brilliant light, like a god in face and shoulders; for his mother's self had shed on her son the grace of clustered locks, the radiant light of youth, and the lustre of joyous eyes; as when ivory takes beauty under the artist's hand, or when silver or Parian stone is inlaid in gold. Then breaking in on all with unexpected speech he thus addresses the queen:

'I whom you seek am here before you, Aeneas of Troy, snatched from the Libyan waves. O thou who alone hast pitied Troy's untold agonies, thou who with us, a remnant of the Grecian foe, the cup of misfortune drained on land and sea, with us in our utter want dost share thy city and home! to render meet recompense is not possible for us, O Dido, nor for all who scattered over the wide world are left of our Dardanian race. The gods grant thee worthy reward, if their deity turn any regard on goodness, if aught avails justice and conscious purity of soul. What happy ages bore thee? what mighty parents gave birth to a soul like thine? While rivers run into the sea, while the mountain shadows move across their slopes, while the stars feed in the fields of heaven, ever shall thine

broidery, and a veil with woven border of yellow acanthus-flower, that once decked Helen of Argos, her mother Leda's wondrous gift; Helen had borne them from Mycenae, when she sought Troy towers and a lawless bridal; the sceptre too that Ilione, Priam's eldest daughter, once had worn, a beaded necklace, and a double circlet of jewelled gold. Achates, hasting on his message, bent his way towards the ships.

But in the Cytherean's breast new arts, new schemes revolve; that Cupid, changed in form and feature, may come in sweet Ascanius' room, and his gifts kindle the queen to madness and set her inmost sense aflame. Verily she fears the uncertain house, the double-tongued race of Tyre; cruel Juno frets her, and at nightfall her care floods back. Therefore to winged Love she speaks these words:

'Son, who art my strength and sovereignty, son, who alone scornest the mighty father's Typhon-quelling shafts, to thee I fly for succour, and sue humbly to thy deity. How Aeneas thy brother is driven about all the sea-coasts by bitter Juno's malignity, thou knowest, and hast often grieved in our grief. Now Dido the Phoenician holds him stayed with soft words, and I tremble to think how the welcome of Juno's house may issue; she will not be idle where all hinges on the event. Wherefore I counsel to prevent her wiles and circle the queen with flame, that, unalterable by any deity, she may be held on my side by passionate love for Aeneas. Take now my thought how to do this. The boy prince, my chiefest care, makes ready at his dear father's summons to go to the Sidonian city, carrying gifts that survive the sea and the flames of Troy. Him will I hide deep asleep in my holy habitation, high on Cythera's hills or in Idalium, that he may not know nor cross our wiles. Do thou but for one night feign his form, and, boy as thou art, put on the familiar face of a boy; so when in festal cheer, amid royal dainties and streaming wine, Dido shall take thee to her lap, shall fold thee in her clasp and kiss thee close and sweet, thou mayest imbreathe a hidden fire and unsuspected poison.'

Love obeys his dear mother's words, lays by his wings, and

honour, thy name and praises endure in whatsoever lands may summon me.' With these words he advances his right hand to dear Ilioneus, his left to Serestus; then to the rest, brave Gyas and brave Cloanthus.

Dido the Sidonian stood astonished, first at the sight of him, then at his strange fortunes, and thus broke into speech:

'What fate follows thee, goddess-born, through perilous ways? what violence throws thee on this evil coast? Art thou that Aeneas whom Venus the bountiful bore to Dardanian Anchises by the wave of Phrygian Simoïs? And well I remember how Teucer came to Sidon, when exiled from his native land he sought Belus' aid to gain new realms; Belus my father even then ravaged rich Cyprus and held it under his conquering sway. From that time forth have I known the fall of the Trojan city, known thy name and the Pelasgian princes. Their very foe would extol the Teucrians with highest praises, and boasted himself a branch of the ancient Teucrian stem. Come therefore, O men, and enter our house. Me too has a like fortune driven through many a woe, and willed at last to find my rest in this land. Not ignorant of ill I learn to succour the afflicted.'

With such tale she leads Aeneas into the royal house, and orders sacrifice in the gods' temples. Therewith she sends to his crews on the shore twenty bulls, an hundred great bristly-backed swine, an hundred fat lambs and their mothers with them, gifts of the day's gladness.... But the palace within is decked with splendour of royal state, and a banquet made ready amid the halls. The coverings are curiously wrought in splendid purple; on the tables is massy silver and deeds of ancestral valour graven in gold, all the long course of history drawn through many a heroic name from the nation's primal antiquity.

Aeneas—for a father's affection let not his spirit rest—sends Achates speeding to his ships, to carry this news to Ascanius, and lead him to the town: in Ascanius is fixed all the parent's loving care. Presents likewise he bids him bring saved from the wreck of Ilium, a mantle stiff with gold em-

walks rejoicingly with Iülus' tread. But Venus pours gentle dew of slumber on Ascanius' limbs, and lifts him lulled in her lap to the tall Idalian groves of her deity, where soft amaracus folds him round with the shadowed sweetness of its odorous blossoms. And now, obedient to her words, Cupid went merrily in Achates' guiding, with the royal gifts for the Tyrians. Already at his coming the queen has taken her seat in the midmost on her golden throne under the splendid tapestries; now lord Aeneas, now too the men of Troy gather, and all recline on the strewn purple. Servants pour water on their hands, deal corn from baskets, and bring napkins with closecut pile. Fifty handmaids are within, whose task is in their course to keep unfailing store and kindle the household fire. An hundred others, and as many pages all of like age, are charged to load the board with food and array the cups. Therewithal the Tyrians are gathered full in the wide feasting chamber, and take their appointed places on the broidered cushions. They marvel at Aeneas' gifts, marvel at Iülus, at the god's burning face and feigned speech, at the mantle and veil broidered with yellow acanthus-flower. Above all the hapless Phoenician, victim to coming doom, cannot satiate her soul, but, stirred alike by the boy and the gifts, she gazes and takes fire. He, when hanging clasped on Aeneas' neck he had satisfied all the deluded parent's love, makes his way to the queen; the queen clings to him with her eyes and all her soul and ever and anon fondles him in her lap, ah, poor Dido! witless how mighty a deity sinks into her breast; but he, mindful of his mother the Acidalian, begins touch by touch to efface Sychaeus, and sows the surprise of a living love in the longsince-unstirred spirit and disaccustomed heart.

Soon as the noise of banquet ceased and the board was cleared, they set down great bowls and enwreathe the wine. The house is filled with hum of voices eddying through the spacious chambers; blazing cressets hang from netted gold, and torches rout the night with flame. Now the queen called for a heavy cup of jewelled gold, and filled it with pure wine; therewith was the use of Belus and all of Belus' race: then the hall was silenced. 'Jupiter,' she cries, 'for thou art reputed lawgiver of hospitality, grant that this be a joyful day to the Tyrians and the voyagers from Troy, a day to live in our children's memory. Bacchus, the giver of gladness, be with us, and gracious Juno; and you, O Tyrians, do full honour to our gathering.' She spoke, and poured liquid libation on the board, which done, she first herself touched it lightly with her lips, then handed it to Bitias in challenge; he valiantly drained the foaming cup, and drew a deep draught from the brimming gold. The other princes followed. Long-haired Iopas, he whom ancient Atlas taught, chants to his gilded lyre; he sings of the wandering moon and the sun's travails; whence is the human race and the brute, whence water and fire; of Arcturus, the rainy Hyades, and the twin Ploughing-oxen; why wintry suns make such haste to dip in ocean, or what delay clogs the lingering nights. Tyrians and Trojans after them redouble applause. Therewithal luckless Dido wore the night in changing talk, and drank long draughts of love, asking many a thing of Priam, many a thing of Hector; now in what armour the son of the Morning came; now of what breed were Diomede's horses; now of the stature of Achilles. 'Nay, come,' she cries, 'tell to us, O guest, from their first beginning the stratagems of the Grecians, thy people's woes, and thine own wanderings; for this is now the seventh summer that bears thee a wanderer over all lands and seas.'

BOOK SECOND

THE STORY OF THE SACK OF TROY

ALL were hushed, and sate with steadfast countenance; thereon, from his cushioned high seat, lord Aeneas thus began:

'Dreadful, O Queen, is the woe thou bidst me recall, how the Grecians pitiably overthrew the wealth and lordship of Troy; and I myself saw these things in all their horror, and I bore great part in them. What Myrmidon or Dolopian, or soldier of stern Ulysses, could in such a tale restrain his tears! and now night falls dewy from the steep of heaven, and the setting stars counsel to slumber. Yet if thy desire be such to know our calamities, and briefly to hear Troy's last agony, though my spirit shudders at the remembrance and recoils in pain, I will essay.

'Broken in war, beaten back by fate, and so many years now slid away, the Grecian captains build by Pallas' divine craft a horse of mountain bulk, and frame its ribs with sawn fir; they feign it vowed for their return, and this rumour goes about. Within the blind sides they stealthily imprison chosen men picked out one by one, and fill the vast cavern of its womb full with armed soldiery.

'There lies in sight an island well known in fame, Tenedos, rich of store while the realm of Priam endured, now but a bay and roadstead treacherous to ships. Hither they launch forth, and hide on the solitary shore: we fancied they were gone, and had run down the wind for Mycenae. So all the Teucrian land put her long grief away. The gates are flung open; men go rejoicingly to see the Doric camp, the deserted stations and abandoned shore. Here the Dolopian troops were tented, here cruel Achilles; here their squadrons lay; here they were wont to meet in battle-line. Some gaze astonished at the deadly gift of Minerva the Virgin, and wonder at the horse's bulk; and Thymoetes begins to advise that it be drawn within our walls and set in the citadel, whether in guile, or that the doom of Troy was even now setting thus. But Capys, and they whose mind was of better counsel, bid us either hurl sheer into the sea the guileful and sinister gift of Greece, and heap flames beneath to consume it, or pierce and explore the hollow hiding-place of its womb. The wavering crowd is torn apart in eager dispute.

'At that, foremost of all and with a great throng about him, Laocoön afire runs down from the fortress height, and cries from far: "Ah, wretched citizens, what height of madness is this? Believe you the foe is gone? or think you any Grecian gift is free of treachery? is it thus we know Ulysses? Either Achaeans are hid in this cage of wood, or the engine is fashioned against our walls to overlook the houses and descend upon the city; or some delusion lurks in it: trust not the horse, O Trojans. Be it what it may, I fear the Grecians even when they offer gifts." Thus speaking, he hurled his huge spear with mighty strength at the creature's side and the curved framework of the belly: the spear stood quivering, and the jarred cavern of the womb sounded hollow and uttered a groan. And had divine ordinance been thus and our soul not infatuate he had moved us to lay violent steel on the Argolic hiding place; and Troy would now stand, and you, tall towers of Priam, yet abide.

'Lo, Dardanian shepherds meanwhile dragged clamorously before the King a man with hands tied behind his back, who to compass this very thing, to lay Troy open to the Achaeans, had gone to meet their ignorant approach, confident of his courage, and doubly prepared to spin his snares or to meet assured death. From all sides, in eagerness to see, the people of Troy run streaming in, and vie in jeers at their prisoner. Know now the treachery of the Grecians, and from a single crime learn them all.... For as he stood amid our gaze confounded, disarmed, and cast his eyes around the Phrygian columns, "Alas!" he cried, "what land now, what seas may receive me? or what is the last doom that yet awaits a wretch like me? who have neither any place among the Grecians, and likewise the Dardanians clamour in wrath for the forfeit of my blood." At that lament our spirit was changed, and all assault stayed: we encourage him to speak, and tell of what blood he is sprung, or what assurance he brings his captors.

'"In all things assuredly," says he, "O King, befall what may, I will confess to thee the truth; nor will I deny myself of Argolic birth—this first—nor, if Fortune has made Sinon unhappy, shall her malice mould him to a cheat and a liar. If the tale of the name of Palamedes, son of Belus, has haply reached thine ears, and of his glorious rumour and renown; whom under false evidence the Pelasgians, because he forbade the war, sent innocent to death by wicked witness; now they bewail him when his light is quenched;—in his company, being near of blood, my father, poor as he was, sent me hither to arms from mine earliest years. While he stood unshaken in royalty and potent in the councils of the kings, we too wore a name and honour. When by subtle Ulysses' malice (no unknown tale do I tell) he left the upper regions, my shattered life crept on in darkness and grief, inly indignant at the fate of my innocent friend. Nor in my madness was I silent: and, should any chance offer, did I ever return a conqueror to my native Argos, I vowed myself his avenger, and with my words I stirred bitter hatred. From this came the first taint of ill; from this did Ulysses ever threaten me with fresh charges, from this flung dark sayings among the crowd and sought confederate arms. Nay, nor did he rest, till by Calchas' service—but yet why do I vainly unroll the unavailing tale, or why hold you in delay? If all Achaeans are ranked together in your mind, and it is enough that I bear the name, take your vengeance none too soon; this the Ithacan would desire, and the sons of Atreus buy at a great ransom."

'Then indeed we press on to ask and inquire the cause, witless of wickedness so great and Pelasgian craft. Tremblingly the false-hearted one pursues his speech:

'"Often would the Grecians have taken to flight, leaving

Troy behind, and disbanded in weariness of the long war; and would God they had! as often the fierce sea-tempest barred their way, and the south wind frightened them from going. Most of all when this horse already stood framed with beams of maple, stormclouds roared over all the sky. In perplexity we send Eurypylus to inquire of Phoebus' oracle; and he brings back from the sanctuary these words of terror: *With blood of a slain maiden, O Grecians, you appeased the winds when first you came to the Ilian coasts; with blood must you seek your return, and an Argive life be the accepted sacrifice.* When that utterance reached the ears of the crowd, their hearts stood still, and a cold shudder ran through their inmost sense: for whom is doom purposed? whom does Apollo demand? At this the Ithacan with loud clamour drags Calchas the soothsayer forth amidst them, and demands of him what is this the gods signify. And now many and one foretold me the villain's craft and cruelty, and silently saw what was to come. Twice five days he is speechless in his tent, and will not have any one denounced by his lips, or given up to death. Scarcely at last, at the loud urgence of the Ithacan, he breaks into speech as was planned, and appoints me for the altar. All consented; and each one's particular fear was turned, ah me! to my single destruction. And now the dreadful day was at hand; the rites were being ordered for me, the salted corn, and the chaplets to wreathe my temples. I broke away, I confess it, from death; I burst my bonds, and lurked all night darkling in the sedge of the marshy pool, till they might set their sails, if haply they should set them. Nor have I any hope more of seeing my old home nor my darling children and the father whom I desire. Of them will they even haply claim vengeance for my flight, and wash away this crime in their wretched death. By the heavenly powers I beseech thee, the deities to whom truth is known, by all the faith yet unsullied that is anywhere left among mortals, pity woes so great, pity a soul that bears intolerable wrong."

'At these his tears we grant him life, and accord our pity. Priam himself at once commands his shackles and strait bonds to be undone, and thus speaks with kindly words: "Whoso thou art, now and henceforth dismiss and forget the Greeks: thou shalt be ours. And unfold the truth to this my question: wherefore have they reared the bulk of this monstrous steed? who is their counsellor? or what their aim? what propitiation, or what engine of war is this?" He ended; the other, stored with the treacherous craft of Pelasgia, lifts to heaven his freed hands. "You, everlasting fires," he cries, "and your inviolable sanctity be my witness; you, O altars and accursed swords I fled, and chaplets of the gods I wore as victim! unblamed may I break the oath of Greek allegiance, unblamed hate them and bring all to light that they conceal; nor am I bound by any laws of country. Do thou only keep by thy promise, O Troy, and preserve faith with thy preserver, as my news shall be true, as my recompense ample.

' "All the hope of Greece, and the confidence in which the war began, ever centred in Pallas' aid. But since the wicked son of Tydeus, and Ulysses, forger of crime, made bold to tear the fated Palladium from her sanctuary, and cut down the sentries on the towered height; since they grasped the holy image, and dared with bloody hands to touch the maiden chaplets of the goddess; since then the hope of Greece ebbed and slid away backwards, their strength was broken, and the mind of the goddess estranged. Whereof the Tritonian gave token by no uncertain signs. Scarcely was the image set in the camp; flame shot sparkling from its lifted eyes, and salt sweat started over its body; thrice, wonderful to tell, it leapt from the ground with shield and spear quivering. Immediately Calchas prophesies that the seas must be explored in flight, nor may Troy towers be overthrown by Argive weapons, except they repeat their auspices at Argos, and bring back that divine presence they have borne away with them in the curved ships overseas. And now they have run down the wind for their native Mycenae, to gather arms and gods to attend them; they will remeasure ocean and be on you unawares. So Calchas expounds the omens. This image at his warning they reared in recompense for the Palladium and the injured deity, to expiate the horror of sacrilege. Yet Calchas bade them raise it to this vast size with oaken crossbeams, and build it up to heaven, that it might not find entry at the gates nor be drawn within the city, nor protect your people beneath the consecration of old. For if hand of yours should violate Minerva's offering, then utter destruction (the gods turn rather on himself his augury!) should be upon Priam's empire and the Phrygian people. But if under your hands it climbed into your city, Asia should advance in mighty war to the walls of Pelops, and a like fate awaited our children's children."

'So by Sinon's wiles and craft and perjury the thing gained belief; and we were ensnared by treachery and forced tears, we whom neither the son of Tydeus nor Achilles of Larissa, whom not ten years nor a thousand ships brought down.

'Hereon another sight, greater, alas! and far more terrible meets us, and alarms our thoughtless senses. Laocoön, allotted priest for Neptune, was slaying a great bull at the accustomed altars. And lo! from Tenedos, over the placid depths (I shudder as I recall) two snakes in enormous coils press down the sea and advance together to the shore; their breasts rise through the surge, and their blood-red crests overtop the waves; the rest trails through the main behind and wreathes back in voluminous curves; the brine gurgles and foams. And now they gained the fields, while their bloodshot eyes blazed with fire, and their tongues lapped and flickered in their hissing mouths. We scatter, blanched at the sight. They in unfaltering train make towards Laocoön. And first the serpents twine in their double embrace his two little children, and bite deep in their wretched limbs; then him likewise, as he comes up to help with arms in his hand, they seize and fasten in their enormous coils; and now twice clasping his waist, twice encircling his neck with their scaly bodies, they tower head and neck above him. He at once strains his hands to tear their knots apart, his fillets spattered with foul black venom; at once raises to heaven awful cries; as when, bellowing, a bull shakes the wavering axe from his neck and rushes wounded from the altar. But the two snakes glide away to the high sanctuary and seek the fierce Tritonian's citadel, and take shelter under the goddess' feet beneath the circle of her shield. Then indeed a strange terror thrills in all our amazed breasts; and Laocoön, men say, has fulfilled his crime's desert, in piercing the consecrated wood and hurling his guilty spear into its body. All cry out that the image must be drawn to its home and supplication made to her deity.... We breach the walls, and lay open the ramparts of the city. All set to the work; they fix sliding rollers under its feet, and tie hempen bands on its neck. The fated engine climbs our walls, big with arms. Around it boys and unwedded girls chant hymns and joyfully lay their hand on the rope. It moves up, and glides menacing into the middle of the town. O native land! O Ilium, house of gods, and Dardanian ramparts renowned in war! four times in the very gateway did it come to a stand, and four times armour rang in its womb. Yet we urge it on, mindless and infatuate, and plant the ill-omened portent in our hallowed citadel. Even then Cassandra opens her lips to the coming doom, lips at a god's bidding never believed by the Trojans. We, the wretched people to whom that day was our last, hang the shrines of the gods with festal boughs throughout the city. Meanwhile the heavens wheel on, and night rises from the sea, wrapping in her vast shadow earth and sky and the wiles of the Myrmidons; about the town the Teucrians are stretched in silence; slumber laps their tired limbs.

'And now the Argive squadron was sailing in order from Tenedos, and in the favouring stillness of the quiet moon sought the shores it knew; when the royal galley ran out a flame, and, protected by the gods' malign decrees, Sinon stealthily lets loose the imprisoned Grecians from their barriers of pine; the horse opens and restores them to the air; and joyfully issuing from the hollow wood, Thessander and Sthenelus the captains, and terrible Ulysses, slide down the dangling rope, with Acamas and Thoas and Neoptolemus son of Peleus, and Machaon first of all, and Menelaus, and Epeüs himself the artificer of the snare. They rush upon a city buried in drunken sleep; the watchmen are cut down, and at the open gates they welcome all their comrades, and unite their confederate bands.

'It was the time when by the gift of God rest comes stealing first and sweetest on unhappy men. In slumber, lo! before mine eyes Hector seemed to stand by, deep in grief and shedding abundant tears; torn by the chariot, as once of old, and black with gory dust, his swoln feet pierced with the thongs. Ah me! in what guise was he! how changed from the Hector who returns from putting on Achilles' spoils, or launching the fires of Phrygia on the Grecian ships! with ragged beard and tresses clotted with blood, and all the many wounds upon him that he received around his ancestral walls. Myself too weeping I seemed to accost him ere he spoke, and utter forth mournful accents: "O light of Dardania, O surest hope of the Trojans, what long delays have withheld thee? from what borders comest thou, Hector our desire? with what weary eyes we see thee, after many deaths of thy kin, after divers woes of people and city! What indignity has marred thy serene visage? or why discern I these wounds?" He replies naught, nor regards my idle questioning; but heavily drawing a heart-deep groan, "Ah, fly, goddess-born," he says, "and rescue thyself from these flames. The foe holds our walls; from her high ridges Troy is toppling down. Thy country and Priam ask no more. If our towers might be defended by strength of hand, this hand too had been their defence. Troy commends to thee her holy things and household gods; take them to accompany thy fate; seek for them a city, which, after all the seas have known thy wanderings, thou shalt at last establish in might." So speaks he, and carries forth in his hands from their inner shrine the chaplets and strength of Vesta, and the everlasting fire.

'Meanwhile the city is stirred with mingled agony; and more and more, though my father Anchises' house lay deep withdrawn and screened by trees, the noises grow clearer and the clash of armour swells. I shake myself from sleep and mount over the sloping roof, and stand there with ears attent: even as when flame catches a corn-field while south winds are furious, or the racing torrent of a mountain stream sweeps the fields, sweeps the smiling crops and labours of the oxen, and hurls the forest with it headlong; the shepherd in ignorant amaze hears the roar from the cliff-top. Then indeed proof is clear, and the treachery of the Grecians opens out. Already the house of Deïphobus has crashed down in wide ruin amid the overpowering flames; already Ucalegon is ablaze hard by: the broad Sigean bay it lit with the fire. Cries of men and blare of trumpets rise up. Madly I seize my arms, nor is there much purpose in arms; but my spirit is on fire to gather a band for fighting and charge for the citadel with my comrades. Fury and wrath drive me headlong, and I think how noble is death in arms.

'And lo! Panthus, eluding the Achaean weapons, Panthus son of Othrys, priest of Phoebus in the citadel, comes hurrying with the sacred vessels and conquered gods and his little grandchild in his hand, and runs distractedly towards my gates. "How stands the state, O Panthus? what stronghold are we to occupy?" Scarcely had I said so, when groaning he thus returns: "The crowning day is come, the irreversible time of the Dardanian land. No more are we a Trojan people; Ilium and the great glory of the Teucrians is no more. Angry Jupiter has cast all into the scale of Argos. The Grecians are lords of the burning town. The horse, standing high amid the city, pours forth armed men, and Sinon scatters fire, insolent in victory. Some are at the wide-flung gates, all the thousands that ever came from populous Mycenae. Others have beset the narrow streets with lowered weapons; edge and glittering point of steel stand drawn, ready for the slaughter; scarcely at the entry do the guards of the gates essay battle, and hold out in the blind fight."

'Heaven's will thus declared by the son of Othrys drives me amid flames and arms, where the baleful Fury calls, and tumult of shouting rises up. Rhipeus and Egyptus, most mighty in arms, join company with me; Hypanis and Dymas meet us in the moonlight and attach themselves to our side, and young Coroebus son of Mygdon. In those days it was he had come to Troy, fired with mad passion for Cassandra, and bore a son's aid to Priam and the Phrygians: hapless, that he listened not to his raving bride's counsels.... Seeing them close-ranked and daring for battle, I therewith began thus: "Men, hearts of supreme and useless bravery, if your desire be fixed to follow in daring the utmost; you see what is the fortune of our state: all the gods by whom this empire was upheld have gone forth, abandoning shrine and altar; your aid comes to a burning city. Let us die, and rush on their encircling weapons. The conquered have one safety, to hope for none."

'So their spirit is heightened to fury. Then, like wolves ravening in a black fog, whom mad malice of hunger has driven blindly forth, and their cubs left behind await with throats unslaked, through the weapons of the enemy we march to certain death, and hold our way straight into the town. Night's hollow shadow flits dark around us. Who may unfold in speech that night's horror and death-agony, or measure its woes in weeping? The ancient city falls with her long years of sovereignty; corpses lie stretched stiff all about the streets and houses and awful courts of the gods. Nor do Teucrians alone pay forfeit of their blood; once and again valour returns even in conquered hearts, and the victorious Grecians fall. Everywhere is cruel agony, everywhere terror, and the multiplied sight of death.

'First, with a great troop of Grecians attending him, Androgeos meets us, taking us in ignorance for an allied band, and opens on us with friendly words: "Hasten, my men; why idly linger so late? others plunder and harry the burning citadel; are you but now on your march from the tall ships?" He spoke, and immediately (for no answer of any assurance was offered) knew he was fallen among the foe. In amazement, he checked foot and voice; even as one who struggling through rough briers has trodden a snake on the ground unwarned, and suddenly starts back in affright as it rises in anger and puffs its dark-green throat out; even thus Androgeos drew away, terror-struck at the sight. We rush in and encircle them with serried arms, and cut them down dispersedly in their ignorance of the ground and seizure of panic. Fortune speeds our first labour. And hereat Coroebus, flushed with success and spirit, cries: "O comrades, follow me where fortune points before us the path of safety, and shews her favour. Let us exchange shields, and accoutre ourselves in Grecian suits; whether craft or courage, who will ask of an enemy? the foe shall arm our hands." Thus speaking, he next dons the plumed helmet and beautifully blazoned shield of Androgeos, and fits the Argive sword to his side. So does Rhipeus, so Dymas in like wise, and all our men in delight arm themselves one by one in the fresh spoils. We advance, mingling with the Grecians under a protection not our own, and join many a battle with those we meet amid the blind night; many a Greek we send down to hell. Some scatter to the ships and run for the safety of the shore; some in craven fear again climb the huge horse, and hide in the belly they knew.

'Alas that none may trust at all to estranged gods! Lo! Cassandra, maiden daughter of Priam, was being dragged with disordered tresses from the temple and sanctuary of Minerva, straining to heaven her blazing eyes in vain; her eyes, for fetters confined her delicate hands. At this sight Coroebus burst forth infuriate, and flung himself on death amid their columns. We all follow him up, and charge with massed arms. Here first from the high temple roof we are overwhelmed with our own people's weapons, and a most pitiful slaughter begins through the fashion of our armour and the mistaken Greek crests; then the Grecians, with angry cries at the maiden's rescue, gather from every side and fall on us; Ajax in all his valour, and the two sons of Atreus, and the whole Dolopian army: as oft when bursting in whirlwind West and South clash with adverse blasts, and the East wind exultant on the coursers of the Dawn; the forests cry, and fierce in foam Nereus with his trident stirs the seas from their lowest depth. Those too appear, whom our stratagem routed through the darkness of dim night and drove all about the town; at once they know the shields and lying weapons, and mark the alien tone on our lips. We go down, overwhelmed by numbers. First Coroebus is stretched by Peneleus' hand at the altar of the goddess armipotent; and Rhipeus falls, the one man who was most righteous and steadfast in justice among the Teucrians: the gods' ways are not as ours. Hypanis and Dymas perish, pierced by friendly hands; nor did all thy goodness, O Panthus, nor Apollo's fillet protect thy fall. O ashes of Ilium and deathflames of my people! you I call to witness that in your ruin I shunned no weapon or encounter, and earned my fall at a Grecian hand, had destiny been thus. We tear ourselves away, I and Iphitus and Pelias, Iphitus now stricken in age, Pelias halting too under the wound of Ulysses, called forward by the clamour to Priam's house.

'Here indeed the fight is fiercest, as if all the rest of the warfare were nowhere, and no slaughter but here throughout the city, so do we descry the battle in full fury, the Grecians rushing on the building, and their shielded column driving up against the beleaguered threshold. Ladders cling to the walls; and hard by the doors and planted on the rungs they hold up their shields in the left hand to ward off our weapons, and with their right clutch the battlements. The Dardanians tear down turrets and whole pinnacles of the palace against them; with these for weapons, since they see the end is come, they prepare to defend themselves even in death's extremity: and hurl down gilded beams, the stately decorations of their fathers of old. Others with drawn swords have beset the doorway below and keep it in crowded column. We renew our courage, to aid the royal dwelling, to support them with our succour, and swell the force of the conquered.

'There was a blind doorway giving passage through the range of Priam's halls by a solitary postern, whereby, while our realm endured, hapless Andromache would often and often glide unattended to her father-in-law's house, and carry the boy Astyanax to his grandsire. I issue out on the sloping height of the ridge, whence wretched Teucrian hands were hurling their ineffectual weapons. A tower stood on the sheer brink, its roof ascending high into heaven, whence was wont to be seen all Troy and the Grecian ships and Achaean camp: attacking it with iron round about, where the joints of the lofty flooring yielded, we wrench it from its high foundations and shake it free; it gives way, and suddenly falls thundering in ruin, crashing wide over the Grecian ranks. But others swarm up; nor meanwhile do stones nor any sort of missile slacken.... Right before the vestibule and in the front doorway Pyrrhus moves rejoicingly in the sparkle of arms and gleaming brass: like as when a snake fed on poisonous herbs, whom chill winter kept hid and swollen underground, now fresh from his weeds outworn and shining in youth wreathes his slippery body into the daylight, his upreared breast meets the sun, and his triple-cloven tongue flickers in his mouth. With him huge Periphas, and Automedon the armour-bearer, driver of Achilles' horses, with him all his Scyrian men climb the roof and hurl flames on the housetop. Himself among the foremost he grasps a poleaxe, bursts through the hard doorway, and wrenches the brazen-plated doors from the hinge; and now he has cut out a plank from the solid oak and pierced a vast gaping hole. The house within is open to sight, and the long halls lie plain; open to sight are the secret chambers of Priam and the kings of old, and they see armed men standing in front of the doorway.

'But the inner house is stirred with shrieks and misery and confusion, and the court echoes deep with women's wailing; the din strikes up to the golden stars. Affrighted mothers stray about the vast house, and cling fast to the doors and print them with kisses. With his father's might Pyrrhus presses on; nor guards nor barriers can hold out. The gate totters under the hard-driven ram, and the doors fall flat, rent from the hinge. The passage is forced; the Greeks burst through the entrance and pour in, slaughtering the foremost, and filling the space with a wide stream of soldiers. Not so furiously when a foaming river bursts his banks and overflows, beating down the opposing dykes with whirling water, is he borne mounded over the fields, and sweeps herds and pens all about the plains. Myself I saw in the gateway Neoptolemus mad with carnage, and the two sons of Atreus, saw Hecuba and the hundred daughters of her house, and Priam polluting with his blood the altar fires of his own consecration. The fifty bridal chambers, the abundant hope of his children's children, their doors magnificent with spoils of barbaric gold, have sunk in ruin; where the fire fails the Greeks are in possession.

'Perchance too thou mayest inquire what was Priam's fate. When he saw the ruin of his captured city, the gates of his house burst open, and the enemy amid his innermost chambers, the old man idly fastens round his aged trembling shoulders his long disused armour, girds on the unavailing sword, and advances on his death among the thronging foe.

'Within the palace and under the bare cope of sky was a massive altar, and hard on the altar an ancient bay tree leaned clasping the household gods in its shadow. Here Hecuba and her daughters crowded vainly about the altar-stones, like doves driven headlong by a black tempest, and crouched clasping the gods' images. And when she saw Priam her lord with the armour of youth on him, "What spirit of madness, my poor husband," she cries, "has moved thee to gird on these weapons? or whither dost thou run? Not such the succour nor these the defenders the time requires: no, were mine own Hector now beside us. Retire, I beseech thee, hither; this altar will protect us all, or thou wilt share our death." With these words on her lips she drew the aged man to her, and set him on the holy seat.

'And lo, escaped from slaughtering Pyrrhus through the weapons of the enemy, Polites, one of Priam's children, flies wounded down the long colonnades and circles the empty halls. Pyrrhus pursues him fiercely with aimed wound, just catching at him, and follows hard on him with his spear. As at last he issued before his parents' eyes and faces, he fell, and shed his life in a pool of blood. At this Priam, although even now fast in the toils of death, yet withheld not nor spared a wrathful cry: "Ah, for thy crime, for this thy hardihood, may the gods, if there is goodness in heaven to care for aught such, pay thee in full thy worthy meed, and return thee the reward that is due! who hast made me look face to face on my child's murder, and polluted a father's countenance with death. Ah, not such to a foe was the Achilles whose parentage thou beliest; but he revered a suppliant's right and trust, restored to the tomb Hector's blood-drained corpse, and sent me back to my own realm." Thus the old man spoke, and launched his weak and unwounding spear, which, recoiling straight from the jarring brass, hung idly from his shield above the boss. Thereat Pyrrhus: "Thou then shalt tell this, and go with the message to my sire the son of Peleus: remember to tell him of my baleful deeds, and the degeneracy of Neoptolemus. Now die." So saying, he drew him quivering to the very altar, slipping in the pool of his child's blood, and wound his hair in the left hand, while in the right the sword flashed out and plunged to the hilt in his side. This was the end of Priam's fortunes; thus did allotted fate find him, with burning Troy and her sunken towers before his eyes, once magnificent lord over so many peoples and lands of Asia. The great corpse lies along the shore, a head severed from the shoulders and a body without a name.

'But then an awful terror began to encircle me; I stood in amaze; there rose before me the sight of my loved father, as I saw the king, old as he, sobbing out his life under the ghastly wound; there rose Creüsa forlorn, my plundered house, and little Iülus' peril. I look back and survey what force is around me. All, outwearied, have given up and leapt headlong to the ground, or flung themselves wretchedly into the fire.

'Yes, and now I only was left; when I espy the daughter of Tyndarus close in the courts of Vesta, crouching silently in the fane's recesses; the bright glow of the fires lights my wandering, as my eyes stray all about. Fearing Teucrian anger for the overthrown towers of Troy, and the Grecians' vengeance and the wrath of the husband she had abandoned, she, the common Fury of Troy and her native country, had hidden herself and cowered unseen by the altars. My spirit kindles to fire, and rises in wrath to avenge my dying land and take repayment for her crimes. Shall she verily see Sparta and her native Mycenae unscathed, and depart a queen and triumphant? Shall she see her spousal and her father's house and children, attended by a crowd of Trojan women and Phrygians to serve her? and Priam have fallen under the sword? Troy blazed in fire? the shore of Dardania so often soaked with blood? Not so. For though there is no name or fame in a woman's punishment, nor honour in the victory, yet shall I have praise in quenching a guilty life and exacting a just recompense; and it will be good to fill my soul with the flame of vengeance, and satisfy the ashes of my people. Thus broke I forth, and advanced infuriate; when my mother came visibly before me, clear to sight as never till then, and shone forth in pure radiance through the night, gracious, evident in godhead, in shape and stature such as she is wont to appear to the heavenly people; she caught me by the hand and stayed me, and pursued thus with roseate lips:

' "Son, what overmastering pain thus wakes thy wrath? Why ravest thou? or whither is thy care for us fled? Wilt thou not first look to it, where thou hast left Anchises, thine aged worn father; or if Creüsa thy wife and the child Ascanius survive? round about whom all the Greek battalions range; and without my preventing care, the flames ere this had consumed them, and the hostile sword drunk their blood. Not the hated face of the Laconian woman, Tyndarus' daughter; not Paris is to blame; the gods, the gods in anger overturn this magnificence, and make Troy topple down. Look, for all the cloud that now veils thy gaze and dulls mortal vision with damp encircling mist, I will rend from before thee. Fear thou no commands of thy mother, nor refuse to obey her counsels. Here, where thou seest sundered piles of masonry and rocks violently torn from rocks, and smoke eddying mixed with dust, Neptune with his great trident shakes wall and foundation out of their places, and upturns all the city from her base. Here Juno in all her terror holds the Scaean gates at the entry, and, girt with steel, calls her allied army furiously from their ships.... Even now on the citadel's height, look back! Tritonian Pallas is planted with glittering bordure and awful

Gorgon head. Their lord himself pours courage and prosperous strength on the Grecians, himself stirs the gods against the arms of Dardania. Haste away, O son, and put an end to the struggle. Nowhere will I desert thee; I will set thee safe in the courts of thy father's house."

'She ended, and plunged in the dense blackness of the night. Awful faces shine forth, and, set against Troy, divine majesties. . . .

'Then indeed I saw all Ilium sinking in flame, and Neptunian Troy uprooted from her base: even as an ancient ash on the mountain heights, hacked all about with steel and fast-glancing axes, when husbandmen emulously strain to cut it down: it nods to the fall, with shaken top and quivering tresses asway; till gradually overmastered with wounds, it utters one last groan, and rending itself away, falls in ruin along the ridge. I descend, and under a god's guidance clear my way between foe and flame; weapons give ground before me, and flames retire.

'And now, when I have reached the courts of my ancestral dwelling, our home of old, my father, whom it was my first desire to carry high into the hills, and whom first I sought, refuses wholly, now Troy is rooted out, to prolong his life through the pains of exile.

' "Ah, you," he cries, "whose blood is at the prime, whose strength stands firm in native vigour, do you take your flight. . . . Had the lords of heaven willed to prolong life for me, they should have preserved this my home. Enough and more is the one desolation we have seen, survivors of a captured city. Thus, oh thus salute me and depart, as a body laid out for burial. Mine own hand shall find me death: the foe will be merciful and seek my spoils: light is the loss of a tomb. This long time hated of heaven, I uselessly delay the years, since the father of gods and king of men blasted me with wind of thunder and scathe of flame."

'Thus held he on in utterance, and remained unstirred. We press him, dissolved in tears, my wife Creüsa, Ascanius, all our household, that our father involve us not all in his ruin, and add his weight to the sinking scale of doom. He refuses, and keeps seated steadfast in his purpose. Again I rush to battle, and choose death in my misery. For what had counsel or chance yet to give? Thoughtest thou my feet, O father, could retire and abandon thee? and fell so unnatural words from a parent's lips? "If heaven wills that naught be left of our mighty city, if this be thy planted purpose, thy pleasure to cast in thyself and thine to the doom of Troy; for this death indeed the gate is wide, and even now Pyrrhus will be here newly bathed in Priam's blood, Pyrrhus who slaughters the son before the father's face, the father at his altars. For this was it, bountiful mother, that thou snatchest me from amid fire and sword, to see the foe in my inmost chambers, and Ascanius and my father, Creüsa by their side, butchered in one another's blood? To arms, my men, to arms! the last day calls on the conquered. Return me to the Greeks; let me revisit and renew the fight. Never to-day shall we all perish unavenged."

'Thereat I again gird on my sword, and fitting my left arm into the clasps of the shield, strode forth of the palace. But lo! my wife clung round my feet on the threshold, and held little Iülus up to his father's sight. "If thou goest to die, let us too hurry with thee to the end. But if thou knowest any hope to place in arms, be this household thy first defence. To what is little Iülus and thy father, to what am I left who once was called thy wife?"'

'So she shrieked, and filled all the house with her weeping; when a sign arises sudden and marvellous to tell. For, between the hands and before the faces of his sorrowing parents, lo! above Iülus' head there seemed to stream a light luminous cone, and a flame whose touch hurt not to flicker in his soft hair and play round his brows. We in hurrying affright shook out the blazing hair and quenched the holy fires with spring water. But lord Anchises joyfully upraised his eyes; and stretching his hands to heaven: "Jupiter omnipotent," he cries, "if thou dost relent at any prayers, look on us this once alone;

and if our goodness deserve it, give a sign hereafter, O lord, and confirm this thine omen."

'Scarcely had the aged man spoken thus, when with sudden crash it thundered on the left, and a star gliding through the dusk shot from heaven drawing a bright trail of light. We watch it slide over the palace roof, leaving the mark of its pathway, and bury its brilliance in the wood of Ida; the long-drawn track shines, and the region all about reeks with sulphur. Then conquered indeed my father rises to address the gods and worship the holy star. "Now, now delay is done with: I follow, and where you lead, I come, gods of my fathers; save my house, save my grandchild. Yours is this omen, and in your deity Troy stands. I yield, O my son, and refuse not to pass forth beside thee."

'He ended; and now more loudly the fire roars along the city, and nearer roll the burning tides. "Up then, beloved father, and place thyself on my neck; these shoulders of mine will sustain thee, nor will a burden so dear weigh me down. Howsoever fortune fall, one and undivided shall be our peril, one the escape of us twain. Little Iülus shall go along with me, and my wife follow our steps afar. You of my household, give heed to what I say. On a mound as you leave the city an ancient temple of Ceres stands lonely, and hard by an aged cypress, guarded many years in ancestral observance: to this gathering-place we will come from diverse quarters. Thou, O father, take the sacred things and the household gods of our ancestors in thine hand. For me, just parted from the desperate battle, with slaughter fresh upon me, to handle them were guilt, until I have washed me in a living stream. . . ." So spoke I, and spread over my neck and broad shoulders a tawny lion-skin for covering, and stoop to my burden. Little Iülus, with his hand fast in mine, keeps uneven pace after his father. Behind my wife follows. We pass on in the shadows. And I, lately moved by no weapons launched against me, nor by the thronging bands of my Grecian foes, am now terrified at every breath, startled by every noise, thrilling with fear alike for my companion and my burden.

'And now I was nearing the gates, and thought I had outsped all the way; when suddenly the crowded trampling of feet came to our ears, and my father, looking forth into the darkness, cries: "My son, my son, fly; they draw near. I espy gleaming shields and the flicker of brass." At this, in my flurry and confusion, some hostile god bereft me of my senses. For while I plunge down byways, and swerve from where the familiar streets ran, Creüsa, alas! whether, torn by fate from her unhappy husband, she stood still, or did she mistake the way, or sink down outwearied? I know not; and never again was she given back to our eyes; nor did I turn to look for my lost one, or cast back a thought, ere we were come to ancient Ceres' mound and hallowed seat; here at last, when all gathered, one was missing, vanished from her child's and her husband's company. What man or god did I spare in frantic reproaches? or what crueller sight did I see in our city's overthrow? I charge my comrades with Ascanius and lord Anchises, and the gods of Teucria, hiding them in the winding vale. Myself I regain the city, girding on my shining armour; fixed to renew every danger, to retrace my way throughout Troy, and fling myself again on its perils. First of all I regain the walls and the dim gateway whence my steps had issued; I scan and follow back my footprints with searching gaze in the night. Everywhere my spirit shudders, dismayed at the very silence. Thence I pass on home, if haply her feet (if haply!) had led her thither. The Grecians had poured in, and filled the palace. The devouring fire goes rolling before the wind high as the roof; the flames tower over it, and the heat surges up into the air. I move on, and revisit the citadel and Priam's dwelling; where now in the spacious porticoes of Juno's sanctuary Phoenix and accursed Ulysses, chosen sentries, were guarding the spoil. Hither from all quarters is flung in masses the treasure of Troy torn from burning shrines, tables of the gods, bowls of solid gold, and captive raiment. Boys and cowering mothers in long file stand round. . . . Yes, and I dared to cry abroad through the darkness; I filled the streets with calling, and again and yet again with vain reiterance cried piteously on Creüsa. As I sought her and rushed endlessly among the houses of the town, there rose before mine eyes a melancholy phantom, the ghost of very Creüsa, in likeness larger than her wont. I was motionless; my hair stood up, and the voice choked in my throat. Then she thus addressed me, and with this speech allayed my distresses: "What help is there in this mad passion of grief, sweet my husband? not without divine influence does this come to pass: nor may it be, nor does the high lord of Olympus allow, that thou shouldest carry Creüsa hence in thy company. Long shall be thine exile, and weary spaces of sea must thou plough; yet thou shalt come to the land Hesperia, where Lydian Tiber flows with soft current through rich and populous fields. There prosperity awaits thee, and a kingdom, and a king's daughter for thy wife. Dispel these tears for thy beloved Creüsa. Never will I look on the proud homes of the Myrmidons or Dolopians, or go to be the slave of Greek matrons, I a daughter of Dardania, a daughter-in-law of Venus the goddess.... But the mighty mother of the gods keeps me in these her borders. And now farewell, and still love thy child and mine." This speech uttered, while I wept and would have said many a thing, she left me and retreated into thin air. Thrice there was I fain to lay mine arms round her neck; thrice the vision I vainly clasped fled out of my hands, even as the light breezes, or most like to fluttering sleep. So at last, when night is spent, I revisit my comrades.

'And here I find a marvellous great company, newly flocked in, mothers and men, a people gathered for exile, a pitiable crowd. From all quarters they are assembled, ready in heart and fortune, to whatsoever land I will conduct them overseas. And now the morning star rose over the high ridges of Ida, and led on the day; and the Grecians held the gateways in leaguer, nor was any hope of help given. I withdrew, and raising my father up, I sought the mountains.'

BOOK THIRD

THE STORY OF THE SEVEN YEARS' WANDERING

'AFTER it pleased heaven's lords to overthrow the state of Asia and Priam's guiltless people, and proud Ilium fell, and Neptunian Troy smokes all along the ground, we are driven by divine omens to seek distant places of exile in waste lands. Right under Antandros and the mountains of Phrygian Ida we build a fleet, uncertain whither the fates carry us or where a resting-place is given, and gather the people together. Scarcely had the first summer set in, when lord Anchises bids us spread our sails to fortune, and weeping I leave the shores and havens of my country, and the plains where once was Troy. I sail to sea an exile, with my comrades and son and the gods of household and state.

'A land of vast plains lies apart, the home of Mavors, in Thracian tillage, and sometime under warrior Lycurgus' reign; friendly of old to Troy, and their gods in alliance while our fortune lasted. Hither I pass, and on the winding shore I lay under unfriendly fates the first foundations of a city, and from my own name fashion its name, Aeneadae.

'I was paying sacrifice to my mother, daughter of Dione, and to all the gods, so to favour the work begun, and slew a shining bull on the shore to the high lord of the heavenly people. Haply there lay a mound hard at hand, crowned with cornel thickets and bristling dense with shafts of myrtle. I drew near; and essaying to tear up the green forest from the soil, that I might cover the altar with leafy boughs, I see a portent ominous and wonderful to tell. For from the first tree whose roots are rent away and broken from the ground, drops of black blood trickle, and gore stains the earth. An icy shudder shakes my limbs, and my blood curdles chill with terror. Yet from another I go on again to tear away a tough shoot, fully to fathom its secret; yet from another black blood follows out of the bark. With many searchings of heart I prayed the woodland nymphs, and lord Gradivus, who rules in the Getic fields, to make the sight propitious as was meet and lighten the omen. But when I assail a third shaft with a stronger effort, pulling with knees pressed against the sand; shall I speak or be silent? from beneath the mound is heard a pitiable moan, and a voice is uttered to my ears: "Woe's me, why rendest thou me, Aeneas? spare me at last in the tomb, spare pollution to thine innocent hands. Troy bore me; not alien to thee am I, nor this blood that oozes from the stem. Ah, fly the cruel land, fly the greedy shore! For I am Polydorus; here the iron harvest of weapons has covered my pierced body, and shot up in sharp javelins." Then indeed, borne down with dubious terror, I was motionless, my hair stood up, and the voice in my throat was choked.

'This Polydorus once with great weight of gold had hapless Priam sent in secret to the nurture of the Thracian king, when now he was losing trust in the arms of Dardania, and saw his city leaguered round about. The king, when the Teucrian power was broken and fortune withdrew, following Agamemnon's estate and triumphant arms, severs every bond of duty; murders Polydorus, and lays strong hands on the gold. O accursed hunger of gold, to what dost thou not compel human hearts! When the terror left my senses, I lay the divine tokens before the chosen princes of the people, with my father at their head, and demand their judgment. All are of one mind, to leave the guilty land, and abandoning a polluted home, to let the gales waft our fleets. So we bury Polydorus anew, and the earth is heaped high over his mound; altars are reared to his ghost, sad with dusky chaplets and black cypress; and around are the Ilian women with hair unbound in their fashion. We offer bubbling bowls of warm milk and cups of consecrated blood, and lay the spirit to rest in her tomb, and with loud voice utter the last call.

'Thereupon, so soon as ocean may be trusted, and the winds leave the seas in quiet, and the soft whispering south wind calls seaward, my comrades launch their ships and crowd the shores. We put out from harbour, and lands and towns sink away. There lies in mid sea a holy land, most dear to the mother of the Nereids and Neptune of Aegae, which strayed about coast and strand till the grateful Archer god chained it fast from high Myconos and Gyaros, and made it lie immoveable and defy the winds. Hither I steer; and it welcomes my weary crew to the quiet shelter of a safe haven. We disembark and worship Apollo's town. Anius the king, king at once of the people and priest of Phoebus, his brows garlanded with fillets and consecrated laurel, hastens to meet us, knowing Anchises, his friend of old; we clasp hands in welcome, and enter his palace.

'I was worshipping the god's temple, an ancient pile of stone. "Lord of Thymbra, give us an enduring dwelling-place; grant a house and family to thy weary servants and a city to abide: keep Troy's second fortress, the remnant left of the Grecians and merciless Achilles. Whom follow we? or whither dost thou bid us go, where fix our seat? Grant an omen, O lord, and inspire our minds." Scarcely had I spoken thus; suddenly all seemed to shake, all the courts and laurels of the god, the whole hill to be stirred round about, and the caldron to moan in the opening sanctuary. We sink low in the ground, and a voice is borne to our ears: "Stubborn race of Dardanus, the same land that bore you by parentage of old shall receive you again on her bountiful breast. Seek out your ancient mother; hence shall the house of Aeneas sway all regions, his children's children and they who shall be born of them." Thus Phoebus; and mingled outcries of great gladness uprose; all ask, what is that city? whither calls Phoebus our wandering, and bids us return? Then my father, unrolling the records of men of old, "Hear, O princes," says he, "and learn your hopes. In mid ocean lies Crete, the island of high Jove, wherein is mount Ida, the cradle of our race. An hundred great towns are inhabited in that opulent realm; from it our forefather Teucer of old, if I recall the tale aright, sailed to the Rhoetean coasts and chose a place for his kingdom. Not yet was Ilium nor the towers of Pergama reared; they dwelt in the valley bottoms. Hence came our Lady, haunter of Cybelus, the Corybantic cymbals and the grove of Ida; hence the rites of inviolate secrecy, and the lions yoked under the chariot of their mistress. Up then, and let us follow where divine commandments lead; let us appease the winds, and seek the realm of Gnosus. Nor is it a far journey away. Only be Jupiter favourable, the third day shall bring our fleet to anchor on the Cretan coast." So spoke he, and slew fit sacrifice on the altars, a bull to Neptune, a bull to thee, fair Apollo, a black sheep to Tempest, a white to the prosperous West winds.

'Rumour flies that Idomeneus the captain is driven forth of his father's realm, and the shores of Crete are abandoned, that the house is void of foes and the dwellings lie empty to our hand. We leave the harbour of Ortygia, and fly along the main, by the revel-trod ridges of Naxos, by green Donusa, Olearos and snow-white Paros, and the sea-strewn Cyclades, threading the channels sown thick with isles. The seamen's clamour rises in emulous dissonance; each cheers his comrade: *Seek we Crete and our forefathers*. A wind rising astern follows us forth on our way, and we glide at last to the ancient coast of the Curetes. So I set eagerly to work on the walls of my chosen town, and call it Pergamea, and exhort my people, joyful at the name, to cherish their homes and rear the castle buildings. And even now the ships were drawn up on the dry beach; the people were busy in marriages and among their new fields; I was giving statutes and homesteads; when suddenly from a tainted space of sky came, noisome on men's bodies and pitiable on trees and crops, pestilence and a year of death. They left their sweet lives or dragged themselves on in misery; Sirius scorched the fields into barrenness; the herbage grew dry, and the sickly harvest denied sustenance. My father counsels to remeasure the sea and go again to Phoebus in his Ortygian oracle, to pray for grace and ask what issue he ordains to our exhausted state; whence he bids us search for aid to our woes, whither bend our course.

'Night fell, and sleep held all things living on the earth.

The sacred images of the gods and the household deities of Phrygia, that I had borne with me from Troy out of the midst of the burning city, seemed to stand before mine eyes as I lay in sleep, clear in the broad light where the full moon poured through latticed windows; then thus addressed me, and with this speech allayed my distresses: "What Apollo has to tell thee when thou dost reach Ortygia, he utters here, and sends us unsought to thy threshold. We who followed thee and thine arms when Dardania went down in fire; we who under thee have traversed on shipboard the swelling sea; we in like wise will exalt to heaven thy children to be, and give empire to their city. Do thou prepare a mighty town for a mighty people, nor draw back from the long wearisome chase. Thou must change thy dwelling. Not to these shores did the god at Delos counsel thee, or Apollo bid thee find rest in Crete. There is a region Greeks name Hesperia, an ancient land, mighty in arms and foison of the clod; Oenotrian men dwell therein; now rumour is that a younger race have called it Italy after their captain's name. This is our true dwelling place; hence is Dardanus sprung, and lord Iasius, the first source of our race. Up, arise, and tell with good cheer to thine aged parent this plain tale, to seek Corythus and the lands of Ausonia. Jupiter denies thee the Dictaean fields."

'Astonished at this vision and divine utterance (nor was that slumber; but openly I seemed to know their countenances, their veiled hair and gracious faces, and therewith a cold sweat broke out all over me) I spring from my bed and raise my voice and upturned hands skyward and pay pure offering on the hearth. The sacrifice done, I joyfully tell Anchises, and relate all in order. He recognises the double descent and twofold parentage, and the later wanderings among ancient lands that had deceived him. Then he speaks: "O son, hard wrought by the destinies of Ilium, Cassandra only foretold me this fortune. Now I recall how she prophesied this destiny to our race, and often cried of Hesperia, often of an Italian realm. But who was to believe that Teucrians should come to Hesperian shores? or whom might

Cassandra then move by prophecy? Yield we to Phoebus, and follow the better way he counsels." So says he, and we all rejoicingly obey his speech. This dwelling likewise we abandon; and leaving some few behind, spread our sails and run over the waste sea in our hollow plank.

'After our ships held the high seas, nor any land now appears, the sky all round us and all round us the deep, a dusky shower drew up overhead carrying night and tempest, and the wave shuddered and gloomed. Straightway the winds upturn the main, and great seas rise; we are tossed asunder over the dreary gulf. Stormclouds enwrap the day, and rainy gloom blots out the sky; out of the bursting clouds fire flashes fast upon fire. Driven from our course, we go wandering on the blind waves. Palinurus himself professes he cannot tell day from night on the sky, nor keep reckoning of the way amid the waters. Three dubious days of blind darkness we wander on the deep, as many nights without a star. Not till the fourth day was land at last seen to rise, discovering distant hills and sending up wreaths of smoke. The sails drop; we swing back to the oars; without delay the sailors strongly toss up the foam, and sweep through the green water. The shores of the Strophades first receive me thus won from the waves, Strophades the Greek name they bear, islands lying in the great Ionian sea, which boding Celaeno and the other Harpies inhabit since Phineus' house was shut on them, and they fled in terror from the board of old. Than these no deadlier portent nor any fiercer plague of divine wrath has issued from the Stygian waters; winged things with maidens' countenance, bellies dropping filth, and clawed hands and faces ever wan with hunger. . . .

'When borne hitherward we enter the haven, lo! we see goodly herds of oxen scattered on the plains, and goats flocking untended over the grass. We attack them with the sword, and call the gods and Jove himself to share our spoil. Then we build seats on the winding shore and banquet on the dainty food. But suddenly the Harpies are upon us, swooping awfully from the mountains, and shaking their wings with loud clangour, plunder the feast, and defile everything with unclean touch, spreading a foul smell, and uttering dreadful cries. Again, in a deep recess under a caverned rock, we array the board and renew the altar fires; again, from their blind ambush in diverse quarters of the sky, the clanging swarm swoop with taloned feet around their prey, defiling the feast with their lips. Then I bid my comrades take up arms, and proclaim war on the accursed race. Even as I bade they do, range their swords in cover among the grass, and hide their shields out of sight. So when they swooped clamorously down along the winding shore, Misenus from his watch-tower on high signals on the hollow brass; my comrades rush in and essay the strange battle, to imbrue their sword in the winged horrors of the sea. But they take no violence on their plumage, nor wounds on their bodies; and soaring into the firmament with rapid flight, leave their foul traces on the spoil they had half consumed. Celaeno alone, prophetess of ill, alights on a towering cliff, and thus breaks forth in speech:

' "War is it for your slaughtered oxen and steers cut down, O children of Laomedon, war is it you would declare, and drive the guiltless Harpies from their ancestral kingdom? Take then to heart and fix fast these words of mine; which the Lord omnipotent foretold to Phoebus, Phoebus Apollo to me, I eldest born of the Furies reveal to you. To Italy you point your course, wooing the winds; to Italy you shall go, and enter her harbours unhindered. Yet shall you not wall round your ordained city, ere this murderous outrage on us compel you, in portentous hunger, to eat your trenchers with gnawing teeth."

'She spoke, and winged her way back to the shelter of the wood. But my comrades' blood froze chill with sudden affright; their spirits fell; and no longer with arms, nay with vows and prayers they bid me entreat favour, whether these be goddesses, or winged things boding and foul. And lord Anchises from the beach calls with outspread hands on the mighty gods, ordering fit sacrifices: "Gods, avert their menaces! Gods, turn this woe away, and graciously save the righteous!" Then he bids pluck the cable from the shore and shake loose the sheets. Southern winds stretch the sails; we scud over the foam-flecked waters, whither wind and pilot called our course. Now wooded Zacynthos appears amid the waves, and Dulichium and Same and the sheer rocks of Neritos. We fly past the cliffs of Ithaca, Laërtes' realm, and curse the land, fostress of cruel Ulysses. Soon too Mount Leucata's cloudy peaks are sighted, and Apollo dreaded of sailors. Hither we steer wearily, and stand in to the little town. The anchor is cast from the prow; the sterns lie aground on the beach.

'So at last having attained to land beyond our hopes, we purify ourselves in Jove's worship, and kindle altars of offering, and make the Actian shore gay with the games of Ilium. My comrades strip, and, slippery with oil, exercise their ancestral contests; glad to have got past so many Argive towns, and held on their flight through the surrounding foe. Meanwhile the sun rounds the great circle of the year, and icy winter ruffles the waters with Northern gales. I fix against the doorway a hollow shield of brass, that tall Abas had borne, and mark the story with a verse: *These arms Aeneas from the conquering Greeks.* Then I bid leave the harbour and sit down at the thwarts; emulously my comrades strike the water, and sweep through the seas. Soon we see the cloud-capped Phaeacian towers sink away, skirt the shores of Epirus, and enter the Chaonian haven and approach high Buthrotum town.

'Here the rumour of a story beyond belief comes on our ears; Helenus son of Priam is reigning over Greek towns, master of the bride and sceptre of Pyrrhus the Aeacid; and Andromache has again fallen to a husband of her people. I stood amazed; and my heart kindled with marvellous desire to accost him and learn of so strange a fortune. I advance from the harbour, leaving the fleet and the shore; just when haply Andromache, in a grove before the town, by the waters of a feigned Simoïs, was making oblation of ritual feasts and gifts of sorrow to Hector's ashes, and calling on his ghost by an empty mound of green turf with two altars, that she had hallowed for a place of weeping. When she caught sight of me coming, and saw distractedly the encircling arms of Troy, terror-stricken at the vision marvellously shewn, her gaze fixed, and warmth left her frame. She swoons away, and hardly at last speaks after long interval: "Comest thou then a real face, a real messenger to me, goddess-born? livest thou? or if sweet light is fled, ah, where is Hector?" She spoke, and bursting into tears filled all the place with her cries. Hardly do I slip in a few words amid her frenzy, and deeply moved gasp out in broken accents: "I live indeed, I live on through all extremities; doubt not, for real are the forms thou seest ... Alas! after such an husband, what fate receives thy fall? or what worthier fortune revisits Hector's Andromache? Keepest thou bonds of marriage with Pyrrhus?" She cast down her countenance, and spoke with lowered voice:

' "O single in happy eminence that maiden daughter of Priam, sentenced to die under high Troy town at an enemy's grave, who never bore the shame of the lot, nor came a captive to her victorious master's bed! We, sailing over strange seas from our burning land, have endured the haughty youthful pride of Achilles' seed, and borne children in slavery: he thereafter, wooing Leda's Hermione and a Lacedaemonian marriage, passed me over to Helenus' keeping, a bondwoman to a bondman. But him Orestes, aflame with passionate desire for his stolen bride, and driven by the furies of crime, catches unguarded and murders at his ancestral altars. At Neoptolemus' death a share of his realm fell to Helenus' hands, who named the plains Chaonian, and called all the land Chaonia after Chaon of Troy, and built withal a Pergama and this Ilian citadel on the hills. But to thee how did winds, how fates give passage? or whose divinity landed thee all unwitting on our coasts? what of the boy Ascanius? lives he yet, and draws breath, thy darling, whom Troy even now ... Yet has the child some thought for his lost mother? does his father Aeneas, does his uncle Hector kindle aught in him of ancient valour and the pride of manhood?"

'Such words she poured forth weeping, and broke out vainly in long lament; when the hero Helenus son of Priam approaches from the town with a great company, knows us for his kin, and leads us joyfully to his gates, shedding a many tears at every word. I advance and recognise a little Troy, and a copy of the great Pergama, and a dry brook with the name of Xanthus, and clasp a Scaean gateway. Therewithal my Teucrians make holiday in the friendly town. The king entertained them in his spacious porches; in the central hall they poured goblets of wine in libation, and held the cups while the feast was served on gold.

'And now a day and another day is sped; the breezes woo our sails, and the canvas blows out to the swelling south. With these words I accost the prophet, and thus make request:

'"Son of Troy, interpreter of the gods, whose sense is open to Phoebus' influences, his tripods and his Clarian laurels, to stars and tongues of birds and auguries of prosperous flight, tell me now,—for the voice of revelation was all favourable to my course, and all divine influence counselled me to seek Italy and explore remote lands; only Celaeno the Harpy prophesies of strange portents, a horror to tell, and cries out of wrath and bale and foul hunger,—what perils are the first to shun? or in what guidance may I overcome these sore labours?"

'Hereat Helenus, first suing for divine favour with fit sacrifice of steers, and unbinding from his head the chaplets of consecration, leads me in his hand to thy courts, O Phoebus, thrilled with the fulness of the deity, and then utters these prophetic words from his augural lips:

'"Goddess-born, since there is clear assurance that under high omens thou dost voyage through the deep; so the king of the gods allots destiny and unfolds change, this is the circle of ordinance; a few things out of many I will unfold to thee in speech, that so thou mayest more safely traverse the seas of thy sojourn, and find rest in the Ausonian haven; for the destinies forbid Helenus to know, and Juno daughter of

Saturn to utter more. First of all, the Italy thou deemest now nigh, and close at hand, unwitting! the harbours thou wouldst enter, far are they sundered by a long and trackless track through a length of lands. First must the Trinacrian wave season thine oar, and thy ships traverse the salt Ausonian plain, by the infernal pools and Aeaean Circe's isle, ere thou mayest build thy city in safety on a peaceful land. I will tell thee the token, and do thou keep it close in thine heart. When in thy perplexity, beside the wave of a sequestered river, a great sow shall be discovered lying under the ilex-wood on the brink, with her newborn litter of thirty, couched white on the ground, her white brood about her teats; that shall be the place of the city, that the appointed rest from thy toils. Neither shrink thou at the bitten tables that await thee; the fates will find a way, and Apollo aid thy call. These lands moreover, on this nearest border of the Italian shore that our own sea's tide washes, flee thou: evil Greeks dwell in all their towns. Here the Locrians of Narycos have placed their city, and here Lyctian Idomeneus beset the Sallentine plains with soldiery; here is the town of the Meliboean captain, Philoctetes' little Petelia propped on her wall. Nay more, when thy fleets have crossed overseas and lie at anchor, when now thou rearest altars and payest vows on the beach, veil thine hair with a purple garment for covering, that no hostile face at thy divine worship may meet thee amid the holy fires and make void the omens. This fashion of sacrifice keep thou, thyself and thy comrades, and let thy children abide taintless in this observance. But when at thy departure the wind has borne thee to the Sicilian coast, and the barred straits of Pelorus open out, steer for the left-hand country and the long circuit of the seas on the left hand; shun the shore and water on thy right. These lands, they say, of old broke asunder, torn and upheaved by vast force (so strong to change is the long antiquity of time), when either country ran on as one; the ocean burst in between, cutting off with its waves the Hesperian from the Sicilian coast, and with narrow tide washes tilth and town along the disparted shore. On the right Scylla keeps guard, on the left unassuaged Charybdis, who thrice swallows the vast flood sheer down her swirling gulf, and ever again hurls it upward, lashing the sky with water. But Scylla lies prisoned in her cavern's blind recesses, thrusting forth her mouths and drawing ships upon the rocks. In front her face is human, and her breast fair as a maiden's to the waist down; behind she is a sea dragon of monstrous frame, with dolphins' tails joined on her wolf-girt belly. Better to track the goal of Trinacrian Pachynus, for all the delay, and fetch a long circuit in thy course, than once catch sight of misshapen Scylla deep in her dreary cavern, and of the rocks that ring to her sea-coloured hounds. Moreover, if Helenus the seer has aught of foresight or of assurance, if Apollo fills his spirit with the truth, this one thing, goddess-born, one thing for all will I foretell thee, and again and again repeat my counsel: to great Juno's deity be thy first prayer and worship; to Juno utter thy willing vows, and overcome the mighty mistress with gifts and supplications; so at last thou shalt leave Trinacria behind, and be sped in triumph to the Italian borders. When borne hither thou drawest nigh the Cymaean city, the haunted lakes and rustling woods of Avernus, thou shalt behold the raving prophetess who deep in the rock chants of fate, and marks down her words on leaves. What verses she writes thereon, the maiden sorts into order and shuts behind her in the cave; they stay in their places unstirred and quit not their rank. But when at the turn of the hinge the light wind from the doorway stirs them, and disarranges the delicate foliage, never after does she trouble to capture them as they flutter about the hollow rock, nor restore their places or join the verses; men depart without counsel, and hate the Sibyl's dwelling. Here let no waste in delay be of such account to thee (though thy company chide, and the passage call thy sails strongly to the deep, and thou mayest fill out their folds to thy desire) that thou do not approach the prophetess, and plead with prayers that she herself utter her oracles and deign to loose the voice from her lips. The nations of Italy and the wars to come, and the fashion whereby every toil may be avoided or endured, she shall unfold to thee, and grant her worshipper prosperous passage. Thus far is our voice allowed to counsel thee: go thy way, and exalt Troy to heaven by thy deeds."

'This the seer uttered with friendly lips; then orders gifts to be carried to my ships, of heavy gold and carved ivory, and loads the hulls with massy silver and caldrons of Dodona, a mail coat triple-woven with links of gold, and a helmet splendid with spike and tressed plumes, the armour of Neoptolemus. My father too has his gifts. Horses besides he brings, and grooms ... fills up the tale of our oarsmen, and equips my crews with arms.

'Meanwhile Anchises bade the fleet set their sails, that the fair wind might meet no delay. Him Phoebus' interpreter accosts with high courtesy: "Anchises, honoured with the splendour of Venus' espousal, the gods' charge, twice rescued from the fallen towers of Troy, lo! the land of Ausonia is before thee; sail thou and seize it. And yet needs must thou glide past it on the sea; far away lies the quarter of Ausonia that Apollo discloses. Go," he continues, "happy in thy son's affection: why do I run on further, and delay the rising winds in talk?" Andromache too, sad at this last parting, brings figured raiment with woof of gold, and a Phrygian scarf for Ascanius, and falls not short in courtesy, loading him with gifts from the loom. "Take these too," so says she, "my child, to be memorials to thee of my hands, and testify long hence the love of Andromache wife of Hector. Take these last gifts of thy kinsfolk, O sole surviving likeness to me of my own Astyanax! Such was he, in eyes and hands and features; and now his equal age were growing into manhood like thine."

'To them as I departed I spoke with starting tears: "Live happily, you whose fortunes have reached their goal! We are summoned ever from fate to fate. For you rest is won, and no ocean floor to furrow, no ever-retreating Ausonian fields to pursue. You see a pictured Xanthus, and a Troy your own hands have built; with better omens, I pray, and to be less open to the Greeks. If ever I enter Tiber and Tiber's bordering fields, and see a city granted to my nation, then both these kindred towns and allied peoples, which have the same Dardanus for founder, and whose story is one, will our hearts make a single Troy, Hesperia one with Epirus. Let that charge await our posterity."

'We put out to sea, keeping the Ceraunian mountains close at hand, whence is the shortest passage and seaway to Italy. The sun sets meanwhile, and the dusky hills grow dim. We choose a place, and fling ourselves on the lap of earth at the water's edge, and, allotting the oars, spread ourselves on the dry beach for refreshment: the dew of slumber falls on our weary limbs. Not yet had Night driven of the Hours climbed her mid arch; Palinurus rises alert from his couch, explores all the winds, and listens to catch a breeze; he marks the constellations gliding together through the silent sky, Arcturus, the rainy Hyades and the twin Oxen, and scans Orion in his armour of gold. When he sees the clear sky quite unbroken, he gives from the stern his shrill signal; we disencamp and explore the way, and spread the wings of our sails. And now reddening Dawn had chased away the stars, when we descry afar dim hills and the low line of Italy. Achates first raises the cry of *Italy;* and with joyous shouts my comrades salute Italy. Then lord Anchises enwreathed a great bowl and filled it up with wine; and called on the gods, standing on the high stern ... "Gods sovereign over sea and land and weather! bring wind to ease our way, and breathe favourably." The breezes freshen at his prayer, and now a harbour opens out nearer at hand, and a temple appears on the Fort of Minerva. My comrades furl the sails and swing the prows to the shore. The harbour is scooped into a bow by the Eastern flood; reefs run out and foam with the salt spray; itself it lies concealed; turreted walls of rock spread their arms on either hand, and the temple retreats from the beach. Here, for a first augury, four horses of snowy whiteness are grazing abroad on the grassy plain. And lord Anchises: "War dost thou carry, land of our sojourn; horses are armed in war, and menace of war is in this herd. But yet these same creatures are wont in time to enter harness, and carry yoke and bit in concord; there is hope of peace too," says he. Then we pray to the holy deity, Pallas of the clangorous arms, the first to welcome our cheers. And before the altars we veil our heads in Phrygian garments, and duly, after the counsel Helenus had urged deepest on us, pay the bidden burnt-sacrifice to Juno of Argos.

'Without delay, once our vows are fully paid, we round to the arms of our sailyards and leave the dwellings and untrusted fields of the Grecian people. Next is descried the bay of Tarentum, town, if rumour is true, of Hercules. Over against it the goddess of Lacinium rears her head, with the towers of Caulon, and Scylaceum wrecker of ships. Then Trinacrian Aetna is descried in the distance rising from the waves, and we hear from afar a great roaring of the sea on beaten rocks, and broken noises by the shore: the channels boil up, and the surge churns with sand. And lord Anchises: "Of a surety here is that Charybdis; of these cliffs, these awful rocks did Helenus prophesy. Out, O comrades, and rise together to the oars." Even as bidden they do; and first Palinurus swung the gurgling prow leftward through the water; to the left all our squadron bent with oar and wind. We are lifted skyward on the arching wave, and again sunk deep into the nether world as the water is sucked away. Thrice amid their rocky caverns the cliffs uttered a cry; thrice we see the foam flung out, and the stars through a dripping veil. Meanwhile the wind falls with sundown; and weary and ignorant of the way we glide on to the Cyclopes' coast.

'There lies a harbour, unstirred by the winds' entrance, and large; but nigh it Aetna thunders awfully in wrack, and ever and again hurls a black cloud into the sky, smoking with boiling pitch and white hot embers, and heaves balls of flame flickering up to the stars: ever and again vomits out on high crags from the torn entrails of the mountain, tosses up masses of molten rock with a groan, and boils forth from the depth below. Rumour is that this mass weighs down the body of Enceladus, half-consumed by the thunderbolt, and mighty Aetna laid over him suspires the flame that bursts from her furnaces; and so often as he changes his weary side, all Trinacria shudders and moans, veiling the sky in smoke. That night we spend in cover of the forest among portentous horrors, and see not what causes the sound. For neither did the stars show their fires, nor was the vault of constellated sky clear; but vapours blotted heaven, and the moon was held in a storm-cloud through dead of night.

'And now the morrow was rising in the early east, and the dewy darkness rolled away from the sky by Dawn, when sudden out of the forest advances a human shape strange and unknown, worn with uttermost hunger and pitiably attired, and stretches entreating hands towards the shore. We turn to look. Filthy and wretched, with shaggy beard and a covering pinned together with thorns, he was yet a Greek, and had been sent of old to Troy in his ancestral armour. And he, when he saw afar the Dardanian habits and arms of Troy, hung back a little in terror at the sight, and stayed his steps; then ran headlong to the shore with weeping and prayers: "By the heavens I beseech you, by the powers above and this luminous sky that gives us breath, take me up, O Trojans, carry me away to any land soever, and it will be enough. I know I am one out of the Grecian fleets, I confess I warred against the household gods of Ilium; for that, if our wrong and guilt is so great, throw me piecemeal on the flood or plunge me in the waste sea. If I perish, gladly will I perish at human hands." He ended; and clung clasping our knees and grovelling on his own. We encourage him to tell who he is and of what blood born, and to reveal how Fortune pursues him since then. Lord Anchises after little delay gives him his hand, and strengthens his courage by visible pledge. At last, laying aside his terror, he speaks thus:

' "I am from an Ithacan home, Achemenides by name, set out for Troy in luckless Ulysses' company; poor was my father Adamastus, and would God fortune had stayed at that! Here my comrades abandoned me in the Cyclops' vast cave, mindless of me while they hurry away from the savage gates.

It is a house of gore and blood-stained feasts, dim and huge within. Himself he is great of stature and knocks at the lofty sky, (gods, take away a curse like this from earth!) to none gracious in aspect or courteous of speech. He feeds on the flesh and dark blood of wretched men. I myself saw, when he caught the bodies of two of us with his great hand, and lying back in the middle of the cave crushed them on the rock, and the courts splashed and swam with gore; I saw when he champed the flesh oozing with dark clots of blood, and the warm limbs quivered under his teeth. Yet not unavenged; Ulysses brooked not this, nor in such straits did the Ithacan forget himself. For so soon as he, gorged with his feast and buried in wine, lay with bent neck sprawling huge over the cave, in his sleep vomiting gore and gobbets mixed with wine and blood, we, with prayers to the great gods and with parts allotted, pour at once all round him, and pierce with a sharp weapon the huge eye that lay sunk single under his savage brow, in fashion of an Argolic shield or the lamp of Phoebus; and at last we exultingly avenge the ghosts of our comrades. But fly, O wretched men, fly and pluck the cable from the beach.... For even in the shape and stature of Polyphemus, when he shuts his fleeced flocks and drains their udders in the cave's covert, an hundred other horrible Cyclopes haunt these winding shores and stray on the mountain heights. Thrice now does the horned moon fill out her light, while I linger in life among desolate lairs and haunts of wild beasts in the woodland, and from a rock survey the giant Cyclopes and shudder at their cries and echoing feet. The boughs yield a miserable sustenance, berries and stony sloes, and plants torn up by the root feed me. Sweeping all the view, I at last espied this fleet standing in to shore. On it, whatsoever it were, I cast myself; it is enough to have escaped the accursed tribe. Do you rather destroy this life by what death you will."

'Scarcely had he spoken thus, when on the mountain top we see shepherding his flocks a vast moving mass, Polyphemus himself seeking the shores he knew, a horror ominous, shapeless, huge, bereft of sight. A lopped pine guides his hand and steadies his footsteps. His fleeced sheep attend him, this his single delight and solace in suffering.... After he has touched the deep flood and come to the sea, he washes in it the blood that oozes from his eye-socket, grinding his teeth with groans; and now he strides through the sea up to his middle, nor yet does the wave wet his towering sides. We hurry far away in quickened flight, taking on board the suppliant who had deserved so well; and silently cut the cable, and bending forward upturn the sea with emulous oars. He heard, and turned his steps towards the echoing sound. But when he may in no wise reach his hand to us, nor can fathom the Ionian waves in pursuit, he raises a vast cry, at which the sea and all his waves shuddered, and the deep land of Italy was startled, and Aetna's vaulted caverns moaned. But the tribe of the Cyclopes, roused from the high wooded hills, run to the harbour and fill the shore. We descry the Aetnean brotherhood standing impotent with scowling eye, their stately heads up to heaven, a dreadful consistory; even as on a mountain summit stand oaks high in air or coned cypresses, a high forest of Jove or covert of Diana. Sharp fear urges us to shake out the sheets in reckless haste, and spread our sails to the favouring wind. Yet Helenus' commands counsel that our course keep not by Scylla and Charybdis, so narrow the remove from death between either way. We are resolved to back our sails, when lo! from the narrow fastness of Pelorus the north wind comes down and reaches us. I sail past Pantagias' mouth in the live rock, the Megarian bay, and low-lying Thapsus. Such names did Achemenides, of luckless Ulysses' company, point out as he retraced his wanderings along the returning shores.

'Stretched in front of a bay of Sicily lies an islet over against wavebeat Plemyrium; they of old called it Ortygia. Hither Alpheus the river of Elis, such is the tale, has cloven a secret passage beneath the sea, and now through thy wellhead, Arethusa, mingles with the Sicilian waves. We adore as bidden the great deities of the ground; and thence I cross the fertile soil of Helorus in the marsh. Next we graze the high reefs and jutting rocks of Pachynus; and far off appears Camarina, forbidden for ever by oracles to move, and the Geloan plains, and vast Gela named after its river. Then Acragas on the steep, once the breeder of noble horses, displays its massive walls in the distance; and with granted breeze I leave thee behind, palm-girt Selinus, and thread the difficult shoals and blind reefs of Lilybaeum. Thereon Drepanum receives me in its haven and joyless border. Here, driven over so many tempestuous seas, I lose, alas! the solace of every care and chance, Anchises my sire. Here thou, dearest father, abandonest me in weariness, alas! rescued in vain from peril and doom. Not Helenus the prophet, though he counselled of many a terror, not boding Celaeno foretold me of this grief. This was the last toil, this the goal of the long ways; thence it was I had departed when a god landed me on your coasts.'

Thus lord Aeneas with all attent retold alone the divine doom and the history of his goings. At last he was hushed, and here ending took his rest.

BOOK FOURTH

THE LOVE OF DIDO, AND HER END

But the Queen, long ere now pierced sore with passion, feeds the wound with her life-blood, and wastes in a hidden fire. Again and again his own valiance and his line's renown flood back upon her spirit; look and accent cling fast in her bosom, and the pain allows not her limbs rest or calm. The morrow's dawn bore the torch of Phoebus across the earth, and had rolled away the dewy darkness from the sky, when, scarce herself, she thus addresses the sister of her heart:

'Anna, my sister, such dreams of terror thrill me through! What guest unknown is this who has entered our dwelling? How high his mien! how great in heart as in arms! I believe it well, with no vain assurance, his blood is divine. Fear proves the vulgar spirit. Alas, by what destinies is he driven! of what wars fought out he told! Were my mind not planted, fixed and immovable, to ally myself to none in wedlock since my first love of old played me false in death; were I not sick to the heart of bridal torch and chamber, to this temptation alone I might haply yield. Anna, I will confess it; since Sychaeus mine husband met his piteous doom, and our household was shattered by a brother's murder, he only has touched mine heart and shaken my soul from its balance. I know the prints of the ancient flame. But rather, I pray, may earth first yawn deep for me, or the Lord omnipotent hurl me with his thunderbolt into gloom, the pallid gloom and profound night of Erebus, ere I soil thee, mine honour, or undo thy laws. He took my love away who made me one with him at first; he shall keep it with him, and guard it in the tomb.' She spoke, and filled her bosom with welling tears.

Anna replies: 'O dearer than the daylight to thy sister, wilt thou waste, sad and alone, all thy length of youth, and know not the sweetness of motherhood, nor love's bounty? Deemest thou the ashes care for that, or the ghost within the tomb? Be it so: in days gone by no wooers bent thy sorrow, not in Libya, not ere then in Tyre; Iarbas was slighted, and other princes nurtured by the triumphal land of Africa; wilt thou contend even with a love to thy liking? nor does it cross thy mind whose are these fields about thy dwelling? On this side are the Gaetulian towns, a race unconquerable in war; the reinless Numidian riders and the grim Syrtis hem thee in; on this lies a thirsty tract of desert, swept by the raiders of Barca. Why speak of the war gathering from Tyre, and thy brother's menaces? ... Under gods' control to my thinking, and with Juno's favour, has the Ilian fleet held on hither before the gale. What a city wilt thou discern here, O sister! what a realm will rise on such a union! the arms of Troy ranged with ours, what glory will exalt the Punic state! Do thou only, asking divine favour with peace-offerings, be bounteous in welcome and multiply reasons for delay, while the storm rages out at sea and Orion is rainy, and his ships are shattered and the sky unvoyageable.' With these words she fired her spirit with resolved love, put hope in her wavering soul, and undid her shame.

First they visit the shrines, and desire grace from altar to altar; they sacrifice sheep fitly chosen to Ceres the Lawgiver, to Phoebus and lord Lyaeus, to Juno before all, guardian of the marriage bond. Dido herself, excellent in beauty, holds the cup in her hand, and pours libation between the horns of a milk-white cow, or moves in state to the rich altars before the gods' presences, day by day renewing her gifts, and plunges her gaze into the breasts of cattle laid open to take counsel from the throbbing entrails. Ah, witless souls of soothsayers! how may vows or shrines help her madness? all the while the subtle flame consumes her inly, and deep in her breast the wound is silent and alive. Stung to misery, Dido wanders in frenzy all down the city, even as an arrow-stricken deer, whom, far and heedless amid the Cretan woodland, a shepherd archer has pierced and left the flying steel in her unaware;

she ranges in flight the Dictaean forest lawns; fast in her side clings the deadly reed. Now she leads Aeneas with her through the town, and displays her Sidonian treasure and ordered city; she essays to speak, and breaks off half-way in utterance. Now, as day wanes, she seeks the repeated banquet, and again in her madness pleads to hear the agonies of Ilium, and again hangs on the teller's lips. Thereafter, when all are gone their ways, and the dim moon in turn quenches her light, and the setting stars counsel to sleep, alone in the empty house she mourns, and flings herself on the couch he left: distant she hears and sees him in the distance; or enthralled by some look of his father, she holds Ascanius on her lap, if so she may steal her love unuttered. No more do the unfinished towers rise, no more do the people exercise in arms, nor work for safety in war on harbour or bastion; the works hang broken off, vast looming walls and engines towering into the sky.

So soon as she perceives her thus fast in the toils, and madly careless of her name, Jove's beloved wife, daughter of Saturn, accosts Venus thus:

'Noble indeed is the fame and splendid the spoils you win, thou and that boy of thine, and mighty the renown of your deity, if two gods have vanquished one woman by treachery. Nor am I so blind to thy terror of our town, thine old jealousy of the high house of Carthage. But what shall be the end? or why all this contest now? Nay, rather let us work an enduring peace and a bridal compact. Thou hast what all thy soul desired; Dido is on fire with love, and has caught the madness through and through. Then rule we this people jointly in equal lordship; allow her to be a Phrygian husband's slave, and to lay her Tyrians for dowry in thine hand.'

To her—for she knew the dissembled purpose in her words, to turn the kingdom of Italy away to the coasts of Libya— Venus thus began in answer: 'Who so mad as to reject these terms, or choose rather to try the fortune of war with thee? if only when done, as thou sayest, fortune follow. But I move uncertain of Jove's ordinance, whether he will that Tyrians and wanderers from Troy be one city, or approve the mingling of peoples or the treaty of union. Thou art his wife, and thy prayers may put his mind to proof. Go on; I will follow.'

Then Queen Juno thus rejoined: 'That task shall be mine. Now, by what means the present need may be fulfilled, attend and I will explain in brief. Aeneas and lovelorn Dido are to go hunting together in the woodland when to-morrow's rising sun goes forth and his rays unveil the world. On them, while the beaters run up and down, and encircle the lawns with toils, will I pour down a blackening rain-cloud mingled with hail, and wake all the sky with thunder. Their company will scatter for shelter in the dim darkness; Dido and the Trojan captain will take covert in the same cavern. I will be there, and if thy goodwill is assured me, I will unite them in wedlock, and make her wholly his; here shall Hymen be present.' The Cytherean gave ready assent to her request, and laughed at the guileful device.

Meanwhile Dawn has arisen forth of ocean. A chosen company issue from the gates while the morning star is high; they pour forth with meshed nets, toils, broad-headed hunting spears, Massylian horsemen and hounds of scent. At her doorway the Punic princes await their queen, who yet lingers in her chamber, and her horse stands splendid in gold and purple with clattering feet and jaws champing on the foamy bit. At last she comes forth amid a great thronging train, girt in a Sidonian mantle, broidered with needlework; her quiver is of gold, her tresses gathered into gold, a golden buckle clasps up her crimson gown. Therewithal the Phrygian train advances with joyous Iülus. Himself first and foremost of all, Aeneas joins her company and mingles his train with hers: even as Apollo, when he leaves wintry Lycia and the streams of Xanthus to visit his mother's Delos, and renews the dance, while Cretans and Dryopes and painted Agathyrsians mingle clamorous about his altar: himself he treads the Cynthian ridges, and plaits his flowing hair with soft heavy sprays and entwines it with gold; the arrows rattle on his shoulder: as lightly as he went Aeneas; such glow of beauty is on his princely face. When they are come to the mountain heights and pathless coverts, lo, wild goats driven from the cliff-tops run down the ridge; in another quarter stags speed over the open plain and gather their flying column in a cloud of dust as they leave the hills. But the boy Ascanius is in the valleys, exultant on his fiery horse, and gallops past one and another, praying that among the unwarlike herds a foaming boar may issue or a tawny lion descend the hill.

Meanwhile the sky begins to thicken and roar aloud. A rain-cloud comes down mingled with hail; the Tyrian train and the men of Troy, and Venus' Dardanian grandchild, scatter in fear and seek shelter far over the fields. Streams pour from the hills. Dido and the Trojan captain take covert in the same cavern. Primeval Earth and Juno the bridesmaid give the sign; fires flash out high in air, witnessing the union, and Nymphs cry aloud on the mountain-top. That day opened the gate of death and the springs of ill. For now Dido recks not of eye or tongue, nor sets her heart on love in secret: she calls it marriage, and with this word shrouds her blame.

Straightway Rumour runs through the great cities of Libya, —Rumour, than whom none other is more swift to mischief; she thrives on restlessness and gains strength by going: at first small and timorous; soon she lifts herself on high and paces the ground with head hidden among the clouds. Her, as they tell, Mother Earth, when stung by wrath against the gods, bore last sister to Coeus and Enceladus, fleet-footed and swift of wing, ominous, awful, vast; for every feather on her body is a waking eye beneath, wonderful to tell, and a tongue, and as many loud lips and straining ears. By night she flits between sky and land, shrilling through the dusk, and droops not her lids in sweet slumber; in daylight she sits on guard upon tall towers or the ridge of the house-roof, and makes great cities afraid; obstinate in perverseness and forgery no less than messenger of truth. She then exultingly filled the countries with manifold talk, and blazoned alike what was done and undone: one Aeneas is come, born of Trojan blood; on him beautiful Dido thinks no shame to fling herself; now they pass the long winter-tide together in revelry, regardless of their realms and enthralled by dishonouring passion. This the pestilent goddess spreads abroad in the mouths of men, and bends her course right on to King Iarbas, and with her words fires his spirit and swells his wrath.

He, the seed of Ammon by a ravished Garamantian Nymph, had built to Jove in his wide realms an hundred great temples, an hundred altars, and consecrated the wakeful fire that keeps watch by night before the gods perpetually, where the soil is fat with blood of beasts and the courts blossom with pied garlands. And he, distraught at heart and on fire at the bitter tidings, before his altars, amid the divine presences often, it is said, bowed in prayer to Jove with uplifted hands:

'Jupiter omnipotent, to whom from the broidered cushions of their banqueting halls the Maurusian people now pour offering of the wine-vat, lookest thou on this? or do we shudder vainly when our father hurls the thunderbolt, and do blind fires in the clouds and idle rumblings appal our soul? The woman wanderer who in our coasts planted a small town on purchased ground, to whom we gave fields by the shore and laws of settlement, has spurned our alliance and taken Aeneas for lord of her realm. And now that Paris, with his effeminate crew, his chin and oozy hair swathed in the turban of Maeonia, takes and keeps her; since to thy temples we bear oblation, and hallow an empty name.'

In such words he pleaded, clasping the altars; the Lord omnipotent heard, and cast his eye on the royal city and the lovers forgetful of their fairer fame. Then he addresses this charge to Mercury:

'Up and away, O son! call the breezes and slide down them on thy wings: accost the Dardanian captain who now loiters in Tyrian Carthage and casts not a look on the cities destined for him; carry down my words through the fleet air. Not such an one did his mother most beautiful vouch him to us, nor for this twice rescue him from Grecian arms; but he was to rule an Italy teeming with empire and loud with war, to transmit the line of Teucer's royal blood, and lay all the world beneath his law. If such glories kindle him in no wise, and he take no trouble for his own honour, does a father grudge his Ascanius the towers of Rome? with what device or in what hope loiters he among a hostile race, and casts not a glance on his Ausonian children and the fields of Lavinium? Let him set sail: this is the sum: thereof be thou our messenger.'

He ended: the other made ready to obey his father's high command. And first he laces to his feet the shoes of gold that bear him winging high over seas or land as fleet as the blast; then takes the rod wherewith he calls wan souls forth of Orcus, or sends them again to the sad depth of hell, gives sleep and takes it away and unseals dead eyes; in whose strength he courses the winds and swims through the tossing clouds. And now in flight he descries the peak and steep sides of toiling Atlas, whose crest sustains the sky; Atlas, whose pine-clad head is girt alway with black clouds and beaten by wind and rain; snow is shed over his shoulders for covering; rivers tumble over his aged chin; and his rough beard is stiff with ice. Here the Cyllenian, poised evenly on his wings, first checked his flight; hence he shot himself sheer to the water. Like a bird that flies low, skirting the sea about the craggy shores of its fishery, even thus the brood of Cyllene left his mother's father, and flew, cutting the winds between sky and land, toward the sandy Libyan shore. So soon as his winged feet touched at the hut-villages, he espies Aeneas founding towers and ordering new dwellings; his sword twinkled with yellow jasper, and a cloak hung from his shoulders ablaze with Tyrian sea-purple, a gift that Dido had made costly and shot the warp with threads of gold. Straightway he breaks in: 'Layest thou now the foundations of high Carthage, and buildest up a fair city in dalliance? ah, forgetful of thine own kingdom and state! From bright Olympus I descend to thee at express command of heaven's sovereign, whose deity sways sky and earth; expressly he bids me carry this charge through the fleet air: with what device or in what hope dost thou loiter idly on Libyan lands? if such glories kindle thee in no wise, yet cast an eye on growing Ascanius, on Iülus thine hope and heir, to whom the kingdom of Italy and the Roman land is due.' As these words left his lips the Cyllenian, yet speaking, quitted mortal sight and vanished into thin air away out of his eyes.

But Aeneas in truth gazed in dumb amazement, his hair thrilled up, and the voice choked in his throat. He burns to flee away and leave the pleasant land, aghast at the high warning and divine ordinance. Alas, what shall he do? how venture now to smooth the tale to the frenzied queen? what prologue shall he find? and this way and that he rapidly throws his mind, and turns it on all hands in swift change of thought. In his perplexity this seemed the better counsel; he calls Mnestheus and Sergestus, and brave Serestus, and bids them silently equip the fleet, gather their crews to the shore, and prepare their armament, keeping the cause of the commotion hid; himself meanwhile, since Dido in her kindness knows not and looks not for severance to so strong a love, will essay to approach her when she may be told most gently, and the way for it be fair. All at once gladly do as bidden, and obey his command.

But the Queen—who may delude a lover?—foreknew his devices, and at once caught the presaging stir, fearing even where no fear was. To her likewise had evil Rumour borne the maddening news of the fleet in equipment and the voyage prepared. Helpless at heart, she reels aflame with rage throughout the city, even as the scared Thyiad in her frenzied triennial orgies, when the holy vessels move forth and the cry of Bacchus re-echoes, and Cithaeron calls her with nightlong din. Thus at last she breaks out upon Aeneas:

'And thou didst hope, traitor, to mask such infamy, and slip away silently from my land? Our love holds thee not, nor the hand thou once gavest, nor the bitter death that is left for Dido's portion? Nay, even in winter weather thou labourest on thy fleet, and hastenest to launch into the deep amid northern gales; ah, cruel! Why, were thy quest not of alien fields and unknown dwellings, did thine ancient Troy remain, should Troy be sought in voyages over tempestuous seas? Fliest thou from me? me who by these tears and thine own hand beseech

thee, since naught else, alas! have I kept mine own—by our
union and the marriage rites begun; if I have done thee any
grace, or aught of mine was once sweet to thee,—pity our sinking house, and if there yet be room for prayers, put off this
purpose of thine. For thy sake Libyan tribes and Nomad kings
are hostile; my Tyrians are estranged; for thy sake, thine, is
mine honour perished, and the former fame, my one title to
the skies. How leavest thou me to die, O my guest? since of
the name of husband all that is left is this. For what do I wait?
till Pygmalion overthrow his sister's city, or Gaetulian Iarbas
lead me to captivity? At least if before thy flight a child of
thine had been clasped in my arms, if a tiny Aeneas were playing in my hall, whose face might yet image thine, I would not
think myself ensnared and deserted utterly.'

She ended; he by counsel of Jove held his gaze unstirred,
and kept his anguish hard down in his heart. At last he briefly
answers:

'Never, O Queen, will I deny that thy goodness has gone
high as thy words can swell the reckoning; nor will I grudge
a memory to Elissa while I remember myself, and breath sways
this body. Little will I say where little is to be said. I never
hoped to slip away in stealthy flight; fancy not that; nor did
I ever hold out the marriage torch or enter thus into alliance.
Did fate allow me to guide my life by mine own government,
and calm my sorrows as I would, my first duty were to the
Trojan city and the dear remnant of my kindred; the high
house of Priam should abide, and my hand had set up Troy
towers anew for a conquered people. But now for broad Italy
has Apollo of Grynos bidden me steer, for Italy the oracles of
Lycia. Here is my desire; this is my native country. If thy
Phoenician eyes are stayed on the fortress of Carthage and thy
Libyan city, what wrong is it, I pray, that we Trojans should
find rest on Ausonian land? We too may seek a foreign realm
unforbidden. In my sleep, often as the dank shades of night
veil the earth, often as the stars lift their fires, the troubled
phantom of my father Anchises comes in warning and dread;
my boy Ascanius comes and the wrong done to one so dear in

cheating him of an Hesperian kingdom and destined fields. Now even the gods' interpreter, sent straight from Jove —I call both to witness—has borne down his commands through the fleet air. Myself in broad daylight I saw the deity passing within the walls, and these ears drank his utterance. Cease to madden me and thyself alike with plaints. Not of my will do I follow Italy. . . .'

Long ere he ended she gazes on him askance, turning her eyes from side to side and perusing him with silent glances; then thus wrathfully speaks:

'No goddess was thy mother, nor Dardanus founder of thy line, traitor! but rough Caucasus bore thee on his iron crags, and Hyrcanian tigresses gave thee suck. For why do I conceal it? For what further outrage do I wait? Has our weeping cost him a sigh, or a lowered glance? Has he broken into tears, or had pity on his lover? Where, where shall I begin? Now neither doth Queen Juno nor our Saturnian lord regard us with righteous eyes. Nowhere is trust safe. Cast ashore and destitute I welcomed him, and madly gave him place and portion in my kingdom; I found him his lost fleet and drew his comrades from death. Alas, the fire of madness speeds me on. Now prophetic Apollo, now oracles of Lycia, now the very gods' interpreter sent straight from Jove through the air carries these rude commands! Truly that is work for the gods, that a care to vex their peace! I detain thee not, nor gainsay thy words: go, follow thine Italy down the wind; seek thy realm overseas. Yet midway my hope is, if righteous gods can do aught at all, thou wilt drain the cup of vengeance on the rocks, and re-echo calls on Dido's name. In murky fires I will follow far away, and when chill death has severed body from soul, my ghost will haunt thee in every region. Wretch, thou shalt repay! I will hear; and the rumour of it shall reach me deep in the under world.'

Even on these words she breaks off her speech unfinished, and, sick at heart, escapes out of the air and sweeps round and away out of sight, leaving him in fear and much hesitance, and with much on his mind to say. Her women catch her in their arms, and carry her swooning limbs to her marble chamber and lay her on her bed.

But good Aeneas, though he would fain soothe and comfort her grief, and quell her passion by speech, with many a sigh, and melted in soul by his great love, yet fulfils the divine commands and returns to his fleet. Then indeed the Teucrians set to work, and haul down their tall ships all along the shore. The hulls are oiled and afloat; they carry from the woodland green boughs for oars and massy logs unhewn, in hot haste to go. ... One might descry them shifting their quarters and pouring out of all the town: even as ants, mindful of winter, plunder a great heap of wheat and store it in their house; a black column advances on the plain as they carry home their spoil on a narrow track through the grass. Some shove and strain with their shoulders at big grains, some marshal the ranks and chastise delay; all the path is aswarm with work. What then were thy thoughts, O Dido, as thou sawest it? What sighs didst thou utter, viewing from the fortress roof the broad beach aswarm, and seeing before thine eyes the whole sea stirred with their noisy din? Injurious Love, to what dost thou not compel mortal hearts! Again she must needs break into tears, again essay entreaty, and bow her spirit down to love, not to leave aught untried and go to death in vain.

'Anna, thou seest the bustle that fills the circle of the shore. They have gathered from every quarter; already their canvas woos the breezes, and the joyous sailors have garlanded the sterns. This great pain, my sister, I shall have strength to bear, as I have had strength to foresee. Yet this one thing, Anna, for love and pity's sake—for of thee alone was the traitor fain, to thee even his secret thoughts were confided, alone thou knewest his moods and tender fits—go, my sister, and humbly accost the haughty stranger: I did not take the Grecian oath in Aulis to root out the race of Troy; I sent no fleet against her fortresses, neither have I disentombed his father Anchises' ashes and ghost. Why does he refuse my words entrance to his stubborn ears? Whither does he run? let him grant this grace—alas, the last!—to his lover, and await fair winds and an easy passage. No more do I pray for the old delusive marriage, nor that he give up fair Latium and abandon a kingdom. A breathing-space I ask, to give my madness rest and room, till my very fortune teach my grief submission. This last grace I implore—sister, be pitiful—let him but grant me this and I will repay it weighted with my death.'

So she pleaded, and so her sister carries and recarries the piteous tale of weeping. But by no weeping is he stirred, and no words that he hears may bend him. Fate withstands, and lays divine bars on unmoved mortal ears. Even as when the eddying blasts of northern Alpine winds are emulous to uproot the secular strength of a mighty oak, it wails on, and the trunk quivers and the high foliage strews the ground; the tree clings fast on the rocks, and high as her top soars into the aëry sky, so deep strike her roots to hell; even thus is the hero buffeted with changeful perpetual accents, and distress thrills his mighty breast, while his purpose stays unstirred, and her tears are shed in vain.

Then indeed, hapless and dismayed by doom, Dido prays for death, and is weary of looking on the arch of heaven. The more to make her fulfil her purpose and quit the light, she saw, when she laid her gifts on the altars alight with incense, awful to tell, the holy streams blacken, and the wine turn as it poured into ghastly blood. Of this sight she spoke to none— no, not to her sister. Likewise there was within the house a marble temple of her ancient lord, kept of her in marvellous honour, and fastened with snowy fleeces and festal boughs. Forth of it she seemed to hear her husband's voice crying and calling when night was dim upon earth, and alone on the house-tops the screech-owl often made moan with funeral note and long-drawn sobbing cry. Therewithal many a warning of wizards of old terrifies her with appalling presage. In her sleep fierce Aeneas drives her wildly, and ever she seems being left by herself alone, ever going uncompanioned on a weary way, and seeking her Tyrians in a solitary land: even as frantic Pentheus sees the arrayed Furies and a double sun, and Thebes shows herself twofold to his eyes: or Agamemnonian Orestes driven over the stage, when his mother pursues him armed with torches and dark serpents, and the Fatal Sisters crouch avenging in the doorway.

So when, overcome by her pangs, she has caught the madness and resolved to die, she works out secretly the time and fashion, and accosts her sorrowing sister with mien hiding her design and hope calm on her brow.

'I have found a way, mine own—wish me joy, sisterlike— to restore him to me or release me of my love for him. Hard by the ocean limit and the set of sun is the extreme Aethiopian land, where ancient Atlas turns on his shoulders the starred burning axletree of heaven. Out of it has been shown to me a priestess of Massylian race, warder of the temple of the Hesperides, even she who gave the dragon his food, and kept the holy boughs on the tree, sprinkling clammy honey and slumberous poppy-seed. She vouches with her spells to relax the purposes of whom she will, but on others to bring passion and pain; to stay the river-waters and turn the stars backward: she calls up ghosts by night; thou shalt see earth moaning under foot and mountain-ashes descending from the hills. I take heaven, sweet, to witness, and thee, mine own darling sister, I do not willingly arm myself with the arts of magic. Do thou secretly raise a pyre in the inner court, and lay upon it the arms of the man that he cruelly left hanging in our chamber, and all the dress he wore, and the bridal bed where I fell. It is good to wipe out all traces of the accursed one, and the priestess orders thus.' So speaks she, and is silent, while pallor overruns her face. Yet Anna deems not her sister drapes death in these strange rites, and grasps not her wild purpose, nor fears aught deeper than at Sychaeus' death. So she makes ready as bidden. . . .

But the Queen, when the pyre is built up of piled faggots and cleft ilex in the inmost of her dwelling, hangs the room with chaplets and garlands it with funeral boughs: on the pillow she lays the dress he wore, the sword he left, and an image of him, knowing what was to come. Altars are reared around, and the priestess, with hair undone, thrice peals from her lips the hundred gods of Erebus and Chaos, and the triform Hecate, the triple-faced maidenhood of Diana. Likewise she had sprinkled pretended waters of Avernus' spring, and rank herbs are sought mown by moonlight with brazen sickles, dark with milky venom, and sought is the tailsman torn from a horse's forehead at birth ere the dam could snatch it.... Herself, the holy cake in her pure hands, hard by the altars, with one foot unshod and garments flowing loose, she invokes the gods ere she die, and the stars that know of doom; then prays to whatsoever deity looks in righteousness and remembrance on lovers ill allied.

Night fell; weary creatures took quiet slumber all over earth, and woodland and wild waters had sunk to rest; now the stars wheel midway on their gliding path, now all the country is silent, and beasts and gay birds that haunt liquid levels of lake or thorny rustic thicket lay couched asleep under the still night. But not so the distressed Phoenician, nor does she ever sink asleep or take the night upon eyes or breast; her pain redoubles, and her love swells to renewed madness, as she tosses on the strong tide of wrath. Even so she begins, and thus revolves with her heart alone:

'Lo, what do I? Shall I again make trial of mine old wooers that will scorn me? and stoop to sue for a Numidian marriage among those whom already over and over I have disdained for husbands? Then shall I follow the Ilian fleets and the uttermost bidding of the Teucrians? because they are glad to have been once raised up by my succour, or the grace of mine old kindness is fresh in their remembrance? And who will permit me, if I would? or take a hated woman on their proud fleet? art thou ignorant, ah me, even in ruin, and knowest not yet the forsworn race of Laomedon? And then? shall I accompany the triumphant sailors, a lonely fugitive? or plunge forth girt with all my Tyrian train? so hardly severed from Sidon city, shall I again drive them seaward, and bid them spread their sails to the tempest? Nay die thou, as thou deservest, and let the steel end thy pain. With thee it began; overborne by my tears, thou, O my sister, dost load me with this madness and agony, and cast me to the enemy. It was not mine to spend a wild life without stain, far from a bridal chamber, and untouched by this passion. O faith ill kept, that was plighted to Sychaeus' ashes!' Thus her heart broke in long lamentation.

Now Aeneas was fixed to go, and now, with all set duly in order, was taking hasty sleep on his high quarterdeck. To him as he slept the god appeared once again in the same fashion of countenance, and thus seemed to renew his warning, in all points like to Mercury, voice and hue and golden hair and limbs gracious in youth. 'Goddess-born, canst thou sleep on in such danger? and seest not the coming perils that hem thee in, madman! nor hearest the breezes blowing fair? She, fixed on death, is revolving craft and crime grimly in her bosom, and swells the changing surge of wrath. Fliest thou not hence headlong, while headlong flight is yet possible? Even now wilt thou see ocean weltering with broken timbers, see the fierce glare of torches and the beach in a riot of flame, if dawn break on thee yet dallying in this land. Up ho! linger no more! Woman is ever a fickle and changing thing.' So spoke he, and melted in the black night.

Then indeed Aeneas, startled by the sudden phantom, leaps out of slumber and bestirs his crew to headlong haste. 'Awake, O men, and sit down to the thwarts; shake out sail speedily. A god sent from high heaven, lo! again spurs us to speed our flight and cut the twisted cables. We follow thee, holy one of heaven, whoso thou art, and again joyfully obey thy command. O be favourable; give gracious aid and bring fair sky and weather.' He spoke, and snatching his sword like lightning from the sheath, strikes at the hawser with the drawn steel. The same zeal catches all at once; rushing and tearing they quit the shore; the sea is hidden under their fleets; strongly they toss up the foam and sweep the blue water.

And now Dawn broke, and, leaving the saffron bed of Tithonus, shed her radiance anew over the world; when the Queen saw from her watch-tower the first light whitening, and the fleet standing out under squared sail, and discerned shore and haven empty of all their oarsmen. Thrice and four times she struck her hand on her lovely breast and rent her yellow hair: 'God!' she cries, 'shall he go? shall an alien make mock of our realm? Will they not issue in armed pursuit from all the city, and some launch ships from the dockyards? Go; bring fire in haste, serve out weapons, ply the oars! What do I talk? or where am I? what mad change is on my purpose? Alas, Dido! now evil deeds touch thee; that had been fitting once, when thou gavest away thy crown. Behold the faith and hand of him! who, they say, carries his household's ancestral gods about with him! who stooped his shoulders to a father outworn with age! Could I not have riven his body in sunder and strewn it on the waves? and slain with the sword his comrades and his dear Ascanius, and served him for the banquet at his father's table? But the chance of battle had been dubious. If it had! whom did I fear in the death-agony? I should have borne firebrands into his camp and filled his decks with flame, blotted out father and son and race together, and flung myself atop of all. Sun, whose fires lighten all the works of the world, and thou, Juno, mediatress and witness of these my distresses, and Hecate, cried on by night in crossways of cities, and you, fatal avenging sisters and gods of dying Elissa, hear me now; bend your just deity to my woes, and listen to our prayers. If it must needs be that the accursed one touch his haven and float up to land, if thus Jove's decrees demand, and this is the appointed term,—yet, distressed in war by an armed and gallant nation, driven homeless from his borders, rent from Iülus' embrace, let him sue for succour and see death on death untimely on his people; nor when he has yielded him to the terms of a harsh peace, may he have joy of his kingdom or the pleasant light; but let him fall before his day and without burial amid its soil. This I pray; this and my blood with it I pour for the last utterance. Then do you, O Tyrians, pursue his seed with your hatred for all ages to come; send this guerdon to our ashes. Let no kindness nor truce be between the nations. Arise, some avenger, out of our dust, to follow the Dardanian settlers with firebrand and steel. Now, then, whensoever strength shall be given, I invoke the enmity of shore to shore, wave to water, sword to sword; let their battles go down to their children's children.'

So speaks she as she kept turning her mind round about, seeking how soonest to break away from the hateful light. Thereon she speaks briefly to Barce, nurse of Sychaeus; for a heap of dusky ashes held her own, in her country of long ago:

'Sweet nurse, bring Anna my sister hither to me. Bid her haste and sprinkle river water over her body, and bring with her the beasts ordained for expiation: so let her come: and thou likewise veil thy brows with a pure chaplet. I would fulfil the rites of Stygian Jove that I have fitly ordered and begun, so set the limit to my distresses and give over to flame the pyre of the Dardanian chief.'

So speaks she; the old woman went eagerly with quickened pace. But Dido, panting and fierce in her awful purpose, with bloodshot restless gaze, and spots on her quivering cheeks burning through the pallor of imminent death, bursts into the inner courts of the house, and mounts in madness the lofty stairs, and unsheathes the sword of Dardania, a gift sought for other use than this. Then after her eyes fell on the Ilian raiment and the bed she knew, dallying a little with her purpose through her tears, she sank on the pillow and spoke the last words of all:

'Dress he wore, sweet while doom and deity allowed! receive my spirit now, and release me from my distresses. I have lived and fulfilled Fortune's allotted course; and now shall I go a queenly phantom under the earth. I have built a renowned city; I have seen my ramparts rise; by my brother's punishment I have avenged my husband of his enemy; happy, ah me! and over happy, had but the keels of Dardania never touched our shores!' She spoke; and burying her face in the pillow, 'Death it will be,' she cries, 'and unavenged; but death be it. Thus, thus is it good to pass into the dark. Let the pitiless Dardanian's gaze drink in this fire out at sea, and my death be the omen he carries on his way.'

She ceased; and even as she spoke her people see her sunk on the steel, and blood reeking on the sword and spattered on her hands. A cry rises in the high halls; Rumour riots down the quaking city. The house resounds with lamentation and sobbing and bitter crying of women; heaven echoes their loud wails; even as though all Carthage or ancient Tyre went down as the foe poured in, and the flames rolled furious over the roofs of house and temple. Death-stricken her sister heard, and in swift hurrying dismay, with torn face and smitten bosom, darts through them all, and calls the dying woman by her name. 'Was it this, mine own? Was my summons a snare? Was it this thy pyre, ah me, this thine altar fires meant? How shall I begin my desolate moan? Didst thou disdain a sister's company in death? Thou shouldst have called me to share thy doom; in the self-same hour, the self-same pang of steel had been our portion. Did these very hands build it, did my voice call on our father's gods, that with thee lying thus I should be away, O merciless? Thou hast destroyed thyself and me together, O my sister, and the Sidonian lords and people, and this thy city. Give her wounds water: I will bathe them and catch on my lips the last breath that haply yet lingers.' So speaking she had climbed the high steps, and, wailing, clasped and caressed her half-lifeless sister in her bosom, and stanched the dark streams of blood with her gown. She, essaying to lift her heavy eyes, swoons back; the deep-driven wound gurgles in her breast. Thrice she rose, and strained to lift herself on her elbow; thrice she rolled back on the pillow, and with wandering eyes sought the light of high heaven, and moaned as she found it.

Then Juno omnipotent, pitying her long pain and difficult decease, sent Iris down from heaven to unloose the struggling life from the body where it clung. For since neither by fate did she perish, nor as one who had earned her death, but woefully before her day, and fired by sudden madness, not yet had Proserpine taken her tress from the golden head, nor sentenced her to the nether Stygian world. So Iris on dewy saffron pinions flits down through the sky athwart the sun in a trail of a thousand changing dyes, and stopping over her head: 'This lock, sacred to Dis, I take as bidden, and release thee from that body of thine.' So speaks she, and cuts it with her hand. And therewith all the warmth ebbed forth from her, and the life passed away upon the winds.

BOOK FIFTH

THE GAMES OF THE FLEET

MEANWHILE Aeneas and his fleet in unwavering track now held mid passage, and cleft the waves that blackened under the North, looking back on the city that even now gleams with hapless Elissa's funeral flame. Why the broad blaze is lit lies unknown; but the bitter pain of a great love trampled, and the knowledge of what woman can do in madness, draw the Teucrians' hearts to gloomy guesses.

When their ships held the deep, nor any land farther appears, the seas all round, and all round the sky, a dusky shower drew up over his head, carrying night and storm, and the wave shuddered and gloomed. Palinurus, master of the fleet, cries from the high stern: 'Alas, why have these heavy storm-clouds girt the sky? lord Neptune, what wilt thou do?' Then he bids clear the rigging and bend strongly to the oars, and brings the sails across the wind, saying thus:

'Noble Aeneas, not did Jupiter give word and warrant would I hope to reach Italy under such a sky. The shifting winds roar athwart our course, and blow stronger out of the black west, and the air thickens into mist: not are we fit to beat up against them or force a passage. Fortune is the stronger; let us follow her, and turn our course whither she calls. Not far away, I think, are the faithful shores of thy brother Eryx, and the Sicilian haven, if my memory retraces rightly the stars I watched but now.'

Then good Aeneas: 'Even I ere now discern that the winds will have it so, and thou urgest against them in vain. Turn thou the course of our sailing. Could any land be welcomer to me, or where I would sooner choose to put in my weary ships, than this that has Dardanian Acestes to greet me, and laps in its embrace lord Anchises' dust?' This said, they steer for harbour, while the following west wind stretches their sails; the fleet runs fast down the flood, and at last they land joyfully on the familiar beach. But Acestes, espying from a high hilltop the friendly squadron approaching from afar, hastens towards them, weaponed and clad in the shaggy skin of a Libyan she-bear. Him a Trojan mother conceived and bore to Crinisus river; not forgetful of his parentage, he wishes them joy of their return, and gladly entertains them on his rustic treasure and comforts their weariness with his friendly store. So soon as the morrow's clear daylight had chased the stars out of the east, Aeneas calls his comrades along the beach together, and from a mounded hillock speaks:

'Great people of Dardanus, born of high blood of gods, the yearly circle of the months is measured out to fulfilment since we laid the dust in earth, all that was left of my divine father, and consecrated our mourning altars. And now the day, if I mistake not, is at hand (this, O gods, was your will), which I will ever keep in grief, ever in honour. Did I spend it an exile on Gaetulian quicksands, or hemmed in on the Argolic sea or in Mycenae town, yet would I fulfil the yearly vows and annual ordinance of festival, and pile the altars with their due gifts. Now we are led hither, to the very dust and ashes of my father, not as I deem without divine purpose and influence, and borne home into the friendly haven. Up then and let us all gather joyfully to the sacrifice: pray we for winds, and that he may grant me to pay these rites to him year by year in an established city and consecrated temple. Two head of oxen Acestes, the seed of Troy, gives to each of your ships by tale: invite to the feast your own ancestral gods of the household, and those whom our host Acestes worships. Further, so the ninth Dawn uplift the gracious day upon men, and her shafts unveil the world, I will ordain contests for my Trojans; first for swift ships; then whoso excels in the foot-race, and whoso, confident in strength, comes forward as champion in shot of light arrows, or adventures to join battle with gloves of raw hide; let all be here, and let merit look for the prize and palm. Now all be hushed, and twine your temples with boughs.'

So speaks he, and shrouds his brows with his mother's myrtle. So Helymus does, so Acestes ripe of years, so the boy Ascanius, and the rest of the people follow. He advances from the assembly to the tomb among a throng of many thousands that crowd about him; here he pours on the ground in fit libation two goblets of pure wine, two of new milk, two of consecrated blood, and scatters bright blossoms, saying thus: 'Hail, holy father, hail once again, ashes of him I saved in vain, and soul and shade of my sire! Thou wert not to share the search for Italian borders and destined fields, nor the dim Ausonian Tiber.' Thus had he spoken; when from beneath the sanctuary a snake slid out in seven vast coils and sevenfold slippery spires, quietly circling the grave and gliding from altar to altar, his green chequered body and the spotted lustre of his scales ablaze with gold, as the bow in the cloud darts a thousand changing dyes athwart the sun: Aeneas stood amazed at the sight. At last he wound his long train among the vessels and polished cups, and tasted the feast, and again leaving the altars where he had fed, crept harmlessly back beneath the tomb. Therefore he renews more devoutly the rites begun for his sire; doubtful if he shall think it the Genius of the ground or his father's ministrant, he slays, as is fit, two sheep of two years old, as many swine and dark-backed steers, pouring the while cups of wine, and calling on the soul of great Anchises and the ghost rearisen from Acheron. Therewithal his comrades joyfully bring gifts each of his own store, heap the altars, and slay steers in sacrifice: others set caldrons arow, and, lying along the grass, put live embers under spits and roast the flesh.

The desired day came, and now Phaëthon's coursers bore up the ninth Dawn clear and bright; and the name and renown of illustrious Acestes had stirred up all the bordering people; their holiday throng had filled the shore, to see Aeneas' men, and some ready to join in contest. First of all the prizes are laid out to view in the middle of the racecourse; tripods of sacrifice, green garlands and palms, the reward of the conquerors, armour and garments dipped in purple, a talent of silver and one of gold: and from a bank in the midst a trumpet-note proclaims the games begun. For the first contest four matched ships, the pick of all the fleet, enter with their heavy oars. Mnestheus' keen rowers drive the swift Sea-Dragon, Mnestheus the Italian to be, from whose name is the Memmian family; Gyas the huge bulk of the hube Chimaera, a floating town, whom her triple-tiered Dardanian crew urge on with oars rising in threefold rank; Sergestus, from whom the Sergian house holds her name, sails in the tall Centaur; and in the sea-green Scylla Cloanthus, whence is thy family, Cluentius of Rome.

Apart in the sea and over against the foaming beach, lies a rock that the swoln waves beat and drown what time the winter north-westers blot out the stars; in calm it rises silent out of the still water, flat-topped, and a haunt where cormorants love best to take the sun. Here lord Aeneas set up a goal of leafy ilex, a mark for the sailors to know whence to return, where to wheel their long course round. Then they choose stations by lot, and on the sterns their captains glitter afar in array of gold and scarlet; the rest of the crews are crowned with poplar sprays, and their naked shoulders glisten wet with oil. They sit down at the thwarts, and their arms are tense on the oars; at full strain they wait the signal, while throbbing fear and high passion of glory drain their riotous blood. Then, when the clear trumpet-note sounds, all in a moment leap forward from the line; the shouts of the sailors strike up to heaven, and the channels are swept into foam by straining arms. They cleave their furrows abreast, and all the sea is torn asunder by oars and triple-pointed prows. Not with speed so headlong do racing pairs whirl the chariots over the course, as they rush streaming from the barriers; not so do their charioteers shake the wavy reins loose over their team, and hang forward on the whip. All the woodland rings with clapping and shouts of men that cheer their favourites, and the sheltered beach eddies back their cries; the noise buffets and re-echoes from the hills. Gyas shoots out in front of the noisy crowd, and glides foremost along the water; whom Cloanthus follows next, rowing better, but held back by his dragging weight of pine. After them, at equal distance, the Sea-Dragon and the Centaur strive to win the foremost room; and now the Sea-Dragon has it, now the vast Centaur outstrips and passes her; now they dart on both together, their figureheads in a line, and their long keels furrowing the salt water-ways. And now they drew nigh the rock, and were hard on the goal; when Gyas as he led, winner over half the flood, cries aloud to Menoetes, the ship's steersman: 'Whither away so far to the right? This way direct her path; kiss the shore, and let the oarblade on the left graze the reefs. Others may keep to deep water.' He spoke; but Menoetes, fearing blind rocks, turns the prow away toward the open sea. 'Whither wanderest thou away? head for the rocks, Menoetes!' again shouts Gyas to bring him back; and lo! glancing round he sees Cloanthus close behind and keeping nearer. Between Gyas' ship and the echoing crags he scrapes through inside on his left, flashes past his leader, and leaving the goal behind is safe in open sea. Then indeed grief burned fierce through his strong frame, and his cheeks ran with tears; heedless of his own dignity and his crew's safety, he flings the too cautious Menoetes sheer into the sea from the high stern, himself succeeds as guide and master of the helm, and cheers on his men, and turns his tiller in to shore. But old Menoetes, when at last he rose struggling from the sea-bottom, wet in his dripping clothes, climbs to the top of the crag, and sits down on a dry rock. The Teucrians laughed out as he fell and as he swam, and laugh to see him spitting the salt water from his chest. At this a joyful hope kindled in the two behind, Sergestus and Mnestheus, of catching up Gyas' wavering course. Sergestus gets the nearer station, closing in on the rock, yet not leading with his whole length of keel; part is ahead, in part the Sea-Dragon's prow overlaps her rival. But striding amidships between his comrades, Mnestheus cheers them on: 'Now, now rise to the oars, comrades of Hector, whom I chose to follow me in Troy's extremity; now put forth the might and courage you showed in Caetulian quicksands, amid Ionian seas and Malea's chasing waves. Not the first place do I now seek for Mnestheus, nor strive to conquer; yet ah!—but be the victory theirs, O Neptune, to whom thou hast given it. To come back last were shame. Win but this, fellow-citizens, and avert that disaster!' His men bent forward, straining every muscle; the brass-plated hull quivers to their mighty strokes, and the ground runs from under her; limbs and parched lips shake with their rapid panting, and sweat flows in streams all over them. Mere chance brought the crew the prize they desired. For while Sergestus drives his prow furiously in towards the rocks and comes up with too scanty room, alas! he grounded on an outstretching reef; the rocks crashed, the oars struck and jarred on the jagged edge, and the broken prow jammed. The sailors leap up and hold her with loud cries, and get out iron-shod poles and sharp-pointed boathooks, and pick up their broken oars out of the eddies. But Mnestheus, rejoicing and flushed by his triumph, with oars fast-dipping and winds at his call, issues into the shelving water and runs down the open sea. As a pigeon suddenly scared from a cavern, whose house and sweet nestlings are in the rock's recesses, wings her flight over the fields and rushes frightened from her house with loud clapping pinions; then gliding noiselessly through the air, slides on her liquid way and moves not her rapid wings; so Mnestheus, so the Sea-Dragon under him swiftly cleaves the last space of sea, so her own speed carries her flying on. And first Sergestus is left behind, struggling on the steep rock and shoal water, and shouting in vain for help and learning to race with broken oars. Next he catches up Gyas and the vast bulk of the Chimaera; she gives way, bereft of a steersman. And now on the very goal Cloanthus alone is left; him he pursues and presses hard, straining all his strength. Then indeed the shouts redouble, as all together eagerly cheer on the pursuer, and the sky echoes their clapping. These scorn to lose the honour that is their own, the glory in their grasp, and would sell life for renown; to these success lends life; they can, because they believe they can. And haply they had carried the prize with prows abreast, had not Cloanthus, stretching both his open hands over the sea, poured forth prayers and called the gods to hear his vows: 'Gods who are sovereign on the sea, over whose waters I run, to your altars on this beach will I joyfully bring a snow-white bull, my vow's penalty, and will cast his entrails into the salt flood and pour liquid wine.' He spoke, and far beneath the flood maiden Panopea heard him, with all Phorcus' choir of Nereids, and lord Portunus with his own mighty hand pushed him on his way. The ship flies to land swifter than the wind or an arrow's flight, and shoots into the deep harbour. Then the seed of Anchises, summoning all in order, declares Cloanthus conqueror by herald's outcry, and dresses his brows in green bay, and gives gifts to each crew, three bullocks of their choice, and wine, and a large talent of silver to take away. For their captains he adds special honours; to the winner a scarf wrought with gold, encircled by a deep double border of Meliboean purple; embroidered on it is the kingly boy on leafy Ida, chasing swift stags with javelin and racing feet, eager and as one panting; him Jove's swooping armour-bearer has caught up aloft from Ida in his talons; his aged guardians stretch their hands vainly upwards, and the baying of hounds rings fierce into the air. But to him who, next in merit, held the second place, he gives to wear a corslet of smooth link-mail triple-woofed with gold, stripped by his own conquering hand from Demoleos under tall Troy by the swift Simoïs, for his ornament and safeguard among arms. Scarce could the straining shoulders of his servants Phegeus and Sagaris carry its heavy folds; yet with it on, Demoleos at full speed would chase the scattered Trojans. The third prize he makes twin caldrons of brass, and bowls wrought in silver and rough with tracery. And now all moved away in the pride and wealth of their prizes, their brows bound with scarlet ribbons; when, hardly torn loose by all his art from the cruel rock, his oars lost, rowing feebly with a single tier, Sergestus brought in his ship jeered at and unhonoured. Even as often a serpent caught on a highway, if a brazen wheel has gone aslant over him or a wayfarer left him half dead and mangled with the blow of a heavy stone, wreathes himself slowly in vain effort to escape, in part undaunted, his eyes ablaze and his hissing throat lifted high; part crippled by the wound keeps him back, coiling in knots and twisting on his own body; so the ship moved rowing slowly on; but she hoists sail and under full sail glides into the harbour mouth. Glad that the ship is saved and the crew brought back, Aeneas presents Sergestus with his promised reward. A slave woman is given him not unskilled in Minerva's labours, Pholoë the Cretan, with twin boys at her breast.

This contest sped, good Aeneas moved to a grassy plain girt all about with winding wooded hills, and amid the valley an amphitheatre, whither, with many thousands, the hero advanced amid the concourse and took his seat on a platform. Here he allures with rewards and offer of prizes those who will try their hap in the fleet foot-race. Trojans and Sicilians gather mingling from all sides, Nisus and Euryalus foremost ... Euryalus famed for beauty and fresh youth, Nisus for pure affection towards the boy. Next follows renowned Diores, of Priam's royal line; after him Salius and Patron together, the one Acarnanian, the other Tegean by family and of Arcadian blood; next two men of Sicily, Helymus and Panopes, foresters and attendants on old Acestes; many besides whose fame is hid in obscurity. Then among them all Aeneas spoke thus: 'Hearken to this, and attend in good cheer. None out of this number will I let go without a gift. To each will I give two Gnosian shafts glittering with polished steel, and an axe chased with silver to bear away; one and all shall be honoured thus. The three foremost shall receive prizes, and have pale olive bound about their head. The first shall have a caparisoned horse, as conqueror; the second an Amazonian quiver filled with arrows of Thrace, girt about by a broad belt of gold, and on the link of the clasp a polished gem; let the third depart satisfied with this helmet of Argolis.' This said, they take their place, and the signal once heard, dart over the course and leave the line, pouring forth like a storm-cloud while they mark the goal. Nisus gets away first, and shoots out far in front of the throng, fleeter than the winds or the winged thunderbolt. Next to him, but next by a long gap, Salius follows; then, left a space behind him, Euryalus third... and Helymus comes after Euryalus; and close behind him, lo! Diores goes flying, just grazing foot with foot, hard on his shoulder; and if a longer space were left, he would slip forward and outpass him, or leave the race drawn. And now almost in the last lap, they began to come up exhausted to the goal, when luckless Nisus trips on the slippery blood of the slain steers, where haply it had spilled over the ground and wetted the green grass. Here, just in the flush of victory, he lost his feet; they slid away on the ground they pressed, and he fell forward right among the ordure and blood of the sacrifice. Yet forgot he not his darling Euryalus; for rising, he flung himself over the slippery ground in front of Salius, and he rolled over and lay all along on the hard sand. Euryalus shoots by and holds the first place, winner by his friend's gift, and flies on amid pursuing claps and cheers. Behind him Helymus comes up, and Diores, now third for the palm. At this Salius fills with loud clamour the whole concourse of the vast ring, and the lords who looked on in front, demanding back his defrauded prize. Euryalus is strong in favour, and beauty in tears, and the merit that gains grace from so fair a form. Diores supports him, who succeeded to the palm, so he loudly cries, and bore off the last prize in vain, if the highest honours shall be given to Salius. Then lord Aeneas speaks: 'For you your rewards remain assured, and none moves the boy's prize from its order: let me be allowed to pity a friend's innocent mischance.' So speaking, he gives to Salius a vast Gaetulian lionskin, with shaggy masses of hair and claws of gold. 'If this,' cries Nisus, 'is the reward of defeat, and thy pity is stirred for the fallen, what fit recompense wilt thou give to Nisus? to my excellence the first crown was due, had not I, like Salius, met Fortune's hostility.' And with the words he displayed his face and limbs befouled with the wet dung. His lord laughed kindly on him, and bade a shield be brought forth, the workmanship of Didymaon, taken from the hallowed gates of Neptune's Grecian temple; with this special prize he rewards his excellence.

Thereafter, when the races are finished and the gifts fulfilled: 'Now,' he cries, 'come, whoso has in him valour and ready heart, and lift up his arms with gauntleted hands.' So speaks he, and sets forth a double prize of battle; for the conqueror a bullock gilt and garlanded; a sword and beautiful helmet to console the conquered. Straightway without pause Dares issues to view in his vast strength, rising amid loud murmurs of the people; he who alone was wont to meet Paris in combat; he who, at the mound where princely Hector lies, struck down as he came the vast bulk upborne by conquering Butes, of Amycus' Bebrycian line, and stretched him dying on the yellow sand. Such was Dares; at once he raises his head high for battle, displays his broad shoulders, and stretches and swings his arms right and left, lashing the air with blows. For him another is required; but none out of all the train durst approach or put the gloves on his hands. So he takes his stand exultant before Aeneas' feet, deeming that all waived the palm; and thereon without more delay grasps the bull's horn with his left hand, and speaks thus: 'Goddess-born, if no man dare trust himself to battle, to what conclusion shall I stand? how long is it seemly to keep me? bid me carry off thy gifts.' Therewith all the Dardanians murmured assent, and bade yield him the promised prize.

At this aged Acestes spoke sharply to Entellus, as he sate next him on the green cushion of grass: 'Entellus, bravest of heroes once of old in vain, wilt thou thus idly let a gift so great be borne away uncontested? Where now prithee is divine Eryx, thy master of fruitless fame? where thy renown over all Sicily, and those spoils hanging in thine house?' Thereat he: 'Desire of glory is not gone, nor ambition checked by fear; but torpid age dulls my chilly blood, and my strength of limb is numb and outworn. If I had what once was mine, if I had now the youth that is yonder braggart's boast and confidence, it had taken no prize of goodly bullock to allure me; nor do I heed gifts.' So he spoke, and thereon flung down a pair of gloves of giant weight, with whose hard hide bound about his wrists valiant Eryx was wont to come armed to battle. They stood amazed; so stiff and grim lay the vast sevenfold oxhide sewn in with lead and iron. Dares most of all shrinks far back in horror, and the noble son of Anchises turns round this way and that their ponderous weight and the vast swathings of their straps. Then the old man thus uttered speech: 'How, had they seen the gloves that were Hercules' own arms, and the fatal fight on this very beach? These arms thy brother Eryx once wore; thou seest them yet stained with blood and spattered brains. In them he stood to face great Alcides; to them was I used while fuller blood supplied me strength, and envious old age had not yet strewn her snows on either temple. But if Dares of Troy will have none of these our arms, and good Aeneas is resolved on it, and Acestes deigns his approval, let us make the battle even. I give up to thee the gauntlets of Eryx; dismiss thy fears; and do thou strip off thy Trojan gloves.' So spoke he, and throwing back the fold of his raiment from his shoulders, he bares the massive joints and limbs, the great bones and muscles, and stands up huge in the middle of the ground. Then Anchises' lordly seed brought out matched gloves and bound the hands of both in equal arms. Straightway each took his stand on tiptoe, and undauntedly raised his arms high in air. They lift their heads right back and away out of reach of blows, and fence hand to hand in preluding skirmish; the one nimbler of foot and confident in his youth, the other mighty in mass of limb, but his knees totter tremulous and slow, and uneasy panting shakes his vast frame. Many a mutual blow the champions deliver in vain, many an one they redouble on chest and side, sounding hollow and loud: hands play fast about ear and temple, and jawbones clash under the hard strokes. Old Entellus stands immovable and astrain, only parrying hits with body and watchful eye. The other, as one who casts mounts against some high city or blockades a hill-fort in arms, tries this and that entrance, and ranges cunningly over all the ground, and presses many an attack in vain. Entellus rose and struck clean out with his right downwards; his quick opponent saw the descending blow before it came, and slid his body rapidly out of its way. Entellus hurled his strength into the air, and all his heavy mass, over-reaching, fell heavily to the earth; as sometime on Erymanthus or mighty Ida falls a hollow uprooted pine. Teucrians and men of Sicily rise eagerly; a cry goes up, and Acestes himself runs forward, and pityingly lifts his friend and birthmate from the ground. But the hero, not balked nor dismayed by his mishap, returns the keener to battle, and grows violent in wrath, while shame and resolved valour kindle his strength. All afire, he hunts Dares headlong over the lists, and redoubles his blows now with right hand, now with left; no breath nor pause; heavy as hailstones rattle on the roof from a storm-cloud, so thickly shower the blows from both his hands as he buffets Dares to and fro. Then lord Aeneas allowed not wrath to swell higher or Entellus to rage out his bitterness, but stopped the fight and rescued the exhausted Dares, saying thus in soothing words: 'Unhappy! what madness is this that has seized thy mind? Knowest thou not the strength is another's and the gods are changed? Yield thou to Heaven.' And with the words he proclaimed the battle over. But him his faithful mates lead to the ships dragging his knees feebly, swaying his head from side to side, and spitting from his mouth clotted gore and teeth mixed with blood. At summons they bear away the helmet and shield, and leave palm and bull to Entellus. At this the conqueror, high in pride and glorying over the bull, cries: 'Goddess-born, and you, O Trojans! learn thus what my strength of body was in its prime, and from what a death Dares is saved by your recall.' He spoke, and stood right opposite in face of the bullock standing by, the prize of battle; then drew back his hand, and swinging the hard gauntlet sheer down between the horns, smashed the bones in upon the shattered brain. The ox rolls over, and quivering and lifeless lies along the ground. Above it he utters speech thus: 'This life, Eryx, I give to thee, a better payment than Dares' death; here I lay down my gloves and skill unconquered.'

Forthwith Aeneas invites all who will to the contest of the swift arrow, and proclaims the prizes. With his mighty hand he uprears the mast of Serestus' ship, and on a cord passed across it hangs from the masthead a fluttering pigeon as mark for their steel. They gather, and a helmet of brass takes the lots as they throw them in. First before them all, amid prosperous cheers, comes out the place of Hippocoön son of Hyrtacus; and Mnestheus follows on him, but now conqueror in the ship race, Mnestheus with his chaplet of green olive. Third is Eurytion, thy brother, O Pandarus great in renown, thou who of old, when prompted to shatter the truce, didst hurl the first shaft amid the Achaeans. Last of all Acestes sank back at the bottom of the helmet, he too venturing to set hand to the task of youth. Then each and all they strongly bend their bows into a curve and pull shafts from their quivers. And first the arrow of the son of Hyrtacus, passing through the sky, smites the air asunder as it flies from the twanging string, and reaches and sticks fast full in the mast's wood: the mast quivered, and the bird fluttered her feathers in affright, and the whole ground rang with loud clapping. Next valiant Mnestheus took his stand with bow bent, aiming high with levelled eye and arrow; yet could not, unfortunate! hit the bird herself with his steel, but cut the knotted hempen bands that tied her foot as she hung from the masthead; she winged her flight into the high windy clouds. Then swiftly Eurytion, who ere now held the arrow ready on his bended bow, called in prayer to his brother, marked the pigeon as she now went down the empty sky exultant on clapping wings; and as she passed under a dark cloud, struck her: she fell breathless, and, leaving her life in the aëry firmament, slid down carrying the arrow that pierced her. Acestes alone was over, and the prize lost; yet he sped his arrow up into the air, to display his lordly skill and resounding bow. At this a sudden sign meets their eyes, mighty in augural presage, as the high event taught thereafter, and in late days boding seers prophesied of the omen. For the flying reed blazed out amid the swimming clouds, traced its path in flame, and burned away on the light winds; even as often stars fall shooting from the sky and draw a flying trail. Trinacrians and Trojans hung in astonishment, praying to the heavenly powers; neither does great

Aeneas reject the omen, but embraces glad Acestes and loads him with lavish gifts, speaking thus: 'Take, my lord: for the high King of heaven by these signs has willed thee to draw a prize uncompeted for. This gift shalt thou have as from aged Anchises' own hand, a bowl embossed with figures, that once Cisseus of Thrace gave my father Anchises to take as a precious gift, the record and pledge of his amity.' So speaking, he twines green bay about his brows, and proclaims Acestes conqueror first before them all. Nor did gentle Eurytion, though he alone struck the bird down from the lofty sky, grudge him his superior honour. Next comes for his prize he who cut the cord; he last, who pierced the mast with his winged reed.

But lord Aeneas, ere yet the contest is sped, calls to him Epytides, guardian and attendant of ungrown Iülus, and thus speaks into his faithful ear: 'Up and away, and tell Ascanius, if he now holds his band of boys ready, and their horses arrayed for the charge, to defile his squadrons to his grandsire's honour in bravery of arms.' So says he, and himself bids all the crowding throng withdraw from the long racecourse and leave the lists free. The boys move in before their parents' faces, glittering in rank on their bitted horses; as they go all the people of Troy and Trinacria murmur and admire. On the hair of them all rests a garland fitly trimmed; each carries two cornel spearshafts tipped with steel; some have polished quivers on their shoulders; above their breast and round their neck goes a flexible circlet of twisted gold. Three in number are the troops of horsemen, and three captains ride out ahead; twice six boys following each glitter in separate files under matched leaders. One youthful line goes rejoicingly behind little Priam, renewer of his grandsire's name, thy renowned seed, O Polites, destined to people Italy; he rides a Thracian horse dappled with spots of white, showing white on his pacing pasterns and white on his high forehead. Second is Atys, from whom the Latin Atii draw their line, little Atys, boy beloved of the boy Iülus. Last and excellent in beauty before them all, Iülus rode in on a Sidonian steed that Dido the fair had given him for token and pledge of love. The rest of the band are mounted on old Acestes' Sicilian horses.... The Dardanians greet their shy entrance with applause, and rejoice at the view, and recognise the features of their parents of old. When they have ridden joyously round all the concourse of their gazing friends, Epytides from afar gives the signal that they await, with shout and crack of whip. They gallop apart in pairs, and open their files three and three in deploying bands, and again at the call wheel about and bear down with levelled arms. Next they enter on other charges and other retreats in opposite spaces, and interlink circle with circle, and wage the armed phantom of battle. And now they discover their backs in flight, now turn their lances to the charge, now plight peace and gallop side by side. As once of old, they say, the labyrinth in high Crete had a tangled path between blind walls, and a thousand ways of doubling treachery, where marks to follow broke off in the maze unmastered and irretraceable: even in such a chase do the children of Troy entangle their footsteps and weave the game of flight and battle; like dolphins who, swimming through the wet seas, cut Carpathian or Libyan....

This manner of riding, these games Ascanius first revived, when he girt Alba the Long about the walls, and taught their celebration to the Old Latins in the fashion of his own boyhood, with the youth of Troy about him. The Albans taught it their children; on from them mighty Rome received it and kept the ancestral observance; and now the boys are called Troy, and the trooping Trojan.

Thus far sped the sacred contests to their holy lord. First from this point Fortune broke faith and grew estranged. While they pay the due rites to the tomb with diverse games, Juno, daughter of Saturn, sends Iris down the sky to the Ilian fleet, and breathes a gale to speed her on, revolving many a device, and not yet satiate of the ancient pain. She, speeding her way along the thousand-coloured bow, runs swiftly, seen of none, down her maiden path. She discerns the vast concourse, and traverses the shore, and sees the haven abandoned and the fleet left alone. But far withdrawn by the solitary verge of the sea the Trojan women wept their lost Anchises, and as they wept gazed all together on the fathomless flood. 'Alas, that so many straits and so vast a sea yet awaits the weary!' such is the single cry of all. They pray for a city, sick of their burden of ocean-toil. So she darts among them, not witless to harm, and lays by face and raiment of a goddess: she becomes Beroë, the aged wife of Tmarian Doryclus, who had once had birth and name and children, and in this guise goes among the Dardanian matrons. 'Ah, wretched we,' she cries, 'whom hostile Achaean hands did not drag to death beneath our native city! ah hapless race, for what destruction does Fortune hold thee back? The seventh summer now rolls on since Troy's overthrow, while we pass measuring out by so many stars the harbourless rocks over every water and land, pursuing all the while over the vast sea an Italy that flies us, and tossing on the waves. Here is the brotherly realm of Eryx, and Acestes' welcome: who denies us to cast up walls and give our citizens a city? O country, O household gods vainly rescued from the foe! shall there never be a Trojan town to tell of? shall I nowhere see a Xanthus and a Simoïs, the rivers of Hector? Nay, up and join me in burning with fire these ill-starred ships. For in sleep the phantom of Cassandra the soothsayer seemed to give me blazing brands: *Here seek your Troy,* she said; *here is your home.* Now is the time to do it; nor do these high portents allow delay. Behold four altars to Neptune; the god himself lends the firebrand and the intent.' Speaking thus, at once she strongly seizes the fiery weapon, and with straining hand whirls it far upreared, and flings: the souls of the Ilian women are startled and their wits amazed. At this one of their multitude, and she the eldest, Pyrgo, nurse in the palace to all Priam's many children: 'This is not Beroë, I tell you, O matrons; this is not the wife of Doryclus of Rhoeteum. Mark the lineaments of divine grace and the gleaming eyes, what a breath is hers, what a countenance, and the sound of her voice and the steps of her going. I, I time agone left Beroë apart, sick and fretting that she alone must have no part in this our service, nor pay Anchises his due sacrifice.' So spoke she.... But the matrons at first gazed dubious on the ships with malignant eyes, wavering between the wretched longing for the land they trod and the call of the destined realm: when the goddess rose through the sky on poised wings, and in her flight drew a vast bow beneath the clouds. Then indeed, amazed at the tokens and driven by madness, they raise a cry and snatch fire from the sacred hearths within; others plunder the altars, and heap on leafy brushwood and faggots. The Fire-god rages with loose rein over thwarts and oars and hulls of painted fir. Eumelus carries the news of the burning ships to the grave of Anchises and the ranges of the theatre; and looking back, their own eyes see the floating cloud of dark ashes. And in a moment Ascanius, even as he rode gaily before his cavalry, spurred his horse to the disordered camp; nor can his breathless guards hold him back. 'What strange madness is this?' he cries; 'whither now hasten you, whither, alas my poor countrywomen? not on the foe nor on some hostile Argive camp; it is your own hopes you burn. Behold me, your Ascanius!' and he flung before his feet the empty helmet, put on when he roused the mimicry of war. Aeneas and the Trojan train together hurry to the spot. But the women scatter apart in fear all over the beach, and slink away to the woods or any cavern among the rocks: they loathe their deed and the daylight, and with changed eyes know their people, and Juno is startled out of their breast. But not thereby does the flame of the burning lay down its untamed strength; under the wet oak the seams are alive, spouting slow coils of smoke; the creeping heat devours the hulls, and the destroyer takes deep hold of all: nor does the heroes' strength avail nor the floods they pour in. Then good Aeneas rent away the raiment from his shoulders and called the gods to aid, stretching forth his hands: 'Jupiter omnipotent, if thou hatest not Troy yet wholly to her last man, if thine ancient pity looks at all on human woes, now, O Lord, grant our fleet to escape the flame, and rescue from doom the slender Teucrian estate; or do thou plunge to death this remnant, if I deserve it, with levelled thunderbolt, and here with thine own hand smite us down.' Scarce had he uttered this, when a black tempest rages in streaming showers; highland and plain tremble to the thunder; the water-flood rushes in torrents from the whole heaven amid black darkness and volleying blasts of the South. The ships are filled from overhead, the half-burnt timbers are soaking; until all the heat is quenched, and all the hulls, but four that are lost, are rescued from destruction.

But lord Aeneas, dismayed by the bitter mischance, shifted this way and that his weight of care, inly revolving whether, forgetting fate, he should rest in Sicilian fields, or reach forth to the borders of Italy. Then old Nautes, whom Tritonian Pallas taught like none other, and made famous in eminence of art—she granted him to reply what the gods' heavy anger menaced or what the order of fate claimed—he then in comforting speech thus begins to Aeneas:

'Goddess-born, follow we fate's ebb and flow, whatsoever it shall be; all fortune may be overcome by being borne. Acestes is of thine own divine Dardanian race; take him, a willing helpmate, into common counsel; deliver to him the remainder, now these ships are lost, and those who are quite weary of thy fortunes and the great quest. Choose out the old men stricken in years, and the matrons sick of the sea, and all that is weak and fearful of peril in thy company. Let this land give a city to the weary; they shall be allowed to call their town Acesta by name.'

Then indeed, though kindled by these words of his aged friend, his spirit is distracted among all his cares. And now black Night rose chariot-borne, and held the sky; when the likeness of his father Anchises seemed to descend from heaven and suddenly utter this:

'O son, dearer to me than life once of old while life was yet mine; O son, hard wrought by the destinies of Ilium! I come hither by Jove's command, who drove the fire from thy fleets, and at last had pity out of high heaven. Obey thou the fair counsel that aged Nautes now gives. Carry through to Italy thy chosen men and bravest souls; in Latium must thou war down a people hard and rough in living. Yet ere then draw thou nigh the nether chambers of Dis, and through deep Avernus come, O son, to meet me. For I am not held in evil Tartarus among wailing ghosts, but inhabit Elysium and the sweet societies of the good. Hither with much blood of dark cattle shall the holy Sibyl lead thee. Then shalt thou learn of all thy line, and what city is given thee. And now farewell; dank Night wheels her mid-career, and even now I feel the stern breath of the panting horses of the East.' He ended, and retreated like a vapour into thin air. 'Ah, whither hurriest thou?' cries Aeneas; 'whither so fast away? From whom fliest thou? or who withholds thee from our embrace?' So speaking, he kindles the sleeping embers of the fire, and with holy meal and laden censer does sacrifice to the tutelar of Pergama and hoar Vesta's secret shrine.

Straightway he summons his crews and Acestes first of all, and instructs them of Jove's command and his beloved father's precepts, and what is now his fixed mind and purpose. They linger not in counsel, nor does Acestes decline his bidden duty: they enrol the matrons in their town, and plant a people there, souls that are content to have none of glory. The rest repair the thwarts and replace the ships' timber that the flames had fed upon, and fit up oars and rigging, little in number, but alert and valiant for war. Meanwhile Aeneas traces the town with the plough and allots the homesteads; this he bids be Ilium, and these lands Troy. Trojan Acestes, rejoicing in his kingdom, appoints a court and gathers his senators to give them statutes. Next, where the crest of Eryx is neighbour to the stars, a sanctuary is founded to Venus the Idalian; and a priest and breadth of holy grove is attached to Anchises' grave.

And now for nine days all the people has feasted, and offering been paid at the altars; quiet breezes have smoothed the ocean floor, and the gathering south wind blows, calling them again to sea. A mighty weeping arises along the winding shore; a night and a day they linger in mutual embraces. The very mothers now, the very men to whom once the sight of the sea seemed cruel and God's will not to be borne, would go on and endure the journey's toil to the end. These Aeneas comforts with kindly words, and commends with tears to his kinsman Acestes' care. Then he bids slay three steers to Eryx and a she-lamb to the Tempests, and loose the hawser as is due. Himself, his head bound with stripped leaves of olive, he stands apart on the prow holding the cup, and casts the entrails into the salt flood and pours liquid wine. A wind rising astern follows them forth on their way. Emulously the crews strike the water, and sweep through the seas.

But Venus meanwhile, wrought upon with distress, accosts Neptune, and thus pours forth her heart's complaint: 'Juno's bitter wrath and heart insatiable compel me, O Neptune, to sink to the uttermost of entreaty: neither length of days nor any goodness softens her, nor does Jove's command nor fate itself break her to desistance. It is not enough that her accursed hatred has devoured the Phrygian city from among the people, and dragged the remnant of Troy through every punishment; still she pursues the bones and ashes of her victim. I pray she know why her passion is so fierce. Thyself art my witness what a sudden coil she raised of late on the Libyan waters, confounding ocean and sky in vain reliance on Aeolus' blasts; this she dared in thy realm.... Lo too, driving the Trojan matrons into guilt, she has foully burned their ships, and forced them, their fleet lost, to leave the crews to an unknown land. Let the remnant, I beseech thee, give their sails to thy safe keeping across the seas; let them reach Laurentine Tiber; if I ask what is permitted, if the Fates grant them a city there.'

Then the son of Saturn, compeller of the ocean deep, uttered thus: 'It is wholly right, O Cytherean, that thy trust should be in my realm, whence thou drawest birth; and I have deserved it: often have I allayed the rage and full fury of sky and sea. Nor less on land, I call Xanthus and Simoïs to witness, has been my care of thine Aeneas. When Achilles pursued the Trojan armies and hurled them breathless on their walls, and sent many thousands to death, when the choked rivers groaned and Xanthus could not find passage or roll out to sea, then I snatched Aeneas away in sheltering mist as he met the brave son of Peleus outmatched in strength and gods, eager though I was to overthrow the walls of perjured Troy that mine own hands had built. Now too my mind rests the same; dismiss thy fears. In safety, as thou desirest, shall he reach the haven of Avernus. One alone thou shalt miss, lost on the flood; one life shall be given for many. . . .'

With these words the goddess' bosom is soothed to joy. Then their lord yokes his wild horses with gold and fastens the foaming bits, and letting all the reins run slack in his hand, flies lightly in his sea-green chariot over the ocean surface. The waves sink to rest, and the swelling sea smooths out its waters under the thundering axle; the storm-clouds scatter from the vast sky. Diverse shapes attend him, monstrous whales, and Glaucus' aged choir, and Palaemon, son of Ino, the swift Tritons, and Phorcus with all his army. Thetis and Melite keep the left, and maiden Panopea, Nesaea and Spio, Thalia and Cymodoce.

Now joy in turn overspreads and lulls lord Aeneas' anxious soul. He bids all the masts be upreared with speed, and the sails stretched on the yards. Together all set their sheets, and all at once slacken their canvas to left and again to right; together they brace and unbrace the yard-arms aloft; prosperous gales waft the fleet along. Foremost, in front of all, Palinurus steered the close column; the rest under orders ply their course by his. And now dewy Night had just reached heaven's midcone; the sailors, stretched on their hard benches under the oars, relaxed their limbs in quiet rest: when Sleep, sliding lightly down from the starry sky, parted the shadowy air and cleft the dark, seeking thee, O Palinurus, carrying dreams of bale to thee who dreamt not of harm, and lit on the high stern, a god in Phorbas' likeness, dropping this speech from his lips: 'Palinurus son of Iasus, the very seas bear our fleet along; the breezes breathe steadily; an hour of rest is given. Lay down thine head, and steal thy worn eyes from their toil. I myself for a little will take thy duty in thy stead.' To whom Palinurus, scarcely lifting his eyes, returns: 'Wouldst thou have me ignorant what the calm face of the brine means, and the stilled waves? Shall I have faith in this perilous thing? How shall I trust Aeneas to fickle breezes and sky, I so often deceived by the treachery of a calm?' Such words he uttered, and clinging fast to the tiller, slackened hold no whit, and fixed his eyes on the stars overhead. Lo! the god shakes over either temple a bough dripping with Lethean dew and made slumberous with the might of Styx, and makes his swimming eyes relax their struggles. Scarcely had sleep begun to slacken his limbs unaware, when bending down, he flung him sheer into the clear water, tearing rudder and half the stern away with him, and many a time crying vainly on his comrades: himself he rose on flying wings into the thin air. None the less does the fleet run safe on its sea-path, and glides on unalarmed in lord Neptune's assurance. And even now they were sailing in to the cliffs of the Sirens, dangerous once of old and white with the bones of many a man; and the hoarse rocks echoed afar in the ceaseless surf; when her lord felt the ship rocking astray for loss of her helmsman, and himself steered her on over the darkling water, sighing often the while, and heavy at heart for his friend's mischance. 'Ah too trustful in calm skies and seas, thou shalt lie, O Palinurus, naked on an alien sand!'

BOOK SIXTH

The Vision of the Under World

So speaks he weeping, and gives his fleet the rein, and at last glides in to Euboïc Cumae's coast. They turn the prows seaward; the ships grounded fast on the anchor-flukes, and the curving sterns line the beach. The warrior band leaps forth eagerly on the Hesperian shore; some seek the seeds of flame hidden in veins of flint, some scour the woods, the thick coverts of wild beasts, and find and shew the streams. But good Aeneas seeks the fortress where Apollo sits high enthroned, and the lone mystery of the awful Sibyl's cavern depth, over whose mind and soul the prophetic Delian breathes high inspiration and reveals futurity.

Now they draw nigh the groves of Trivia and the roof of gold. Daedalus, as the story runs, when in flight from Minos' realm he dared to spread his fleet wings to the sky, glided on his unwonted way towards the icy northern star, and at length lit gently on the Chalcidian fastness. Here, on the first land he retrod, he dedicated his winged oarage to thee, O Phoebus, in the vast temple he built. On the doors is Androgeos' death; thereby the children of Cecrops, bidden, ah me! to pay for yearly ransom seven souls of their sons; the urn stands there, and the lots are drawn. Right opposite, the land of Gnosus rises from the sea; on it is the cruel love of the bull, the disguised stealth of Pasiphaë, and the mingled breed and double issue of the Minotaur, record of a shameful passion; on it the famous dwelling's laborious inextricable maze; but Daedalus, pitying the great love of the princess, himself unlocked the tangled treachery of the palace, guiding with the clue her lover's blind footsteps. Thou too hadst no slight part in the work he wrought, O Icarus, did grief allow. Twice had he essayed to portray thy fate in gold; twice the father's hands dropped down. Nay, their eyes would scan all the story in order, were not Achates already returned from his errand, and with him the priestess of Phoebus and Trivia, Deïphobe daughter of Glaucus, who thus accosts the king: 'Other than this are the sights the time demands: now were it well to sacrifice seven unbroken bullocks of the herd, as many fitly chosen sheep of two years old.' Thus speaks she to Aeneas; nor do they delay to do her sacred bidding; and the priestess calls the Teucrians into the lofty shrine.

A vast cavern is scooped in the side of the Euboïc cliff, whither lead an hundred wide passages by an hundred gates, whence peal forth as manifold the responses of the Sibyl. They had reached the threshold, when the maiden cries: 'It is time to enquire thy fate: the god, lo! the god.' And even as she spoke thus in the gateway, suddenly countenance nor colour nor ranged tresses stayed the same; her wild heart heaves madly in her panting bosom; and she expands to sight, and her voice is more than mortal, now the god breathes on her in nearer deity. 'Lingerest thou to vow and pray,' she cries, 'Aeneas of Troy? Lingerest thou? for not till then will the vast portals of the spell-bound house swing open.' So spoke she, and sank to silence. A cold shiver ran through the Teucrians' iron frames, and the king pours heart-deep supplication:

'Phoebus, who has ever pitied the sore travail of Troy, who didst guide the Dardanian shaft from Paris' hand full on the son of Aeacus, in thy leading have I pierced all these seas that skirt mighty lands, the Massylian nations far withdrawn, and fields that the Syrtes fringe; now at last we catch at the flying skirts of Italy; thus far let the fortune of Troy follow us. You too may now unforbidden spare the nation of Pergama, gods and goddesses to whomsoever Ilium and the great glory of Dardania did wrong. And thou, O prophetess most holy, foreknower of the future, grant (for no unearned realm does my destiny claim) a resting-place in Latium to the Teucrians, to their wandering gods and the storm-tossed deities of Troy. Then will I ordain to Phoebus and Trivia a temple of solid marble, and festal days in Phoebus' name. Thee likewise a mighty sanctuary awaits in our realm. For here will I place thine oracles and the secrets of destiny uttered to my people, and consecrate chosen men, O gracious one. Only commit not thou thy verses to leaves, lest they fly disordered, the sport of rushing winds; thyself utter them, I beseech thee.' His lips made an end of utterance.

But the prophetess, not yet tame to Phoebus' hand, rages fiercely in the cavern, so she may shake the mighty godhead from her breast; so much the more does he tire her maddened mouth and subdue her wild breast and shape her to his pressure. And now the hundred mighty portals of the house open of their own accord, and bring through the air the answer of the soothsayer:

'O thou for whom the great perils of the sea are at last over, though heavier yet by land await thee, the Dardanians shall come to the realm of Lavinium; relieve thy heart of this care; but not so shall they have joy of their coming. Wars, grim wars I discern, and Tiber afoam with streams of blood. A Simoïs shall not fail thee, a Xanthus, a Dorian camp; another Achilles is already provided in Latium, he too goddess-born; nor shall Juno's presence ever leave the Teucrians; while thou in thy need, to what nations or what towns of Italy shalt thou not sue! Again is an alien bride the source of all that Teucrian woe, again a foreign marriage-chamber. . . . Yield not thou to distresses, but all the bolder go forth to meet them, as thy fortune shall allow thee way. The path of rescue, little as thou deemest it, shall first open from a Grecian town.'

In such words the Sibyl of Cumae chants from the shrine her perplexing terrors, echoing through the cavern truth wrapped in obscurity: so does Apollo clash the reins and ply the goad in her maddened breast. So soon as the spasm ceased and the raving lips sank to silence, Aeneas the hero begins: 'No shape of toil, O maiden, rises strange or sudden on my sight; all this ere now have I guessed and inly rehearsed in spirit. One thing I pray; since here is the gate named of the infernal king, and the darkling marsh of Acheron's overflow, be it given me to go to my beloved father, to see him face to face; teach thou the way, and open the consecrated portals. Him on these shoulders I rescued from encircling flames and a thousand pursuing weapons, and brought him safe from amid the enemy; he shared my journey over all the seas, and bore with me all the threats of ocean and sky, in weakness, beyond his age's strength and due. Nay, he it was who besought and enjoined me to seek thy grace and draw nigh the courts. Have pity, I beseech thee, on son and father, O gracious one! for thou art all-powerful, nor in vain has Hecate given thee rule in the groves of Avernus. If Orpheus could call up his wife's ghost in the strength of his Thracian lyre and the music of the strings, if Pollux redeemed his brother by exchange of death, and passes and repasses so often,—why make mention of great Theseus, why of Alcides? I too am of Jove's sovereign race.'

In such words he pleaded and clasped the altars; when the soothsayer thus began to speak:

'O sprung of gods' blood, child of Anchises of Troy, easy is the descent into hell; all night and day the gate of dark Dis stands open; but to recall thy steps and issue to upper air, this is the task, this the burden. Some few of gods' lineage have availed, such as Jupiter's gracious favour or virtue's ardour has upborne to heaven. Midway all is muffled in forest, and the black sliding coils of Cocytus circle it round. Yet if thy soul is so passionate and so desirous twice to float across the Stygian lake, twice to see dark Tartarus, and thy pleasure is to plunge into the mad task, learn what must first be accomplished. Hidden in a shady tree is a bough with leafage and pliant shoot all of gold, consecrate to nether Juno, wrapped in the depth of woodland and shut in by dim dusky vales. But to him only who first has plucked the golden-tressed fruitage from the tree is it given to enter the hidden places of the earth. This has beautiful Proserpine ordained to be borne to her for her proper gift. The first torn away, a second fills the place in gold, and the spray burgeons with even such ore again. So let thine eyes trace it home, and thine hand pluck it duly when found; for lightly and unreluctant will it follow if thine is fate's summons; else will no strength of thine avail to conquer it nor hard steel to cut it away. Yet again, a friend of thine lies a lifeless corpse, alas! thou knowest it not, and defiles all the fleet with death, while thou seekest our counsel and lingerest in our courts. First lay him in his resting-place and hide him in the tomb; lead thither black cattle; be this first thine expiation; so at last shalt thou behold the Stygian groves and the realm untrodden of the living.' She spoke, and her lips shut to silence.

Aeneas goes forth, and leaves the cavern with lowered eyes and sad countenance, his soul revolving inly the unseen issues. By his side goes faithful Achates, and plants his footsteps in equal perplexity. Long they ran on in mutual change of talk; of what lifeless comrade spoke the soothsayer, of what body for burial? And even as they came, they see on the dry beach Misenus cut off by untimely death, Misenus the Aeolid, excelled of none other in stirring men with brazen breath and kindling battle with his trumpet-note. He had been attendant on mighty Hector; in Hector's train he waged battle, renowned alike for bugle and spear: after victorious Achilles robbed him of life the valiant hero had joined Dardanian Aeneas' company, and followed no meaner leader. But now, while he makes his hollow shell echo over the seas, ah fool! and calls the gods to rival his blast, jealous Triton, if belief is due, had caught him among the rocks and sunk him in the foaming waves. So all surrounded him with loud murmur and cries, good Aeneas the foremost. Then weeping they quickly hasten on the Sibyl's orders, and work hard to pile trees for the altar of burial, and heap it up into the sky. They pass into the ancient forest, the deep coverts of game; pitch-pines fall flat, ilex rings to the stroke of axes, and ashen beams and oak are split in clefts with wedges; they roll in huge mountain-ashes from the hills. Aeneas likewise is first in the work, and cheers on his crew and arms himself with their weapons. And alone with his sad heart he ponders it all, gazing on the endless forest, and thus idly prays: 'If but now that bough of gold would shew itself to us on the tree in this depth of woodland! since all the soothsayer's tale of thee, Misenus, was, alas! too truly spoken.' Scarcely has he said thus, when twin doves haply came flying down the sky, and lit on the green sod right under his eyes. Then the kingly hero knows them for his mother's birds, and joyfully prays: 'Ah, be my guides, if way there be, and direct your aëry passage into the groves where the rich bough overshadows the fertile ground! and thou, O goddess mother, fail not our wavering fortune!' So spoke he and stayed his steps, marking what they signify, whither they urge their way. Feeding and flying they advance at such distance as following eyes could keep them in view; then, when they came to Avernus' pestilent gorge, they tower swiftly, and sliding down through the liquid air, choose their seat and light side by side on a tree, through whose boughs shone out the contrasting sheen of gold. As in chill mid-winter the woodland is wont to blossom with the strange leafage of the mistletoe, sown on an alien tree and wreathing the smooth stems with burgeoning saffron; so on the shadowy ilex seemed that leafy gold, so the foil tinkled in the light breeze. Immediately Aeneas seizes it and eagerly breaks off its resistance, and carries it beneath the Sibyl's roof.

And therewithal the Teucrians on the beach wept Misenus, and bore the last rites to the thankless ashes. First they build up a vast pyre of resinous billets and cleft oak, whose sides they entwine with dark leaves and plant funereal cypresses in front, and adorn it above with his shining armour. Some prepare warm water in caldrons bubbling over the flames, and wash and anoint the chill body, and make their moan; then, their weeping done, lay his limbs on the pillow, and spread over it crimson raiment, the accustomed pall. Some uplift the heavy bier, a melancholy service, and with averted faces in their ancestral fashion hold and thrust in the torch. Gifts of frankincense, food, bowls of olive oil, are poured and piled upon the fire. After the embers sank in and the flame died away, they soaked with wine the remnant of thirsty ashes, and Corynaeus gathered the bones and shut them in an urn of brass; and he too thrice encircled his comrades with fresh water, and cleansed them with light spray sprinkled from a bough of fruitful olive, and spoke the words of farewell. But good Aeneas heaps a mighty mounded tomb over him, with his own armour and his oar and trumpet, beneath a skyey mountain, that now is called Misenus after him, and keeps his name immortal from age to age.

This done, he hastens to fulfil the Sibyl's ordinance. A deep cave yawned dreary and vast, shingle-strewn, sheltered by the black lake and the gloom of the forests; over it no flying things could wing their way scathless, such a vapour streamed from the dark gorge and rose into the overarching sky. Here the priestess first arrays four black-bodied bullocks and pours wine upon their forehead; and plucking the topmost hairs from between the horns, lays them on the sacred fire for first-offering, calling aloud on Hecate, mistress of heaven and hell. Others lay knives to their throats, and catch the warm blood in cups. Aeneas himself smites with the sword a black-fleeced she-lamb to the mother of the Eumenides and her mighty sister, and a barren heifer to thee, O Proserpine. Then he uprears darkling altars to the Stygian king, and lays whole carcases of bulls upon the flames, pouring fat oil over the blazing entrails. And lo! about the first rays of sunrise the ground moaned underfoot, and the woodland ridges began to stir, and dogs seemed to howl through the dusk as the goddess came. 'Apart, ah keep apart, O ye unsanctified!' cries the soothsayer; 'retire from all the grove; and thou, stride on and unsheath thy steel; now is need of courage, O Aeneas, now of strong resolve.' So much she spoke, and plunged in ecstasy into the cavern's opening; he with unflinching steps keeps pace with his advancing guide.

Gods who are sovereign over souls! silent ghosts, and Chaos and Phlegethon, the wide dumb realm of night! as I have heard, so let me tell, and according to your will unfold things sunken deep under earth in gloom.

They went darkling through the dusk beneath the solitary night, through the empty dwellings and bodiless realm of

Dis; even as one walks in the forest beneath the jealous light of a doubtful moon, when Jupiter shrouds the sky in shadow and black night blots out the world. Right in front of the doorway, in the entry of the jaws of hell, Grief and avenging Cares have made their bed; there dwell wan Sickness and gloomy Eld, and Fear, and ill-counselling Hunger, and loathly Penury, shapes terrible to see; and Death and Travail, and thereby Sleep, Death's kinsman, and the Soul's guilty Joys, and death-dealing War full in the gateway, and the Furies in their iron cells, and mad Discord with bloodstained fillets enwreathing her serpent locks.

Midway an elm, shadowy and high, spreads her boughs and secular arms, where, one saith, idle Dreams dwell clustering, and cling under every leaf. And monstrous creatures besides, many and diverse, keep covert at the gates, Centaurs and twy-shaped Scyllas, and the hundred-fold Briareus, and the beast of Lerna hissing horribly, and the Chimaera armed with flame, Gorgons and Harpies, and the form of the triple-bodied shade. Here Aeneas snatches at his sword in a sudden spasm of terror, and turns the naked edge on them as they come; and did not his wise fellow-passenger remind him that these lives flit thin and unessential in the hollow mask of body, he would rush on and vainly lash through the phantoms with his steel.

Hence a road leads to Tartarus and Acheron's wave. Here the dreary pool swirls thick in muddy eddies and disgorges into Cocytus all its load of sand. Charon, the dread ferryman, guards these flowing streams, ragged and awful, his chin covered with untrimmed masses of hoary hair, and his eyes a steady flame; his soiled raiment hangs knotted from his shoulders. Himself he plies the pole and trims the sails of his vessel, the steel-blue galley with freight of dead; stricken now in years, but a god's old age is lusty and green. Hither all crowded, and rushed streaming to the bank, matrons and men and high-hearted heroes dead and done with life, boys and unwedded girls, and children laid young on the bier before their parents' eyes, multitudinous as leaves fall dropping in the forests at autumn's earliest frost, or birds swarm landward from the deep gulf, when the chill of the year routs them overseas and drives them to sunny lands. They stood pleading for the first passage across, and stretched forth passionate hands to the farther shore. But the grim mariner admits now one and now another, while some he pushes back far apart on the strand. Moved with marvel at the confused throng: 'Say, O maiden,' cries Aeneas, 'what means this flocking to the river? of what are the souls so fain? or what difference makes these retire from the banks, those go with sweeping oars over the leaden waterways?'

To him the ancient priestess thus briefly returned: 'Seed of Anchises, most sure progeny of gods, thou seest the deep pools of Cocytus and the Stygian marsh, by whose divinity the gods fear to swear falsely. All this crowd thou discernest is helpless and unsepultured; Charon is the ferryman; they who ride on the wave found a tomb. Nor is it given to cross the awful banks and hoarse streams ere the dust has found a resting-place. An hundred years they wander here flitting about the shore; then at last they gain entrance, and revisit the pools so sorely desired.'

Anchises' son stood still, and ponderingly stayed his footsteps, pitying at heart their cruel lot. There he discerns, mournful and unhonoured dead, Leucaspis and Orontes, captains of the Lycian squadron, whom, as they sailed together from Troy over gusty seas, the south-wester overwhelmed and wrapped the waters round ship and men.

Lo, there went by Palinurus the steersman, who of late, while he watched the stars in their Libyan passage, had slipped from the stern and fallen amid the waves. To him, soon as he barely knew the melancholy form in that depth of shade, he thus opens speech: 'What god, O Palinurus, reft thee from us and sank thee amid the seas? forth and tell. For in this single answer Apollo deceived me, never found false before, when he prophesied thee safety on ocean and arrival on the Ausonian coasts. Lo, is this his promise-keeping?'

And he: 'Neither did Phoebus on his oracular seat delude

thee, O prince, Anchises' son, nor did any god plunge me in the sea. For while I clung to my appointed charge and governed our course, I pulled the tiller with me in my fall, and the shock as I slipped wrenched it away. By the rough seas I swear, fear for myself never wrung me so sore as for thy ship, lest, the rudder lost and the pilot struck away, those gathering waves might master it. Three wintry nights in the water the blustering south drove me over the endless sea; scarcely on the fourth dawn I descried Italy as I rose on the climbing wave. Little by little I swam shoreward; already I clung safe; but while, encumbered with my dripping raiment, I caught with crooked fingers at the jagged mountain-headlands, the barbarous people attacked me in arms and ignorantly deemed me a prize. Now the wave holds me, and the winds toss me on the shore. By heaven's pleasant light and breezes I beseech thee, by thy father, by Iülus thy rising hope, rescue me from these distresses, O unconquered one! Either do thou, for thou canst, cast earth over me and again seek the haven of Velia; or do thou, if any wise that may be, if in any wise the goddess who bore thee shews a way,—for not without divine will do I deem thou wilt float across these vast rivers and the Stygian pool,—lend me a pitying hand, and bear me over the waves in thy company, that at least in death I may find a quiet resting-place.'

Thus he ended, and the soothsayer thus began: 'Whence, O Palinurus, this fierce longing of thine? Shalt thou without burial behold the Stygian waters and the awful river of the Furies, or draw nigh the bank unbidden? Cease to hope prayers may bend the decrees of heaven. But take my words to thy memory, for comfort in thy woeful case: far and wide shall the bordering cities be driven by celestial portents to appease thy dust; they shall rear a tomb, and pay the tomb a yearly offering, and for evermore shall the place keep Palinurus' name.' The words soothed away his distress, and for a while drove grief away from his sorrowing heart; the land is glad in his name.

So they complete their journey's beginning, and draw nigh

the river: and now the waterman descried them from the Stygian wave advancing through the silent woodland and turning their feet towards the bank, and open on them in these words of challenge and chiding: 'Whoso thou art who marchest in arms towards our river, forth and say, there as thou art, why thou comest, and stay thine advance. This is the land of Shadows, of Sleep, and slumberous Night; no living body may pass in the Stygian ferry-boat. Nor truly had I joy of taking Alcides on the lake for passenger, nor Theseus and Pirithoüs, born of gods though they were and unconquered in might. He laid fettering hand on the warder of Tartarus, and dragged him cowering from the very King's throne; they essayed to ravish our mistress from the bridal chamber of Dis.' Thereto the Amphrysian soothsayer made brief reply: 'No such plot is here; be not moved; nor do our weapons offer violence; the huge gatekeeper may bark on for ever in his cavern and affright the bloodless ghosts. Proserpine may keep her honour within her uncle's gates. Aeneas of Troy, renowned in goodness as in arms, goes down to meet his father in the deep shades of Erebus. If the sight of such affection stirs thee in nowise, yet this bough' (she discovers the bough hidden in her raiment) 'thou must know.' Then his heaving breast allays its anger, and he says no more; but marvelling at the awful gift, the fated rod so long unseen, he steers in his dusky vessel and draws to shore. Next he routs out the souls that sate on the long benches, and clears the thwarts, while he takes mighty Aeneas on board. The galley groaned under the weight in all her seams, and the marsh-water leaked fast in. At length prophetess and prince are landed unscathed on the ugly ooze and livid sedge.

This realm rings with the triple-throated baying of vast Cerberus, couched huge in the cavern opposite; to whom the prophetess, seeing the serpents already bristling up on his neck, throws a cake made slumberous with honey and drugged grain. He, with threefold jaws gaping in ravenous hunger, catches it when thrown, and sinks to earth with monstrous body outstretched, and sprawling huge over all his den. The warder overwhelmed, Aeneas makes entrance, and quickly overstrides the bank of the irremeable wave.

Immediately wailing voices are loud in their ears, the souls of babies crying, whom, taken from sweet life at the doorway and torn from the breast, a dark day cut off and drowned in bitter death. Hard by them are those condemned to death on false accusation. Neither indeed are these dwellings assigned without lot and judgment; Minos presides and shakes the urn; he summons a council of the silent people, and inquires of their lives and impeachments. Next in order have these mourners their place whose own innocent hands dealt them death, who flung away their souls in hatred of the day. How fain were they now in upper air to endure their poverty and sore travail! It may not be; the gloomy pool of that unlovely wave confines them, and Styx pours her ninefold barrier between. And not far from here are shewn stretching on every side the Wailing Fields; so they call them by name. Here they whom pitiless love has wasted in cruel decay hide among untrodden ways, shrouded in embosoming myrtle thickets; not death itself ends their distresses. In this region he discerns Phaedra and Procris and woeful Eriphyle, shewing on her the wounds of her merciless son, and Evadne and Pasiphaë; Laodamia goes in their company, and she who was once Caeneus and a man, now woman, and again returned by fate into her shape of old. Among whom Dido the Phoenician, fresh from her death-wound, wandered into the vast forest; by her the Trojan hero stood, and knew the dim form through the darkness, even as the moon at the month's beginning to him who sees or thinks he sees her rising through the vapours; he let tears fall, and spoke to her lovingly and sweet:

'Alas, Dido! so the news was true that reached me; thou didst perish, and the sword sealed thy doom! Ah me, was I cause of thy death? By the stars I swear, by the heavenly powers and all that is sacred beneath the earth, unwillingly, O queen, I left thy shore. But the gods' commands, which now compel me to pass through this shadowy place, this land of mouldering overgrowth and deep night, drove me imperiously forth; nor could I deem my departure would bring thee pain so great. Stay thy footstep, and withdraw not from our gaze. From whom fliest thou? the last speech of thee fate ordains me is this.'

In such words and with starting tears Aeneas soothed the burning and fierce-eyed spirit. She turned away with looks fixed fast on the ground, stirred no more in countenance by the speech he essays than if she stood in iron flint or Marpesian stone. At length she started, and fled wrathfully into the shadowy woodland, where Sychaeus, in responsive passion and equal love, is her husband as long ago. Yet Aeneas, dismayed by her cruel doom, follows her far on her way with pitying tears.

Thence he pursues his appointed path. And now they trod those utmost fields where the renowned in war have their haunt apart. Here Tydeus meets him; here Parthenopaeus, glorious in arms, and the pallid phantom of Adrastus; here the Dardanians long wept on earth and fallen in the war; sighing he discerns all their long array, Glaucus and Medon and Thersilochus, the three sons of Antenor, and Polyboetes, Ceres' priest, and Idaeus yet charioted, yet grasping his arms. The souls throng round him to right and left; nor is one look enough; it delights them to linger on, to pace by his side and learn wherefore he is come. But the princess of the Grecians and Agamemnon's armies, when they see him glittering in arms through the gloom, hurry terror-stricken away; some turn backward, as when of old they fled to the ships; some raise their voice faintly, and gasp out a broken ineffectual cry.

And here he saw Deïphobus son of Priam, all his body hacked and his face barbarously torn, face and both hands, and ears lopped from his mangled temples, and nostrils maimed by a shameful wound. Barely he knew the cowering form that hid its dreadful punishment; then he springs to accost it in familiar speech:

'Deïphobus, mighty in arms, seed of Teucer's royal blood whose wantonness of vengeance was so cruel? who was allowed to use thee thus? Rumour reached me that on that last night, outwearied with endless slaughter of the Pelasgians, thou hadst sunk on the heap of mingled carnage. Then mine own hand reared an empty tomb on the Rhoetean shore, mine own voice thrice called aloud upon thy ghost. Thy name and armour keep the spot; thee, O my friend, I could not see nor lay in the native earth I left.'

Whereto the son of Priam: 'In nothing, O my friend, wert thou wanting; thou hast paid the full to Deïphobus and the dead man's shade. But me my fate and the Laconian woman's murderous guilt thus dragged down to doom; these are the records of her leaving. For how we spent that last night in delusive gladness thou knowest, and must needs remember too well. When the fated horse overleapt the sheer ramparts of Troy, bearing armed infantry for the burden of its womb, she, in feigned procession, led round our Phrygian women with Bacchic cries; herself she upreared a mighty flame amid them, and called the Grecians out of the fortress height. Then was I fast in mine ill-fated bridal chamber, deep asleep and outworn with my charge, and lay overwhelmed in slumber sweet and profound and most like to easeful death. Meanwhile that crown of wives removes all the arms from my dwelling, and slips out the faithful sword from beneath my head; she calls Menelaus into the house and flings wide the gateway: be sure she hoped her lover would magnify the gift, and so she might quench the fame of her ill deeds of old. Why do I linger? They burst into the chamber, they and the Aeolid, counsellor of crime, added to their company. Gods, recompense the Greeks even thus, if with righteous lips I call for vengeance! But come, tell in turn what chances have brought thee hither yet alive. Comest thou driven on ocean wanderings, or by promptings from heaven? or what fortune keeps thee from rest, that thou shouldst draw nigh these sad sunless dwellings, this disordered land?'

In this change of talk Dawn had already crossed heaven's mid axle on her rose-charioted way; and haply had they thus drawn out all the allotted time; but the Sibyl made brief warning speech to her companion: 'Night falls, Aeneas; we waste the hours in weeping. Here is the place where the road disparts; by this that runs to the right under the city of great Dis is our path to Elysium; but the leftward wreaks vengeance on the wicked and sends them to unrelenting hell.' But Deïphobus: 'Be not angered, mighty priestess; I will depart, I will refill my place and return into darkness. Go, glory of our people, go, enjoy a fairer fate than mine.' Thus much he spoke, and on the word turned away his footsteps.

Aeneas looks back on a sudden, and sees beneath the cliff on the left hand a wide city, girt with a triple wall and encircled by a swift river of boiling flame, Tartarean Phlegethon, rolling its loud boulders down. In front is the gate, huge and pillared with solid adamant, that no warring force of men nor the very habitants of heaven may avail to overthrow; the iron tower uprears itself, and Tisiphone sitting girt in bloodstained pall keeps sleepless watch at the entry by night and day. Hence moans are heard and fierce lashes resound, with the clank of iron and dragging chains. Aeneas stopped and drank in the tumult dismayed. 'What shapes of crime are here? declare, O maiden; or what the punishment that pursues them, and all this clashing in mine ears?' Then the soothsayer thus began to speak: 'Illustrious chief of Troy, no pure foot may tread these guilty courts; but me Hecate herself, when she gave me rule over the groves of Avernus, taught how the gods punish, and guided through all her realm. Gnosian Rhadamanthus here holds unrelaxing sway, chastises secret crime revealed, and exacts confession, wheresoever in the upper world one vainly exultant in stolen guilt has put off, till death makes it too late, the expiation of his crimes. Straightway avenging Tisiphone, girt with her scourge, tramples down the shivering sinners, menaces them with the grim snakes in her left hand, and summons forth her sisters in merciless train. Then at last the sacred gates are flung open and grate on jarring hinge. Markest thou what sentry is seated in the doorway? what shape guards the threshold? More grim within sits the monstrous Hydra with her fifty black yawning throats: and

Tartarus' self gapes sheer and strikes into the gloom through twice the space that one looks upward to Olympus and the skyey heaven. Here Earth's ancient children, the Titans' brood, hurled down by the thunderbolt, lie wallowing in the abyss. Here likewise I saw the twin Aloïds, enormous of frame, who essayed with violent hands to pluck down high heaven and thrust Jove from his upper realm. Likewise I saw Salmoneus paying the grim penalty for mocking Jove's flame and Olympus' thunders. Borne by four horses and brandishing a torch, he rode in triumph amid the Grecian people and through Elis town, and claimed for himself the worship of deity; madman! who would mimic the storm-cloud and the inimitable bolt with brass that rang under his trampling horse-hoofs. But the Lord omnipotent hurled his shaft through thickening clouds (no firebrand his, nor smoky glare of torches) and dashed him headlong in the fury of the whirlwind. Therewithal Tityos might be seen, fostering of Earth the mother of all, whose body stretches over nine full acres, and a monstrous vulture with crooked beak eats away the imperishable liver and the entrails that breed in suffering, and plunges deep into the breast that gives it food and dwelling; nor is any rest given to the fibres that ever grow anew. Why tell of the Lapithae, of Ixion and Pirithoüs? over whom a black stone hangs just slipping and just as though it fell; or the high banqueting couches gleam golden-pillared, and the feast is spread in royal luxury before their faces; couched hard by, the eldest of the Furies wards the tables from their touch and rises with torch upreared and thunderous lips. Here are they who hated their brethren while life endured, or struck a parent or entangled a client in wrong, or who brooded alone over found treasure and shared it not with their fellows, this the greatest multitude of all; and they who were slain for adultery, and who followed unrighteous arms, and feared not to betray their masters' plighted hand. Imprisoned they await their doom. Seek not to be told what doom, or in what guise fortune has overwhelmed them. Some roll a vast stone, or hang outstretched on the spokes of wheels; hapless Theseus sits and shall sit for ever, and Phlegyas in his misery gives counsel to all and witnesses aloud through the gloom. *Learn by this warning to do justly and not to slight the gods.* This man sold his country for gold, and laid her under a tyrant's sway; he set up and pulled down laws at a price; this other forced his daughter's bridal chamber and a forbidden marriage; all ventured some monstrous wickedness, and gained their venture. Not had I an hundred tongues, an hundred mouths, and a voice of iron, could I sum up all the shapes of crime or name over all their punishments.'

Thus spoke Phoebus' ancient priestess; then 'But come now', she cries; 'hasten on the way and perfect the service begun; let us go faster; I descry the ramparts cast in Cyclopean furnaces, and in front the arched gateway where they bid us lay the gifts foreordained.' She ended, and advancing side by side along the shadowy ways, they overtake the space between, and draw nigh the gates. Aeneas makes entrance, and sprinkling his body with fresh water, plants the bough in front of the gateway.

Now at length, this fully done, and the service of the goddess perfected, they came to the happy place, the green pleasances and blissful seats of the Fortunate Woodlands. Here an ampler air clothes the meadows in lustrous sheen, and they know their own sun and a starlight of their own. Some exercise their limbs in tournament on the greensward, contend in games, and wrestle on the yellow sand. Some dance with beating footfall and lips that sing; with them is the Thracian priest in sweeping robe, and makes music to their measures with the notes' sevenfold interval, the notes struck now with his fingers, now with his ivory rod. Here is Teucer's ancient brood, a generation excellent in beauty, heroic souls born in happier years, Ilus and Assaracus, and Dardanus, founder of Troy. Afar he marvels at the armour and chariots empty of their lords: their spears stand fixed in the ground, and their unyoked horses pasture at large over the plain: their life's delight in chariot and armour, their care in pasturing their sleek horses, follows them in like wise to their place under earth.

Others, lo! he beholds feasting on the sward to right and left, and singing in chorus the glad Paean-cry, within a scented laurel-grove whence Eridanus river surges upward full-volumed through the wood. Here is the band of them who bore wounds in fighting for their country, and they who were pure in priesthood while life endured, and the good poets whose speech abased not Apollo; and they who made life beautiful by the arts of their invention, and who won by service a memory among others, the brows of all girt with the snow-white fillet. To their encircling throng the Sibyl spoke thus, and to Musaeus before them all; for he is midmost of all the multitude, and stands out head and shoulders among their upward gaze:

'Tell, O blissful souls, and thou, poet most gracious, what region, what place has Anchises for his own? For his sake are we come, and have sailed across the wide rivers of Erebus.'

And to her the hero thus made brief reply: 'None has a fixed dwelling; we live in the shady woodlands; soft-swelling banks and meadows kept fresh with streams are our habitation. But you, if this be your heart's desire, scale this ridge, and I will even now set you on an easy pathway.' He spoke, and paced on before them, and from above shews the shining plains; thereafter they leave the mountain heights.

But lord Anchises, deep in the green valley, was musing in earnest survey over the imprisoned souls destined to the daylight above, and haply reviewing his beloved children and all the tale of his people, them and their fates and fortunes, their works and ways. And he, when he saw Aeneas advancing to meet him over the greensward, stretched forth both hand eagerly, while tears rolled over his cheeks, and his lips parted in a cry: 'Art thou come at last, and has thy love, child of my desire, conquered the difficult road? Is it granted, O my son, to gaze on thy face, to hear and to answer in the speech we know? Thus indeed did I forecast in spirit, counting the days between; nor has my care misled me. What lands, what space of seas hast thou traversed to reach me, through what surge of perils, O my son! How I dreaded lest the realm of Libya might work thee harm!'

And he: 'Thy melancholy phantom, thine, O my father, came before me often and often, and moved me to steer to these portals. My fleet is anchored on the Tyrrhenian brine. Give thine hand to clasp, O my father, give it, and withdraw not from our embrace.'

So spoke he, his face wet the while with abundant weeping. Thrice there did he essay to fling his arms about his neck; thrice the phantom vainly grasped fled out of his hands even as light wind, and most like to fluttering sleep.

Meanwhile Aeneas sees deep withdrawn in the covert of the vale a woodland and rustling forest thickets, and the river of Lethe that floats past the peaceful dwellings. Around it flittered nations and peoples innumerable; even as in the meadows when in clear summer weather bees settle on the variegated flowers and stream round the snow-white lilies, all the plain is murmurous with their humming. Aeneas starts at the sudden view, and asks the reason he knows not; what are those spreading streams, or who are they whose endless train fills the banks? Then lord Anchises: 'Souls, for whom second bodies are destined and due, drink at the wave of the Lethean stream the heedless water of long forgetfulness. These of a truth have I long desired to tell thee and shew thee face to face, and number all the generation of thy children, that so thou mayest the more rejoice with me in finding Italy.'—'O father, must we think that any souls travel hence into upper air, and return again to bodily fetters? why this strange sad longing for the light?' 'I will tell,' rejoins Anchises, 'nor will I hold thee in suspense, O my son.' And he unfolds all things in order one by one.

'First of all, heaven and earth and the liquid fields, the shining orb of the moon and the Titanian star, doth a spirit sustain inly, and a soul shed abroad in them sways all their members and mingles in the mighty frame. Thence is the generation of man and beast, the life of winged things, and the monstrous forms that ocean breeds under his glittering floor. Those seeds have fiery force and divine birth, so far as they are not clogged by sinful bodies and dulled by earthy frames and limbs ready to die. From these is it that they fear and desire, sorrow and rejoice; nor do their eyes pierce the air while barred in the blind darkness of their prison-house. Nay, even when the last ray of life is gone, nor yet, alas! does all their woe, nor do all the plagues of the body wholly leave them free; and needs must be that many a long hardened evil should take root marvellously deep. Therefore they are schooled in punishment, and pay all the forfeit of a lifelong ill; some are hung stretched to the viewless winds; some have the taint of guilt washed away beneath the dreary deep, or burned out in fire. We suffer, each in his own ghost; thereafter we are sent to the broad spaces of Elysium, some few of us to possess the happy fields; till length of days completing time's circle takes out the clotted soilure and leaves untainted the ethereal sense and pure spiritual flame. All these before thee, when the wheel of a thousand years has come fully round, a God summons in vast train to the river of Lethe, that so they may regain in forgetfulness the slopes of upper earth again, and begin to desire to return into the body.'

Anchises ceased, and leads his son and the Sibyl likewise amid the assembled murmurous throng, and mounts a hillock whence he might scan all the long ranks and learn their countenances as they came.

'Now come, the glory hereafter to follow our Dardanian progeny, the posterity to abide in our Italian people, illustrious souls and inheritors of our name to be, these will I rehearse, and instruct thee of thy destinies. He yonder, seest thou? the warrior who leans on his pointless spear, holds the place allotted nearest to daylight, and shall rise first into the air of heaven from the mingling blood of Italy, Silvius of Alban name, the child of thine age, whom late in thy length of days thy wife Lavinia shall nurture in the woodland, king and father of kings; from him in Alba the Long shall our house have dominion. He next him is Procas, glory of the Trojan race; and Capys and Numitor; and he who shall renew thy name, Silvius Aeneas, eminent alike in goodness or in arms, if ever he shall receive his kingdom in Alba. Men of men! see what strength they display, and wear the civic oak shading their brows. They shall establish Nomentum and Gabii and Fidena city, they the Collatine hill-fortress, Pometii and the Fort of Inuus, Bola and Cora: these shall be names that are nameless lands now. Nay, Romulus likewise, seed of Mavors, shall join his grandsire's company, from his mother Ilia's nurture and Assaracus' blood. Seest thou how the twin plumes stand upright on his crest, and his father's own emblazonment already marks him for upper air? Behold, O son! in his auspices shall Rome the renowned fill earth with her empire and heaven with her pride, and gird about seven fortresses with her single wall, prosperous mother of men; even as our lady of Berecyntus rides in her chariot turret-crowned through the Phrygian cities, glad in the gods she has borne, clasping an hundred of her children's children, all habitants of the sky, all dwellers upon the heights of heaven. Hither now bend thy twin-eyed gaze; behold this people, the Romans that are thine. Here is Caesar and all Iülus' posterity that shall arise under the mighty cope of heaven. Here is he, he of whose promise thou hearest so often, Caesar Augustus, a god's son, who shall again establish the ages of gold in Latium over the fields that once were the realm of Saturn, and carry his empire afar to Garamant and Indian, to the land that lies beyond our stars, beyond the sun's year-long ways, where Atlas the sky-bearer wheels on his shoulder the glittering star-spangled pole. Before his coming even now the kingdoms of the Caspian shudder at oracular answers, and the Maeotic land and the mouths of sevenfold Nile shudder in alarm. Nor indeed did Alcides traverse such spaces of earth, though he pierced the brazen-footed deer, or though he still the Erymanthian woodlands and made Lerna tremble at his bow: nor he who sways his yoked team with reins of vine, Liber the conqueror, when he drives his tigers from Nysa's lofty crest. And do we yet hesitate to give valour scope in deeds, or shrink in fear from setting foot on Ausonian land?

Ah, and who is he apart, marked out with sprays of olive, offering sacrifice? I know the locks and hoary chin of the king of Rome who shall establish the infant city in his laws, sent from little Cures' sterile land to the majesty of empire. To him Tullus shall next succeed, who shall break the peace of his country and stir to arms men rusted from war and armies now disused to triumphs; and hard on him over-vaunting Ancus follows, even now too elate in popular breath. Wilt thou see also the Tarquin kings, and the haughty soul of Brutus the Avenger, and the fasces regained? He shall first receive a consul's power and the merciless axes, and when his children would stir fresh war, the father, for fair freedom's sake, shall summon them to doom. Unhappy! yet howsoever posterity shall take the deed, love of country and limitless passion for honour shall prevail. Nay, behold apart the Decii and the Drusi, Torquatus with his cruel axe, and Camillus returning with the standards. Yonder souls likewise, whom thou discernest gleaming in equal arms, at one now, while shut in Night, ah me! what mutual war, what battle-lines and bloodshed shall they summon forth, so they attain the light of the living! father-in-law descending from the Alpine barriers and the fortress of the Dweller Alone, son-in-law facing him with the embattled East. Nay, O my children, harden not your hearts to such warfare, neither turn upon her own heart the mastering might of your country; and thou, be thou first to forgive, who drawest thy descent from heaven; cast down the weapons from thy hand, O blood of mine. . . . He shall drive his conquering chariot to the Capitoline height triumphant over Corinth, glorious in Achaean slaughter. He shall uproot Argos and Agamemnonian Mycenae, and the Aeacid's own heir, the seed of Achilles mighty in arms, avenging his ancestors in Troy and Minerva's polluted temple. Who might leave thee, lordly Cato, or thee, Cossus, to silence? who the Gracchan family, or these two sons of the Scipios, a double thunderbolt of war, Libya's bale? and Fabricius potent in poverty, or thee, Serranus, sowing in the furrow? Whither whirl you me all breathless, O Fabii? thou art he, the most mighty, the one man whose lingering retrieves our State. Others shall beat out the breathing bronze to softer lines, I believe it well; shall draw living lineaments from the marble; the cause shall be more eloquent on their lips; their pencil shall portray the pathways of heaven, and tell the stars in their arising: be thy charge, O Roman, to rule the nations in thine empire; this shall be thine art, to ordain the law of peace, to be merciful to the conquered and beat the haughty down.'

Thus lord Anchises, and as they marvel, he so pursues: 'Look how Marcellus the conqueror marches glorious in the splendid spoils, towering high above them all! He shall stay the Roman State, reeling beneath the invading shock, shall ride down Carthaginian and insurgent Gaul, and a third time hang up the captured armour before Quirinus his sire.'

And at this Aeneas, for he saw going by his side one excellent in beauty and glittering in arms, but his brow had little cheer, and his eyes looked down:

'Who, O my father, is he who thus attends him on his way? son, or other of his children's princely race? What hum of comrades is around him! how goodly of presence he is! but dark Night flutters round his head with melancholy shade.'

Then lord Anchises with welling tears began: 'O my son, ask not of the great sorrow of thy people. Him shall fate but shew to earth, and suffer not to stay further. Too mighty, lords of heaven, did you deem the brood of Rome, had this your gift been abiding. What moaning of men shall arise from the Field of Mavors by the imperial city! what a funeral train shalt thou see, O Tiber, as thou flowest by the new-made grave! Neither shall the boyhood of any of Ilian race raise his Latin forefathers' hope so high; nor shall the land of Romulus ever boast of any fosterling like this. Alas his goodness, alas his antique honour, and right hand invincible in war! none had faced him unscathed in armed shock, whether he met the foe on foot, or ran his spurs into the flanks of his foaming horse. Ah poor boy! if thou mayest break the grim bar of fate, thou shalt be Marcellus. Give me lilies in full hands; let me strew bright blossoms, and these gifts at least let me lavish on my descendant's soul, and do an unavailing service.'

Thus they wander up and down over the whole region of broad vaporous plains, and scan all the scene. And when Anchises had led his son over it, each point by each, and kindled his spirit with passion for the glories on their way, he tells him thereafter of the war he next must wage, and instructs him of the Laurentine peoples and the city of Latinus, and in what wise he may avoid or endure every burden.

There are twin portals of Sleep, whereof the one is fabled of horn, and by it real shadows are given easy outlet; the other shining white of polished ivory, but false visions issue upward from the ghostly world. With these words then Anchises follows forth his son and the Sibyl together there, and dismisses them by the ivory gate. He pursues his way to the ships and revisits his comrades; then bears on to Caieta's haven straight along the shore. The anchor is cast from the prow; the sterns lie aground on the beach.

BOOK SEVENTH

THE LANDING IN LATIUM, AND THE ROLL OF THE ARMIES OF ITALY

THOU also, Caieta, nurse of Aeneas, gavest our shores an everlasting renown in death; and still thine honour haunts thy resting-place, and a name in broad Hesperia, if that glory is aught, marks thy dust. But when the last rites are duly paid, and the mound smoothed over the grave, good Aeneas, now the high seas are hushed, bears on under sail and leaves his haven. Breezes blow into the night, and the white moonshine speeds them on; the sea glitters in her quivering radiance. Soon they skirt the shores of Circe's land, where the rich daughter of the Sun makes her untrodden groves echo with ceaseless song; and her stately house glows nightlong with burning odorous cedarwood, as she runs over her delicate web with the ringing comb. Hence are heard afar angry cries of lions chafing at their fetters and roaring in the deep night; bears and bristly swine rage in their pens, and vast shapes of wolves howl; whom with her potent herbs Circe the cruel goddess had disfashioned, face and body, into wild beasts from the likeness of men. But lest the good Trojans might suffer so dread a change, might enter her haven or draw nigh the awful shores, Neptune filled their sails with favourable winds, and gave them escape, and bore them past the seething shallows.

And now the sea reddened with shafts of light, and high in heaven yellow Dawn shone in her rosy car; when the winds fell, and every breath sank suddenly, and the oar-blades toil through the heavy ocean-floor. And on this Aeneas descries from sea a mighty forest. Midway in it the pleasant Tiber stream breaks to sea in swirling eddies, laden with yellow sand. Around and above fowl many in sort, that haunt his banks and the channel of his flood, solaced heaven with song and flew about the forest. He orders his crew to bend their course and turn their prows to land, and glides joyfully into the shady river.

Forth now, Erato! and I will unfold who were the kings, what the times, how it was with the state of ancient Latium when first that foreign army drew their fleet ashore on the Ausonian coast, and will recall the preluding of battle. Thou, divine one, instruct thou thy poet. I will tell of grim wars, tell of embattled lines, of kings whom honour drove on death, of the Tyrrhenian forces, and all Hesperia enrolled in arms. A greater history opens before me, to a greater work I set my hand.

Latinus the King, now growing old, ruled in a long peace over quiet tilth and town. He, men say, was sprung of Faunus and the nymph Marica of Laurentum. Faunus' father was Picus; and he boasts himself, Saturn, thy son; thou art the first source of their blood. Son of his, by divine ordinance, and male descent was none, cut off in the early spring of youth. One alone kept the household and its august home, a daughter now ripe for a husband and of full years for marriage. Many wooed her from wide Latium and all Ausonia. Fairest and foremost of all is Turnus, of long and lordly ancestry, whose union to her daughter the queen-consort urged with wondrous desire; but boding signs from heaven, many and terrible, bar the way. Within the palace, in the lofty inner courts, was a laurel of sacred foliage, guarded in awe through many years, which lord Latinus, it was said, himself found and dedicated to Phoebus when first he would build his citadel; and from it gave his settlers their name of Laurentines. High atop of it, wonderful to tell, bees borne with loud humming across the liquid air girt it thickly about, and with interlinked feet hung in a sudden swarm from the leafy bough. Straightway the prophet cries: 'I see a foreigner draw nigh, an army from the same quarter seek the same quarter, and reign high in our citadel.' Furthermore, while maiden Lavinia stands beside her father feeding the altars with holy fuel, she seemed, O horror! to catch fire in her long tresses, and burn with flickering flame in all her array, her queenly hair lit up, lit up her jewelled circlet; till, enwreathed in smoke and ruddy light, she scattered fire over all the palace. That sight was rumoured wonderful and terrible; herself, they prophesied, she should be glorious in fame and fortune; but a great war was foreshadowed for her people. But the King, troubled by the omen, visits the oracle of his father Faunus the soothsayer, and the groves deep under Albunea, where, queen of the woods, she echoes from her holy well, and breathes forth a dim and deadly vapour. Hence do the tribes of Italy and all the Oenotrian land seek answers in perplexity; hither the priest bears his gifts, and when he has lain down and sought slumber under the silent night on the spread fleeces of slaughtered sheep, sees many flitting phantoms of wonderful wise, hears manifold voices, and attains converse of the gods, and holds speech with Acheron and the deep tract of hell. Here then, likewise seeking an answer, lord Latinus paid fit sacrifice of an hundred woolly ewes, and lay couched on the strewn fleeces they had worn. Out of the lofty grove a sudden voice was uttered: 'Seek not, O my child, to unite thy daughter in Latin espousals, nor trust her to the bridal chambers ready to thine hand; foreigners shall come to be thy sons, whose blood shall raise our name to heaven, and the children of whose race shall see, where the circling sun looks on either ocean, all the rolling world swayed beneath their feet.' This his father Faunus' answer and counsel given in the silent night Latinus keeps not within locked lips; but wide-flitting Rumour had already borne it round among the Ausonian cities, when the seed of Laomedon moored their fleet to the grassy slope of the river bank.

Aeneas, with the foremost of his captains and fair Iülus, lay them down under the boughs of a high tree and array the feast. They spread wheaten cakes along the sward under their meats—so Jove on high prompted—and crown the platter of corn with wilding fruits. Here haply when the rest was spent, and dearth of food set them to eat their scanty bread, and with hand and venturous teeth break the round of the fate-fraught cake and spare not the broad slabs: 'Ha, we are eating tables and all!' cries Iülus jesting, that and no more. The voice no sooner heard set their toils a limit; and soon as he spoke his father caught it from his lips and hushed him, in amazement at the omen. Straightway 'Hail, O land,' he cries, 'my destined inheritance! and hail, O household gods, faithful to your Troy! here is home; this is our native country. For my father Anchises, now I remember it, bequeathed me this secret of fate: "When hunger shall drive thee, O son, to consume the tables where the feast falls short, on the unknown shores whither thou shalt sail, then in thy weariness hope for home, and there let thine hand remember to build thy bulkwarks and place thy first dwelling." This was the hunger, this the last that awaited us, to set the promised end to our desolations... Up then, and, glad with the first sunbeam, let us explore and search all abroad from our harbour, what is the country, who its habitants, where is the town of the nation. Now pour your cups to Jove, and call in prayer on Anchises our father, setting the wine again upon the board.' So speaks he, and binding his brows with a leafy bough, he makes supplication to the Genius of the ground, and Earth first of deities, and the Nymphs, and the Rivers yet unknown; then calls on Night and Night's rising signs, and next on Jove of Ida, and our lady of Phrygia, and on his twain parents, in heaven and in the underworld. At this the Lord omnipotent thrice thundered sharp from high heaven, and with his own hand shook out for a sign in the sky a cloud ablaze with luminous shafts of gold. The sudden rumour spreads among the Trojan array, that the day is come to found their destined city. Emulously they renew the feast, and, glad at the high omen, array the flagons and engarland the wine.

Soon as the morrow bathed the lands in its dawning light,

they part to search out the town, and the borders and shores of the nation: these are the pools and spring of Numicus; this is the Tiber river; here dwell the brave Latins. Then the seed of Anchises commands an hundred envoys chosen of every degree to go to the stately royal city, all with the wreathed boughs of Pallas, to bear him gifts and desire grace for the Teucrians. Without delay they hasten on their message, and advance with swift step. Himself he traces the city walls with a shallow trench, and sets to work on the site, girdling this first settlement on the shore, camp-fashion, with mound and battlements. And now his men had traversed their way; they espied the towers and steep roofs of the Latins, and drew near the wall. Before the city boys and men in their early bloom exercise on horseback, and break in their teams on the dusty ground, or draw ringing bows, or hurl tough javelins from the shoulder, and contend in running and boxing: when a messenger riding forward brings news to the ears of the aged King that mighty men are come thither in unknown raiment. He gives orders to call them within his house, and takes his seat in the midst on his ancestral throne. His house, stately and vast, crowned the city, upreared on an hundred columns, once the palace of Laurentian Picus, amid awful groves of ancestral sanctity. Here the tradition was for their kings to receive the sceptre, and have the fasces first raised before them; this temple was their senate-house; this their sacred banqueting-hall; here, after sacrifice of rams, the elders were wont to sit down at long tables. Further, there stood a row in the entry images of the forefathers of old in ancient cedar, Italus, and lord Stabinus, planter of the vine, still holding in show the curved pruning-hook, and grey Saturn, and the likeness of Janus the double-facing, and the rest of their primal kings, and they who had borne wounds of war in fighting for their country. Armour besides hangs thickly on the sacred doors, captured chariots and curved axes, helmet-crests and massy gateway-bars, lances and shields, and beaks torn from warships. He too sat there, with the divining-rod of Quirinus, girt in the short augural gown, and carrying on his left arm the sacred shield, Picus the tamer of horses; he whom Circe, desperate with amorous desire, smote with her golden rod and turned by her poisons into a bird with patches of colour on his wings. Of such wise was the temple of the gods wherein Latinus, sitting on his fathers' seat, summoned the Teucrians to his house and presence; and when they entered in, he thus opened with placid mien:

'Tell, O Dardanians, for we are not ignorant of your city and race, nor unheard of do you bend your course overseas, what seek you? what the cause or whereof the need that has borne you over all these blue waterways to the Ausonian shore? Whether wandering in your course, or tempest-driven (such perils manifold on the high seas do sailors suffer), you have entered the river banks and lie in harbour, shun not our welcome, and be not ignorant that the Latins are Saturn's people, whom no laws fetter to justice, upright of their own free will and the custom of the god of old. And now I remember, though the story is dimmed with years, thus Auruncan elders told, how Dardanus, born in this our country, made his way to the towns of Phrygian Ida and to the Thracian Samos that is now called Samothrace. Here was the home he left, Tyrrhenian Corythus; now the palace of heaven, glittering with golden stars, enthrones him and adds one to the ranged altars of the gods.'

He ended; and Ilioneus pursued his speech with these words:

'King, Faunus' illustrious progeny, neither has black tempest driven us with stress of waves to shelter in your lands, nor has star or shore misled us on the way we went. Of set purpose and willing mind do we draw nigh this thy city, outcasts from a realm once the greatest that the sun looked on as he came from Olympus' utmost border. From Jove is the source of our race; in Jove the men of Dardania rejoice as ancestor; our King himself of Jove's supreme family, Aeneas of Troy, has sent us to thy courts. How terrible the tempest that burst from fierce Mycenae over the plains of Ida, driven by what fate Europe and Asia met in the shock of two worlds, even he has heard who is sundered in the utmost land where the ocean surge recoils, and he whom stretching midmost of the four zones the zone of the intolerable sun holds in severance. Escaped from that deluge and borne over many desolate seas, we crave a scant dwelling for our country's gods, an unmolested landing-place, and the air and water that are open to all. We shall not disgrace the kingdom; nor will the rumour of your renown be lightly gone or the grace of a deed so great fade away; nor will Ausonia be sorry to have taken Troy to her breast. By the fortunes of Aeneas I swear, by that right hand mighty, whether tried in friendship or in warlike arms, many and many a people and nation—scorn us not because we advance with hands proffering chaplets and words of supplication—has sought us for itself and desired our alliance; but yours is the land that heaven's high ordinance drove us forth to find. Hence Dardanus had his birth: hither Apollo recalls us, and pushes us on with imperious orders to Tyrrhenian Tiber and the holy pools of Numicus' spring. Further, he presents to thee these small guerdons of our past estate, relics saved from burning Troy. From this gold did lord Anchises pour libation at the altars; this was Priam's array when he delivered statutes to the nations assembled in order; the sceptre, the sacred mitre, the raiment wrought by the women of Ilium. . . .'

At these words of Ilioneus Latinus holds his countenance in a steady gaze, and stays motionless on the floor, casting his intent eyes around. Nor does the embroidered purple nor the sceptre of Priam so greatly move the King, as he ponders his daughter's marriage and bridal chamber, and turns over in his heart the oracle of ancient Faunus. This is he, the wanderer from a foreign home, foreshewn of fate for his son-in-law, and called to a realm of equal dominion, whose race should be excellent in valour and their might overbear all the world. At last he speaks with good cheer:

'The gods prosper our undertaking and their own augury! What thou desirest, Trojan, shall be given; nor do I spurn your gifts. While Latinus reigns you shall not lack foison of rich land nor Troy's own wealth. Only let Aeneas himself come hither, if desire of us be so strong, if he be in haste to join our friendship and be called our ally. Let him not shrink in terror from friendly faces. In my terms of peace shall be the touch of your monarch's hand. Do you now convey in answer my message to your King. I have a daughter whom the oracles of my ancestral shrine and many a celestial token alike forbid me to unite to one of our own nation; a bridegroom shall come, they prophesy, from foreign coasts, such is the destiny of Latium, whose blood shall exalt our name to heaven. He it is on whom fate calls; so I deem, so I would have it, if there be any truth in my soul's foreshadowing.'

Thus he speaks, and chooses horses for all the company. Three hundred stood sleek in their high stalls; for all the Teucrians in order he straightway commands them to be led forth, fleet-footed, covered with cloths of embroidered purple: golden chains hang drooping over their chests, golden their housings, and they champ on bits of ruddy gold: for the absent Aeneas a chariot and pair of chariot horses of celestial breed, with nostrils breathing flame, of the race of those which subtle Circe bred by sleight on her father, the bastard issue of a stolen union. With these gifts and words the Aeneadae ride back from Latinus carrying peace.

And lo! the fierce consort of Jove was returning from Inachian Argos, and held her way along the air, when out of the distant sky, far as from Sicilian Pachynus, she espied the rejoicing of Aeneas and the Dardanian fleet. She sees them already building homes, already trusting in the land, their ships left empty. She stops, shot with sharp pain; then shaking her head, she pours forth these words:

'Ah, hated brood, and doom of the Phrygians that thwarts our doom! Could they perish on the Sigean plains? Could they be ensnared when taken? Did the fires of Troy consume her people? Through the midst of armies and through the midst of flames they have found their way. But, I think, my deity lies at last outwearied, or my hatred is fed full and satisfied? Nay, it is I who have been fierce to follow them over the waves when hurled from their country, and on all the seas to cross their flight. Against the Teucrians the forces of sky and sea are spent. What have availed me Syrtes or Scylla, what desolate Charybdis? they find shelter in their desired Tiber-bed, careless of ocean and of me. Mars availed to destroy the giant race of the Lapithae; the very father of the gods gave over ancient Calydon to Diana's wrath: for forfeit of what crime in the Lapithae, what in Calydon? But I, Jove's imperial consort, who have borne, ah me! to leave naught undared, who have shifted to every device, I am vanquished by Aeneas. If my deity is not great enough, I will not assuredly falter to seek succour where it may be found; if I cannot bend the gods, I will stir up Acheron. It may not be to debar him of a Latin realm; be it so; and Lavinia is destined his bride unalterably. But it may be yet to draw out and breed delay in these high affairs; but it may be yet to waste away the nation of either king; at such forfeit of their people may son-in-law and father-in-law enter into union. Blood of Troy and Rutulia shall be thy dower, O maiden, and Bellona is the bridesmaid who awaits thee. Nor did Cisseus' daughter alone conceive a firebrand and travail of bridal flames. Nay, even such a birth has Venus of her own, a second Paris, another balefire for Troy towers reborn.'

These words uttered, she descends to earth in all her terrors, and calls dolorous Allecto from the home of the awful goddesses in nether gloom, whose delight is in woeful wars, in wrath and treachery and evil feuds: hateful to lord Pluto himself, hateful and horrible to her hell-born sisters; into so many faces does she turn, so savage the guise of each, so thick her black viper-growth. With these words Juno spurs her on, saying thus:

'Grant me, virgin born of Night, this thy proper task and service, that our renown may not be broken or our fame dwindle, nor the Aeneadae have power to win Latinus by marriage or beset the borders of Italy. Thou canst set in armed conflict brothers once united, and overturn families with hatreds; thou canst launch into houses thy whips and deadly brands; thine are a thousand names, a thousand devices of injury. Stir up thy teeming breast, sunder the peace they have joined, and sow seeds of quarrel; let their warriors at once desire and demand and fly to arms.'

Thereon Allecto, steeped in Gorgonian venom, first seeks Latium and the high house of the Laurentine monarch, and silently sits down before Amata's doors, whom a woman's distress and anger heated to frenzy over the Teucrians' coming and the marriage of Turnus. At her the goddess flings a snake out of her dusky tresses, and slips it into her bosom to her very inmost heart, that she may embroil all her house under its maddening magic. Sliding between her raiment and smooth breasts, it coils without touch, and instils its viperous breath unseen; the great serpent turns into the twisted gold about her neck, turns into the long ribbon of her chaplet, inweaves her hair, and winds slippery over her body. And while the gliding infection of the clammy poison begins to penetrate her sense and run in fire through her frame, nor as yet has all her breast caught the fire, softly she spoke and in mothers' wonted wise, with many a tear over her daughter's Phrygian bridal:

'Is it to exiles, to Teucrians, that Lavinia is proffered in marriage, O father? and hast thou no compassion on thy daughter and on thyself? no compassion on her mother, whom with the first northern wind the treacherous rover will abandon, steering to sea with his maiden prize? But is it not thus the Phrygian herdsman, winding his way to Lacedaemon, carried Leda's Helen to the Trojan towns? What of thy plighted faith? What of thine ancient care for thy people, and the hand Turnus thy kinsman has clasped so often? If one of alien race from the Latins is sought to be our son, if this stands fixed, and thy father Faunus' commands are heavy upon thee, all the land whose freedom severs it from our sway is to my mind alien, and of this is the divine word. And Turnus, if one retrace the earliest source of his line, is born of Inachus and Acrisius, and of the midmost of Mycenae.'

When in this vain essay of words she sees Latinus fixed against her, and the serpent's maddening poison is sunk deep in her vitals and runs through and through her, then indeed, stung by infinite horrors, hapless and frenzied, she rages wildly through the endless city. As whilom a top flying under the twisted whipcord, which boys busy at their play drive circling wide round an empty hall, runs before the lash and spins in wide gyrations; with witless ungrown band hang wondering over it and admire the whirling boxwood; the strokes lend it life: with pace no slacker is she borne midway through towns and valiant nations. Nay, she flies into the woodland under feigned Bacchic influence, assumes a greater guilt, arouses a greater frenzy, and hides her daughter in the mountain coverts to rob the Teucrians of their bridal and stay the marriage torches. 'Hail, Bacchus!' she shrieks and clamours; 'thou only art worthy of the maiden; for to thee she takes up the lissom wands, about thee she circles in the dance, to thee she trains and consecrates her tresses.' Rumour flies abroad; and the matrons, their breasts kindled with madness, run at once with a single ardour to seek out strange dwellings. They have left their homes empty, they throw neck and hair free to the winds; while others fill the air with ringing cries, girt about with fawnskins, and carrying spears of vine. Amid them the infuriate queen holds her blazing pine-torch on high, and chants the wedding of Turnus and her daughter; and rolling her bloodshot gaze, cries sudden and harsh: 'Hear, O mothers of Latium, wheresoever you be; if unhappy Amata has yet any favour in your affection, if care for a mother's right pierces you, untie the fillets from your hair, begin the orgies with me.' Thus, amid woods and wild beasts' solitary places, does Allecto drive the queen on and on with the Bacchic sting.

When their frenzy seemed heightened and her first task complete, the purpose and all the house of Latinus turned upside down, the dolorous goddess next flies onward, soaring on dusky wing, to the walls of the gallant Rutulian. That city Danaë, they say, borne down on the streaming southern gale, built and planted with settlers of Acrision's blood. The place was called Ardea once of old; and still Ardea remains a mighty name; but its fortune is past. Here in his high house Turnus now took rest in the black midnight. Allecto puts off her grim feature and the body of a Fury; she transforms her face to an aged woman's, and furrows her brow with ugly wrinkles; she puts on white tresses fillet-bound, and entwines them with an olive spray; she becomes aged Calybe, priestess of Juno's temple, and presents herself before his eyes, uttering thus:

'Turnus, wilt thou brook all these toils poured out in vain, and the conveyance of thy crown to Dardanian settlers? The King denies thee thy bride and the dower thy blood had earned; and a foreigner is sought for heir to the kingdom. Forth now, dupe, and face thankless perils; forth, mow down the Tyrrhenian lines; give the Latins peace in thy protection. This Saturn's omnipotent daughter in very presence commanded me to pronounce to thee, as thou wert lying in the still night. Wherefore arise, and make ready with good cheer to arm thy people and march through thy gates to battle; consume those Phrygian captains that lie with their painted hulls in the beautiful river. All the force of heaven orders thee on. Let King Latinus himself, unless he consents to give thee thy bridal, and abide by his words, be aware and at last make proof of Turnus' arms.'

But he, deriding her inspiration, with the words of his mouth thus answers her again:

'The fleets ride on the Tiber wave; that news has not, as thou deemest, escaped mine ears. Frame not such terrors before me. Neither is Queen Juno forgetful of us. . . . But thee, O mother, overworn old age, exhausted and untrue, frets with vain distress, and amid embattled kings mocks thy presage with false dismay. Thy charge it is to keep the divine images and temples; war and peace shall be in the hands of men whose task is warfare.'

At such words Allecto's wrath blazed out. But amid his utterance a quick shudder overruns his limbs; his eyes are fixed in horror; so thickly hiss the snakes of the Fury, so vast her form expands. Then rolling her fiery eyes, she thrust him back as he would stammer out more, raised two serpents in her hair, and, sounding her whip, resumed with furious tone:

'Behold me the overworn! me whom old age, exhausted and untrue, mocks with false dismay amid embattled kings! Look on this! I am come from the home of the Dread Sisters: war and death are in my hand....'

So speaking, she hurled her torch at him, and pierced his breast with the lurid smoking brand. He breaks from sleep in overpowering fear, his limbs and frame bathed in sweat that starts out all over his body; he shrieks madly for arms, searches for arms on his bed and in his palace. The passion of the sword rages high, the accursed fury of war, and wrath over all: even as when flaming sticks are heaped roaring loud under the sides of a seething caldron, and the boiling tides leap up; the river of water within smokes furiously and swells high in overflowing foam, and now the wave contains itself no longer; the dark steam flies aloft. So, in breach of peace, he orders his chief warriors to march on King Latinus, and bids prepare for battle, to defend Italy and drive the foe from their borders; himself will suffice for Trojans and Latins together. When he uttered these words and called the gods to hear his vows, the Rutulians stir one another up to arms. One the splendour of his youthful beauty, one his royal ancestry fires, another the noble deeds of his hand.

While Turnus fills the Rutulians with daring courage, Allecto on Stygian wing hastens towards the Trojans. With fresh wiles she marked the spot where beautiful Iülus was trapping and coursing game on the bank; here the infernal maiden suddenly crosses his hounds with the maddening touch of a familiar scent, and drives them hotly on the stag-hunt. This was the source and spring of trouble, and kindled the rustic hearts to war. The stag, beautiful and high-antlered, Tyrrheus' boys had stolen from his mother's udder and reared, they and their father Tyrrheus, master of the royal herds, and ranger of the plain far and wide. Their sister Silvia tamed him to her rule, and lavished her care on his adornment, twining his antlers with delicate garlands, and combed his wild coat and washed him in the clear spring. Tame to her hand, and familiar to his master's table, he would wander the woods, and, however late the night, return home uncalled to the door he knew. Far astray, he floated idly down the stream, and allayed his heat on the green bank, when Iülus' furious hounds started him in their hunting; and Ascanius himself, kindled with desire of the chief honour, aimed a shaft from his bended bow. A present deity suffered not his hand to stray, and the loud whistling reed came driven through belly and flanks. But the wounded beast fled within the familiar roof and crept moaning to the courtyard, dabbled with blood, and filling all the house with moans as of one beseeching. Silvia, smiting her arms with open hands, begins to call for aid, and gathers with cries the hardy rustic brotherhood. They, for a fell destroyer is hidden in the silent woodland, are there before her expectation, one armed with a stake hardened in the fire, one with a heavy knotted trunk; what each one finds in searching, wrath turns into a weapon. Tyrrheus calls up their band, breathing vengeance, as he was haply splitting an oaken log in four clefts with cross-driven wedges, the axe caught up in his hand.

But the grim goddess, seizing from her watch-tower the moment of mischief, seeks the steep farm-roof and sounds the pastoral war-note from the ridge, straining her hellish voice on the twisted horn; it spread shuddering over all the woodland, and echoed through the deep forests: the lake of Trivia heard it afar; Nar, the river white with sulphurous water, and the springs of Velinus heard; and frightened mothers clasped their children to their breasts. Then, hurrying to the voice of the terrible trumpet-note, on all sides the wild rustics snatch their arms and stream in: therewithal the

Trojan array fling open their camp-gates and pour forth to succour Ascanius. They range their battle-lines; not now in rustic strife is the fight waged with hardwood billets or fire-seasoned stakes; the two-edged steel sways the contest, the broad corn-fields bristle dark with drawn swords, and brass flashes smitten by the sunlight, and casts a gleam high into the cloudy air: as when the flood begins to whiten under the rising wind, gradually the sea lifts his waves higher and yet higher, then mounts to the sky from the depths below. Here in the front rank young Almo, once Tyrrheus' eldest son, is struck down by a whistling arrow; for the wound, staying in his throat, cut off in blood the moist voice's passage and the thin life. Around many a one lies dead, aged Galaesus among them, slain as he throws himself between them for a peacemaker, once incomparable in justice and wealth of Ausonian fields; for him five flocks bleated, a five-fold herd returned from pasture, and an hundred ploughs upturned the soil.

But while thus equal battle is waged on the broad plain, the goddess, her promise fulfilled, now she has dyed the war in blood, and mingled death in the first encounter, quits Hesperia, and, glancing through the sky, addresses Juno in accents proud with victory:

'Lo, discord is ripened at thy desire into baleful war: bid them now mix in amity and join alliance! Insomuch as I have stained the Trojans with Ausonian blood, this likewise will I add, if I have assurance of thy will. With my rumours I will sweep the bordering towns into war, and kindle their spirit with furious desire for battle, that from all quarters help may come; I will sow the land with arms.'

Then Juno answering: 'Terror and harm is wrought abundantly. The springs of war are unsealed: they fight sword in hand; fresh blood stains the weapons that chance first supplied. Let this be the union, this the bridal that Venus' illustrious progeny and Latinus the king shall celebrate. Our Lord who reigns on Olympus' summit would not have thee stray too freely in heaven's upper air. Withdraw thy presence. Whatsoever fortune remains in the struggle, that I myself will sway.'

Such accents uttered the daughter of Saturn; and the other raises her rustling snaky wings and darts away from the high upper air to Cocytus her home. There is a place midmost of Italy, deep in the hills, notable and famed of rumour in many a country, the Vale of Amsanctus; on either hand a wooded ridge, dark with thick foliage, hems it in, and midway a torrent in swirling eddies echoes in thunder over the rocks. Here is shewn a ghastly pool, a breathing-hole of the grim lord of hell, and a vast chasm breaking into Acheron yawns with pestilential throat. In it the Fury sank, and relieved earth and heaven of her hateful influence.

But therewithal the queenly daughter of Saturn puts the last touch to war. The shepherds pour in full tale from the battlefield into the town, bearing back their slain, the boy Almo and Galaesus' disfigured face, and cry to the gods and call on Latinus. Turnus is there, and amid the burning outcry at the slaughter redoubles the terror, crying that Teucrians are bidden to the kingdom, that a Phrygian race is mingling with theirs, and that he is thrust from their gates. They too, the matrons of whose kin, stricken by Bacchus, trample in choirs down the pathless woods—nor is Amata's name a little thing—they too gather together from all sides and shout themselves hoarse for battle. Omens and oracles of gods go down before them, and all clamour for dread war under the malign influence. Emulously they surround Latinus' royal house. He withstands, even as a rock in ocean unremoved, as a rock in ocean when the great crash comes down, firm in its own mass among many waves bellowing all about: the crags and boulders idly hiss round it in foam, and against its side the seaweed is flung up and sucked away. But when he may in nowise overbear their blind counsel, and all goes at fierce Juno's beck, with many an appeal to gods and void sky, 'Alas!' he cries, 'we are broken by fate and driven helpless in the storm. With your own impious blood will you pay the price of this, O wretched men! Thee, O Turnus, thy crime, thee thine awful punishment shall await; too late wilt thou address to heaven thy prayers and supplication. For my own rest was won, and full on the harbour-bar, I am robbed but of a happy death.' And without further speech he shut himself in the palace, and dropped the reins of state.

There was a use in Hesperian Latium, which the Alban towns kept in holy observance, now Rome keeps, the mistress of the world, when they rouse the War-God to enter battle; whether their hands prepare to carry woeful war among Getae or Hyrcanians or Arabs, or to reach to India and pursue the Dawn, and reclaim their standards from the Parthian. There are twain gates of War, so runs their name, consecrate in grim Mars' sanctity and terror. An hundred bolts of brass and masses of everlasting iron shut them fast, and Janus the guardian never lifts foot from their threshold. There, when the sentence of the Fathers stands fixed for battle, the Consul, arrayed in the robe of Quirinus and the Gabine cincture, with his own hand unbars the grating doors, with his own lips calls battles forth; then all the rest follow on, and the brazen trumpets blare harsh with consenting breath. With this use then likewise they bade Latinus proclaim war on the Aeneadae, and unclose the baleful gates. Their lord withheld his hand, and shrank away averse from the abhorred service, and hid himself blindly in the dark. Then the Saturnian queen of heaven gliding from the sky with her own hand thrust open the lingering gates, and swung sharply back on their hinges the iron-bound doors of war. Ausonia is ablaze, till then unstirred and immoveable. Some make ready to march afoot over the plains; some, mounted on lofty steeds, ride amain in clouds of dust. All seek out arms; and now they rub their shields smooth and make their spearheads glitter with fat lard, and grind their axes on the whetstone: rejoicingly they advance under their standards and hear the trumpet note. Five great cities set up the anvil and sharpen the sword, strong Atina and proud Tibur, Ardea and Crustumeri, and turreted Antemnae. They hollow out head-gear to guard them, and plait wickerwork round shield-bosses; others forge breastplates of brass or smooth greaves of flexible silver. To this is come the honour of share and pruning-hook, to this all the love of the plough: they re-temper their fathers' swords in the furnace. And now the trumpets blare; the watchword for war passes along. One snatches a helmet hurriedly from his house, another backs his neighing horses into the yoke; and arrays himself in shield and mail-coat triple-linked with gold, and girds on his trusty sword.

Open now the gates of Helicon, goddesses, and stir the song of the kings that were called up for war, the array that followed each and filled the plains, the men that even then blossomed, the arms that blazed in Italy the bountiful land; for you remember, divine ones, and you can recall; to us but a breath of rumour, scant and slight, is wafted down.

First from the Tyrrhene coast savage Mezentius, scorner of the gods, opens the war and arrays his columns. By him is Lausus, his son, unexcelled in bodily beauty by any save Laurentine Turnus, Lausus tamer of horses and destroyer of wild beasts; he leads a thousand men who followed him in vain from Agylla town; worthy to be happier in ancestral rule, and to have other than Mezentius for father.

After them beautiful Aventinus, born of beautiful Hercules, displays on the sward his palm-crowned chariot and victorious horses, and carries on his shield his father's device, the hundred snake of the Hydra's serpent-wreath. Him, in the wood of the hill Aventine, Rhea the priestess bore by stealth into the borders of light, a woman mingled with a god, after the Tirynthian Conqueror had slain Geryon and set foot on the fields of Laurentum, and bathed his Iberian oxen in the Tuscan river. These carry for war javelins and grim stabbing weapons, and fight with the tapered shaft and sharp point of the Sabellian pike. Himself he went on foot swathed in a vast lion skin, shaggy with bristling terrors, whose teeth encircled his head; in such wild dress, the garb of Hercules clasped over his shoulders, he entered the royal house.

Next twin brothers leave Tibur town, and the people called by their brother Tiburtus' name, Catillus and valiant Coras, the Argives, and advance in the forefront of battle among the throng of spears: as when two cloud-born Centaurs descend from a lofty mountain peak, leaving Homole or snowy Othrys in rapid race; the mighty forest yields before them as they go, and the crashing thickets give them way.

Nor was the founder of Praeneste city absent, the king who, as every age has believed, was born of Vulcan among the pasturing herds, and found beside the hearth, Caeculus. On him a rustic battalion attends in loose order, they who dwell in steep Praeneste and the fields of Juno of Gabii, on the cool Anio and the Hernican rocks dewy with streams; they whom rich Anagnia feeds, and thou, lord Amesenus. Not all of them have armour, nor shields and clattering chariots. The most part shower bullets of dull lead; some wield in their hand two darts, and have for a head-covering caps of tawny wolf-skin; their left foot is bare wherewith to plant their steps; the other is covered with a boot of raw hide.

But Messapus, tamer of horses, the seed of Neptune, whom none might ever strike down with steel or fire, calls quickly to arms his long unstirred peoples and bands disused to war, and again handles the sword. These hold the Fescennine edges and Faliscan levels, these Soracte's fortress and the fields of Flavina, and Ciminus' lake and hill, and the groves of Capena. They marched in even time, singing their King; as whilome snowy swans among the watery clouds, when they return from pasturage, and utter resonant notes through their long necks; far off echoes the river and the smitten Asian fen.... Nor would one deem that these vast streaming masses were ranks clad in brass; rather that, high in air, a cloud of hoarse birds from the deep gulf was pressing to the shore.

Lo, Clausus of the ancient Sabine blood, leading a great host, a great host himself; from whom now the Claudian tribe and family is spread abroad since Rome was shared with the Sabines. Alongside is the great battalion of Amiternum, and the Old Latins, and all the force of Eretum and the Mutuscan olive-orchards; they who dwell in Nomentum town, and the Rosean country by Velinus, who keep the crags of rough Tetrica and Mount Severus, Casperia and Foruli, and the river of Himella; they who drink of Tiber and Fabaris, they whom cold Nursia has sent, and the squadrons of Orta and the tribes of Latinium; and they whom Allia, ill-omened name, washes with severing stream; as many as the waves that roll on the Libyan sea-floor when fierce Orion sets in the wintry surge; as thick as the ears that ripen in the morning sunlight on the plain of the Hermus or the yellowing Lycian tilth. Their shields clatter, and earth is amazed under the trampling of their feet.

Next Agamemnonian Halaesus, foe of the Trojan name, yokes his chariot horses, and draws a thousand warlike peoples to Turnus; those who turn with spades the Massic soil that is glad with wine; whom the elders of Aurunca have sent from their high hills, and the Sidicine low country hard by; and those who leave Cales, and the dweller by the shallows of Volturnus river, and side by side the rough Saticulan and the Oscan bands. Polished maces are their weapons, and these it is their wont to fit with a tough thong; a target covers their left side, and for close fighting they have crooked swords.

Nor shalt thou, Oebalus, depart untold of in our verses, who wast borne, men say, by the nymph Sebethis to Telon, when he grew old in rule over Capreae the Teleboïc realm: but not so content with his ancestral fields, his son even then held in wide sway the Sarrastian peoples and the meadows watered by Sarnus, and the dwellers in Rufrae and Batulum, and the fields of Celemnae, and they on whom the ramparts of Abella look down through apple orchards. Their wont was to hurl lances in Teutonic fashion; their head covering was stripped bark of the cork tree, their shield-plates glittering brass, glittering brass their sword.

Thee too, Ufens, mountainous Nersae sent forth to battle, of noble fame and prosperous arms, whose race on the stiff Aequiculan clods is rough beyond all other, and bred to continual hunting in the woodland; they till the soil in arms, and it is ever their delight to drive in fresh spoils and live on plunder.

Furthermore, sent by King Archippus, there came the priest of the Marruvian people, dressed with prosperous olive leaves over his helmet, Umbro excellent in valour, who was wont with charm and touch to sprinkle slumberous dew on the viper's brood and water-snakes of noisome breath, and charmed their anger and allayed their bite by his art. Yet he availed not to heal the stroke of the Dardanian spear-point, nor was he helped against wounds by his sleepy charms and herbs culled on the Massic hills. Thee the woodland of Angitia, thee Fucinus' glassy wave, thee the clear pools wept. . . .

Likewise the seed of Hippolytus marched to war, Virbius most excellent in beauty, sent by his mother Aricia. The groves of Egeria nursed him round the spongy shore where Diana's altar stands rich and gracious. For they say in story that Hippolytus, after he fell by his stepmother's treachery, torn asunder by his frightened horses to fulfil in blood a father's revenge, came again to the daylight and heaven's upper air, recalled by Diana's love and the drugs of the Healer. Then the Lord omnipotent, indignant that any mortal should rise from the nether shades to the light of life, launched his thunder and hurled down to the Stygian water the Phoebus-born, the discoverer of such craft and cure. But Trivia the bountiful hides Hippolytus in a secret habitation, and sends him away to the nymph Egeria and the woodland's keeping, where, solitary in Italian forests, he should spend an inglorious life, and have Virbius for his altered name. Whence also hoofed horses are kept away from Trivia's temple and consecrated groves, because, affrighted at the portents of the sea, they overset the chariot and flung him out upon the shore. Notwithstanding did his son train his fiery steeds on the level plain, and sped charioted to war.

Himself too among the foremost, splended in beauty of body, Turnus moves armed and towers a whole head over all. His lofty helmet, triple-tressed with horse-hair, holds high a Chimaera breathing from her throat Aetnean fires, raging the more and exasperate with baleful flames, as the battle and bloodshed grow fiercer. But on his polished shield was emblazoned in gold Io with uplifted horns, already a heifer and overgrown with hair, the proud crest of his race, and Argus the maiden's warder, and Inachus her sire pouring his stream from his embossed urn. Behind comes a cloud of infantry, and shielded columns thicken over all the plains; the Argive men and Auruncan forces, the Rutulians and old Sicanians, the Sacranian ranks and Labicians with painted shields; they who till thy dells, O Tiber, and Numicus' sacred shore, and whose ploughshare goes up and down on the Rutulian hills and the Circaean headland, over whose fields Jupiter of Anxur watches, and Feronia glad in her greenwood: and where the marsh of Satura lies black, and cold Ufens winds his way along the valley-bottoms and sinks into the sea.

Therewithal came Camilla the Volscian, leading a train of cavalry, squadrons splendid with brass: a virgin warrior who had never used her woman's hands to Minerva's distaff or wool-baskets, but a maiden hard to endure the battle shock and outstrip the winds with racing feet. She might have flown across the topmost blades of unmown corn and left the tender ears unhurt as she ran; or sped her way over mid sea upborne by the swelling flood, nor dipt her swift feet in the water. All the people pour from house and field, and mothers crowd to wonder and gaze at her as she goes, in rapturous astonishment at the royal lustre of purple that drapes her smooth shoulders, at the clasp of gold that intertwines her tresses, at the Lycian quiver she carries, and the pastoral myrtle shaft topped with steel.

BOOK EIGHTH

THE EMBASSAGE TO EVANDER

When Turnus ran up the flag of war on the towers of Laurentum, and the trumpets blared with harsh music, when he spurred his fiery steeds and clashed his armour, straightway men's hearts are in tumult; all Latium at once bands together in stir of uprisal, and youthful rage maddens her warriors. Their chiefs, Massapus, and Ufens, and Mezentius, scorner of the gods, begin to enrol forces on all sides, and dispeople the wide fields of husbandmen. Venulus too is sent to the town of mighty Diomede to seek succour; to instruct him that Teucrians set foot in Latium; that Aeneas in his fleet invades them with the vanquished gods of his home, and proclaims himself the King summoned of fate; that many tribes join the Dardanian, and his name swells high in Latium. What he will rear on these foundations, what issue he covets for the fight, if Fortune attend him, lies clearer to his own sight than to King Turnus or King Latinus.

Thus was it in Latium. And the hero of Laomedon's blood, seeing it all, tosses on a heavy surge of care, and throws his mind rapidly this way and that, and turns it on all hands in swift change of thought: even as when the quivering light of water brimming in brass, struck back from the sunlight or the moon's glittering sheen, flickers abroad over all the room, and now mounts aloft and strikes the high panelled roof. Night fell, and over all lands weary creatures were fast in deep slumber, the race of fowl and of cattle; when lord Aeneas, vexed at heart by the dismal warfare, stretched him on the river bank under the cope of the cold sky, and let sleep, though late, overspread his limbs. To him the very god of the ground, the pleasant Tiber stream, seemed to raise his aged form among the poplar boughs; thin lawn veiled him with its grey covering, and shadowy reeds hid his hair. Thereon he addressed him thus, and with these words allayed his distresses:

'O born of the family of the gods, thou who bearest back our Trojan city from hostile hands, and keepest Troy towers in eternal life; O long looked for on Laurentine ground and Latin fields! here is thine assured home, thine home's assured gods. Draw not thou back, nor be alarmed by menace of war. All the anger and wrath of the gods is passed away... And even now for thine assurance, that thou think not this the idle fashioning of sleep, a great sow shall be found lying under the oaks on the shore, with her new-born litter of thirty head: white she couches on the ground, and the brood about her teats is white. By this token in thirty revolving years shall Ascanius found a city, Alba of bright name. My prophecy is sure. Now hearken, and I will briefly instruct thee how thou mayest unravel and overcome thy present task. An Arcadian people sprung of Pallas, following in their king Evander's company beneath his banners, have chosen a place in these coasts, and set a city on the hills, called Pallanteum after Pallas their forefather. These wage perpetual war with the Latin race; these do thou take to thy camp as allies, and join with them in league. Myself I will lead thee by my banks and straight along my stream, that thou mayest oar thy way upward against the river. Up and arise, goddess-born, and even with the setting stars address thy prayers to Juno as is meet, and vanquish her wrath and menaces with humble vows. To me thou shalt pay a conqueror's sacrifice. I am he whom thou seest washing the banks with full flood and severing the rich tilth, glassy Tiber, best beloved by heaven of rivers. Here is my stately home; my fountain-head is among high cities.'

Thus spoke the River, and sank in the depth of the pool: night and sleep left Aeneas. He arises, and, looking towards the radiant sky of the sunrising, holds up water from the river in fitly-hollowed palms, and pours to heaven these accents: 'Nymphs, Laurentine Nymphs, from whom is the generation of rivers, and thou, O father Tiber, with thine holy flood, receive Aeneas and deign to save him out of danger. What pool soever holds thy source, who pitiest our discomforts, from whatsoever soil thou dost spring excellent in beauty, ever shall my worship, ever my gifts frequent thee, the horned river lord of Hesperian waters. Ah, be thou only by me, and let thy presence confirm thy will.' So speaks he, and chooses two galleys from his fleet, and mans them with rowers, and withal equips a crew with arms.

And lo! suddenly, ominous and wonderful to tell, the milk-white sow, of one colour with her white brood, is espied through the forest couched on the green brink; whom to thee, yes to thee, queenly Juno, Aeneas offers in pious sacrifice, and sets with her offspring before thine altar. All that night long Tiber assuaged his swelling stream, and silently stayed his refluent wave, smoothing the surface of his waters to the fashion of still pool and quiet mere, to spare labour to the oar. So they set out and speed on their way; with prosperous cries the painted fir slides along the water-way; the waves and unwonted woods marvel at their far-gleaming shields, and the gay hulls afloat on the river. They outwear a night and a day in rowing, ascend the long reaches, and pass under the chequered shadows of the trees, and cut through the green woodland in the calm water. The fiery sun had climbed midway in the circle of the sky when they see afar fortress walls and scattered house roofs, where now the might of Rome has risen high as heaven; then Evander held a slender state. Quickening their pace, they turn their prows to land and draw near the town.

It chanced on that day the Arcadian king paid his accustomed sacrifice to the great son of Amphitryon and all the gods in a grove before the city. With him his son Pallas, with him all the chief of his people and his poor senate were offering incense, and the blood steamed warm at their altars. When they saw the high ships gliding up between the shady woodlands and resting on their silent oars, the sudden sight appals them, and all at once they rise and stop the banquet. Pallas courageously forbids them to break off the rites; snatching up a spear, he flies forward, and from a hillock cries afar: 'O men, what cause has driven you to explore these unknown ways? or whither do you steer? What is your kin, whence your habitation? Is it peace or arms you carry hither?' Then from the lofty stern lord Aeneas thus speaks, stretching forth in his hand a peace-bearing olive bough:

'Thou seest men born of Troy and arms hostile to the Latins, who have driven us to flight in insolent warfare. We seek Evander; carry this message, and tell him that chosen men of the Dardanian captains are come pleading for an armed alliance.'

Pallas stood amazed at the august name. 'Descend,' he cries, 'whoso thou art, and speak with my father face to face, and enter our home and hospitality.' And giving him the grasp of welcome, he caught and clung to his hand. Advancing, they enter the grove and leave the river. Then Aeneas in courteous words addresses the King:

'Best of the Grecian race, thou whom by fortune's decree I supplicate, holding before me boughs dressed in fillets, no fear stayed me because thou wert a Grecian chief and an Arcadian, or allied by descent to the twin sons of Atreus. Nay, mine own prowess and the sanctity of divine oracles, our ancestral kinship, and the fame of thee that is spread abroad over the earth, have allied me to thee and led me willingly on the path of fate. Dardanus, who sailed to the Teucrian land, the first father and founder of the Ilian city, was born, as Greeks relate, of Electra the Atlantid; Electra's sire is ancient Atlas, whose shoulder sustains the heavenly spheres. Your father is Mercury, whom white Maia conceived and bore on the cold summit of Cyllene; but Maia, if we give any credence to report, is daughter of Atlas, that same Atlas who bears up the starry heavens; so both our families branch from a single blood. In this confidence I sent no embassy, I framed no crafty overtures; myself I have presented mine own person, and come a suppliant to thy courts. The same Daunian race pursues us and thee in merciless warfare; we once expelled, they trust nothing will withhold them from laying all

Hesperia wholly beneath their yoke, and holding the two seas that wash it above and below. Accept and return our friendship. We can give brave hearts in war, high souls and men approved in deeds.'

Aeneas ended. The other ere now scanned in a long gaze the face and eyes and all the form of the speaker; then thus briefly returns:

'How gladly, bravest of the Teucrians, do I hail and own thee! how I recall thy father's words and the very tone and glance of great Anchises! For I remember how Priam son of Laomedon, when he sought Salamis on his way to the realm of his sister Hesione, went on to visit the cold borders of Arcadia. Then early youth clad my cheeks with bloom: I admired the Teucrian captains, admired their lord, the son of Laomedon; but Anchises moved high above them all. My heart burned with youthful passion to accost him and clasp hand in hand; I made my way to him, and led him eagerly to Pheneus' high town. Departing he gave me an adorned quiver and Lycian arrows, a scarf interwoven with gold, and a pair of golden bits that now my Pallas possesses. Therefore my hand is already joined in the alliance you seek, and soon as to-morrow's dawn rises again over earth, I will send you away rejoicing in mine aid, and supply you from my store. Meanwhile, since you are come hither in friendship, solemnise with us these yearly rites which we may not defer, and even now learn to be familiar at your comrades' board.'

This said, he commands the feast and the wine-cups to be replaced whence they were taken, and with his own hand ranges them on the grassy seat, and welcomes Aeneas to the place of honour, with a lion's shaggy fell for cushion and a hospitable chair of maple. Then chosen men with the priest of the altar in emulous haste bring roasted flesh of bulls, and pile baskets with the gift of dressed corn, and serve the wine. Aeneas and the men of Troy with him feed on the long chines of oxen and the entrails of the sacrifice.

After hunger is driven away and the desire of food stayed, King Evander speaks: 'No idle superstition that knows not the gods of old has ordered these our solemn rites, this customary feast, this altar of august sanctity; saved from bitter perils, O Trojan guest, do we worship, and most due are the rites that we inaugurate. Look now first on this overhanging cliff of stone, where shattered masses lie strewn, and the mountain dwelling stands desolate, and rocks are rent away in vast ruin. Here was a cavern, awful and deep-withdrawn, impenetrable to the sunbeams, where the monstrous half-human shape of Cacus had his hold: the ground was ever warm with fresh slaughter, and pallid faces of men, ghastly with gore, hung nailed on the haughty doors. This monster was the son of Vulcan, and spouted Vulcan's black fires from his mouth as he moved in giant bulk. To our prayers likewise time bore a god's aid and arrival. For princely Alcides the avenger came glorious in the spoils of triple Geryon slain; this way the Conqueror drove the huge bulls, and his oxen filled the river valley. But savage Cacus, infatuate to leave nothing undared or unhandled in craft or crime, drives four bulls of choice shape away from their pasturage, and as many heifers of excellent beauty. And these, that there should be no straightforward footprints, he dragged by the tail into his cavern, the track of their compelled path reversed, and hid them behind the screen of rock. No marks were there to lead a seeker to the cavern. Meanwhile the son of Amphitryon, his herds filled with food, was now breaking up his pasturage and making ready to go. The oxen low as they depart; all the woodland is filled with their complaint as they clamorously quit the hills. One heifer returned the cry, and, lowing from the depth of the dreary cave, baffled the hope of Cacus from her imprisonment. At this the grief and choler of Alcides blazed forth dark and infuriate. Seizing in his hand his club of heavy knotted oak, he seeks with swift pace the aëry mountain steep. Then, as never before, did our eyes see Cacus afraid and troubled; he goes flying swifter than the wind and seeks his cavern; fear wings his feet. As he shut himself in, and, bursting the chains, dropped the vast rock slung in iron by his father's craft, and made fast the bars that fortified the doorway, lo! the Tirynthian came in furious wrath, and, scanning all the entry, turned his face this way and that and ground his teeth. Thrice, hot with rage, he circles all Mount Aventine; thrice he assails the rocky portals in vain, thrice he sinks down outwearied in the valley. There stood a peak of flint with sides cut sheer away, rising over the cavern's ridge a vast height to see, fit haunt for foul birds to nest in. This— for, sloping from the ridge, it leaned on the left towards the river—he rocked, pressing on it from the right till he tore it loose from its deep foundations; then suddenly shook it free: with the shock the vast sky thunders, the banks leap apart, and the amazed river recoils. But the den, Cacus' huge palace, lay open and revealed, and the depths of gloomy cavern were made manifest; even as though some force tearing earth apart should unlock the infernal house, and disclose the pallid realms abhorred of heaven, and deep down the monstrous gulf be descried where the ghosts flutter in the streaming daylight. On him then, surprised by unexpected light, shut in the rock's recesses and howling in strange fashion, Alcides from above hurls missiles and calls all his arms to aid, and presses hard on him with boughs and enormous millstones. And he, for none other escape from peril is left, vomits from his throat vast jets of smoke, wonderful to tell, and enwreathes his dwelling in blind gloom, blotting view from the eyes, while in the cave's depth night thickens with smoke-bursts in a darkness shot with fire. Alcides broke forth in anger, and with a bound hurled himself sheer amid the flames, where the smoke rolls billowing and voluminous, and the cloud surges black through the enormous den. Here, as Cacus in the darkness spouts forth his idle fires, he grasps and twines tight round him, till his eyes start out and his throat is drained of blood under the strangling pressure. Straightway the doors are torn open and the dark house laid plain; the stolen oxen and forsworn plunder are shewn forth to heaven, and the misshapen carcase dragged forward by the feet. Men cannot satisfy their soul with gazing on the terrible eyes, the monstrous face and shaggy bristling chest, and the throat with its quenched fires. Thenceforth this sacrifice is solemnised, and a younger generation have gladly kept the day; Potitius the inaugurator, and the Pinarian family, guardians of the rites of Hercules, have set in the grove this altar, which shall ever be called of us Most High, and shall be our highest evermore. Wherefore arise, O men, and for guerdon of that great achievement enwreathe your hair with leafy sprays, and stretch forth the cups in your hands; call on our common god and pour wine in good cheer.' As he ended, the twy-coloured poplar of Hercules hid his shaded hair with drooping twine of leafage, and the sacred goblet filled his hand. Speedily all pour glad libation on the board, and supplicate the gods.

Meanwhile the evening star draws nigher down the slope of heaven, and now the priests went in procession, Potitius at their head, girt with skins after their fashion, and bore torches aflame. They renew the banquet, and bring the grateful gift of a second repast, and heap the altars with loaded platters. Then the Salii stand round the lit altar-fires to sing, their brows bound with poplar boughs, one chorus of young men, one of elders, and extol in song the praises and deeds of Hercules; how first he strangled in his gripe the twin terrors, the snakes of his stepmother; how he likewise shattered in war famous cities, Troy and Oechalia; how under Eurystheus the King he bore the toil of a thousand labours by Juno's malign decrees. Thine hand, unconquered, slays the cloud-born double-bodied race, Hylaeus and Pholus, the Cretan monster, and the huge lion under the Nemean rock. Before thee the Stygian pools shook for fear, before thee the warder of hell, couched on half-gnawn bones in his blood-stained cavern; to thee not any form was terrible, not Typhoeus' self towering in arms; thou wast not bereft of counsel when the snake of Lerna encompassed thee with thronging heads. Hail, true seed of Jove, added glory to the courts of heaven! graciously visit us and these thy rites with favourable feet. Such are their songs of praise; they crown all with the cavern of Cacus and its fire-breathing lord. All the woodland echoes with their clamour, and the hills resound.

Thence all at once, the sacred rites accomplished, retrace their way to the city. The age-worn King walked holding Aeneas and his son by his side for companions on his way, and lightened the road with changing talk. Aeneas admires and turns his eyes lightly round about, pleased with the country; and gladly on spot after spot inquires and hears of the memorials of earlier men. Then King Evander, founder of the fortress of Rome:

'In these woodlands dwelt Fauns and Nymphs sprung of the soil, and a tribe of men born of stocks and hard oak; who had neither law nor grace of life, nor did they know to yoke bulls or lay up stores or save their gains, but were nurtured by the forest boughs and the hard living of the huntsman. Long ago Saturn came from heaven on high in flight before Jove's arms, an exile from his lost realm. He gathered together the unruly race scattered on the mountain heights, and gave them statutes, and chose Latium to be their name, since in these borders he had found a safe hiding-place. Beneath his reign were the ages named of gold; thus, in peace and quietness, did he rule the nations; till gradually there crept in a sunken and stained time, the rage of war, and the lust of possession. Then came the Ausonian clan and the tribes of Sicania, and many a time the land of Saturn put away her name. Then were kings, and fierce Thybris with his giant bulk, from whose name we of Italy afterwards called the Tiber river, when it lost the true name of old, Albula. Me, cast out from my country and following the utmost limits of the sea, all-powerful Fortune and irreversible doom settled in this region; and my mother the Nymph Carmentis' awful warnings and Apollo's divine counsel drove me hither.'

Scarce was this said; next advancing he points out the altar and the Carmental Gate, which the Romans call anciently by that name in honour of the Nymph Carmentis, seer and soothsayer, who sang of old the coming greatness of the Aeneadae and the glory of Pallanteum. Next he points out the wide grove where valiant Romulus set his sanctuary, and the Lupercal in the cool hollow of the rock, dedicate to Lycean Pan after the manner of Parrhasia. Therewithal he shows the holy wood of Argiletum, and calls the spot to witness as he tells the slaying of his guest Argus. Hence he leads him to the Tarpeian house, and the Capitol golden now, of old rough with forest thickets. Even then the awful sanctity of the spot held the frightened rustics in awe; even then men trembled before the wood and rock. 'This grove,' he cries, 'this hill with its leafy crown, is a god's dwelling, what god's we know not; the Arcadians believe they have seen Jove himself, when often he shook the darkening aegis in his hand and gathered the stormclouds. Thou seest these two towns likewise with walls overthrown, relics and memorials of men of old. This fortress lord Janus built, this Saturn; the name of this was once Janiculum, of that Saturnia.'

With such mutual words they drew nigh the house of poor Evander, and saw scattered herds lowing on the Roman Forum and down the splendid Carinae. When they reached his dwelling, 'This threshold,' he cries, 'Alcides the Conqueror stooped to cross; in this palace he rested. Dare thou, my guest, to despise riches; mould thyself to like dignity of godhead, and come not harsh to our poverty.' He spoke, and led mighty Aeneas under the low roof of his narrow dwelling, and laid him on a couch of stuffed leaves and the skin of a Libyan shebear. Night falls and clasps the earth in her dusky wings.

But Venus, stirred in spirit by no vain mother's alarms, and moved by the threats and stern uprisal of the Laurentines, addresses herself to Vulcan, and in her golden bridal chamber begins thus, breathing divine passion in her speech:

'While Argolic kings wasted in war the doomed towers of Troy, the fortress fated to fall in hostile fires, no succour did I require for her wretched people, no weapons of thine art and aid: nor would I task, dear my lord, thee or thy toils for naught, though I owed many and many a debt to the children of Priam, and had often wept the sore labour of Aeneas. Now by Jove's commands he has set foot in the Rutulian borders; I now therefore come with entreaty, and ask armour of thee in reverence, a mother for a son. The daughter of Nereus, the consort of Tithonus, availed to melt thee with their tears. Look what nations are gathering, what cities bar their gates and sharpen the sword against me for the desolation of my children.'

The goddess ended, and, as he hesitates, clasps him round in the soft embrace of her snowy arms. He suddenly caught the wonted flame, and the heat known of old pierced him to the heart and overran his melting frame: even as when, bursting from the thunder-peal, a sparkling cleft of fire shoots through the storm-clouds with dazzling light. His consort knew, rejoiced in her wiles, and felt her beauty. Then her lord speaks, enchained by Love the immortal:

'Why these far-fetched pleas? Whither, O goddess, is thy trust in me gone? Had like distress been thine, even then we might unblamed have armed thy Trojans, nor did doom nor the Lord omnipotent forbid Troy to stand, and Priam to survive yet ten other years. And now, if thou purposest war, and this is thy counsel, whatever charge I can undertake in my craft, in aught that may be made of iron or molten electrum, whatever fire and air can do, cease thou to entreat as one doubtful of thy strength.' These words spoken, he clasped his wife in the desired embrace, and, sinking in her lap, wooed quiet slumber to overspread his limbs.

Thereon, so soon as sleep, now in mid-career of waning night, had given rest and gone; soon as a woman, whose task is to sustain life with her distaff and the slender labours of the loom, kindles the ashes of her slumbering fire, her toil encroaching on the night, and sets a long task of lamp-lit spinning to her maidens, that so she may keep her husband's bed unsullied and nourish her little children,—even so the Lord of Fire, nor slacker in his hours than she, rises from his soft couch to the work of his smithy. An island rises by the side of Sicily and Aeolian Lipare, steep with smoking cliffs, whereunder the vaulted and thunderous Aetnean caverns are hollowed out for Cyclopean forges, strong strokes on the anvils echo in groans, ore of steel hisses in the vaults, and the fire pants in the furnaces: the house of Vulcan, and Vulcania the land's name. Hither now the Lord of Fire descends from heaven's height. In the vast cavern the Cyclopes were forging iron, Brontes and Steropes and Pyracmon with bared limbs. Shaped in their hands was a thunderbolt, in part already polished, such as the Father of Heaven hurls down on earth in multitudes, part yet unfinished. Three coils of frozen rain, three of watery mist they had enwrought in it, three of ruddy fire and winged south wind; now they were mingling in their work the awful splendours, the sound and terror, and the angry pursuing flames. Elsewhere they hurried on for Mars a chariot with flying wheels, wherewith he stirs up men and cities; and busily burnished the golden serpent-scales of the awful aegis, the armour of wrathful Pallas, and the entwined snakes on the breast of the goddess, the Gorgon head with severed neck and rolling eyes. 'Away with all!' he cries: 'stop your tasks unfinished, Cyclopes of Aetna, and attend to this; a warrior's armour must be made. Now must strength, now quickness of hand be tried, now all our art lend her guidance. Fling off delay.' He spoke no more; but they all bent rapidly to the work, allotting their labours equally. Brass and ore of gold flow in streams, and wounding steel is molten in the vast furnace. They shape a mighty shield, to receive singly all the weapons of the Latins, and weld it sevenfold, circle on circle. Some fill and empty the windy bellows of their blast, some dip the hissing brass in the trough. The cavern groans under their anvils; they raise their arms mightily in answering time, and turn the mass of metal about in the grasp of their tongs.

While the lord of Lemnos is busied thus in the borders of Aeolia, gracious daylight and the matin songs of birds from the eaves rouse Evander from his low dwelling. The old man arises, and draws on his body raiment, and ties the Tyrrhene shoe-latchets about his feet; then buckles to his side and shoulder his Tegean sword, and swathes himself in a panther-skin that droops upon his left. Therewithal two watch-dogs go before him from the high threshold, and accompany their master's steps. The hero sought his guest Aeneas alone in his dwelling, mindful of their talk and his promised bounty.

Nor did Aeneas fail to be astir with the dawn. With the one went his son Pallas, with the other Achates. They meet and clasp hands, and, sitting down within the house, at length enjoy unchecked converse. The King begins thus:

'Princely chief of the Teucrians, in whose lifetime I will never allow the state or realm of Troy vanquished, our strength is scant to succour in war for so great a name. On this side the Tuscan river shuts us in; on that the Rutulian drives us hard, and thunders in arms about our walls. But I purpose to unite to thee mighty peoples and the camp of a wealthy realm; an unforeseen chance offers this for thy salvation. Thou comest at Fate's call. Not far from here stands fast Agylla city, an ancient pile of stone, where of old the Lydian race, eminent in war, settled on the Etruscan ridges. For many years it flourished, till King Mezentius ruled it with insolent sway and armed terror. Why should I relate the horrible murders, the savage deeds of the monarch? May the gods keep them in store for himself and his line! Nay, he would even link dead bodies to living, fitting hand to hand and face to face (the torture!), and in the oozy foulness and corruption of the dreadful embrace so slay them by a lingering death. But at last his citizens, outwearied by his mad excesses, surround him and his house in arms, cut down his comrades, and hurl fire in his roof. Amid the massacre he escaped to the refuge of Rutulian land and the armed defence of Turnus' friendship. So all Etruria has risen in righteous fury, and in immediate battle claim their king for punishment. Over these thousands will I make thee chief, O Aeneas; for their noisy ships crowd all the shore, and they bid the standards advance, while the aged diviner stays them with prophecies: "O chosen men of Maeonia, flower and strength of them of old time, whom righteous anger urges on the enemy, and Mezentius inflames with just wrath, to no Italian is it permitted to hold this great nation in control: choose foreigners to lead you." At that, terrified by the divine warning, the Etruscan lines have encamped on the plain; Tarchon himself has sent ambassadors to me with the crown and sceptre of the kingdom, and offers the royal attire will I but enter their camp and accept the Tyrrhene realm. But old age, frozen to dulness, and exhausted with length of life, denies me the load of empire, and my prowess is past its day. I would urge it on my son, did not the mixture of blood by his Sabellian mother make him half a native here. Thou, to whose years and race alike the fates extend their favour, on whom fortune calls, enter thou in, a leader supreme in bravery over Teucrians and Italians. Mine own Pallas likewise, our hope and comfort, I will send with thee; let him grow used to endure warfare and the stern work of battle under thy teaching, to regard thine actions, and from his earliest years look up to thee. To him will I give two hundred Arcadian cavalry, the choice of our warlike strength, and Pallas as many more to thee in his own name.'

Scarce had he ended; Aeneas, son of Anchises, and trusty Achates gazed with steadfast face, and, sad at heart, were revolving inly many a labour, had not the Cytherean sent a sign from the clear sky. For suddenly a flash and peal come quivering from heaven, and all seemed in a moment to totter, and the Tyrrhene trumpet-blast to roar along the sky. They look up; again and yet again the heavy crash re-echoes. They see in a serene space of sky armour gleam red through a cloud in the clear air, and ring clashing out. The others stood in amaze; but the Trojan hero knew the sound and the promise of his goddess mother; then he speaks: 'Ask not, O friend, ask not in any wise what fortune this presage announces; it is I who am summoned. This sign the goddess who bore me foretold she would send from heaven if war were gathering, and would bring through the air to my succour armour from Vulcan's hands.... Ah, what slaughter awaits the wretched Laurentines! what a price, O Turnus, wilt thou pay me! how many shields and helmets and brave bodies of men shalt thou, Lord Tiber, roll under thy waves! Let them call for armed array and break the treaty!'

These words uttered, he rises from the high seat, and first wakes with fresh fire the slumbering altars of Hercules, and gladly draws nigh his tutelar god of yesternight and the small deities of the household. Alike Evander, and alike the men of Troy offer up duly chosen sheep of two years old. Thereafter he goes to the ships and rivisits his crew, of whose company he chooses the foremost in valour to attend him to war; the rest glide down the water and float idly with the descending stream, to come with news to Ascanius of his father's state. They give horses to the Teucrians who seek the fields of Tyrrhenia; a chosen one is brought for Aeneas, housed in a tawny lion skin that glitters with claws of gold. Rumour flies suddenly, spreading over the little town, that they ride in haste to the courts of the Tyrrhene king. Mothers redouble their prayers in terror, as fear treads closer on peril and the likeness of the War God looms larger in sight. Then Evander, clasping the hand of his departing son, clings to him weeping unsated, and speaks thus:

'Oh, if Jupiter would restore me the years that are past, as I was when, close under Praeneste, I cut down their foremost ranks and burned the piled shields of the conquered! then this right hand sent King Erulus down to hell, though to him at his birth his mother Feronia (awful to tell) had given three lives and triple arms to wield; thrice must he be laid low in death; yet then this hand took all his lives and as often stripped him of his arms: in nowise should I now, O son, be severed from thy dear embrace; never had the insolent sword of Mezentius on my borders dealt so many cruel deaths, widowed the city of so many citizens. But you, O heavenly powers, and thou, Jupiter, Lord and Governor of Heaven, have compassion, I pray, on the Arcadian king, and hear a father's prayers. If your deity and decrees keep my Pallas safe for me, if I live that I may see him and meet him yet, I pray for life; any burden soever I have patience to endure. But if, O Fortune, thou threatenest some dread calamity, now, ah now, may I break off a cruel life, while anxiety still wavers and expectation is in doubt, while thou, dear boy, the one delight of my age, art yet clasped in my embrace; let no bitterer message wound mine ear.' These words the father poured forth at the final parting; his servants bore him swooning within.

And now the cavalry had issued from the open gates, Aeneas and trusty Achates among the foremost, then other of the Trojan princes, Pallas conspicuous amid the column in scarf and inlaid armour, even as when the Morning Star, newly washed in the ocean wave, whom Venus cherishes before the other starry fires, shews his holy face in heaven, and melts the darkness away. Fearful mothers stand on the walls and follow with their eyes the cloud of dust and the squadrons gleaming in brass. They, where the goal of their way lies nearest, bear through the brushwood in armed array. Forming in column, they advance noisily, and the horse hoof shakes the crumbling plain with four-footed trampling. There is a high grove by the cold river of Caere, widely revered in ancestral awe; sheltering hills shut it in all about and girdle the woodland with their dark firs. Rumour is that the old Pelasgians, who once long ago held the Latin borders, consecrated the grove and its festal day to Silvanus, god of the tilth and flock. Not far from it Tarchon and his Tyrrhenians were encamped in a protected place; and now from the hill-top the tents of all their army might be seen outspread on the fields. Lord Aeneas and his chosen warriors draw hither and refresh their weary horses and limbs.

But Venus the white goddess drew nigh, bearing her gifts through the clouds of heaven; and when she saw her son withdrawn far apart in the valley's recess by the cool river, cast herself in his way, and addressed him thus: 'Behold perfected the presents of my husband's promised craftsmanship: so shalt thou not shun, O my child, soon to challenge the haughty Laurentines or fiery Turnus to battle.' The Cytherean spoke, and sought her son's embrace, and laid the armour glittering under an oak over against him. He, rejoicing in the magnificence of the goddess' gift, cannot have his fill of turning his eyes over it piece by piece, and admires and handles between his arms the helmet, dread with plumes and spouting flame, the death-dealing sword, the stiff corslet of brass, blood-red and vast as when a blue cloud takes fire in the sunbeams and gleams afar; then the smooth greaves of electrum and refined gold, the spear, and the shield's ineffable design. There the Lord of Fire has fashioned the story of Italy and the triumphs of the Romans, not witless of prophecy or ignorant of the age to be; there all the race of Ascanius' future seed and their wars fought one after one. Likewise had he fashioned the she-wolf couched after the birth in the green cave of Mars; round her teats the twin boys hung playing, and fearlessly mouthed their foster-mother; she, with sleek neck bent back, stroked them by turns and shaped their bodies with her tongue. Thereto not far from this he had set Rome and the lawless rape of the Sabines in the concourse of the theatre when the great Circensian games were held, and a fresh war suddenly arising between the people of Romulus and aged Tatius and austere Cures. Next these same kings laid down their mutual strife and stood armed before Jove's altar with cup in hand, and joined treaty over a slain sow. Not far from there four-horse chariots driven apart had torn Mettus asunder (but thou, O Alban, shouldst have kept by thy words!), and Tullus tore the flesh of the liar through the forest, his splashed blood dripping from the briars. Therewithal Porsena commanded to admit the exiled Tarquin, and held the city in the grasp of a strong blockade; the Aeneadae rushed on the sword for liberty. Him thou couldst espy like one who chafes and like one who threatens, because Cocles dared to tear down the bridge, and Cloelia broke her bonds and swam the river. Highest of all Manlius, warder of the Tarpeian fortress, stood with the temple behind him and held the high Capitoline; and Romulus' palace stood fresh in its crisp thatch. And here the silver goose, fluttering in the gilded colonnades, cried that the Gauls were there on the threshold. The Gauls were there among the brushwood, hard on the fortress, secure in the darkness and the dower of dim night. Their clustering locks are of gold, and of gold their attire; their striped cloaks glitter, and their milk-white necks are entwined with gold. Two Alpine pikes sparkle in the hand of each, and long shields guard their bodies. Here he had embossed the dancing Salii and the naked Luperci, the mitres wreathed in wool, and the sacred shields that fell from heaven; in cushioned cars the virtuous matrons led on their rites through the city. Far hence he adds the habitations of hell also, the high gates of Dis and the dooms of guilt; and thee, O Catiline, clinging on the beetling rock, and shuddering at the faces of the Furies; and far apart the good, Cato delivering them statutes. Amidst it all flows wide the likeness of the swelling sea, wrought in gold, though the foam surged grey upon blue water; and round about dolphins, in shining silver, swept the seas with their tails in circle as they cleft through the tide. In the centre were visible the brazen war-fleets of Actium; thou mightest see all Leucate swarm in embattled array, and the waves gleam with gold. Here Caesar Augustus, leading Italy to battle with Fathers and People, with gods of household and of state, stands on the lofty stern; from his rejoicing brows a double flame streams out, and his ancestral star dawns overhead. Elsewhere Agrippa, with favouring winds and gods, leads on his towering column; on his brows glitters the prow-girt naval crown, the haughty emblazonment of the war. Here Antonius with barbarian aid and motley arms, from the conquered nations of the Dawn and the shore of the southern sea, carries with him Egypt and the Eastern forces of utmost Bactra, and the shameful Egyptian woman follows as his consort. All at once rush on, and the whole ocean is torn into foam by back-sweeping oars and triple-beaked prows. They steer to sea; one might think that the Cyclades were uptorn and floated on the main, or that lofty mountains clashed with mountains, so mightily do their crews urge on the turreted ships. Flaming tow and the winged steel of darts shower thickly from their hands; the fields of ocean redden with fresh slaughter. Midmost the Queen calls on her squadron with the timbrel of her country, nor yet casts back a glance on the twin snakes behind her. Howling Anubis, and gods monstrous and multiform, level their arms against Neptune and Venus and against Minerva; Mars rages amid the havoc, graven in iron, and the Fatal Sisters hang aloft, and Discord strides rejoicing with garment rent, and Bellona attends her with blood-stained scourge. Looking thereon, Actian Apollo above drew his bow; with the terror of it all Egypt and India, every Arab and Sabaean, turned back in flight. The Queen herself seemed to call the winds and spread her sails, and even now let her sheets run slack. Her the Lord of Fire had fashioned amid the carnage, wan with the shadow of death, borne along by the waves and the north-west wind; and over against her the vast bulk of mourning Nile, opening out his folds and calling with all his raiment the conquered people into his blue lap and the coverture of his streams. But Caesar rode into the city of Rome in triple triumph, and dedicated his vowed offering to the gods to stand for ever, three hundred stately shrines all about the city. The streets were loud with gladness and games and cheering. In all the temples was a band of matrons, in all were altars, and before the altars slain steers strewed the ground. Himself he sits on the snowy threshold of Phoebus the bright, reviews the gifts of the nations and ranges them on the haughty doors. The conquered tribes move in long line, diverse as in tongue, so in fashion of dress and armour. Here Mulciber had designed the Nomad race and the ungirt Africans, here the Leleges and Carians and archer Gelonians. Euphrates went by now with smoother waves, and the Morini utmost of men, and the twy-horned Rhine, the untamed Dahae, and Araxes chafing under his bridge.

These things he admires on the shield of Vulcan, his mother's gift, and rejoicing in the portraiture of unknown history, lifts on his shoulder the destined glories of his children.

BOOK NINTH

THE SIEGE OF THE TROJAN CAMP

And while thus things pass far in the distance, Juno daughter of Saturn sent Iris down the sky to gallant Turnus, then haply seated in his forefather Pilumnus' holy forest dell. To him the child of Thaumas spoke thus with roseate lips:

'Turnus, what no god had dared promise to thy prayer, behold is brought unasked by the circling day. Aeneas has quitted town and comrades and fleet to seek Evander's throne and Palatine dwelling place. Nor is it enough; he has pierced to Corythus' utmost cities, and is mustering in arms a troop of Lydian rustics. Why hesitate? now, now is the time to call for chariot and horses. Break through all hindrance and seize the bewildered camp.'

She spoke, and rose into the sky on poised wings, and flashed under the clouds in a long flying bow. He knew her, and lifting either hand to heaven, with this cry pursued her flight: 'Iris, grace of the sky, who has driven thee down the clouds to me and borne thee to earth? Whence is this sudden sheen of weather? I see the sky parting asunder, and the wandering stars in the firmament. I follow the high omen, whoso thou art that callest me to arms.' And with these words he drew nigh the wave, and caught up water from its brimming eddy, making many prayers to the gods and burdening the air with vows.

And now all the army was advancing on the open plain, rich in horses, rich in raiment of broidered gold. Messapus rules the foremost ranks, the sons of Tyrrheus the rear. Turnus commands the centre: even as Ganges rising high in silence when his seven streams are still, or the rich flood of Nile when he ebbs from the plains, and is now sunk into his channel. On this the Teucrians descry a sudden cloud of dark dust gathering, and the blackness rising on the plain. Caïcus raises a cry from the front rampart: 'What mass of misty gloom, O citizens, is rolling hitherward? to arms in haste! serve out weapons, climb the walls. The enemy approaches, ho!' With mighty clamour the Teucrians pour in through all the gates and line the works. For so at his departure Aeneas the great captain had enjoined; were aught to chance meanwhile, they should not venture to range their battle-line or trust the open field, but keep their camp and the safety of the entrenched walls. So, though shame and wrath beckon them on to battle, they yet bar the gates and do his bidding, and await the foe armed and in shelter of the towers. Turnus, who had flown forward in advance of his tardy column, comes up suddenly to the town with a train of twenty chosen cavalry, borne on a Thracian horse dappled with white, and covered by a golden helmet with scarlet plume. 'Who will be with me, my men, to be first on the foe? See!' he cries; and sends a javelin spinning into the air to open battle, and advances towering on the plain. His comrades take up the cry, and follow with dreadful din, wondering at the Teucrians' coward hearts, that they issue not on even field nor face them in arms, but keep in shelter of the camp. Hither and thither he rides furiously, tracing the walls, and seeking entrance where way is none. And as a wolf prowling about some crowded sheepfold, when, beaten sore of winds and rains, he howls at the pens by midnight; safe beneath their mothers the lambs keep bleating on; he, savage and insatiate, rages in anger against the flock he cannot reach, tired by long-gathering madness for food, and a throat unslaked with blood: even so the Rutulian, as he gazes on the walled camp, kindles in anger, and indignation is hot in his iron frame. By what means may he essay entrance? by what passage hurl the imprisoned Trojans from the rampart and fling them on the plain? Close under the flanking camp lay the fleet, fenced about with earthworks and the waters of the river; it he attacks, and calls for fire to his exultant comrades, and eagerly catches a blazing pine in his hand. Then indeed they press on, quickened by Turnus' presence, and all the band arm them with black torches. The hearth-fires are plundered; the smoky brand trails a resinous glare, and the Fire-god sends clouds of glowing ashes upward.

What god, O Muses, guarded the Trojans from the rage of the fire? who repelled the fierce flame from their ships? Tell it; ancient is the assurance thereof, but the fame everlasting. What time Aeneas began to shape his fleet on Phrygian Ida, and prepared to seek the high seas, the Berecyntian, they say, the very Mother of gods, spoke to high Jove in these words: 'Grant, O son, to my prayer, what she who bore thee and laid Olympus under thy feet asks of thy love. On the fortress-height was a grove whither men bore my holy things, dim with dusky pine and pillared maples. These, when he required a fleet, I gave gladly to the Dardanian; now fear wrings me with sharp distress. Relieve my terrors, and grant a mother's prayers such power that they may yield to no stress of voyaging or of stormy gust: be birth on our hills their avail.'

Thus her son in answer, who wheels the starry worlds: 'O mother, whither callest thou fate? or what dost thou seek for these of thine? May hulls have the right of immortality that were fashioned by mortal hand? and may Aeneas traverse perils secure in insecurity? To what god is power so great given? Nay, but when, their duty done, they shall lie at last in their Ausonian haven, from all that have outgone the waves and borne their Dardanian captain to the fields of Laurentum will I take their mortal body, and bid them be goddesses of the mighty deep, even as Doto the Nereïd and Galatea, when they cut the sea that falls away from their breasts in foam.' He ended; and by his brother's Stygian streams, by the banks of the pitchy black-boiling chasm he nodded confirmation, and shook all Olympus with his nod.

So the promised day was come, and the Destinies had fulfilled their due time, when Turnus' assault stirred the Mother to ward the brands from her holy ships. First then a strange light flashed on all eyes, and a great glory from the Dawn seemed to dart over the sky, with the choirs of Ida; then an awful voice fell through air, filling the Trojan and Rutulian ranks: 'Disquiet not yourselves, O Teucrians, to guard ships of mine, neither arm your hands: sooner shall Turnus burn the seas than these holy pines. You, go free; go, goddesses of the seas; the Mother bids it.' And immediately each ship breaks the bond that held it, as with dipping prows they plunge like dolphins deep into the water: from it again (O wonderful and strange!) they rise with maidens' faces in like number, and stand out to sea.

The Rutulians stood dumb; Messapus himself is terror-stricken among his disordered cavalry; even the stream of Tiber pauses with hoarse murmur, and recoils from the main. But bold Turnus fails not a whit in confidence; nay, he raises their courage with words, nay, he chides them: 'On the Trojans are these portents aimed; Jupiter himself has bereft them of their wonted succour; nor do they abide Rutulian spear and fire. So are the seas pathless for the Teucrians, nor is there any hope in flight; they have lost half their world. And we hold the land: in all their thousands the nations of Italy are under arms. In no wise am I dismayed by those divine oracles of doom that the Phrygians insolently advance. Fate and Venus are satisfied, in that the Trojans have touched our fruitful Ausonian fields. I too have my destiny against theirs, to put utterly to the sword the guilty nation who have robbed me of my bride; not the sons of Atreus alone feel that pain, nor may Mycenae alone take arms. *But to have perished once is enough!* To have sinned once should have been enough, in all but utter hatred of the whole of womankind. Trust in the sundering rampart, and the hindrance of their trenches, so narrow a remove from death, gives these their courage: yet have they not seen Troy town, the work of Neptune's hand, sink into fire? But you, my chosen, who of you makes ready to breach their palisade at the sword's point, and falls with me on their panic-stricken camp? I have no need of Vulcanian arms, of a thousand ships, to meet the Teucrians. All Etruria may join on with them in alliance:

let them not fear darkness and cowardly thefts, nor will we hide ourselves unseen in a horse's belly; in daylight and unconcealed are we resolved to girdle their walls with flame. Not with Grecians will I make them say they have to do, nor a Pelasgian force kept off till the tenth year by Hector. Now, since the better part of day is spent, for what remains refresh your bodies, O warriors, glad to have done so well, and expect the order of battle.'

Meanwhile charge is given to Messapus to blockade the gates with pickets of sentries, and encircle the works with watchfires. Twice seven Rutulians are chosen to guard the walls with soldiery; but each leads an hundred men, crimson-plumed and sparkling in gold. They spread themselves about and keep alternate watch, and, lying along the grass, drink deep and upturn brazen bowls. The fires glow, and the sentinels spend the night awake in games. . . .

Down on this the Trojans look forth from the rampart, as they hold the height in arms; withal in fearful haste they try the gates and lay gangways from bastion to bastion, and bring up missiles. Mnestheus and valiant Serestus speed the work, whom lord Aeneas appointed, should misfortune call, to be rulers of the younger and governors of the state. All their battalions, sharing the lot of peril, keep watch along the walls, and take charge in turn of what each has to guard.

Nisus was sentry at the gate, Hyrtacus' son most valiant in arms, whom Ida the huntress had sent in Aeneas' company with fleet javelin and light arrows; and by his side Euryalus, fairest of all the Aeneadae and the wearers of Trojan arms, showing on his unshaven boy's face the first bloom of youth. These two were one in affection, and charged side by side in battle; now likewise their common guard kept the gate. Nisus cries: 'Lend the gods this fervour to the soul, Euryalus? or does fatal passion become a proper god to each? Long ere now my soul is restless to begin some great deed of arms, and quiet peace delights it not. Thou seest how confident in fortune are the Rutulians. Their lights glimmer far apart; relaxed in drunken sleep they have sunk to rest; silence stretches over the field. Learn then what I ponder, what that Aeneas be summoned, and men be sent to carry him tidings. If they promise what I ask in thy name—for to me tidings. If they promise what I ask in thy name—for to me the glory of the deed is enough—methinks I can find beneath yonder hillock a path to the walls of Pallanteum town.'

Euryalus stood fixed, struck through with high ambition, and therewith speaks thus to his fiery friend: 'Dost thou shun me then, Nisus, to share thy company in highest deeds? shall I send thee alone into so great perils? Not thus did my warrior father Opheltes rear and nurture me amid the Argolic terror and the agony of Troy, nor thus have I borne myself by thy side while following noble Aeneas to his utmost fate. Here is a spirit, yes here, that scorns the light of day, that deems lightly bought at a life's price that honour to which thou dost aspire.'

To this Nisus: 'Assuredly I had no such fear of thee; I could not, no; so may great Jupiter, or whoso looks on earth with equal eyes, restore me to thee triumphant. But if haply—as thou seest often and often in so forlorn a hope—if haply chance or deity sweep me to adverse doom, I would have thee survive; thine age is worthier to live. Be there one to commit me to earth, rescued or ransomed from the battlefield: or, if Fortune in her wonted way deny that, to pay me far away the rites of funeral and the grace of a tomb. Neither would I bring such pain on thy poor mother, she who singly of many matrons has dared to follow her boy to the end, and recks not of great Acestes' city.'

And he: 'In vain dost thou string idle reasons; nor does my purpose yield or change its place so soon. Let us make haste.' He speaks, and rouses the watch; they come up, and relieve the guard; quitting their post, he and Nisus stride on to seek the prince.

The rest of living things over all lands were soothing their cares in sleep, and their hearts forgot their pain; the foremost Trojan captains, a chosen band, held counsel for the safety of the kingdom; what to do, or who should now be their messenger to Aeneas. They stand, leaning on their long spears and grasping their shields, in mid level of the camp. Then Nisus and Euryalus together pray with urgent haste to be given audience; their matter is weighty and will be worth the delay. Iülus at once granted their hurried plea, and bade Nisus speak. Thereon the son of Hyrtacus: 'Hear, O people of Aeneas, with favourable mind, nor regard our years in what we offer. Relaxed in drunken sleep, the Rutulians are silent; we have stealthily spied the open ground that lies in the path through the gate next the sea. The line of fires is broken, and their smoke rises darkly upwards. If you let us take our fortune to seek Aeneas in Pallanteum town, you will soon descry us here at hand with the spoils of the great slaughter we have dealt. Nor shall we miss the way we go; up the dim valleys we have caught a glimpse of the town, and learned all the river in continual hunting.'

Thereon aged Aletes, ripe in counsel: 'Gods of our fathers, under whose deity Troy ever stands, not wholly yet do you purpose to blot out the Trojan race, when you have brought us young honour and hearts so sure as these.' So speaking, he caught both by shoulder and hand, with tears showering down over face and feature. 'What guerdon shall I deem may be given you, O men, what recompense for these feats of honour? First and fairest shall be your reward from the gods and your own conduct; and Aeneas' goodness shall speedily repay the rest, and Ascanius with all life before him never forget so great a service.'—'Nay,' breaks in Ascanius, 'I whose sole safety is in my father's return, I adjure thee and him, O Nisus, by our great household gods, by the tutelar spirit of Assaracus and hoar Vesta's sanctuary—on your knees I lay all my fortune and trust—recall my father; give him back to sight; all sorrow disappears in his recovery. I will give a pair of cups my father took in vanquished Arisba, wrought in silver and rough with tracery, twin tripods, and two large talents of gold, and an ancient bowl of Sidonian Dido's giving. If it be indeed our lot to possess Italy and grasp a conquering sceptre, and to assign the spoil; thou sawest the horse and armour of Turnus as he went all in gold; that same horse, the shield and the ruddy plume, will I reserve from partition, thy reward, O Nisus, even from now. My father will give besides twelve mothers of the choicest beauty, and men captives, all in their due array; above these, the space of meadowland that is now King Latinus' own domain. Thee, O noble boy, whom mine age follows at a nearer interval, even now I welcome to all my heart, and embrace as my companion in every fortune. No glory of mine shall be sought without thee; whether peace or war be in conduct, my chiefest trust for deed and word shall be in thee.'

Answering whom Euryalus speaks thus: 'No day shall come to prove me degenerate from this daring valour; let but fortune fall prosperous, not adverse. But above all thy gifts, one thing I ask of thee. My poor mother of Priam's ancient race, whom neither the Ilian land nor King Acestes' city kept from following me forth, I leave now ignorant of this danger, such as it is, and without a farewell, because—night and thine hand be witness!—I cannot bear a parent's tears. But thou, I pray, support her want and relieve her loneliness. Let me take with me this hope in thee, I shall more daringly meet every chance.' Deeply stirred at heart, the Dardanians shed tears, fair Iülus before them all, as the sight of filial affection touched his spirit. Then he speaks thus: ... 'Assure thyself all that is due to thy mighty enterprise; for she shall be a mother to me, and only in name fail to be Crëusa; nor slight is the honour reserved for the mother of such a son. What chances soever follow this deed, I swear by this head whereby my father was wont to swear, what I promise to thee on thy prosperous return shall abide the same for thy mother and kindred.' So speaks he weeping, and ungirds from his shoulder the sword inlaid with gold, fashioned with marvellous skill by Lycaon of Gnosus and set in a fitted sheath of ivory. Mnestheus gives Nisus the shaggy spoils of a lion's hide; faithful Aletes exchanges his helmet. They move forth in arms, and as they go all the company of captains, young and old, speed them to the gates with good wishes. Likewise fair

Iülus, with a man's thought and a spirit beyond his years, gave many messages to be carried to his father. But the breezes shred all asunder and give them unaccomplished to the clouds.

They issue and cross the trenches, and through the shadow of night seek the fatal camp, themselves first to be the death of many a man. All about they see bodies strewn along the grass in drunken sleep, chariots atilt on the shore, the men lying among their traces and wheels, with their armour by them, and their wine. The son of Hyrtacus began thus: 'Euryalus, now for daring hands; all invites them; here lies our way; see thou that none raise a hand from behind against us, and keep far-sighted watch. Here will I deal desolation, and make a broad path for thee to follow.' So speaks he and checks his voice; therewith he drives his sword at lordly Rhamnes, who haply on carpets heaped high was drawing the full breath of sleep; a king himself, and King Turnus' best-beloved augur, but not all his augury could avert his doom. Three of his household beside him, lying carelessly among their arms, and the armour-bearer and charioteer of Remus go down before him, caught at the horses' feet. Their drooping necks he severs with the sword, then beheads their lord likewise and leaves the trunk spouting blood; the dark warm gore soaks ground and cushions. Therewithal Lamyrus and Lamus, and beautiful young Serranus, who that night had played long and late, and lay with the conquering god heavy on every limb; happy, had he played out the night, and kept up his game till day! Even thus an unfed lion riots through full sheepfolds, for mad hunger urges him, and champs and rends the fleecy flock that are dumb with fear, and roars with blood-stained mouth. Nor less is the slaughter of Euryalus; he too rages all aflame; an unnamed multitude go down before his path, and Fadus and Herbesus and Rhoetus and Aboris, and Abaris, unaware; Rhoetus awake and seeing all, but he hid in fear behind a great bowl; right in whose breast, as he rose close by, he plunged the sword all its length, and drew it back red with the flood of death.

He vomits forth his life-blood, and throws up wine mixed with blood in the death agony, while the other presses hotly on his stealthy errand. And now he bent his way towards Messapus' comrades, where he saw the last flicker of the fires go down, and the horses tethered in order cropping the grass; when Nisus briefly speaks thus, for he saw him beside himself for lust of slaying: 'Let us stop; for unfriendly daylight draws nigh. Vengeance is sated to the full; a path is cut through the enemy.' Much they leave behind, men's armour wrought in solid silver, and bowls therewith, and beautiful carpets. Euryalus tears away the decorations of Rhamnes and his sword-belt embossed with gold, a gift which Caedicus, wealthiest of men of old, sends to Remulus of Tibur when plighting friendship far away; he on his death-bed gives them to his grandson for his own; these he fits on the shoulders valiant in vain, then puts on Messapus' light helmet with its graceful plumes. They issue from the camp and make for safety.

Meanwhile an advanced guard of cavalry were on their way from the Latin city, while the rest of their marshalled battalions linger on the plains, and bore a reply to King Turnus; three hundred men all under shield, in Volscens' leading. And now they approached the camp and drew near the walls, when they descry the two turning away by the pathway to the left; and in the glimmering darkness of night the forgotten helmet betrayed Euryalus, glittering as it met the light. It was seen and marked. Volscens cries aloud from his column: 'Stand, men! why on the march? or who are you in arms? or whither hold you your way?' They offer no reply, but quicken their flight into the forest, and throw themselves on the night. On this side and this the horsemen bar the familiar crossways, and encircle every outlet with sentinels. The forest spread wide in tangled thickets and dark ilex; thick growth of briars choked it all about, and the muffled pathway glimmered in a broken track. Hampered by the shadowy boughs and his cumbrous spoil, Euryalus in his fright misses the line of way. Nisus gets clear;

and now unawares he had passed the enemy, and the place afterwards called Albani from Alba's name; then the deep coverts were of King Latinus' domain: when he stopped, and looked back in vain for his lost friend. 'Euryalus, unhappy! on what ground have I left thee? or where shall I follow?' Therewithal, again unwinding all the entanglement of the treacherous woodland way, he marks and retraces his footsteps, and wanders down the silent thickets. He hears the horses, hears the clatter and signal-notes of the pursuers. Nor had he long to wait, when shouts reach his ears, and he sees Euryalus, whom even now, in the perplexity of ground and darkness, the whole squadron have borne down in a sudden onset, and seize in spite of all his vain struggles. What shall he do? with what force, what arms dare his rescue? or shall he rush on his doom amid their swords, and find in their wounds a speedy and glorious death? Quickly he draws back his arm with poised spear, and looking up to the moon on high, utters this prayer: 'Do thou give present aid to our enterprise, O Latonian goddess, glory of the stars and guardian of the woodlands: by all the gifts my father Hyrtacus ever bore for my sake to thine altars, by all mine own hand hath added from my hunting, or hung in thy dome, or fixed on thy holy roof, grant me to confound these masses, and guide my javelin through the air.' He ended, and with all the force of his body hurls the steel. The flying spear whistles through the darkness of the night, and comes full on the back of Sulmo from behind, and there snaps, and the broken shaft passes on through his heart. Spouting a warm tide from his breast he rolls over chill in death, and his sides throb with long-drawn gasps. Hither and thither they gaze round. Lo, he all the fiercer was poising another weapon high by his ear; while they waver, the spear went whizzing through both Tagus' temples, and pierced and stuck fast in the warm brain. Volscens is mad with rage, and nowhere espies the sender of the weapon, nor where to direct his fury. 'Yet meanwhile thou with thy warm blood shalt pay me for both,' he cries; and unsheathing his sword, he leapt on Euryalus. Then indeed frantic with terror Nisus shrieks out; no longer could he shroud himself in darkness or endure such agony. 'On me, on me, I am here, I did it, on me turn your steel, O Rutulians! Mine is all the guilt; he dared not, no, nor could not; to this heaven I appeal and the stars that know; he but loved his hapless friend too well.' Such words he was uttering; but the sword driven hard home is gone clean through his ribs and pierces the white breast. Euryalus rolls dead, and the blood runs over his lovely limbs, and his neck sinks and settles on his shoulder; even as when a lustrous flower cut away by the plough droops in death, or weary-necked poppies bow down their head if overweighted with a random shower. But Nisus rushes amidst them, and alone among them all makes at Volscens, stays at Volscens alone: round him the foe cluster, closing in from right and left to hurl him back: none the less he presses on, and whirls his sword like lightning, till he plunges it full in the face of the shrieking Rutulian, and slays his enemy as he dies. Then, stabbed through and through, he flung himself above his lifeless friend, and there at last found the quiet sleep of death.

Happy pair! if my verse is aught of avail, no length of days shall ever blot you from the memory of time, while the house of Aeneas shall dwell by the steadfast Capitolian rock, and the lord of Rome hold sovereignty.

The victorious Rutulians, with their spoils and the plunder regained, bore dead Volscens weeping to the camp. Nor in the camp was the wailing less, when Rhamnes was found a bloodless corpse, and Serranus and Numa and all their princes destroyed in a single slaughter. Crowds throng towards the corpses and the men wounded to death, the ground fresh with warm slaughter and the swoln runlets of frothing blood. They mutually recognise the spoils, Messapus' shining helmet and the trappings won at such cost of sweat.

And now Dawn, leaving the saffron bed of Tithonus, scattered over earth her fresh shafts of early light; now the sunlight streams in, now daylight unveils the world. Turnus, himself fully armed, awakes his men to arms, and each leader marshals to battle his brazen lines and whets their anger with varying rumours. Nay, pitiable sight! they fix on spear-points and uprear and follow with loud shouts the heads of Euryalus and Nisus. . . . The Aeneadae stubbornly face them, lining the left hand wall (for their right is girdled by the river), hold the deep trenches and stand gloomily on the high towers, stirred withal by the pierced faces they know, alas, too well, in their dark dripping gore.

Meanwhile Rumour on fluttering wings rushes with the news through the alarmed town and glides to the ears of Euryalus' mother. But instantly the warmth leaves her woeful body, the shuttle starts from her hand and the threads unroll. She darts forth in agony, and with woman's wailing and torn hair runs distractedly towards the walls and the foremost columns, recking naught of men, naught of peril or weapons; thereon she fills the air with her complaint: 'Is it thus I behold thee, O Euryalus? Couldst thou, the latest solace of mine age, leave me alone so cruelly? nor when sent into such danger was one last word to thee allowed thine unhappy mother? Alas, thou liest in a strange land, given for a prey to the dogs and fowls of Latium! nor was I thy mother there for chief mourner, to lay thee out or close thine eyes or wash thy wounds, and cover thee with the garment I hastened on for thee whole nights and days, an anxious old woman taking comfort from the loom. Whither shall I follow? or what land now holds thy mangled corpse, thy body torn limb from limb? Is this all of what thou wert that returns to me, O my son? is it this I have followed by land and sea? Strike me through of your pity, on me cast all your weapons, Rutulians; make me the first sacrifice of your steel. Or do thou, mighty lord of heaven, be merciful, and with thine own weapon hurl this hateful life to the nether deep, since in no wise else may I break away from life's cruelty.' At this weeping cry their courage falters, and a sigh of sorrow passes all along; their strength is benumbed and broken for battle. Her, while her grief kindled, at Ilioneus' and weeping Iülus' bidding Idaeus and Actor catch up and carry home in their arms.

But the terrible trumpet-note afar rang on the shrill brass; a shout follows, and is echoed from the sky. The Volscians hasten up in even line under their advancing roof of shields, and set to fill up the trenches and tear down the palisades. Some seek entrance by scaling the walls with ladders, where the defenders' battle-line is thin, and light shows through gaps in the ring of men. The Teucrians in return shower weapons of every sort, and push them down with stiff poles, practised by long warfare in defending ramparts: and fiercely hurl heavy stones, so be they may break the shielded line; while they, crowded under their shell, lightly bear all the downpour. But now they fail; for where the vast mass presses close, the Teucrians roll a huge block tumbling down that makes a wide gap in the Rutulians and crashes through their armoured roof. Nor do the bold Rutulians care longer to continue the blind fight, but strive to clear the rampart with missiles. . . . Elsewhere in dreadful guise Mezentius brandishes his Etruscan pine and hurls smoking brands; but Messapus, tamer of horses, seed of Neptune, tears away the palisading and calls for ladders to the ramparts.

Thy sisterhood, O Calliope, I pray inspire me while I sing the destruction spread then and there by Turnus' sword, the deaths dealt from his hand, and whom each warrior sent down to the under world; and unroll with me the broad borders of war.

A tower loomed vast with lofty gangways at a point of vantage; this all the Italians strove with main strength to storm, and set all their might and device to overthrow it; the Trojans in return defended it with stones and hurled showers of darts through the loopholes. Turnus, leading the attack, threw a blazing torch that caught flaming on the side wall; swoln by the wind, the flame seized the planking and clung devouring to the standards. Those within, in hurry and confusion, desire retreat from their distress; in vain; while they cluster together and fall back to the side free from the destroyer, the tower sinks prone under the sudden weight with a crash that thunders through all the sky. Pierced by their own weapons, and impaled on hard splinters of wood, they come half slain to the ground with the vast mass behind them. Scarcely do Helenor alone and Lycus struggle out; Helenor in his early prime, whom a slave woman of Licymnos bore in secret to the Maeonian king, and sent to Troy in forbidden weapons, lightly armed with sheathless sword and white unemblazoned shield. And he, when he saw himself among Turnus' encircling thousands, ranks on this side and ranks on this of Latins, as a wild beast which, girt with a crowded ring of hunters, dashes at their weapons, hurls herself unblinded on death, and comes with a bound upon the spears; even so he rushes to his death amid the enemy, and presses on where he sees their weapons thickest. But Lycus, far fleeter of foot, holds by the walls in flight midway among foes and arms, and strives to catch the coping in his grasp and reach the hands of his comrades. And Turnus pursuing and aiming as he ran, thus upbraids him in triumph: 'Didst thou hope, madman, thou mightest escape our hands?' and catches him as he clings, and tears him and a great piece of the wall away: as when, with a hare or snowy-bodied swan in his crooked talons, Jove's armour-bearer soars aloft, or the wolf of Mars snatches from the folds some lamb sought of his mother with incessant bleating. On all sides a shout goes up. They advance and fill the trenches with heaps of earth; some toss glowing brands on the roofs. Ilioneus strikes down Lucetius with a great fragment of mountain rock as, carrying fire, he draws nigh the gate. Liger slays Emathion, Asylas Corinaeus, the one skilled with the javelin, the other with the stealthy arrow from afar. Caeneus slays Ortygius; Turnus victorious Caeneus; Turnus Itys and Clonius, Dioxippus, and Promolus, and Sagaris, and Idas where he stood in front of the turret top; Cayps Privernus; him Themillas' spear had first grazed lightly; the madman threw down his shield to carry his hand to the wound; so the arrow winged her way, and pinning his hand to his left side, broke into the lungs with deadly wound. The son of Arcens stood splendid in arms, and scarf embroidered with needlework and bright with Iberian blue, the beautiful boy sent by his father Arcens from nurture in the grove of Mars about the streams of Symaethus, where Palicus' altar is rich and gracious. Laying down his spears, Mezentius whirled thrice round his head the tightened cord of his whistling sling, pierced him full between the temples with the molten bullet, and stretched him all his length upon the sand.

Then, it is said, Ascanius first aimed his flying shaft in war, wont before to frighten beasts of the chase, and struck down a brave Numanian, Remulus by name, but lately allied in bridal to Turnus' younger sister. He advancing before his ranks clamoured things fit and unfit to tell, and strode along lofty and voluble, his heart lifted up with his fresh royalty.

'Take you not shame to be again held leaguered in your ramparts, O Phrygians twice taken, and to make walls your fence from death? Behold them who demand in war our wives for theirs! What god, what madness, has driven you to Italy? Here are no sons of Atreus nor false-tongued Ulysses. A race of hardy breed, we carry our newborn children to the streams and harden them in the bitter icy water; as boys they spend wakeful nights over the chase, and tire out the woodland; but in manhood, unwearied by toil and trained to poverty, they subdue the soil with their mattocks, or shake towns in war. Every age wears iron, and we goad the flanks of our oxen with reversed spear; nor does creeping old age weaken our strength of spirit or abate our force. White hairs bear the weight of the helmet; and it is ever our delight to drive in fresh spoil and live on our plunder. Yours is embroidered raiment of saffron and shining sea-purple. Indolence is your pleasure, your delight the luxurious dance; you wear sleeved tunics and ribboned turbans. O right Phrygian women, not even Phrygian men! traverse the heights of Dindymus, where the double-mouthed flute breathes familiar music; the drums call you, and the Berecyntian boxwood of the mother of Ida; leave arms to men, and lay down the sword.'

As he flung forth such words of ill-ominous strain, Ascanius brooked it not, and aimed an arrow on him from the stretched horse sinew; and as he drew his arms asunder, first stayed to supplicate Jove in lowly vows: 'Jupiter omnipotent, deign to favour this daring deed. My hands shall bear yearly gifts to thee in thy temple, and bring to stand before thine altars a steer with gilded forehead, snow-white, carrying his head high as his mother's, already pushing with his horn and making the sand fly up under his feet.' The Father heard and from a clear space of sky thundered on the left; at once the fatal bow rings, the grim-whistling arrow flies from the tense string, and goes through the head of Remulus, the steel piercing through from temple to temple. 'Go, mock valour with insolence of speech! Phrygians twice taken return this answer to Rutulians.' Thus and no further Ascanius; the Teucrians respond in cheers, and shout for joy in rising height of courage. Then haply in the tract of heaven tressed Apollo sate looking down from his cloud on the Ausonian ranks and town, and thus addresses triumphant Iülus: 'Good speed to thy young valor, O boy! this is the way to heaven, child of gods and parent of gods to be! Rightly shall all wars fated to come sink to peace beneath the line of Assaracus; nor art thou bounded in a Troy.' So speaking, he darts from heaven's height, and cleaving the breezy air, seeks Ascanius. Then he changes the fashion of his countenance, and becomes aged Butes, armour-bearer of old to Dardanian Anchises, and the faithful porter of his threshold; thereafter his lord gave him for Ascanius' attendant. In all points like the old man Apollo came, voice and colour, white hair, and grimly clashing arms, and speaks these words to eager Iülus: 'Be it enough, son of Aeneas, that the Numanian has fallen unavenged beneath thine arrows; this first honour great Apollo allows thee, nor envies the arms that match his own. Further, O boy, let war alone.' Thus Apollo began, and yet speaking retreated from mortal view, vanishing into thin air away out of their eyes. The Dardanian princes knew the god and the arms of deity, and heard the clash of his quiver as he went. So they restrain Ascanius' keenness for battle by the words of Phoebus' will; themselves they again close in conflict, and cast their lives nto the perilous breach. Shouts run all along the battlemented walls; ringing bows are drawn and javelin thongs twisted: all the ground is strewn with missiles. Shields and hollow helmets ring to blows; the battle swells fierce; heavy as the shower lashes the ground that sets in when the Kids are rainy in the West; thick as hail pours down from storm-clouds on the shallows, when the rough lord of the winds congeals his watery deluge and breaks up the hollow vapours in the sky.

Pandarus and Bitias, sprung of Alcanor of Ida, whom woodland Iaera bore in the grove of Jupiter, grown now tall as their ancestral pines and hills, fling open the gates barred by their captain's order, and confident in arms, wilfully invite the enemy within the walls. Themselves within they stand to right and left in front of the towers, sheathed in iron, the plumes flickering over their stately heads: even as high in air around the gliding streams, whether on Padus' banks or by pleasant Athesis, twin oaks rise lifting their unshorn heads into the sky with high tops asway. The Rutulians pour in when they see the entrance open. Straightway Quercens and Aquicolus beautiful in arms, and desperate Tmarus, and Haemon, seed of Mars, either gave back in rout with all their columns, or in the very gateway laid down their life. Then the spirits of the combatants swell in rising wrath, and now the Trojans gather swarming to the spot, and dare to close hand to hand and to sally farther out.

News is brought to Turnus the captain, as he rages afar among the routed foe, that the enemy surges forth into fresh slaughter and flings wide his gates. He breaks off unfinished, and, fired with immense anger, rushes towards the haughty brethren at the Dardanian gate. And on Antiphates first, for first he came, the bastard son of mighty Sarpedon by a Theban mother, he hurls his javelin and strikes him down; the Italian cornel flies through the yielding air, and, piercing the gullet, runs deep into his breast; a frothing tide pours from the dark yawning wound, and the steel grows warm where it pierces the lung. Then Meropes and Erymas, then Aphidnus goes down before his hand; then Bitias, fiery-eyed and exultant, not with a javelin; for not to a javelin had he yielded his life; but the loud-whistling pike came hurled with a thunderbolt's force; neither twofold bull's hide kept it back, nor the trusty corslet with double scales of gold: his vast limbs sink in a heap; earth utters a groan, and the great shield clashes over him. Thus once and again on the Euboïc shore of Baiae falls a mass of stone, built up of great blocks and so cast into the sea; thus does it tumble prone, crashes into the shoal water and sinks deep to rest; the seas are stirred, and the dark sand eddies up; therewith the depth of Prochyta quivers at the sound, and the couchant rocks of Inarime, piled above Typhoeus by Jove's commands.

On this Mars armipotent raised the spirit and strength of the Latins, and goaded their hearts to rage, and sent Flight and dark Fear among the Teucrians. From all quarters they gather, since battle is freely offered; and the warrior god inspires.... Pandarus descries his brother's fall, sees how fortune stands, what hap rules the day; and swinging the gate round on its hinge with all his force, pushes it to with his broad shoulders, leaving many of his own people shut outside the walls in the desperate conflict, but shutting others in with him as they pour back in retreat. Madman! who saw not the Rutulian prince burst in amid the crowd, and fairly shut him into the town, like a monstrous tiger among the silly flocks. At once strange light flashed from his eyes, and his armour rang terribly; the blood-red plumes flicker on his head, and lightnings shoot sparkling from his shield. In sudden dismay the Aenaedae know the hated form and giant limbs. Then tall Pandarus leaps forward, in burning rage at his brother's death: 'This is not the palace of Amata's dower,' he cries, 'nor does Ardea enclose Turnus in her native walls. Thou seest a hostile camp; escape hence is hopeless.' To him Turnus, smiling and cool: 'Begin with all thy valiance, and close hand to hand; here too shalt thou tell that a Priam found his Achilles.' He ended; the other, putting out all his strength, hurls his rough spear, knotty and unpeeled. The breezes caught it; Juno, daughter of Saturn, made the wound glance off as it came, and the spear sticks fast in the gate. 'But this weapon that my strong hand whirls, this thou shalt not escape; for not such is he who sends weapon and wound.' So speaks he, and rises high on his uplifted sword; the steel severs the forehead midway right between the temples, and divides the beardless cheeks with ghastly wound. He crashes down; earth shakes under the vast weight; dying limbs and brain-spattered armour tumble in a heap to the ground, and the head, evenly severed, dangles this way and that from either shoulder. The Trojans scatter and turn in hasty terror; and had the conqueror forthwith taken thought to burst the bars and let in his comrades at the gate, that had been the last day of the war and of the nation. But rage and mad thirst of slaughter drive him like fire on the foe. . . . First he catches up Phalaris; then Gyges, and hamstrings him; he plucks away their spears, and hurls them on the backs of the flying crowd; Juno lends strength and courage. Halys he sends to join them, and Phegeus, pierced right through the shield; then, as they ignorantly raised their war-cry on the walls, Alcander and Halius, Noëmon and Prytanis. Lynceus advanced to meet him, calling up his comrades; from the rampart he sweeps his glittering sword to the left and catches him; struck off by the one downright blow, head and helmet lay far away. Next Amycus fell, the deadly huntsman, incomparable in skill of hand to anoint his arrows and arm their steel with venom; and Clytius the Aeolid, and Cretheus beloved of the Muses, Cretheus of the Muses' company, whose delight was ever in songs and harps and stringing of verses; ever he sang of steeds and armed men and battles.

At last, hearing of the slaughter of their men, the Teucrian captains, Mnestheus and gallant Serestus, come up, and see their comrades in disordered flight and the foe let in. And Mnestheus: 'Whither next, whither press you in flight? what other walls, what farther city have you yet? Shall one man, and he girt in on all sides, fellow-citizens, by your entrenchments, thus unchecked deal devastation throughout our city, and send all our best warriors to the under world? Have you no pity, no shame, cowards, for your unhappy country, for your ancient gods, for great Aeneas?'

Kindled by such words, they take heart and rally in dense array. Little by little Turnus drew away from the fight towards the river, and the side encircled by the stream: the more bravely the Teucrians press on him with loud shouts and thickening masses, even as a band that fall on a wrathful lion with levelled weapons, but he, daunted, retires surly and grim-glaring; and neither does wrath nor courage let him turn his back, nor can he make head, for all that he desires it, against the surrounding arms and men. Even thus Turnus draws lingeringly backward, with unhastened steps, and soul boiling in anger. Nay, twice even then did he charge amid the enemy, twice drove them in flying rout along the walls. But all the force of the camp gathers hastily up; nor does Juno, daughter of Saturn, dare to supply him strength to countervail; for Jupiter sent Iris down through the aëry sky, bearing stern orders to his sister that Turnus shall withdraw from the high Trojan town. Therefore neither with shield nor hand can he keep his ground, so overpoweringly from all sides comes upon him the storm of weapons. About the hollows of his temples the helmet rings with incessant clash, and the solid brass is riven beneath the stones; the horsehair crest is rent away; the shield-boss avails not under the blows; Mnestheus thunders on with his Trojans, and pours in a storm of spears. All over him the sweat trickles and pours in swart stream, and no breathing space is given; sick gasps shake his exhausted limbs. Then at last, with a headlong bound, he leapt fully armed into the river; the river's yellow eddies opened for him as he came, and the buoyant water brought him up, and, washing away the slaughter, returned him triumphant to his comrades.

BOOK TENTH

THE BATTLE ON THE BEACH

MEANWHILE the heavenly house omnipotent unfolds her doors, and the father of gods and king of men calls a council in the starry dwelling; whence he looks sheer down on the whole earth, the Dardanian camp, and the peoples of Latium. They sit down within from doorway to doorway: their lord begins:

'Potentates of heaven, wherefore is your decree turned back, and your minds thus jealously at strife? I forbade Italy to join battle with the Teucrians; why this quarrel in face of my injunction? What terror has bidden one or another run after arms and tempt the sword? The due time of battle will arrive, call it not forth, when furious Carthage shall one day sunder the Alps to hurl ruin full on the towers of Rome. Then hatred may grapple with hatred, then hostilities be opened; now let them be, and cheerfully join in the treaty we ordain.'

Thus Jupiter in brief; but not briefly golden Venus returns in answer: ...

'O Lord, O everlasting Governor of men and things—for what else may we yet supplicate?—beholdest thou how the Rutulians brave it, and Turnus, borne charioted through the ranks, proudly sweeps down the tide of battle? Bar and bulwark no longer shelter the Trojans; nay, within the gates and even on the mounded walls they clash in battle and make the trenches swim with blood. Aeneas is away and ignorant. Wilt thou never then let our leaguer be raised? Again a foe overhangs the walls of infant Troy; and another army, and a second son of Tydeus rises from Aetolian Arpi against the Trojans. Truly I think my wounds are yet to come, and I thy child am keeping some mortal weapons idle. If the Trojans have sought Italy without thy leave and defiant of thy deity, let them expiate their sin; aid not such with thy succour. But if so many oracles guided them, given by god and ghost, why may aught now reverse thine ordinance or write destiny anew? Why should I recall the fleets burned on the coast of Eryx? why the king of storms, and the raging winds roused from Aeolia, or Iris sped down the clouds? Now hell too is stirred (this share of the world was yet untried) and Allecto suddenly let loose above to riot through the Italian towns. In no wise am I moved for empire; that was our hope while Fortune stood; let those conquer whom thou wilt. If thy cruel wife leave no region free to Teucrians, by the smoking ruins of desolated Troy, O father, I beseech thee, grant Ascanius unhurt retreat from arms, grant that my son's child survive. Aeneas may well be tossed over unknown seas and follow wheresoever fortune open a path; him let me avail to shelter and withdraw from the turmoil of battle. Amathus is mine, high Paphos and Cythera, and my house of Idalia; there, far from arms, let him spend an inglorious life. Bid Carthage in high lordship rule Ausonia; thence will nothing arise to check the Tyrian cities. What help was it for the Trojans to escape war's doom and thread their flight through Argive fires, to have exhausted all those perils of sea and desolate lands, while they seek Latium and the towers of a Troy rebuilt? Were it not better to have clung to the last ashes of their country, and the ground where once was Troy? Give back, I pray, Xanthus and Simoïs to a wretched people, and let the Teucrians again, O Lord, circle through the fates of Ilium.'

Then Queen Juno, swift and passionate:

'Why forcest thou me to break long silence and proclaim my hidden pain? Has any man or god constrained Aeneas to court war or make armed attack on King Latinus? In oracular guidance he steered for Italy: be it so: he whom raving Cassandra sent on his way! Did we urge him to quit the camp or entrust his life to the winds? to give the issue of war and the charge of his ramparts to a child? to stir the loyalty of Tyrrhenia or throw peaceful nations into tumult? What god, what potent cruelty of ours, has driven him on his hurt?

Where is Juno in this, or Iris sped down the clouds? It shocks thee that Italians should engird an infant Troy with flame, and Turnus stand on his own ancestral soil—he, grandchild of Pilumnus, son of Venilia the goddess: how, that the dark brands of Troy assail the Latins? that Trojans subjugate and plunder fields not their own? how, that they choose their brides and tear plighted bosom from bosom? that their gestures plead for peace, and their ships are lined with arms? Thou canst steal thine Aeneas from Grecian hands, and spread before them a human semblance of mist and empty air; thou canst turn his fleet into nymphs of like number: is it dreadful if we answer with some aid to the Rutulians? *Aeneas is away and ignorant;* away and ignorant let him be. Paphos is thine and Idalium, thine high Cythera; why meddlest thou with fierce spirits and a city big with war? Is it we who would overthrow the tottering state of Phrygia? we? or he who brought the Achaeans down on the hapless Trojans? who made Europe and Asia bristle up in arms, and whose theft shattered the alliance? Was it in my guidance the adulterous Dardanian broke into Sparta? or did I send the shafts of passion that kindled war? Then terror for thy children had graced thee; too late now dost thou rise with unjust complaints, and reproaches leave thy lips in vain.'

Thus Juno pleaded; and all the heavenly people murmured in diverse consent; even as rising gusts murmur when caught in the forests, and eddy in blind moanings, betraying to sailors the gale's approach. Then the Lord omnipotent and primal Power of the world begins; as he speaks the high house of the gods and trembling floor of earth sink to silence; silent is the deep sky, and the breezes are stilled; ocean hushes his waters into calm.

'Take then to heart and lay deep these words of mine. Since it may not be that Ausonians and Teucrians join alliance, and your quarrel finds no term, to-day, what fortune each wins, what hope each follows, be he Trojan or Rutulian, I will hold in even poise; whether it be Italy's fate or Trojan infatuation and evil counsel that holds the camp in leaguer. Nor do I acquit the Rutulians. Each as he has begun shall work out his destiny. Jupiter is one and king over all; the fates will find their way.' By his brother's infernal streams, by the banks of the pitchy black-boiling chasm he signed assent, and made all Olympus quiver at his nod. Here speaking ended: thereon Jupiter rises from his golden throne, and the heavenly people surround and escort him to the doorway.

Meanwhile the Rutulians press round all the gates, dealing grim slaughter and girdling the walls with flame. But the army of the Aeneadae are held leaguered within their trenches, with no hope of retreat. They stand helpless and disconsolate on their high towers, and their thin ring girdles the walls,—Asius, son of Imbrasus, and Thymoetes, son of Hicetaon, and the two Assaraci, and Castor, and old Thymbris together in the front rank: by them Clarus and Thaemon, both full brothers to Sarpedon, out of high Lycia. Acmon of Lyrnesus, great as his father Clytius, or his brother Mnestheus, carries a stone, straining all his vast frame to the huge mountain fragment. Emulously they keep their guard, these with javelins, those with stones, and wield fire and fit arrows on the string. Amid them he, Venus' fittest care, lo! the Dardanian boy, his graceful head uncovered, shines even as a gem set in red gold on ornament of throat or head, or even as gleaming ivory cunningly inlaid in boxwood or Orician terebinth; his tresses lie spread over his milk-white neck, bound by a flexible circle of gold. Thee, too, Ismarus, proud nations saw aiming wounds and arming thy shafts with poison; thee, of house illustrious in Maeonia, where the rich tilth is wrought by men's hands, and Pactolus waters it with gold. There too was Mnestheus, exalted in fame as he who erewhile had driven Turnus from the ramparts; and Capys, from whom is drawn the name of the Campanian city.

They had closed in grim war's mutual conflict; Aeneas, while night was yet deep, clove the seas. For when, leaving Evander for the Etruscan camp, he has audience of the king, and tells the king of his name and race, and what he asks or offers, instructs him of the arms Mezentius is winning to his side, and of Turnus' overbearing spirit, reminds him what is all the certainty of human things, and mingles all with entreaties; delaying not, Tarchon joins forces and strikes alliance. Then, freed from the oracle, the Lydian people man their fleet, laid by divine ordinance in the foreign captain's hand. Aeneas' galley keeps in front, with the lions of Phrygia fastened on her prow, above them overhanging Ida, sight most welcome to the Trojan exiles. Here great Aeneas sits revolving the changing issues of war; and Pallas, clinging on his left side, asks now of the stars and their pathway through the dark night, now of his fortunes by land and sea.

Open now the gates of Helicon, goddesses, and stir the song of the band that come the while with Aeneas from the Tuscan borders, and sail in armed ships overseas.

First in the brazen-plated Tiger Massicus cuts the flood; beneath him are ranked a thousand men who have left Clusium town and the city of Cosae; their weapons are arrows, and light quivers on the shoulder, and their deadly bow. With him goes grim Abas, all his train in shining armour, and a gilded Apollo glittering astern. To him Populonia had given six hundred of her children, tried in war, but Ilva three hundred, the island rich in unexhausted mines of steel. Third Asilas, interpreter between men and gods, master of the entrails of beasts and the stars in heaven, of speech of birds and ominous lightning flashes, draws a thousand men after him in serried lines bristling with spears, bidden to his command from Pisae, the city of Alphaean foundation on Etruscan soil. Astyr follows, excellent in beauty, Astyr, confident in his horse and glancing arms. Three hundred more—all have one heart to follow—come from the households of Caere and the fields of Minio, and ancient Pyrgi, and fever-stricken Graviscae.

Let me not pass thee by, O Cinyrus, bravest in war of Ligurian captains, and thee, Cupavo, with thy scant company, from whose crest rise the swan plumes, fault, O Love, of thee and thine, and blazonment of his father's form. For they tell that Cycnus, in grief for his beloved Phaëthon, while he sings and soothes his woeful love with music amid the shady sisterhood of poplar boughs, drew over him the soft plumage of white old age, and left earth and passed crying through the sky. His son, followed on shipboard with a band of like age, sweeps the huge Centaur forward with his oars; he leans over the water, and threatens the waves with a vast rock he holds on high, and furrows the deep seas with his length of keel.

He too calls a train from his native coasts, Ocnus, son of prophetic Manto and the river of Tuscany, who gave thee, O Mantua, ramparts and his mother's name; Mantua, rich in ancestry, yet not all of one blood; threefold is her race, and under each race four cantons; herself she is the cantons' head, and her strength is of Tuscan blood. From her likewise has Mezentius five hundred in arms against him, whom Mincius, child of Benacus, draped in grey reeds, led to battle in his advancing pine. Aulestes moves on heavily, smiting the wave with the swinging forest of an hundred oars; the channels foam as they sweep the sea-floor. He sails in the vast Triton, who amazes the blue waterways with his shell, and swims on with shaggy front, in human show from the flank upward; his belly ends in a dragon; beneath the monster's breast the wave gurgles into foam. So many were the chosen princes who went in thirty ships to aid Troy, and severed the salt plains with brazen prow.

And now day had faded from the sky, and gracious Phoebe trod mid-heaven in her night-wandering chariot: Aeneas, for his charge allows not rest to his limbs, himself sits guiding the tiller and managing the sails. And lo, in middle course a band of his own fellow-voyagers meets him, the nymphs whom bountiful Cybebe had bidden be gods of the sea, and turn to nymphs from ships; they swam on in even order, and cleft the flood, as many as erewhile, brazen-plated prows, had anchored on the beach. From far they know their king, and wheel their bands about him, and Cymodocea, their readiest in speech, comes up behind, catching the stern with her right hand: her back rises out, and her left hand oars her passage through the silent water. Then she thus accosts her amazed lord: 'Wakest thou, seed of gods, Aeneas? wake, and loosen the sheets of thy sails. We are thy fleet, Idaean pines from the holy hill, now nymphs of the sea. When the treacherous Rutulian urged us headlong with sword and fire, reluctantly we broke thy bonds, and for thee we search over ocean. This new guise our Lady made for us in pity, and granted us to be goddesses and spend our life under the waves. But thy boy Ascanius is held within wall and trench among the weapons and fiery warriors of Latium. Already the Arcadian cavalry and the brave Etruscan together hold the appointed ground. Turnus' plan is determined, to bar their way with his squadrons, that they may not reach the camp. Up and arise, and ere the coming of the Dawn bid thy crews be called to arms; and take thou the shield which the Lord of Fire forged for victory and rimmed about with gold. To-morrow's daylight, if thou deem not my words vain, shall see Rutulians heaped high in slaughter.' She ended, and, as she went, pushed the tall ship on with her hand wisely and well; the ship shoots through the water fleeter than javelin or windswift arrow. Thereat the rest quicken their speed. The son of Anchises of Troy is himself deep in bewilderment; yet the omen cheers his courage. Then looking on the heavenly vault, he briefly prays: 'O gracious upon Ida, mother of gods, whose delight is in Dindymus and turreted cities and lions coupled to thy rein, do thou lead me in battle, do thou meetly prosper thine augury, and draw nigh thy Phrygians, goddess, with favourable feet.' Thus much he spoke; and meanwhile the broad light of returning day was now pouring in, and had chased away the night. First he commands his comrades to follow his signals, brace their courage to arms and prepare for battle. And now his Trojans and his camp are in sight as he stands high astern, when next he lifts the blazing shield on his left arm. The Dardanians on the walls raise a shout to the sky. Hope comes to kindle wrath; they hurl their missiles strongly; even as under black clouds cranes from the Strymon utter their signal notes and sail clamouring across the sky, and noisily stream down on the gale. But this seemed marvellous to the Rutulian king and the captains of Ausonia, till looking back they see the ships steering for the beach, and all the sea as a single fleet sailing in. His helmet-spike blazes, flame pours from the cresting plumes, and the golden shield-boss spouts floods of fire; even as when in transparent night comets glow blood-red and drear, or the splendour of Sirius, that brings drought and sicknesses on wretched men, rises and saddens the sky with malignant beams.

Yet gallant Turnus in unfailing confidence will prevent them on the shore and repel their approach to land. 'What your prayers have sought is given, to break them at the sword's point. The god of battles is in your hands, O men. Now remember each his wife and home: now recall the high deeds of our fathers' honour. Let us challenge meeting at the water's edge, while they waver and their feet yet slip as they disembark. Fortune aids daring.... So speaks he, and counsels inly whom he shall lead to meet them, whom leave in charge of the leaguered walls.

Meanwhile Aeneas lands his allies by gangways from the high ships. Many watch the retreat and slack of the sea, and leap boldly into the shoal water; others slide down the oars. Tarchon, marking the shore where he is secure of shoals and no broken surge plashes, but the sea glides up and spreads its tide unhindered, turns his prow sharply to land and implores his comrades: 'Now, O chosen crew, bend strongly to your oars; lift your ships, make them go; let the prows cleave this hostile land and the keel plough herself a furrow. I accept even shipwreck on such harbourage if once we take the land.' When Tarchon had spoken in such wise, his comrades rise on their oar-blades and carry their ships in foam towards the Latin fields, till the prows are fast on dry land and all the keels are aground unhurt. But not thy galley, Tarchon; for she strikes on the cruel ridge of a shoal, and swings long swaying and beating the flood, then breaks up, and lands her crew among the waves. Splintered oars and floating thwarts entangle them, and the ebbing wave sucks their feet away.

Nor does Turnus keep idly dallying, but swiftly hurries

his whole array against the Trojans and ranges it to face the beach. The trumpets blow. At once Aeneas charges and confounds the rustic squadrons of the Latins, and slays Theron for omen of battle. The giant advances to challenge Aeneas; but through sewed plates of brass and tunic rough with gold the sword plunges in his open side. Next he strikes Lichas, cut from his mother already dead, and consecrated, Phoebus, to thee; to what profit was his infancy granted escape from the perilous steel? Near thereby he struck dead brawny Cisseus and vast Gyas, whose clubs were mowing whole files down: naught availed them the arms of Hercules and their strength of hand, nor Melampus their father, ever of Alcides' company while earth yielded him sore travail. Lo! while Pharus flings deedless vaunts the hurled javelin strikes on his shouting mouth. Thou too, while thou followest thy new delight, Clytius, whose cheeks are golden with youthful down —thou, luckless Cydon, struck down by the Dardanian hand, wert lying past thought, ah pitiable! of the young loves that were ever thine, did not the close array of thy brethren interpose, the children of Phorcus, seven in number, and send a sevenfold shower of darts. Some glance ineffectual from helmet and shield; some Venus the bountiful turned aside as they grazed his body. Aeneas calls to trusty Achates: 'Give me store of weapons; none that has been planted in Grecian body on the plains of Ilium shall my hand hurl at Rutulian in vain.' Then he catches and throws his great spear; the spear flies grinding through the brass of Maeon's shield, and breaks through corslet and through breast. His brother Alcanor runs up and sustains with his right arm his sinking brother; through his arm the spear passes speeding straight on its message, and holds its bloody way, and the hand dangles by the sinews lifeless from the shoulder. Then Numitor, seizing his dead brother's javelin, aims at Aeneas, but might not fairly pierce him, and grazed tall Achates on the thigh. Here Clausus of Cures comes confident in his pride of strength, and with a long reach strikes Dryops under the chin, and, urging the stiff spear-shaft home, stops the accents of his speech and his life together, piercing the throat; but he strikes the earth with his forehead, and vomits clots of blood. Three Thracians likewise of Boreas' sovereign race, and three sent by their father Idas from their native Ismarus, fall in divers wise before him. Halaesus and his Auruncan troops hasten hither; Messapus too, seed of Neptune, comes up charioted. This side and that strive to hurl back the enemy, and fight hard on the very edge of Ausonia. As when in the depth of air adverse winds rise in battle with equal spirit and strength; not they, not clouds nor sea, yield one to another; long the battle is doubtful; all stands locked in counterpoise: even thus clash the ranks of Troy and ranks of Latium, foot caught on foot, and man crowded up on man.

But in another quarter, where a torrent had driven a wide path of rolling stones and bushes torn away from the banks, Pallas saw his Arcadians, unaccustomed to advance on foot, giving back before the Latin pressure, when the roughness of the ground bade them dismount. This only was left in his strait, to kindle them to valour, now by entreaties, now by taunts: 'Whither flee you, comrades? by your deeds of bravery, by your leader Evander's name, by your triumphant campaigns, and my hope that now rises to rival my father's honour, trust not to flight. Our swords must hew a way through the enemy. Where yonder mass of men presses thickest, there your proud country calls you with Pallas at your head. No gods are they who bear us down; mortals, we feel the pressure of a mortal foe; we have as many lives and hands as he. Lo, the deep shuts us in with vast sea barrier; even now land fails our flight; shall we make ocean or Troy our goal?'

So speaks he, and bursts amid the serried foe. First Lagus meets him, drawn thither by malign destiny; him, as he tugs at a ponderous stone, hurling his spear where the spine ran dissevering the ribs, he pierces and wrenches out the spear where it stuck fast in the bone. Nor does Hisbo catch him stooping, for all that he hoped it; for Pallas, as he rushes unguarded on, furious at his comrade's cruel death, receives him on his sword and buries it in his distended lungs. Next he attacks Sthenius, and Anchemolus of Rhoetus' ancient family, who dared to violate the bridal chamber of his stepmother. You, too, the twins Larides and Thymber, fell on the Rutulian fields, children of Daucus, indistinguishable for likeness and a sweet perplexity to your parents. But now Pallas made cruel difference between you; for thy head, Thymber, is swept off by Evander's sword; thy right hand, Larides, severed, seeks its master, and the dying fingers jerk and clutch at the steel. Mingled wrath and shame arm the Arcadians against the foe, kindled by his exhortation as they view his mighty deeds. Then Pallas pieces Rhoeteus as he flies past in his chariot. This space, this much of respite was given to Ilus; for at Ilus he had aimed the strong spear from afar, and Rhoeteus intercepts its passage, in flight from thee, noble Teuthras and Tyres thy brother; he rolls from the chariot in death, and his heels strike the Rutulian fields. And as the shepherd, when summer winds have risen to his desire, kindles the woods dispersedly; on a sudden the mid spaces catch, and a single flickering line of fire spreads wide over the plain; he sits looking down on his conquest and the revel of the flames; even so, Pallas, do thy brave comrades gather close to sustain thee. But warrior Halaesus advances full on them, gathering himself behind his armour; he slays Ladon, Pheres, Demodocus; his gleaming sword shears off Strymonius' hand as it rises to his throat; he strikes Thoas on the face with a stone, and drives the bones asunder in a shattered mass of blood and brains. Halaesus had his father, prophesying fate, kept hidden in the woodland: when the old man's glazing eyes sank to death, the Destinies laid hand on him and devoted him to the arms of Evander. Pallas aims at him, first praying thus: 'Grant now, lord Tiber, to the steel I poise and hurl, a prosperous way through brawny Halaesus' breast; thine oak shall bear these arms and the dress he wore.' The god heard it; while Halaesus covers Imaon, he leaves, alas! his breast unarmed to the Arcadian's weapon. Yet at his grievous death Lausus, himself a great arm of the war, lets not his columns be dismayed; at once he meets and cuts down Abas, the check and stay of their battle. The men of Arcadia go down before him; down go the Etruscans, and you, O Teucrians, invincible by Greece. The armies close, matched in strength and in captains; the rear ranks crowd in; weapons and hands are locked in the press. Here Pallas strains and pushes on, here Lausus opposite, nearly matched in age, excellent in beauty; but fortune had denied both return to their own land. Yet that they should meet face to face the sovereign of high Olympus allowed not; an early fate awaits them beneath a mightier foe.

Meanwhile Turnus' gracious sister bids him come to Lausus' aid, and his fleet chariot parts the ranks. When he saw his comrades, 'It is time,' he cried, 'to stay from battle. I alone must assail Pallas; to me and none other Pallas is due; I would his father himself were here to see.' So speaks he, and his Rutulians draw back from a level space at his bidding. But then as they withdrew, he, wondering at the haughty command, stands in amaze at Turnus, his eyes scanning the vast frame, and his fierce glance perusing him from afar. And with these words he returns the words of the monarch: 'For me, my praise shall even now be in the lordly spoils I win, or in illustrious death: my father will bear calmly either lot: away with menaces.' He speaks, and advances into the level ring. The Arcadians' blood gathers chill about their hearts. Turnus leaps from his chariot and prepares to close with him. And as a lion sees from some lofty outlook a bull stand far off on the plain revolving battle, and flies at him, even such to see is Turnus' coming. When Pallas deemed him within reach of a spear-throw, he advances, if so chance may assist the daring of his overmatched strength, and thus cries into the depth of sky: 'By my father's hospitality and the board whereto thou camest a wanderer, on thee I call, Alcides; be favourable to my high emprise; let Turnus even in death discern me stripping his blood-stained armour, and his swooning eyes endure the sight of his conqueror.' Alcides heard him, and deep in his heart he stifled a heavy sigh, and let idle tears fall. Then with kindly words the father accosts his son: 'Each has his own appointed day; short and irrecoverable is the span of life for all: but to spread renown by deeds is the task of valour. Under high Troy town many and many a god's son fell; nay, mine own child Sarpedon likewise perished. Turnus too his own fate summons, and his allotted period has reached the goal.' So speaks he, and turns his eyes away from the Rutulian fields. But Pallas hurls his spear with all his strength, and pulls his sword flashing out of the hollow scabbard. The flying spear lights where the armour rises high above the shoulder, and, forcing a way through the shield's rim, stayed not till it drew blood from mighty Turnus. At this Turnus long poises the spear-shaft with its sharp steel head, and hurls it on Pallas with these words: 'See thou if our weapon have not a keener point.' He ended; but for all the shield's plating of iron and brass, for all the bull-hide that covers it round about, the quivering spear-head smashes it fair through and through, passes the guard of the corslet, and pierces the breast with a gaping hole. He tears the warm weapon from the wound; in vain; together and at once lifeblood and sense follow it. He falls heavily on the ground, his armour clashes over him, and his bloodstained face sinks in death on the hostile soil. And Turnus standing over him . . . : 'Arcadians,' he cries, 'remember these my words, and bear them to Evander. I send him back his Pallas as was due. All the meed of the tomb, all the solace of sepulture, I give freely. Dearly must he pay his welcome to Aeneas.' And with these words, planting his left foot on the dead, he tore away the broad heavy sword-belt engraven with a tale of crime, the array of grooms foully slain together on their bridal night, and the nuptial chambers dabbled with blood, which Clonus, son of Eurytus, had wrought richly in gold. Now Turnus exults in spoiling him of it, and rejoices at his prize. Ah spirit of man, ignorant of fate and the allotted future, or to keep bounds when elate with prosperity!—the day will come when Turnus shall desire to have bought Pallas' safety at a great ransom, and curse the spoils of this fatal day

But with many moans and tears Pallas' comrades lay him on his shield and bear him away amid their ranks. O grief and glory and grace of the father to whom thou shalt return! This one day sent the first to war, this one day takes thee away, while yet thou leavest heaped high thy Rutulian dead.

And now no rumour of the dreadful loss, but a surer messenger flies to Aeneas, telling him his troops are on the thin edge of doom; it is time to succour the routed Teucrians. He mows down all that meets him, and hews a broad path through the columns with furious sword, as he seeks thee, O Turnus, in thy fresh pride of slaughter. Pallas, Evander, all flash before his eyes; the board whereto but then he had first come a wanderer, and the clasped hands. Here four of Sulmo's children, as many more of Ufens' nurture, are taken by him alive to slaughter in sacrifice to the shade below, and slake the flames of the pyre with captive blood. Next he levelled his spear full on Magus from far. He stoops cunningly; the spear flies quivering over him; and, clasping his knees, he speaks thus beseechingly: 'By thy father's ghost, by Iülus thy growing hope, I entreat thee, save this life for a child and a parent. My house is stately; deep in it lies buried wealth of engraven silver; I have masses of wrought and unwrought gold. The victory of Troy does not turn on this, nor will a single life make so great a difference.' He ended; to him Aeneas thus returns answer: 'All the wealth of silver and gold thou tellest of, spare thou for thy children. Turnus has broken off this thy trafficking in war, even then when Pallas fell. Thus judges the ghost of my father Anchises, thus Iülus.' So speaking, he grasps his helmet with his left hand, and, bending back his neck, drives his sword up to the hilt in the suppliant. Hard by is Haemonides, priest of Phoebus and Trivia, his temples wound with the holy ribboned chaplet, all glittering white in vesture and ornaments. Him he meets and chases down the plain, and, standing over his fallen foe, slaughters him and wraps him in great darkness; Serestus gathers the armour and carries it away on his shoulders, a trophy, King Gradivus, to thee. Caeculus, born of Vulcan's race, and Umbro, arriving from the Marsian hills, fill up the line. The Dardanian rushes full on them. His sword-blade had hewn off Anxur's left arm, with all the circle of the shield—he had uttered brave words and deemed his prowess would second his vaunts, and perchance with spirit lifted up had promised himself hoar age and length of years—when Tarquitus in the pride of his glittering arms met his fiery course, whom the nymph Dryope had borne to Faunus, haunter of the woodland. Drawing back his spear, he pins the ponderous shield to the corslet; then, as he vainly pleaded and would say many a thing, strikes his head to the ground, and, rolling away the warm body, cries thus over his enemy: 'Lie there now, terrible one! no mother's love shall lay thee in the sod, or place thy limbs beneath thine heavy ancestral tomb. To birds of prey shalt thou be left, or borne down sunk in the eddying water, where hungry fish shall suck thy wounds.' Next he pursues Antaeus and Lucas, the first of Turnus' train, and brave Numa and tawny-haired Camers, born of noble Volscens, who was wealthiest in land of the Ausonians, and reigned in silent Amyclae. Even as Aegaeon, who, men say, had an hundred arms, an hundred hands, fifty mouths and breasts ablaze with fire, and arrayed against Jove's thunders as many clashing shields and drawn swords: so Aeneas, when once his sword's point grew warm, rages victorious over all the field. Nay, lo! he darts full in face of Niphaeus' four-horse chariot; before his long strides and dreadful cry they turned in terror and dashed back, throwing out their driver and tearing the chariot down the beach. Meanwhile the brothers Lucagus and Liger drive up with their pair of white horses. Lucagus valiantly waves his drawn sword, while his brother wheels his horses with the rein. Aeneas, wrathful at their mad onslaught, rushes on them, towering high with levelled spear. To him Liger ... 'Not Diomede's horses dost thou discern, nor Achilles' chariot, nor the plains of Phrygia: now on this soil of ours the war and thy life shall end together.' Thus fly mad Liger's random words. But not in words does the Trojan hero frame his reply: for he hurls his javelin at the foemen. As Lucagus spurred on his horses, bending forward over the whip, with left foot advanced ready for battle, the spear passes through the lower rim of his shining shield and pierces his left groin, hurls him out of the chariot, and stretches him in death on the fields. To him good Aeneas speaks in bitter words: 'Lucagus, no slackness in thy coursers' flight has betrayed thee, or vain shadow of the foe turned them back; thyself thou leapest off the harnessed wheels.' In such wise he spoke, and caught the horses. His brother, slipping down from the chariot, pitiably outstretched helpless hands: 'Ah, by the parents who gave thee birth, great Trojan, spare this life and pity my prayer.' More he was pleading; but Aeneas: 'Not such were the words thou wert uttering. Die, and be brother undivided from brother.' With that his sword's point pierces the breast where the life lies hid. Thus the Dardanian captain dealt death over the plain, like some raging torrent stream or black whirlwind. At last the boy Ascanius and his troops burst through the ineffectual leaguer and issue from the camp.

Meanwhile Jupiter breaks silence to accost Juno: 'O sister and wife best beloved, it is Venus, as thou deemedst, nor is thy judgment astray, who sustains the forces of Troy; not their own valour of hand in war, and untameable spirit and endurance in peril.' To whom Juno beseechingly:

'Why, fair my lord, vexest thou one sick at heart and trembling at thy bitter words? If that force were in my love that once was, and that was well, never had thine omnipotence denied me leave to withdraw Turnus from battle and preserve him for his father Daunus in safety. Now let him perish, and pay forfeit to the Trojans of his innocent blood. Yet he traces his birth from our name, and Pilumnus was his father in the fourth generation, and oft and again his bountiful hand has heaped thy courts with gifts.'

To her the king of high heaven thus briefly spoke: 'If thy prayer for him is delay of present death and respite from his fall, and thou dost understand that I ordain it thus, remove thy Turnus in flight, and snatch him from the fate that is upon him. For so much indulgence there is room. But if any ampler grace mask itself in these thy prayers, and thou dreamest to move or change the whole issue of the war, idle is the hope thou nursest.'

And Juno, weeping: 'Ah yet, if thy mind were gracious where thy lips are stern, and this gift of life might remain confirmed to Turnus! Now his portion is bitter and guiltless death, or I wander idly from the truth. Yet, oh that I rather deluded myself with false alarms, and thou who canst wouldst bend thy course to better counsels.'

These words uttered, she darted through the air straight from high heaven, cloud-girt in driving tempest, and sought the Ilian ranks and camp of Laurentum. Then the goddess, strange and ominous to see, fashions into the likeness of Aeneas a thin and pithless shade of hollow mist, decks it with Dardanian weapons, and gives it the mimicry of shield and divine helmet plume, gives unsubstantial words and senseless utterance, and the mould and motion of his tread: like shapes rumoured to flit when death is past, or dreams that delude the slumbering senses. But in front of the battle-ranks the phantom dances rejoicingly, and with arms and mocking accents provokes the foe. Turnus hastens up and sends his spear whistling from far on it; it gives back and turns its footsteps. Then indeed Turnus, when he believed Aeneas turned and fled from him, and his spirit madly drank in the illusive hope: 'Whither fliest thou, Aeneas? forsake not thy plighted bridal chamber. This hand shall give thee the land thou has sought overseas.' So clamouring he pursues, and brandishes his drawn sword, and sees not that his rejoicing is drifting with the winds. The ship lay haply moored to a high ledge of rock, with ladders run out and gangway ready, wherein king Osinius sailed from the coasts of Clusium. Here the fluttering phantom of flying Aeneas darts and hides itself. Nor is Turnus slack to follow; he overleaps the barriers and springs across the high gangways. Scarcely had he lighted on the prow; the daughter of Saturn snaps the hawser, and the ship, parted from her cable, runs out on the ebbing tide. Then the light phantom seeks not yet any further hiding-place, but, flitting aloft, melts in a dark cloud. And him Aeneas seeks for battle and finds not, and sends many a man that meets him to death; and a blast comes down meanwhile and sweeps Turnus through the seas. He looks back, witless of his case and thankless for his salvation, and, wailing, stretches both hands to heaven: 'Father omnipotent, was I so guilty in thine eyes, and is this the punishment thou hast ordained? Whither am I borne? whence came I? what flight is this, or in what guise do I return? Shall I look again on the camp or walls of Laurentum? What of that array of men who followed me to arms? whom—oh horrible!—I have abandoned all amid a dreadful death; and now I see the stragglers and catch the groans of those who fall. What am I doing? or how may earth yawn for me deep enough now? Do you rather, O winds, be pitiful, carry my bark on rock or reef; it is I, Turnus, who desire and implore you; or drive me on the cruel shoals of the Syrtis, where no Rutulian may follow nor rumour know my name.' Thus speaking, he wavers in mind this way and that: maddened by the shame, shall he plunge on his sword's harsh point and drive it through his side, or fling himself among the waves, and seek by swimming to gain the winding shore, again to return on the Trojan arms? Thrice he essayed either way; thrice queenly Juno checked and restrained him in pity of heart. Cleaving the deep, he floats with the tide down the flood, and is borne on to his father Daunus' ancient city.

But meanwhile at Jove's prompting fiery Mezentius takes his place in the battle and assails the triumphant Teucrians. The Tyrrhene ranks gather round him, and all at once in unison shower their darts down on the hated foe. As a cliff that juts into the waste of waves, meeting the raging winds and breasting the deep, endures all the threatening force of sky and sea, itself fixed immoveable, so he dashes to earth Hebrus son of Dolichaon, and with him Latagus, and Palmus as he fled; catching Latagus full front in the face with a vast fragment of mountain rock, while Palmus he hamstrings, and leaves him rolling helpless; his armour he gives Lausus to wear on his shoulders, and the plumes to fix on his crest. With them fall Evanthes the Phrygian, and Mimas, fellow and birth-mate of Paris; for on one night Theano bore him to his father Amycus, and the queen, Cisseus' daughter, Paris the firebrand of her womb; Paris sleeps in his fathers' city; Mimas lies a stranger on the Laurentian coast. And as the boar driven by snapping hounds from the mountain heights, many a year hidden by Vesulus in his pines, many an one fed in the Laurentian marsh among the reedy forest, once come among the nets, halts and snorts savagely, with shoulders bristling up, and none of them dare be wrathful or draw closer, but they shower from a safe distance their darts and cries; even thus none of those whose anger Mezentius has earned have courage to meet him with drawn weapon: far off they provoke him with missiles and huge clamour, and he turns slow and fearless round about, grinding his teeth as he shakes the spears off his shield. From the bounds of ancient Corythus Acron the Greek had come, leaving for exile a bride half won. Seeing him afar dealing confusion amid the ranks, in crimson plumes and his plighted wife's purple,— as an unpastured lion often ranging the deep coverts, for madness of hunger urges him, if he haply catches sight of a timorous roe or high-antlered stag, he gapes hugely for joy, and, with mane on end, clings crouching over its flesh, his cruel mouth bathed in reeking gore ... so Mezentius darts lightly among the thick of the enemy. Hapless Acron goes down, and, spurning the dark ground, gasps out his life, and covers the broken javelin with his blood. But the victor deigned to bring down Orodes with the blind wound of his flying lance as he fled; full face to face he meets him, and engages man with man, conqueror not by stealth but armed valour. Then, as with planted foot, he thrust him off the spear: 'O men,' he cries, 'haughty Orodes lies low, no little part of the war.' His comrades give an answering cheer, and raise the chant of victory. But the dying man: 'Not unavenged nor long, whoso thou art, shalt thou be glad in victory: thee

too an equal fate marks down, and in these fields thou shalt
soon lie.' Smiling thereat half wrathfully, Mezentius: 'Now
die thou. But of me let the father of gods and king of men take
counsel.' So saying, he drew the weapon out of his body. Grim
rest and iron slumber seal his eyes; his lids close on everlasting
night. Caedicus slays Alcathoüs, Sacrator Hydaspes, Rapo
Parthenius and the grim strength of Orses, Messapus Clonius
and Erichaetes son of Lycaon, the one when his reinless
horse stumbling had flung him to the ground, the other on
foot. And on foot Agis the Lycian advanced only to be struck
down by Valerus, brave as his ancestry; and Thronius by
Salius, and Salius by Nealces, the good archer with unseen
shot from afar.

Now the heavy hand of war dealt equal woe and counter-
change of death; in even balance conquerors and conquered
slew and fell; nor one nor other knows of retreat. The gods
in Jove's house pity the vain rage of either and all the ago-
nising of mortals. From one side Venus, from one opposite
Juno, daughter of Saturn, looks on; pale Tisiphone rages
among the many thousand men. But now, brandishing his
huge spear, Mezentius strides glooming over the plain, vast
as Orion when, with planted foot, he cleaves his way through
the vast pools of mid-ocean and his shoulder overtops the
waves, or carrying an ancient mountain-ash from the hill-
tops, paces the ground and hides his head among the clouds:
so moves Mezentius, huge in arms. Aeneas, espying him in
the deep columns, makes on to meet him. He remains, unter-
rified, awaiting his noble foe, steady in his own bulk, and
measures with his eye the sufficient range for a spear. 'This
right hand's divinity, and the weapon I poise and hurl, now be
favourable! thee, Lausus, I vow for the live trophy of Aeneas,
dressed in the spoils stripped from the pirate's body.' He
spoke, and cast the spear whistling from far; it flies on, glancing from the shield, and pierces illustrious Antores hard by
him sidelong in the flank; Antores, companion of Hercules,
who, sent thither from Argos, had stayed by Evander, and
settled in an Italian town. Hapless he goes down with a wound

not his own, and looks on heaven, remembering sweet Argos as he dies. Then good Aeneas throws his spear; through the sheltering circle of threefold brass, through the canvas lining and fabric of triple-sewn bull-hide it went, and sank deep in his groin; yet carried not its strength home. Quickly Aeneas, joyful at the sight of the Tyrrhenian's blood, snatches his sword from his thigh and presses hotly on his struggling enemy. Lausus saw, and groaned deeply for love of his dear father, and tears rolled over his face. Here will I not keep silence of thy hard death-doom and thine excellent deeds (if in any wise things wrought in the old time may win belief), nor of thyself, O fitly remembered! He, helpless and trammelled, withdrew backward, the deadly spear-shaft trailing from his shield. The youth dashed forward and plunged into the fight; and even as Aeneas' hand rose to bring down the blow, he caught up his point and held him in delay. His comrades follow up with loud cries, so the father may withdraw in shelter of his son's shield, while they shower their darts and bear back the enemy with missiles from a distance. Aeneas wrathfully keeps covered. And as when storm-clouds pour down in streaming hail, all the ploughmen and country-folk scatter off the fields, and the wayfarer cowers safe in his fortress, a stream's bank or deep arch of rock, while the rain falls, that they may do their day's labour when sunlight reappears; thus under the circling storm of weapons Aeneas sustains the cloud of war till it thunders itself all away, and calls on Lausus with chiding, on Lausus with menace: 'Whither runnest thou on thy death, with daring beyond thy strength? thine affection betrays thee into rashness.' But none the less he leaps madly on; and now wrath rises higher and fiercer in the Dardanian captain, and the Fates pass Lausus' last threads through their hand; for Aeneas drives the sword strongly right through him up all its length: the point pierced the light shield that armed his assailant, and the tunic sewn by his mother with flexible gold: blood filled his breast, and the life left the body and passed mourning through the air to the under world. But when Anchises' son saw the look on the dying face, the face pale in wonderful wise, he sighed deeply in pity, and reached forth his hand, as the sight of filial affection rose into his soul. 'What now shall good Aeneas give thee, what, O poor boy, for this thy praise, for guerdon of a nature so noble? Keep for thine own the armour thou didst delight in; and I restore thee, if that matters aught at all, to the ghosts and ashes of thy parents. Yet thou shalt have this sad comfort in thy piteous death, thou fallest by great Aeneas' hand.' Then, chiding his hesitating comrades, he lifts him from the ground, dabbling the comely-ranged tresses with blood.

Meanwhile his father, by the wave of the Tiber river, stanched his wound with water, and rested his body against a tree-trunk. Hard by his brazen helmet hangs from the boughs, and the heavy armour lies quietly on the meadow. Chosen men stand round; he, sick and panting, leans his neck and lets his beard spread down over his chest. Many a time he asks for Lausus, and sends many an one to call him back and carry a grieving parent's commands. But Lausus his weeping comrades were bearing lifeless on his armour, mighty and mightily wounded to death. Afar the soul prophetic of ill knew their lamentation: he soils his grey hairs plenteously with dust, and stretches both hands on high, and clings on the dead. 'Was life's hold on me so sweet, O my son, that I let him I bore receive the hostile stroke in my room? Am I, thy father, saved by these wounds of thine, and living by thy death? Alas and woe! now at last death is bitter! now the wound is driven deep! And I, even I, O my son, stained thy name with crime, driven in hatred from the throne and sceptre of my fathers. I owed vengeance to my country and my people's resentment; might mine own guilty life but have paid it by every form of death! Now I live, and leave not yet man and day; but I will.' As he speaks thus he raises himself painfully on his thigh, and though the violence of the deep wound cripples him, yet unbroken he bids his horse be brought, his beauty, his comfort, that ever had carried him victorious out of war, and says these words to the grieving beast: 'Rhoebus, we have lived long, if aught at all lasts long with mortals. This day either shalt thou bring back in triumph the gory spoils and head of Aeneas, and we will avenge Lausus' agonies; or if no force opens a way, thou wilt die with me: for I deem not, bravest, thou wilt deign to bear an alien rule and a Teucrian lord.' He spoke, and took his welcome seat on the back he knew, loading both hands with keen javelins, his head sheathed in glittering brass and shaggy horse-hair plumes. Thus he galloped in. Through his heart sweep together the vast tides of shame and mingling madness and grief. And with that he thrice loudly calls Aeneas. Aeneas knew the call, and makes glad invocation: 'So the father of gods speed me, so Apollo on high: do thou essay to close hand to hand. . . .' Thus much he utters, and moves up to meet him with levelled spear. And he: 'Why seek to frighten me, fierce man, now my son is gone? this was thy one road to my ruin. We shrink not from death, nor relent before any of thy gods. Cease; for I come to my death, first carrying these gifts for thee.' He spoke, and hurled a weapon at his enemy; then plants another and yet another as he darts round in a wide circle; but they are stayed on the boss of gold. Thrice he rode wheeling close round him by the left, and sent his weapons strongly in; thrice the Trojan hero turns round, taking the grim forest on his brazen guard. Then, weary of lingering in delay on delay, and plucking out spear-head after spear-head, and hard pressed in the uneven match of battle, with much counselling of spirit now at last he bursts forth, and sends his spear at the war-horse between the hollows of the temples. The creature raises itself erect, beating the air with its feet, throws its rider, and coming down after him in an entangled mass, slips its shoulder as it tumbles forward. The cries of Trojans and Latins kindle the sky. Aeneas rushes up, drawing his sword from the scabbard, and thus above him: 'Where now is fierce Mezentius and all that wild courage of his?' Thereto the Tyrrhenian, as he came to himself and gazing up drank the air of heaven: 'Bitter foe, why these taunts and menaces of death? Naught forbids my slaughter; neither on such terms came I to battle, nor did my Lausus make treaty for this between me and thee. This one thing I beseech thee, by whatsoever grace a vanquished enemy may claim: allow my body sepulture. I know I am girt by the bitter hatred of my people. Stay, I implore, their fury, and grant me and my son union in the tomb.' So speaks he, and takes the sword in his throat unfalteringly, and the lifeblood spreads in a wave over his armour.

BOOK ELEVENTH

THE COUNCIL OF THE LATINS, AND THE LIFE
AND DEATH OF CAMILLA

MEANWHILE Dawn arising left the Ocean: Aeneas, though the charge presses to give a space for burial of his comrades, and his mind is harassed with death, was paying the gods his vows of victory with the breaking of the East. He plants on a mound a mighty oak with boughs lopped away on every hand, and arrays it in the gleaming arms stripped from Mezentius the captain, a trophy to thee, mighty Lord of War; he fixes on it the plumes dripping with blood, the broken spears, and the corslet struck and pierced in twelve places; he ties the shield of brass on his left hand, and hangs from his neck the ivory sword. Then among his triumphant comrades (for all the throng of his captains girt him close about) he begins in these words of cheer:

'The greatest deed is done, O men; be all fear gone for what remains. These are the spoils of a haughty king, the firstfruits won from him; my hands have set Mezentius here. Now our way lies to the walls of the Latin king. Prepare your arms; let your courage and hope anticipate the war; let no ignorant delay hinder, no tardy thoughts of fear keep us back, so soon as heaven give us the sign to pluck up the standards and lead our army from the camp. Meanwhile let us commit to earth the unburied bodies of our comrades, since deep in Acheron this honour is left alone. Go,' says he, 'grace with the last gifts those noble souls whose blood won us this land for ours; and first let Pallas be sent to Evander's mourning city, he whose valour failed not when the day of darkness took him, and the bitter wave of death.'

So speaks he weeping, and retraces his steps to the door, where aged Acoetes watched Pallas's lifeless body laid out for burial; once armour-bearer to Evander in Parrhasia, but now gone forth with darker omens, appointed attendant to his darling foster-child. Around is the whole train of servants, with a crowd of Trojans, and the Ilian women with hair unbound in mourning after their fashion. When Aeneas entered at the high doorway they beat their breasts and raise a loud wail aloft, and the palace moans to their grievous lamentation. Himself, when he saw the pillowed head and fair face of Pallas, and on his smooth breast the gaping wound of the Ausonian spear-head, speaks thus with welling tears:

'Did Fortune in her joyous coming,' he cries, 'O luckless boy, grudge thee to see our realm, and ride victorious to thy father's dwelling? Not this promise of thee had I given to Evander thy sire at my departure, when he embraced me as I went and bade me speed to a wide empire, and yet warned me in fear that the men were valiant, the people obstinate in battle. And now he, fast ensnared by empty hope, perchance offers vows and heaps gifts on his altars; we, a mourning train, go in hollow honour by his corpse, who now owes no more to aught in heaven. Unhappy! thou wilt see thy son cruelly slain; is this the triumphal return we awaited? is this my strong assurance? Yet thou shalt not see him, Evander, with the shameful wounds of flight, nor shall death's terrors be welcome to the father because the son lives. Ah me, what a shield is lost, Iülus, to Ausonia and to thee!'

This lament done, he bids raise the piteous body, and sends a thousand men chosen from all his army for the last honour of escort, to mingle in the father's tears; a small comfort in a great sorrow, yet the unhappy parent's due. Others quickly plait a soft wicker bier of arbutus rods and oak shoots, and shadow the heaped pillows with a leafy covering. Here they lay him, high on their rustic strewing; even as some tender violet or drooping hyacinth-blossom plucked by a maiden's finger, whose sheen and whose grace is not yet departed, but no more does Earth the mother feed it or lend it strength. Then Aeneas bore forth two purple garments stiff with gold, that Sidonian Dido's own hands, happy over their work, had once wrought for him, and shot the warp with thread of gold. One of these he sadly folds round him, a last honour, and veils in its covering the tresses destined to the fire; and heaps up besides many a Laurentine battle-prize, and bids his spoils be led forth in long train; with them the horses and arms whereof he had stripped the enemy, and those, with hands tied behind their back, whom he would send as nether offering to his ghost, and sprinkle the blood of their slaying on the flame, and bids his captains carry stems dressed in the armour of the foe, with the hostile names fixed on them. Unhappy Acoetes is led along, outworn with age; he smites his breast and rends his face, and flings himself forward all along the ground. Likewise they lead forth the chariot bathed in Rutulian blood; behind goes weeping Aethon the war-horse, his trappings removed, and big drops wet his face. Others bear his spear and helmet, for all else is Turnus' prize. Then follow in mourning array the Teucrians and all the Tyrrhenians, and the Arcadians with arms reversed. When the whole long escorting file had advanced, Aeneas stopped, and sighing deep, pursued thus: 'Once again war's dreadful destiny calls us hence to other tears: hail thou for evermore, O princely Pallas, and for evermore farewell.' And without more words he bent his way to the high walls and advanced towards his camp.

And now envoys were there from the Latin city with wreathed boughs of olive, praying him of his grace to restore the dead that lay strewn by the sword over the plain, and let them go to their earthy grave: no war lasts with men conquered and bereft of breath; let this indulgence be given to men once called friends and fathers of their brides. To them Aeneas grants leave in kind and courteous wise, spurning not their prayer, and goes on in these words: 'What spite of fortune, O Latins, has entangled you in the toils of war, and made you fly our friendship? Plead you for peace to the lifeless bodies that the battle-lot has slain? I would fain grant it even to the living. Neither have I come but because destiny had given me this place to dwell in; nor wage I war with your people; your king it is who has broken our covenant and preferred to trust himself to Turnus' arms. Fitter it were that Turnus had faced death to-day. If he will fight out the war and expel the Teucrians, it had been well to meet me here in arms; so had he lived to whom life were granted of heaven or his own right hand. Now go, and kindle the fire beneath your hapless countrymen.' Aeneas ended: they stood dumb in silence, with faces bent steadfastly in mutual gaze. Then aged Drances, ever young Turnus' assailant in hatred and accusation, with the words of his mouth thus answers him again:

'O Trojan, great in renown, yet greater in arms, with what praises may I extol thy divine goodness? Shall thy righteousness first wake my wonder, or thy toils in war? We indeed will gratefully carry these words to our fathers' city, and, if fortune grant a way, will make thee at one with King Latinus. Let Turnus seek his own alliances. Nay, it will be our delight to rear the massy walls of destiny and stoop our shoulders under the stones of Troy.'

He ended thus, and all with one voice murmured assent. Twelve days' truce is struck, and in mediation of the peace Teucrians and Latins stray mingling unharmed on the forest-clad ridges. The tall ash echoes the strokes of the steel axe; they overturn pines that soar into the sky, and cease not to cleave hearts of oak and scented cedar with wedges, nor to hale mountain-ashes on creaking wains.

And now flying Rumour, harbinger of the heavy woe, fills Evander and Evander's house and city with the same voice that but now told of Pallas victorious over Latium. The Arcadians stream to the gates, snatching funeral torches after their ancient use; the road gleams with the long line of flame, and parts the fields with a broad pathway of light; the arriving crowd of Phrygians meets them and mingles in mourning array. When the matrons saw all the train approach their dwellings they kindle the town with loud wailing. But no force may withhold Evander; he comes amid them; the bier is set down; he flings himself on Pallas, and clasps him with tears and sighs, and scarcely at last does grief let loose his utterance. 'Not this, O Pallas! was the promise that thou hadst given thy father. Hadst thou been content to plunge less recklessly into the fury of battle! I knew well how strong was the fresh pride of arms and the sweetness of honour in a first battle. Ah, unhappy first-fruits of his youth and bitter prelude of the war upon our borders! ah, vows and prayers of mine that no god heard! and thou, holiest of wives, happy that thou art dead and not spared for this sorrow! But I have outgone my destiny in living, to stay here the survivor of my child. Would I had followed the allied arms of Troy, to be overwhelmed by Rutulian weapons! Would my life had been given, and I and not my Pallas were borne home in this procession! I would not blame you, O Teucrians, nor our treaty and the friendly hands we clasped: our old age had that appointed debt to pay. Yet if untimely death awaited my son, we will be glad that he perished leading the Teucrians into Latium, and slew his Volscian thousands before he fell. Nay, no other funeral would I deem thy due, my Pallas, than good Aeneas does, than the mighty Phrygians, than the Tyrrhene captains and all the army of Tyrrhenia. Great are the trophies they bring on whom thine hand deals death; thou also, Turnus, wert standing now a great trunk dressed in arms, had his age and his strength of years equalled thine. But why does my misery keep back the Trojans from arms? Go, and forget not to carry this message to your king: Thine hand keeps me lingering in a life that is hateful since Pallas fell, and Turnus is the debt thou seest son and father claim: for thy virtue and thy fortune this scope alone is left. I ask not joy in life; I may not; but to carry this to my son deep in the under world.'

Meanwhile Dawn had raised her gracious light on weary men, bringing back task and toil: now lord Aeneas, now Tarchon, have built the pyres on the winding shore. Hither in ancestral fashion has each born the bodies of his kin; the dark fire is lit beneath, and the vapour hides high heaven in gloom. Thrice, girt in glittering arms, they have marched about the blazing piles, thrice compassed on horseback the sad fire of death, and uttered their wail. Tears fall fast upon earth and armour; cries of men and blare of trumpets roll skyward. Then some fling on the fire Latin spoils stripped from the slain, helmets and shapely swords, bridles and glowing chariot wheels; others familiar gifts, the very shields and luckless weapons of the dead. Around are slain in sacrifice oxen many in number, and bristly swine and cattle gathered out of all the country are slaughtered over the flames. Then, crowding the shore, they gaze on their burning comrades, and guard the embers of the pyres, and cannot tear themselves away till dewy Night wheels on the star-spangled glittering sky.

Therewithal the unhappy Latins far apart build countless pyres, and many slain men they bury in the ground, and many more they lift and bear away to the neighbouring lands, or send them back to the city; the rest, a vast heap of undistinguishable slaughter, they burn uncounted and unhonoured; on all sides the broad fields gleam with crowded rivalry of fires. The third Dawn had rolled away the chill shadow from the sky; mournfully they piled high the ashes and mingled bones from the embers, and heaped a load of warm earth above them. Now in the dwellings of rich Latinus' city the noise is loudest, and most the long lamentation. Here mothers and their sons' unhappy brides, here beloved sisters sadhearted and orphaned boys curse the disastrous war and Turnus' bridal, and bid him his own self arm and decide the issue with the sword, since he claims for himself the first rank and the lordship of Italy. Fierce Drances embitters their cry, and vouches that Turnus alone is called, alone is claimed for battle. Yet therewith many a diverse-worded counsel is for Turnus, and the great name of the queen overshadows him and he rises high in renown of trophies fitly won.

Among their stir, and while confusion is fiercest, lo! to crown all, the envoys from great Diomede's city bring their gloomy message: nothing is come of all the toil and labour spent; gifts and gold and strong entreaties have been of no avail; Latium must seek other arms, or sue for peace to the Trojan king. For heavy grief King Latinus himself swoons away. The wrath of heaven and the fresh graves before his eyes warn him that Aeneas is borne on by fate's evident will. So he sends imperial summons to his high council, the foremost of his people, and gathers them within his lofty courts. They assemble, and stream up the crowded streets to the royal dwelling. Latinus, eldest in years and first in royalty, sits amid them with cheerless brow, and bids the envoys sent back from the Aetolian city tell the news they bring, and demands a full and ordered reply. Then tongues are hushed; and Venulus, obeying his word, thus begins to speak:

'We have seen, O citizens, Diomede in his Argive camp, and outsped our way and passed all its dangers, and touched the hand whereunder the land of Ilium fell. He was founding a town, named Argyripa after his ancestral people, on the conquered fields of Iapygian Garganus. After we entered in, and license of open speech was given, we display our gifts, we instruct him of our name and country, who are its invaders, and why we are drawn to Arpi. He heard us, and replied thus with calm utterance:

' "O fortunate races, realm of Saturn, Ausonians of old, how does fortune vex your quiet and woo you to tempt wars you know not? We that have drawn sword on the fields of Ilium—I forbear to tell the drains of war beneath her high walls, the men sunken in yonder Simoïs—have all over the world paid to the full our punishment and the reward of guilt such a crew as Priam's self might pity; as Minerva's baleful star knows, and the Euboïc reefs and Caphereus the avenger. From that warfaring driven to alien shores, Menelaus son of Atreus is in exile far as Proteus' Pillars, Ulysses has seen the Cyclopes of Aetna. Shall I make mention of the realm of Neoptolemus, and Idomeneus' household gods overthrown? or of the Locrians who dwell on the Libyan beach? Even the lord of Mycenae, the mighty Achaeans' general, sank on his own threshold edge under his accursed wife's hand; an adulterer took his seat on the spoils of Asia. Aye, or that the gods grudged it me to return to my ancestral altars, to see the bride of my desire, and lovely Calydon! Now likewise sights of appalling presage pursue me; my comrades, lost to me, have soared on wings into the sky, and flitting birds about the rivers—ah me, dread punishment of my people!—fill the cliffs with their melancholy cries. This it was I had to look for even from the time when I madly assailed celestial limbs with steel, and sullied the hand of Venus with a wound. Do not, ah, do not urge me to such battles. Neither have I any war with Troy since her towers are overthrown, nor do I remember with delight the woes of old. Turn to Aeneas with the gifts you bear to me from your ancestral borders. We have stood to face his grim weapons, and met him hand to hand; believe one who has proved it, how mightily he rises over his shield, in what a whirlwind he hurls his spear. Had the land of Ida borne two more like him, Dardanus had marched to attack the towns of Inachus, and Greece were mourning fate's reverse. In all our delay before that obstinate Trojan city, it was Hector and Aeneas whose hand stayed the Grecian victory and held back its advance till the tenth year. Both were splendid in courage, both eminent in arms; Aeneas was first in duty. Let your hands join in treaty as they may; but beware that your weapons close not with his."

'Thou hast heard, most gracious king, at once what is the king's answer, and what his counsel for our great struggle.'

Scarcely thus the envoys, when a diverse murmur ran through the troubled lips of the Ausonians; even as, when rocks delay some running river, it plashes in the barred pool, and the banks murmur nigh to the babbling wave. So soon as their minds were quieted, and their hurrying lips hushed, the king, first calling on the gods, begins from his lofty throne:

'Ere now could I wish, O Latins, we had determined our course of state, and it had been better thus; not to meet in council at such a time as now, with the enemy seated before our walls. We wage an ill-timed war, fellow-citizens, with a divine race, invincible, unbroken in battle, who brook not even when conquered to drop the sword. If you had hope in appeal to Aetolian arms, abandon it; though each man's hope is his own, you discern how narrow a path it is. Beyond that you see with your eyes and handle with your hands the total ruin of our fortunes. I blame no one; what valour's utmost could do is done; we have fought with our whole kingdom's strength. Now I will unfold what I doubtfully advise and purpose, and instruct you of it—give heed!—in brief. There is an ancient land of mine bordering the Tuscan river, stretching far westward beyond the Sicanian borders. Auruncans and Rutulians sow on it, work the stiff hills with the ploughshare, and pasture them where they are roughest. Let all this tract, with a pine-clad belt of mountain height, pass to the Teucrians in friendship; let us name fair terms of treaty, and invite them as allies to our realm; let them settle, if they desire it so, and found a city. But if they have a mind to try other coasts and another people, and can abide to leave our soil, let us build twice ten ships of Italian oak, or as many more as they can man; timber lies at the water's edge for all; let them assign the number and fashion of the vessels, and we will supply brass, labour, dockyards. Further, it is our advice that an hundred ambassadors of the highest rank in Latium shall go to bear our words and ratify the treaty, holding forth in their hands the boughs of peace, and carrying for gifts weight of gold and ivory, and the chair and striped robe, our royal array. Give counsel openly, and succour our exhausted state.'

Then Drances again, he whose jealous ill-will was wrought to anger and stung with bitterness by Turnus' fame, lavish of wealth and quick of tongue though his hand was cold in war, held no empty counsellor and potent in faction—his mother's rank ennobled a lineage whose paternal source was obscure—rises, and with these words heaps and heightens their passion:

'Dark to no man and needing no voice of ours, O gracious king, is that whereon thou takest counsel. All confess they know how our nation's fortune sways; but they speak in whispers. Let him grant freedom of speech and abate his breath, he by whose disastrous government and perverse way (I will speak out, though he menace me with arms and death) we see so many stars of battle gone down and all our city sunk in mourning; while he, confident in flight, assails the Trojan camp and makes heaven quail before his arms. Add yet one to those gifts of thine, to all the riches thou bidst us send or promise to the Dardanians, most gracious of kings, but one; let no man's passion overbear thee from giving thine own daughter to an illustrious son-in-law and a worthy marriage, and confirming this peace by perpetual treaty. Yet if we are thus terror-stricken heart and soul, let us implore him in person, in person plead him of his grace to give way, to restore king and country their proper right. Why again and again hurlest thou these unhappy citizens on peril so evident, O source and spring of Latium's woes? In war is no safety; peace we all implore of thee, Turnus, and the one pledge that makes peace inviolable. I the first, I whom thou picturest thine enemy, as I care not if I am, see, I bow at thy feet. Pity thine allies; relent, and retire before thy conqueror. Enough have we seen of rout and death, and desolation over our broad lands. Or if glory stir thee, if such strength kindle in thy breast, and if a palace so delight thee for thy dower, be bold, and advance stout-hearted upon the foe. We verily, that Turnus may have his royal bride, must lie scattered on the plains, worthless lives, a crowd unburied and unwept. Do thou also, if thou hast aught of might, if the War-god be in thee as in thy fathers, look him in the face who challenges....'

At these words Turnus' passion blazed out. He utters a groan, and breaks forth into speech thus:

'Copious indeed, Drances, and fluent is ever thy speech at the moment when war calls for action; and when the fathers are summoned thou art there the first. But we need no words to fill our senate-house, safely as thou wingest them while the mounded walls keep off the enemy, and the trenches swim not yet with blood. Thunder on in rhetoric, thy wonted way: accuse thou me of fear, Drances, thou whose hand has heaped so many Teucrians in slaughter, and whose glorious trophies dot the fields. Trial is open of what live valour can do; nor indeed is our foe far to seek; on all sides they surround our walls. Are we going to meet them? Why linger? Will thy bravery ever be in that windy tongue and those timorous feet of thine? ... *My conqueror?* Caitiff, shall any justly flout me as conquered, who sees Tiber swoln fuller with Ilian blood, and all the house and people of Evander laid low, and the Arcadians stripped of their armour? Not such did Bitias and huge Pandarus prove me, and the thousand men whom on one day my conquering hand sent down to hell, shut as I was in their walls and closed in the enemy's ramparts. *In war is no safety.* Fool! be thy boding on the Dardanian's head and thine own fortunes. Go on; cease not to throw all into confusion with thy terrors, to exalt the strength of a twice vanquished race, and abase the arms of Latinus before it. Now the princes of the Myrmidons tremble before Phrygian arms, and Aufidus river recoils from the Adriatic wave. Or when the villain schemer pretends to shrink at my abuse, and sharpens calumny by terror! never shall this hand—keep quiet!—rob thee of such a soul; with thee let it abide, and dwell in that breast of thine. Now I return to thee, my lord, and thy weighty resolves. If thou dost repose no further hope in our arms, if all has indeed left us, and one repulse been our utter ruin, and our fortune is beyond recovery, let us plead for peace and stretch forth unarmed hands. Yet ah! had we aught of our wonted manhood, his toil beyond all other is blessed and his spirit eminent, who rather than see it thus, has fallen prone in death and once bitten the ground. But if we have yet resources and an army still unbroken, and cities and peoples of Italy remain for our aid; but if even the Trojans have won their glory at great cost of blood (they too have their deaths, and the storm fell equally on all), why do we shamefully faint even on the threshold? Why does a shudder seize our limbs before the trumpet sound? Often do the Days and the varying change of toiling Time restore prosperity; often Fortune in broken visits makes man her sport and again establishes him. The Aetolian will not help us from Arpi; but Messapus will, and Tolumnius the fortunate, and the captains sent by many a nation; nor will fame be scant to follow the flower of Latium and the Laurentine land. Camilla the Volscian princess too is with us, leading her train of cavalry, squadrons splendid in brass. But if I only am claimed by the Teucrians for combat, if that is your pleasure, and I am the barrier to the public good, Victory does not so hate and shun my hands that I should renounce any enterprise for so great a hope. I will meet him in courage, did he outmatch great Achilles and wear arms like his forged by Vulcan's hands. To you and to my father Latinus I Turnus, unexcelled in bravery by any of old, consecrate my life. *Aeneas calls on him alone:* let him call, I implore: let not Drances rather appease with his life this wrath of heaven, if such it be, or win the renown of valour.'

Thus they one with another strove together in uncertainty; Aeneas moved from his camp to battle. Lo, a messenger rushes spreading confusion through the royal house, and fills the town with great alarms: the Teucrians, ranged in battle-line with the Tyrrhene forces, are marching down by the Tiber river and filling the plain. Immediately spirits are stirred and hearts shaken and wrath roused in fierce excitement among the crowd. Hurrying hands grasp at arms; for arms their young men clamour; the fathers shed tears and mutter gloomily. With that a great noise rises aloft in diverse contention, even as when flocks of birds haply settle on a lofty grove, or swans utter their hoarse cry among the vocal pools on the river-fisheries of Padusa. 'Yes, citizens!' cries Turnus, seizing his time: 'gather in council and sit praising peace, while they rush on dominion in arms!' Without more words he sprang up and issued swiftly from the high halls. 'Thou, Volsus,' he cries, 'bid the Volscian battalions arm, and lead out the Rutulians. Messapus, and Coras with thy brother, spread your armed cavalry widely over the plain. Let a division entrench the city gates and man the towers: the rest of our array attack with me where I command.' The whole town goes rushing to the walls; lord Latinus himself, dismayed by the woeful emergency, quits the council and puts off his high designs, and chides himself sorely for not having given Aeneas unasked welcome, and made him son and bulwark of the city. Some entrench the gates, or bring up supply of stones and poles. The hoarse clarion gives bloody signal for war. A motley ring of boys and matrons girdle the walls; the supreme task summons all. Therewithal the queen with a crowd of mothers ascends bearing gifts to Pallas' towered temple, and by her side goes maiden Lavinia, source of all that woe, her beautiful eyes cast down. The mothers enter in, and while the temple steams with their incense, pour from the high doorway their mournful cry: 'Maiden armipotent, Tritonian, sovereign of war, break with thine hand the spear of the Phrygian robber, hurl him prone to earth and dash him down beneath our lofty gates.' Turnus arrays himself in hot haste for battle, and even now has done on his sparkling breastplate with its rough scales of brass, and clasped his golden greaves, his brows yet bare and his sword buckled to his side; he runs down from the fortress height glittering in gold, and exultantly anticipates the foe. Thus when a horse snaps his tether, and, free at last, rushes from the stalls and gains the open plain, he either darts towards the pastures of the herded mares, or bathing, as is his wont, in the familiar river waters, dashes out and neighs with neck stretched high, glorying, and his mane tosses over collar and shoulder. Camilla with her Volscian array meets him face to face in the gateway; the princess leaps from her horse, and all her squadron at her example slip from horseback to the ground. Then she speaks thus:

'Turnus, if bravery has any just self-confidence, I dare and promise to engage Aeneas' cavalry, and advance to meet the Tyrrhene horse. Permit my hand to try war's first perils: do thou on foot keep by the walls and guard the city.'

To this Turnus, with eyes fixed on the terrible maiden:

'O maiden flower of Italy, how may I essay to express, how to prove my gratitude? But now, since that spirit of thine excels all praise, share thou the toil with me. Aeneas, as rumour assures and the scouts sent out report, has sent on his light-armed horse to annoy us and scour the plains; himself he marches on the city across the lonely ridge of the mountain steep. I am arranging a stratagem of war in his pathway on the wooded slope, to block a gorge on the highroad with armed troops. Do thou receive and join battle with the Tyrrhene cavalry; with thee shall be gallant Messapus, the Latin squadrons, and Tiburtus' division: do thou likewise assume a captain's charge.'

So speaks he, and with like words heartens Messapus and the allied captains to battle, and advances towards the enemy. There is a sweeping curve of glen, made for ambushes and devices of arms. Dark thick foliage hems it in on either hand, and into it a bare footpath leads by a narrow gorge and difficult entrance. Right above it on the watch-towers of the hill-top lies an unexpected level, hidden away in shelter, whether one would charge from right and left or stand on the ridge and roll down heavy stones. Hither he passes by a line of way he knew, and, seizing his ground, occupies the treacherous woods.

Meanwhile in the heavenly dwellings Latona's daughter addressed fleet Opis, one of her maiden fellowship and sacred band, and sadly uttered these accents: 'Camilla moves to fierce war, O maiden, and vainly girds on our arms, dear as she is beyond others to me. For her love of Diana is not newly born, nor her spirit stirred by sudden affection. Driven from his kingdom through jealousy of his haughty power, Metabus left ancient Privernum town, and bore his infant with him in his flight through war and battle, the companion of his exile, and called her by her mother Casmilla's name, with a little change, Camilla. Carrying her before him on his breast, he sought a long ridge of lonely woodland; on all sides angry weapons pressed on him, and Volscian soldiery spread hurrying round about. Lo, in mid flight swoln Amasenus ran foaming with banks abrim, so heavily had the clouds burst in rain. He would swim it; but love of the infant holds him back in alarm for so dear a burden. Inly revolving all, he settled reluctantly on a sudden resolve: the great spear that the warrior haply carried in his stout hand, of hard-knotted and seasoned oak, to it he ties his daughter swathed in cork-tree bark of the woodland, and binds her balanced round the mid spear; then poising it in his great right hand he thus cries aloft: "Gracious one, haunter of the woodland, maiden daughter of Latona, a father devotes this babe to thy service; thine is this weapon she holds, thine infant suppliant, flying through the air from her enemies. Accept her, I implore, O goddess, for thine own, whom now I entrust to the chance of air." He spoke, and drawing back his arm, darts the spinning spear-shaft: the waters roar: over the racing river poor Camilla shoots on the whistling weapon. But Metabus, while a strong band now presses nigher, plunges into the river, and triumphantly pulls spear and girl, his gift to Trivia, from the grassy turf. No cities ever received him within house or rampart, nor had his savagery submitted to it; he led his life on the lonely pastoral hills. Here he nursed his daughter in the underwood among tangled coverts, on the milk of a wild brood-mare's teats, squeezing the udder into her tender lips. And so soon as the baby stood and went straight on her feet, he armed her hands with a sharp javelin, and hung quiver and bow from her little shoulders. Instead of gold to clasp her tresses, instead of the long skirted gown, a tiger's spoils hang down her back. Even then her tender hand hurled childish darts, and whirled about her head the twisted thong of her sling, and struck down the crane from Strymon or the milk-white swan. Many a mother among Tyrrhenian towns destined her for their sons in vain; content with Diana alone, she keeps unsoiled for ever the love of her darts and maidenhood. Would she had not plunged thus into warfare and provoked the Trojans by attack! so were she now dear to me and one of my company. But since bitter doom is upon her, up, glide from heaven, O Nymph, and seek the Latin borders, where under evil omen they join in baleful battle. Take these, and draw from the quiver an avenging shaft; by it shall he pay me forfeit of his blood, whoso, Trojan or Italian alike, shall sully her sacred body with a wound. Thereafter will I in a sheltering cloud bear body and armour of the hapless girl unspoiled to the tomb, and lay them in her native land.' She spoke; but the other sped lightly down the aëry sky, girt about with dark whirlwind on her echoing way.

But meanwhile the Trojan force nears the walls, with the Etruscan captains and their whole cavalry arrayed in ordered squadrons. Their horses' trampling hoofs thunder on all the field, as, swerving this way and that, they chafe at the reins' pressure; the iron field bristles wide with spears, and the plains blaze with uplifted arms. Likewise Messapus and the Latin horse, and Coras and his brother, and maiden Camilla's squadron, come forth against them on the plain, and draw back their hands and level the quivering points of their long lances, in a fire of neighing horses and advancing men. And now each had drawn within javelin-cast of each, and drew up; with a sudden shout they dart forth, and urge on their furious horses; from all sides at once weapons shower thick like snow, and veil the sky with their shadow. In a moment Tyrrhenus and fiery Aconteus charge violently with levelled spears, and are the first to fall; they go down with a heavy crash, and their chargers break and shatter chest upon chest. Aconteus, hurled off like a thunderbolt or some mass slung from an engine, is dashed away, and scatters his life in air. Immediately the lines waver, and the Latins wheeling about throw their shields behind them and turn their horses towards the town. The Trojans pursue; Asilas heads and leads on their squadrons. And now they drew nigh the gates, and again the Latins raise a shout and wheel their supple necks about; the pursuers fly, and gallop right back with loosened rein. As when the sea, running up in ebb and flow, now rushes shoreward and strikes over the cliffs in a wave of foam, drenching the edge of the sand in its curving sweep; now runs swirling back, and as the surge sucks the rolling stones away, leaves the shore bare in ebbing shallow; so twice the Tuscans turn and drive the Rutulians towards the town; twice they are repelled, and look back behind them from cover of their shields. But when now meeting in a third encounter, the lines are locked together all their length, and man singles out his man; then indeed, amid groans of the dying, deep in blood roll armour and bodies, and horses half slain mixed up with human carnage; the battle swells fierce. Orsilochus hurled his spear at the horse of Remulus, whom himself he shrank to meet, and left the steel in it under the ear; at the stroke the charger rears madly, and, mastered by the wound, lifts his chest and flings up his legs: the rider is thrown and rolls over on the ground. Catillus strikes down Iollas, and Herminius mighty in courage, mighty in limbs and arms, bareheaded, tawny-haired, bare-shouldered; undismayed by wounds, he leaves his vast body open against arms. Through his broad shoulders the quivering spear runs piercing him through, and doubles him up with pain. Everywhere the dark blood flows; they deal death with the sword in battle, and seek a noble death by wounds.

But amid the slaughter Camilla rages, a quivered Amazon, with one side stripped for battle, and now sends tough javelins showering from her hand, now snatches the strong battle-axe in her unwearying grasp; the golden bow, the armour of Diana, clashes on her shoulders; and even when forced backward in retreat, she turns in flight and aims darts from her bow. But around her are her chosen comrades, maiden Larina, Tulla, Tarpeia brandishing an axe plated with bronze, girls of Italy, whom Camilla the bright chose for her own escort, good at service in peace and war: even as Thracian Amazons when the streams of Thermodon clash beneath them as they go to war in painted arms, whether around Hippolyte, or while martial Penthesilea returns in her chariot, and the crescent-shielded columns of women dance with loud confused cry. Whom first, whom last, fierce maiden, does thy dart strike down? or how many dost thou stretch dying bodies on the earth? First Euneus, son of Clytius; for as he meets her the long fir shaft crashes through his open breast. He falls spouting streams of blood, and bites the gory ground, and dying writhes himself upon his wound. Then Liris and Pagasus above him; who fall headlong and together, the one thrown as he gathers up the reins of his ensanguined steed, the other while he runs forward and stretches his unarmed hand to stay his fall. To these she joins Amastrus, son of Hippotas, and follows from far with her spear Tereus and Harpalycus and Demophoön and Chromis: and as many darts as the maiden sends whirling from her hand, so many Phrygians fall. Ornytus the hunter rides near in strange arms on his Iapygian horse, his broad warrior's shoulders swathed in the hide stripped from a bullock, his head covered by a wolf's widegrinning mouth and white-tusked jaws; a rustic pike arms his hand; himself he moves amid the squadrons a full head over all. Catching him up (for that was easy amid the rout), she runs him through, and thus cries above her enemy: 'Thou wert hunting wild beasts in the forest, thoughtest thou, Tyrrhenian? the day is come for a woman's arms to refute thy words. Yet no light fame shalt thou carry to thy fathers' ghosts, to have fallen under the weapon of Camilla.' Next Orsilochus and Butes, the two mightiest of mould among the Teucrians; Butes she pierces in the back with her spear-point between corslet and helmet, where the neck shews as he sits, and the shield hangs from his left shoulder; Orsilochus she flies, and darting in a wide circle, slips into the inner ring and pursues her pursuer; then rising her full height, she drives the strong axe deep through armour and bone, as he pleads and makes much entreaty; warm brain from the wound splashes his face. One met her thus and hung startled by the sudden sight, the warrior son of Aunus haunter of the Apennine, not the meanest in Liguria while fate allowed him to deceive. And he, when he discerns that no fleetness of foot may now save him from battle or turn the princess from pursuit, essays to wind a subtle device of treachery, and thus begins: 'How hast thou glory, if a woman trust in her horse's strength? Debar retreat; trust thyself to level ground at close quarters with me, and prepare to fight on foot. Soon wilt thou know how windy boasting brings one to harm.' He spoke; but she, furious and stung with fiery indignation, hands her horse to an attendant, and takes her stand in equal arms on foot and undismayed, with naked sword and shield unemblazoned. But he, thinking his craft had won the day, himself flies off on the instant, and turning his rein, darts off in flight, pricking his beast to speed with iron-armed heel. 'False Ligurian, in vain elated in thy pride! for naught hast thou attempted thy slippery native arts, nor will thy craft bring thee home unhurt to treacherous Aunus.' So speaks the maiden, and with running feet swift as fire crosses his horse, and catching the bridle, meets him in front and takes her vengeance in her enemy's blood: as lightly as the falcon, bird of bale, swoops down from aloft on a pigeon high in a cloud, and pounces on and holds her, and disembowels her with taloned feet, while blood and torn feathers flutter down the sky.

But the creator of men and gods sits high on Olympus' summit watching this, not with eyes unseeing: he kindles Tyrrhenian Tarchon to the fierce battle, and sharply goads him on to wrath. So Tarchon gallops amid the slaughter where his squadrons retreat, and urges his troops in changing tones, calling man after man by name, and rallies the fliers to fight. 'What terror, what dastardy has fallen on your spirits, O never to be stung to shame, O ever sluggish Tyrrhenians? a woman drives you in disorder and routs our armies! Why wear we steel? for what are these idle weapons in our hands? Yet you slack not in Venus' service and wars by night, or when the curving flute proclaims Bacchus' revels. Look forward to the feast and the cups on the loaded board (this your passion, this your desire) while the soothsayer pronounce the offering favourable, and the fatted victim invite you to the deep groves!' So speaking, he spurs his horse into the midmost, ready himself to die, and bears violently down full on Venulus; and tearing him from horseback, grasps his enemy and carries him away with him on the saddle-bow by main force. A cry rises up, and all the Latins turn their eyes. Tarchon flies like fire over the plain, carrying the armed man, and breaks off the steel head from his own spear and searches the uncovered places, trying where he may deal the mortal blow; the other struggling against him keeps his hand off his throat, and strongly parries his attack. And, as when a golden eagle snatches and soars with a serpent in his clutch, and his feet are fast in it, and his talons cling; but the wounded snake writhes in coiling spires, and its scales rise and roughen, and its mouth hisses as it towers upward; the bird none the less attacks his struggling prize with crooked beak, while his vans beat the air: even so Tarchon carries him out of Tiburtine ranks, triumphant in his prize. Following their captain's example and success the men of Maeonia charge in. Then Arruns, due to his doom, circles in advance of fleet Camilla with artful javelin, and tries what chance may be easiest. Where the maiden darts furious amid the ranks, there Arruns slips up and silently tracks her footsteps; where she returns victorious and retires from amid the enemy, there he stealthily bends his rapid reins. Here he approaches, and here again he approaches, and strays all round and about, and untiringly shakes his certain spear. Haply Chloreus, consecrated and a priest once on Cybelus, glittered afar, splendid in Phrygian armour; a skin feathered with brazen scales and clasped with gold clothed the horse that foamed under his spur; himself he shone in foreign blue and scarlet, and sped fleet Gortynian shafts from a Lycian horn; a golden bow was on his shoulder, and the soothsayer's helmet was of gold; red gold knotted up his yellow scarf with its rustling lawny folds; his tunics and barbarian leggings were wrought in needlework. Him, whether that she might nail armour of Troy on her temples, or herself ride hunting in captive gold, the maiden pursued in blind chase alone of all the battle conflict, and down the whole line, reckless and fired by a woman's passion for spoils and plunder: when at last out of his ambush Arruns chooses his time and darts his javelin, praying thus aloud to heaven: 'Apollo, most high of gods, holy Soracte's warder, to whom we beyond all pay worship, for whom the blaze is fed from the pine-heap, where we thy worshippers in pious faith print our steps amid the deep embers of the fire, grant, O Lord omnipotent, that our arms wipe off this disgrace. I seek not the dress the maiden wore, nor trophy or any spoil of victory; other deeds shall bring me praise; let but this dread scourge fall stricken beneath my wound, I will return inglorious to my native towns.' Phoebus heard, and inly granted half his vow to prosper, half he shred into the flying breezes. To surprise and strike down Camilla in sudden death, this he yielded to his prayer; that his high home might see his return he gave not, and a gust swept his accents off on the gale. So, when the spear sped from his hand hurtled through the air, all the Volscians marked it well and turned their eyes on the queen; and she alone knew not wind or sound of the weapon on its aëry path, till the spear passed home and sank under her bared breast, and, its flight stayed, drank deep of her maiden blood. Her companions run hastily up and catch their sinking mistress. Arruns takes to flight more alarmed than all, in mingled fear and exultation, and no longer dares to trust his spear or face the maiden's weapons. And as the wolf, some shepherd or great bullock slain, plunges at once among the trackless mountain heights ere hostile darts are in pursuit, and knows how reckless he has been, and drooping his tail lays it quivering under his belly, and seeks the woods; even so does Arruns withdraw from sight in dismay, and, satisfied to escape, mingles in the throng of arms. The dying woman pulls at the weapon with her hand; but the iron head is fixed deep in the wound up between the rib-bones. She swoons away with loss of blood; her death-cold eyes sink; the once lustrous colour leaves her face. Then gasping, she thus accosts Acca, one of her birthmates, who alone before all was true to Camilla, with whom her cares were divided; and even so she speaks: 'Thus far, Acca my sister, have I availed; now the bitter wound overmasters me, and all about me darkens in mist. Haste away, and carry to Turnus my last message; to take my place in battle, and repel the Trojans from the town. And now goodbye.' Even with the words she dropped the reins and slid to ground unconscious. Then in the gradual chill she released herself wholly from the body, her neck slackened and her death-stricken head sank; the weapons leave her hands, and the life with a moan flies indignant into the dark. Then indeed an infinite cry rises and smites the golden stars; the battle grows bloodier now Camilla is down; at once in serried ranks all the Teucrian forces pour in, with the Tyrrhene captains and Evander's Arcadian squadrons.

But Opis, Trivia's sentinel, long ere now sits high on the hill-tops, gazing on the battle undismayed. And when afar amid the din of angry men she espied Camilla done woefully to death, she sighed and uttered a heart-deep cry: 'Ah too, too cruel, O maiden, the forfeit thou hast paid for adventuring attack on the Teucrians! and nothing has availed thee thy lonely following of Diana in the woodlands, nor wearing our quiver on thy shoulder. Yet thy Queen has not left thee unhonoured now thy latter end is come; nor will this thy death be unnamed among the nations, nor shalt thou bear the fame of one unavenged; for whosoever has sullied thy body with a wound shall pay death for due.' Under the mountain height was a great earthen mound, tomb of Dercennus, a Laurentine king of old, muffled in shadowy ilex. Hither the goddess most beautiful first swoops down, and marks Arruns from the mounded height. As she saw him glittering in arms and idly exultant: 'Why,' she cries, 'wanderest thou away? hitherward direct thy steps; came hither to thy doom, to receive thy fit reward for Camilla. Shalt thou also die by Diana's weapons?' The Thracian spoke, and slid out a fleet arrow from her gilded quiver, and stretched it level on the bow, and drew it far, till the curving tips met one another, and now as her hands pulled asunder, the left touched the steel edge, the string in the right her breast. At once and in a moment Arruns heard the whistle of the dart and the resounding air, as the steel sank in his body. His comrades leave him forgotten on the unknown dust of the plain, moaning his last and gasping his life away; Opis wings her flight to the skyey heaven.

At once the light squadron of Camilla retreat now they have lost their mistress; the Rutulians retreat in confusion, brave Atinas retreats. Scattered captains and thinned companies make for safety, and wheeling back, gallop to the town. Nor does any avail to make stand against the swarming death-dealing Teucrians, or bear their shock in arms; but their unstrung bows droop on their shoulders, and the four-footed galloping horse-hoof shakes the crumbling plain. Eddying dust rolls up thick and black towards the walls, and on the watchtowers mothers beat their breasts and the cries of women rise up to heaven. On such as first in the rout broke in at the open gates the mingling hostile throng follows hard; nor do they escape death, alas! but in the very gateway, in their native city and within their sheltering homes, they are pierced through and gasp out their life. Some shut the gates, and dare not open to their pleading comrades nor receive them in the town; and a most pitiful slaughter begins between the armed men who guard the entry and the others who rush upon their arms. Barred out before their weeping parents' eyes and faces, some, swept on by the rout, roll headlong into the trenches; some, blindly rushing with loosened rein, batter at the gates and stiffly-bolted doorway. The very mothers from the walls in eager heat (true love of country points the way, when they see Camilla) dart weapons with trembling hand, and eagerly make hard stocks of wood and fire-hardened poles serve for steel, and burn to die among the foremost for their city.

Meanwhile among the forests the terrible news pours in on Turnus, and Acca brings him news of the mighty rout; the Volscian lines are destroyed; Camilla is fallen; the enemy thicken and press on, and have swept all before them down the tide of battle; already the terror draws nigh the city. Mad with vexation—Jove's stern will ordains it so—he abandons the hills that he had beset, and quits the rough woodland. Scarcely had he marched out of sight and gained the plain when lord Aeneas enters the open defiles, surmounts the ridge, and issues from the dim forest. So both advance swiftly to the town with all their columns, no long march apart, and at once Aeneas descried afar the plains all smoking with dust, and saw the Laurentine columns, and Turnus knew Aeneas terrible in arms, and heard the advancing feet and the neighing of the horses. And straightway would they join battle and essay the conflict, but that ruddy Phoebus even now dips his weary coursers in the Iberian flood, and night draws on over the fading day. They encamp before the city, and draw their trenches round the walls.

BOOK TWELFTH

THE SLAYING OF TURNUS

When Turnus sees the Latins broken and fainting in the disastrous warfare, his promise claimed for fulfilment, and men's eyes pointed on him, his own spirit rises in unappeasable flame. As the lion in Punic fields, his breast heavily wounded by the huntsmen, at last starts into arms, and shakes out the shaggy masses from his exultant neck, and undismayed snaps the brigand's planted weapon, roaring with blood-stained mouth; even so Turnus kindles and swells in passion. Then he thus addresses the king, and so furiously begins:

'Turnus stops not the way; there is no excuse for the coward Aeneadae to take back their words or renounce their compact. I join battle; bring the holy things, my lord, and swear the treaty. Either this hand shall hurl to hell the Dardanian who skulks from Asia, and the Latins sit and see my single sword wipe out the nation's reproach; or let him rule his conquest, and Lavinia pass to his espousal.'

To him Latinus calmly replied: 'O high in youth and courage, the more thy hot valour abounds, the more intently must I counsel, and weigh fearfully what may befall. Thou hast thy father Daunus' realm, hast many towns taken by thine hand, nor is Latinus lacking in gold and goodwill. There are other maidens unwedded in Latium and Laurentine fields, and of no mean birth. Let me unfold this hard saying in all sincerity: and do thou drink it into thy soul. I might not ally my daughter to any of her old wooers; such was the universal oracle of gods and men. Overborne by love for thee, overborne by kinship of blood and my mourning wife's tears, I broke all fetters, I severed the maiden from her promised husband, I took up unrighteous arms. Since then, Turnus, thou seest what calamities, what wars pursue me, what woes thyself before all dost suffer. Twice vanquished in pitched battle, we scarce guard within our city the hopes of Italy: the streams of Tiber yet run warm with our blood, and our bones whiten the boundless plain. Why fall I away again and again? what madness bends my purpose? If I am ready to take them into alliance after Turnus' destruction, why do I not rather bar the strife while he lives? What will thy Rutulian kinsmen, will all Italy say, if thy death—Fortune make void the word!—comes by my betrayal, while thou suest for our daughter in marriage? Cast a glance on war's changing fortune; pity thine aged father, who now far away sits sad in his native Ardea.'

In no wise do the words bend Turnus' passion: he rages the more fiercely, and sickens of the cure. So soon as he found speech he thus made utterance:

'The care thou hast for me, most gracious lord, for me lay down, I implore thee, and let me purchase honour with death. Our hand too rains weapons, our steel is strong; and our wounds too draw blood. Far from him will be his goddess mother's presence to cover his flight, womanlike, in a cloud and an empty phantom's hiding.'

But the queen, dismayed by the new terms of battle, wept, and clung in a death-clasp to her fiery son-in-law: 'Turnus, by these tears, by Amata's regard, if that touches thee at all— thou art now the one hope, the repose of mine unhappy age; in thine hand is Latinus' honour and empire, on thee is the weight of all our sinking house—one thing I beseech thee; forbear to join battle with the Teucrians. What fate soever awaits thee in the strife thou seekest, it awaits me, Turnus, too: with thee will I leave the hateful light, nor shall my captive eyes see Aeneas my daughter's lord.' Lavinia tearfully heard her mother's words with cheeks all aflame, as deep blushes set her on fire and ran hotly over her face. Even as Indian ivory, if one stain it with sanguine dye, or where white lilies are red with many a rose amid: such colour came on the maiden's face. Love throws him into tumult, and stays his countenance on the maid: he burns fiercer for arms, and briefly answers Amata:

'Do not, I pray thee, do not weep for me, neither pursue me thus ominously as I go to the stern shock of war. Turnus is not free to put off death. Thou, Idmon, bear my message to the Phrygian monarch in this harsh wording: So soon as to-morrow's Dawn rises in the sky blushing on her crimson wheels, let him not loose Teucrian on Rutulian: let Teucrian arms and Rutulians have rest, and our blood decide the war; on that field let Lavinia be sought in marriage.'

These words uttered, withdrawing swiftly homeward, he orders out his horses, and rejoicingly beholds them snorting before his face: those that Orithyia's self gave Pilumnus for guerdon, to excel the snows in whiteness and the gales in speed. The busy charioteers stand round and pat their chests with clapping hollowed hands, and comb their tressed manes. Himself next he girds on his shoulders the corslet stiff with gold and pale fine bronze, and buckles on the sword and shield and scarlet-plumed helmet-spikes: that sword the divine Lord of Fire had himself forged for his father Daunus and dipped glowing in the Stygian wave. Next, where it stood amid his dwelling leaning on a massy pillar, he strongly seizes his stout spear, the spoil of Actor the Auruncan, and brandishes it quivering, and cries aloud: 'Now, O spear that never hast failed at my call, now the time is come; thee princely Actor once, thee Turnus now wields in his grasp. Grant this strong hand to strike down the effeminate Phrygian, to rend and shatter the corslet, and defile in dust the locks curled with hot iron and wet with myrrh.' Thus madly he runs on: sparkles leap out from all his blazing face, and his keen eyes flash fire: even as when a bull raises horrid bellowings ere the fight begin, and drives against a tree's trunk to make trial of his angry horns, and buffets the air with blows or scatters the sand in prelude of battle.

And therewithal Aeneas, terrible in his mother's armour, kindles for warfare and awakes into wrath, rejoicing that offer of treaty stays the war. Comforting his comrades and sorrowing Iülus' fear, he instructs them of destiny, and bids bear answer of assurance to King Latinus, and name the terms of peace.

Scarcely did the morrow shed on the mountain-tops the beams of risen day, as the horses of the sun begin to rise from the deep flood and breathe light from their lifted nostrils; Rutulian and Teucrian men measured out and made ready lists for battle under the great city's ramparts, and amid them hearth-fires and grassy altars to the gods of both peoples; while others bore spring water and fire, draped in priestly dress and their brows bound with grass of the field. The Ausonian army issue forth, and crowd through the gates in streaming serried columns. On this side all the Trojan and Tyrrhenian host pour in diverse armament, girt with iron even as though the harsh battle-strife called them forth. Therewith amid their thousands the captains flit up and down, splendid in gold and purple, Mnestheus, seed of Assaracus, and brave Asilas, and Messapus, tamer of horses, brood of Neptune: then each on signal given retiring to his own ground, they plant their spears in the earth and lean their shields against them. Mothers in eager abandonment, and the unarmed crowd and feeble elders, beset towers and house-roofs, or stand at the lofty gates.

But Juno, on the summit that is now called the Alban—then the mountain had neither name nor fame or honour—looked forth from the hill and surveyed the plain and double lines of Laurentine and Trojan, and Latinus' town. Straightway spoke she thus to Turnus' sister, goddess to goddess, lady of pools and noisy rivers: such worship did Jupiter the high king of air consecrate to her for her stolen virginity:

'Nymph, grace of rivers, best beloved of our soul, thou knowest how out of all the Latin women that ever rose to high-hearted Jove's thankless bed, thee only have I preferred and gladly given part and place in heaven. Learn thy woe, that thou blame not me for it, Juturna. Where fortune seemed to allow and the Destinies granted Latinus' estate to prosper, I shielded Turnus and thy city. Now I see him joining battle with unequal fates, and the day of doom and deadly force draws nigh. Mine eyes cannot look on this battle and treaty: thou, if thou darest aught of more present help for the brother of thy blood, go on; it befits thee. Haply relief shall follow misery.'

Scarcely thus: when Juturna's eyes overbrimmed with tears, and thrice and again she smote her hand on her gracious breast. 'This is not time for tears,' cries Juno, daughter of Saturn: 'hasten and snatch thy brother, if it may be, from his death or do thou waken war, and make the treaty abortive. I encourage thee to dare.' With such urgence she left her, doubting and dismayed, and grievously wounded in soul.

Meanwhile the kings go forth; Latinus in mighty pomp rides in his four-horse chariot; twelve gilded rays go glittering round his brows, symbol of the Sun his ancestor; Turnus moves behind a white pair, clenching in his hand two broadheaded spears. On this side lord Aeneas, fount of the Roman race, ablaze in starlike shield and celestial arms, and close by Ascanius, second hope of mighty Rome, issue from the camp; and the priest, in spotless raiment, has brought the young of a bristly boar and an unshorn sheep of two years old, and set his beasts by the blazing altars. They, turning their eyes towards the sunrising, scatter salted corn from their hands and clip the beasts with steel over the temples, and pour cups on the altars. Then Aeneas the good, with sword drawn, thus makes invocation:

'Be the Sun now witness, and this Earth to my call, for whose sake I have borne to suffer so sore travail, and the Lord omnipotent, and thou his wife, at last, divine daughter of Saturn, at last I pray more favourable; and thou, mighty Mavors, who wieldest all warfare in lordship beneath thy sway; and on the Springs and Rivers I call, and the Dread of high heaven, and the divinities of the blue seas: if haply victory fall to Turnus the Ausonian, the vanquished make covenant to withdraw to Evander's city; Iülus shall quit the land; nor ever hereafter shall the Aeneadae return in arms to renew warfare, or attack this realm with the sword. But if Victory grant battle to us and ours (as I think the rather, and so the rather may the gods confirm it by their will), I will not bid Italy obey my Teucrians, nor do I claim the realm for mine; let both nations, unconquered, join treaty for ever under equal law. Gods and worship shall be of my giving: my father Latinus shall bear the sword, and have a father's prescribed command. For me my Teucrians shall establish a city, and Lavinia give the town her name.'

Thus Aeneas first: thereon Latinus thus follows, looking up skyward and stretching his hand to heaven:

'By these same I swear, O Aeneas, by Earth, Sea, Sky, and the twin brood of Latona and Janus the double-facing, and the might of nether gods and grim Pluto's shrine; this let our Father hear, who seals treaties with his thunderbolt. I touch the altars, I take to witness the fires and the gods between us; no time shall break this peace and truce in Italy, howsoever fortune fall; nor shall any force turn my will aside, not if it dissolve land into water in turmoil of deluge, or melt heaven in hell: so surely as this sceptre' (for haply he bore a sceptre in his hand) 'shall never burgeon into thin leafage and shady shoot, since once in the forest cut down to the stock it lost its mother, and the steel lopped away its tressed arms: a tree of old: now the craftsman's hand has bound it in adornment of brass and given it to our Latin fathers' bearing.'

With such words they sealed mutual treaty midway in sight of the princes. Then they duly slay the consecrated beasts over the flames, and tear out their live entrails, and pile the altars with laden chargers.

But long ere this the Rutulians deemed the battle unequal, and their hearts are stirred in changeful motion; and now the more, as they discern nigher . . . heightened by Turnus, as advancing with noiseless pace he humbly worships at the altar with downcast eye, by his wasted cheeks and the pallor on his youthful frame. Soon as Juturna his sister saw this talk spread, and the people's mind waver in uncertainty, into the mid ranks, in feigned form of Camers—his family was high in long ancestry, and his father's name for valour renowned, and himself most valiant in arms—into the mid ranks she glides, not ignorant of her task, and scatters diverse rumours, saying thus: 'Shame, O Rutulians! shall we set one life in the breach for so many such as these? are we unequal in numbers or bravery? See, Troy and Arcadia is all they bring, and those fated forces that Etruria hurls on Turnus. Scarce is there an enemy to meet every other man of ours. He indeed will ascend to the gods for whose altars he devotes himself, and move living in the lips of men: we, our country lost, shall bow to the haughty rigour of our lords, if we now sit slackly on the field.'

By such words the soldiers' counsel was kindled yet higher and higher, and a murmur crept through their columns; the very Laurentians, the very Latins are changed; and they who but now hoped for rest from battle and rescue of fortune now desire arms and pray that the treaty were undone, and pity Turnus' cruel lot. To this Juturna adds a yet stronger impulse, and high in heaven shews a sign more potent than any to confuse Italian souls with delusive augury. For on the crimsoned sky Jove's tawny bird flew chasing, in a screaming crowd, fowl of the shore that winged their column; then suddenly stooping to the water, pounces greedily on a noble swan with crooked talons. The startled Italians watch, while all the birds together clamorously wheel round from flight, wonderful to see, and dim the sky with their pinions, and ir thickening cloud urge their foe through air, till, conquered by their attack and his heavy prey, he yielded and dropped it from his talons into the river, and winged his way deep into the clouds. Then indeed the Rutulians clamorously greet the omen, and their hands flash out. And Tolumnius the augur cries before them all: 'This it was, this, that my vows often have sought; I welcome and know a deity; follow me, follow, snatch up the sword, O hapless people whom the greedy alien frightens with his arms like silly birds, and with strong hand ravages your shores. He too will take to flight, and spread his sails afar over ocean. Do you with one heart close up your squadrons, and defend in battle your lost king.' He spoke, and darting forward, hurled a weapon full on the enemy; the whistling cornel-shaft sings, and unerringly cleaves the air. At once and with it a vast shout goes up, and all their rows are amazed and their hearts hotly stirred. The spear flies on; where haply stood opposite in ninefold brotherhood all the beautiful sons of one faithful Tyrrhene wife, borne of her to Gylippus the Arcadian, one of these, midway where the sewn belt rubs on the flank and the clasp bites the fastenings of the side, one of these, excellent in beauty and glittering in arms, it pierces clean through the ribs and stretches on the yellow sand. But of his banded brethren, their courage fired by grief, some grasp and draw their swords, some snatch lances to hurl, and rush blindly forward. The Laurentine columns charge forth against them; again from the other side Trojans and Agyllines and Arcadians in painted armour flood thickly in: so has one passion seized all to make decision by the sword. They strip the altars; through all the air goes a thick storm of weapons, and faster falls the iron rain. Bowls and hearth-fires are carried off; Latinus himself retreats, bearing the outraged gods of the broken treaty. Others harness their chariots, or vault upon their horses and come up with swords drawn. Messapus, eager to shatter the treaty, rides menacingly down on Aulestes the Tyrrhenian, a king in a king's array. Retreating hastily, and tripped on the altars that meet him behind, the hapless man goes down on his head and shoulders. But Messapus flies up with wrathful spear, and strikes him, as he pleads sore, a deep downward blow from horseback with his beam-like spear, saying thus: 'That for him: the high gods are given this better victim.' The Italians crowd in and strip his warm limbs. Corynaeus seizes a charred brand from the altar, and meeting Ebysus as he advances to strike, darts the flame in his face; his heavy beard flamed up, and gave out a scorched smell. Following up his enemy's confusion, the other seizes him with his left hand by the hair, and bears him to earth with a thrust of his planted knee, and there drives the unyielding sword into his side. Podalirius pursues and overhangs with naked sword the shepherd Alsus as he rushes amid the foremost line of weapons; Alsus swings back his axe, and severs brow and chin full in front, wetting his armour all over with spattered blood. Grim rest and iron slumber seal his eyes; his lids close on everlasting night.

But good Aeneas, his head bared, kept stretching his unarmed hand and calling loudly to his men: 'Whither run you? What is this strife that so spreads and swells? Ah, restrain your wrath! truce is already stricken, and all its laws ordained; mine alone is the right of battle. Leave me alone, and fear not; my hand shall confirm the treaty; these rites already make Turnus mine.' Amid these accents, amid words like these, lo! a whistling arrow winged its way to him, sped from what hand or how tempest-driven, none knows, or what chance or deity brought such honour to the Rutulians; the renown of the high deed was buried, nor did any boast to have dealt Aeneas' wound. Turnus, when he saw Aeneas retreating from the ranks and his captains in dismay, burns hot with sudden hope. At once he calls for his horses and armour, and with a bound leaps proudly into his chariot and handles the reins. He darts on, dealing many brave men's bodies to death; many an one he rolls half-slain, or crushes whole files under his chariot, or seizes and showers spears on the fugitives. As when by the streams of icy Hebrus Mavors kindles to bloodshed and clashes on his shield, and stirs war and speeds his furious coursers; they outwing south winds and west on the open plain; utmost Thrace groans under their hoof-beats; and around in the god's train rush the faces of dark Terror, and Wraths and Ambushes; even so amid the battle Turnus briskly lashes on his reeking horses, trampling on the foes that lie piteously slain; the galloping hoof scatters bloody dew, and spurns mingled gore and sand. And now has he dealt Sthenelus to death, and Thamyrus and Pholus, him and him at close quarters, the other from afar; from afar both the sons of Imbrasus, Glaucus and Lades, whom Imbrasus himself had nurtured in Lycia and equipped in equal arms, whether to meet hand to hand or to outstrip the winds on horseback. Elsewhere Eumedes advances amid the fray, ancient Dolon's offspring, illustrious in war, renewing his grandfather's name, his father's courage and strength of hand, who of old dared to claim Pelides' chariot as his price if he went to spy out the Grecian camp; to him the son of Tydeus told out another price for his venture, and he dreams no more of Achilles' horses. Him Turnus descried far on the open plain, and first following him with light javelin through long space of air, stops his double-harnessed horses and leaps from the chariot, and descends on his fallen half-lifeless foe, and, planting his foot on his neck, wrests the blade out of his hand and dyes its glitter deep in his throat, adding these words withal: 'Behold, thou liest, Trojan, meting out those Hesperian fields thou didst seek in war. Such guerdon is theirs who dare to tempt my sword; thus do they found their city.' Then with a spear-cast he sends Asbutes to follow him, and Chloreus and Sybaris, Dares and Thersilochus, and Thymoetes fallen flung over his horse's neck. And as when the Edonian north wind's wrath roars on the deep Aegean, and the wave follows it shoreward; where the blast comes down, the clouds race over the sky; so, wheresoever Turnus cleaves his way, columns retreat and lines turn and run; his own speed bears him on, and his flying plume tosses as his chariot meets the breeze. Phegeus disdained his furious onset; he faced the chariot, and caught and twisted away in his right hand the mouths of his horses, spurred into speed and foaming on the bit. Dragged along and hanging by the yoke he is left uncovered; the broad lance-head reaches him, pins and pierces the corslet of double-twined mail, and lightly wounds the surface of his body. Yet turning, he advanced on the enemy behind his shield, and sought succour in the naked point; when the wheel running forward on its swift axle struck him headlong and flung him to ground, and Turnus' sword following it smote off his head between the helmet-rim and the upper border of the breastplate, and left the body on the sand.

And while Turnus thus victoriously deals death over the plains, Mnestheus meantime and faithful Achates, and Ascanius by their side, set down Aeneas in the camp, dabbled with blood and leaning at every other step on his long spear. He storms, and tries hard to pull out the dart where the reed had broken, and calls for the nearest way of remedy, to cut open the wound with broad blade, and tear apart the weapon's lurking-place, and so send him back to battle. And now Iapix son of Iasus came, beloved beyond others of Phoebus, to whom once of old, smitten with sharp desire, Apollo gladly offered his own arts and gifts, augury and the lyre and swift arrows: he, to lengthen out the destiny of a parent given over to die, chose rather to know the potency of herbs and the practice of healing, and deal in a silent art unrenowned. Aenas stood chafing bitterly, propped on his vast spear, encircled by mourning Iülus and a great crowd of men, unstirred by their tears. The aged man, with garment drawn back and girt about him in Paeonian fashion, makes many a hurried effort with healing hand and the potent herbs of Phoebus, all in vain; in vain his hand solicits the arrow-head, and his pincers' grasp pulls at the steel. Fortune leads him forward in no wise; Apollo aids not with counsel; and more and more the fierce clash swells over the plains, and the havoc draws nigher on. Already they see the sky a mass of dust, the cavalry approaching, and shafts falling thickly amid the camp; the dismal cry uprises of warriors fighting and falling under the War-god's heavy hand. At this, stirred deep by her son's cruel pain, Venus his mother plucked from Cretan Ida a stalk of dittamy with downy leaves and bright-tressed flowers, the plant not unknown to wild goats when winged arrows are fast in their body. This Venus bore down, her face shrouded in a dim halo; this she steeps with secret healing in the river-water poured out and sparkling abrim, and sprinkles life-giving juice of ambrosia and scented balm. With that water aged Iapix washed the wound, unwitting; and suddenly, lo! all the pain left his body, all the blood in the deep wound was stanched. And now following his hand the arrow fell out unforced, and strength returned afresh as of old. 'Hasten! arms for him quickly! why stand you still?' cries Iapix aloud, and at once kindles their courage against the enemy; 'this comes not by human resource or schooling of art, nor does my hand save thee, Aeneas: a higher god is at work, and sends thee back to higher deeds.'

He, eager for battle, had already clasped on the greaves of gold right and left, and scorning delay, brandishes his spear. When the shield is adjusted by his side and the corslet on his back, he clasps Ascanius in his armed embrace, and lightly kissing him through the helmet, cries: 'Learn of me, O boy, valour and toil in deed, fortune of others. Now mine hand shall give thee defence in war, and lead thee to great reward: do thou, when hereafter thine age ripens to fulness, keep this in remembrance, and as thou recallest the pattern of thy kindred, let thy father Aeneas, thine uncle Hector arouse thy courage.'

These words uttered, he issued towering from the gates, brandishing his mighty spear: with him in serried column rush Antheus and Mnestheus, and all the throng streams forth of the camp. The field drifts with blinding dust, and the startled earth trembles under the tramp of feet. From his earthworks opposite Turnus saw and the Ausonians saw them come, and an icy shudder ran deep through their frame; first and before all the Latins Juturna heard and knew the sound, and in terror fled away. He flies on, and hurries his dark column over the open plain. As when in fierce weather a storm-cloud moves over mid sea to land, with presaging heart, alas! the hapless husbandmen shudder from afar; it will deal havoc to their trees and destruction to their crops, and make a broad path of ruin; the winds fly before it, and bear its roar to the beach; so the Rhoeteian captain drives his army full on the foe; one and all they close up in serried wedges, and mass their ranks. Thymbraeus smites massive Osiris with the sword, Mnestheus slays Arcetius, Achates Epulo, Gyas Ufens: Tolumnius the augur himself goes down, he who had hurled the first weapon against the foe. Their cry rises to heaven, and in turn the routed Rutulians give back, flying in a cloud of dust across the fields. Himself he deigns not to cut down the fugitives, nor pursue such as meet him fair on foot of approach in arms: Turnus alone he tracks and searches in the thick haze, him alone calls to conflict. Then panic-stricken the warrior maiden Juturna flings Metiscus, Turnus' charioteer, out over his reins, and leaving him far where he slips from the chariot-pole, herself succeeds and manages the wavy reins, her voice and body and armour all those that Metiscus wore. As when a black swallow flits through some rich lord's spacious house, and circles in flight the lofty halls, gathering her tiny food for sustenance to her twittering nestlings, and now swoops down the spacious colonnades, now round the wet ponds; in like wise dart Juturna's horses amid the enemy, and her fleet chariot passes flying over all the field. And now here and now here she displays her triumphant brother, nor yet allows him to close, but flies far and away. None the less does Aeneas thread the circling maze to meet him, and tracks his man, and with loud cries on him through the scattered ranks. Often as he cast eyes on his enemy and essayed to outrun the speed of the flying-footed horses, so often Juturna wheeled her chariot away. Alas, what can he do? Vainly he tosses on the ebb and flow, and in his spirit diverse cares make conflicting call; when Messapus, who haply bore in his left hand two tough spear-shafts topped with steel, runs lightly up and aims and hurls one of them upon him with unerring stroke. Aeneas stood still, and gathered himself behind his armour, sinking on bended knee; yet the rushing spear bore off his helmet-spike, and dashed the helmet-plume from the crest. Then indeed his wrath swells; and forced to it by their treachery, while he sees chariot and horses disappear, he calls Jove and the altars of the violated treaty again and again to witness, and now at last plunges amid their lines. Sweeping terrible down the tide of battle he wakens fierce indiscriminate carnage, and flings loose all the reins of wrath.

What god may now unfold for me in verse so many woes, so many diverse slaughters and death of captains whom now Turnus, now again the Trojan hero, drives over all the field? Was it thy will, O God, that nations destined to everlasting peace should clash in so vast a shock? Sucro the Rutulian delayed not Aeneas long, though that combat stayed the first rush of the Teucrians; he catches him on the side, and, where fate comes quickest, drives the harsh sword clean through the ribs where they fence the breast. Turnus unhorsing Amycus meets him on foot, him and his brother Diores: one he strikes with his long spear as he comes, one with his sword-point, and hangs both severed heads on his chariot and carries them off dripping with blood. The one sends to death Talos and Tanaïs and brave Cethegus, three at one meeting, and woeful Onites, of Echionian name, and Peridia the mother that bore him; the other those brethren sent from Lycia and Apollo's fields, and Menoetes the Arcadian, him who loathed warfare in vain; who once had his art and humble home about the river-fisheries of Lerna, and knew not the courts of the great, but his father was tenant of the land he tilled. And as fires kindled dispersedly in a dry forest and rustling laurel thickets, or foaming rivers where they leap swift and loud from high hills, and speed to sea each in his own path of havoc; as fiercely the two, Aeneas and Turnus, dash amid the battle; now, now wrath surges within them, and hearts break rather than know defeat; now in all their might they rush upon wounds. The one dashes Murranus down and stretches him on the soil with a vast whirling mass of rock, as he cries the names of his fathers and forefathers of old, a whole line drawn through Latin kings; under traces and yoke the wheels spurned him, and the fast-beating hoofs of his rushing horses trample down their forgotten lord. The other meets Hyllus rushing on in gigantic pride, and hurls his weapon at his gold-bound temples; the spear pierced through the helmet and stood fast in the brain. Neither did thy right hand save thee from Turnus, O Cretheus, bravest of the Greeks; nor did his gods shield Cupencus when Aeneas came; he gave his breast full to the steel, nor, alas! was the brazen shield's delay aught of avail. Thee likewise, Aeolus, the Laurentine plains saw sink backward and cover a wide space of earth; thou fallest, whom Argive battalions could not lay low, nor Achilles the destroyer of Priam's realm. Here was thy goal of death; thine high house was under Ida, at Lyrnesus thine high house, on Laurentine soil thy tomb. The whole battle-lines gather up, all Latium and all Dardania, Mnestheus and valiant Serestus, with Messapus, tamer of horses, and brave Asilas, the Tuscan battle-line and Evander's Arcadian squadrons; man by man they struggle with all their might; no rest nor pause in the vast strain of conflict.

At this Aeneas' mother most beautiful inspired him to advance on the walls, directing his columns on the town and dismaying the Latins with sudden and swift disaster. As in search for Turnus he bent his glance this way and that round the separate ranks, he descries the city free from all this warfare, unpunished and unstirred. Straightway he kindles at the view of a greater battle; he summons Mnestheus and Sergestus and brave Serestus his captains, and mounts a hillock; there the rest of the Teucrian army gathers thickly, still grasping shield and spear. Standing on the high mound amid them, he speaks: 'Be there no delay to my words; Jupiter is with us; neither let any be slower to move that the design is sudden. This city to-day, the source of war, the royal seat of Latinus, unless they yield them to receive our yoke and obey their conquerors, will I raze to ground, and lay her smoking roofs level with the dust. Must I wait forsooth till Turnus please to stoop to combat, and choose again to face his conqueror? This, O citizens, is the head and sum of the accursed war. Bring firebrands speedily, and reclaim the treaty in flame.' He ended; all with spirit alike emulous form a wedge and advance in serried mass to the walls. Ladders are run up, and fire leaps sudden to sight. Some rush to the several gates, and cut down the guards of the entry, others hurl their steel and darken the sky with weapons. Aeneas himself among the foremost, upstretching his hand to the city walls, loudly reproaches Latinus, and takes the gods to witness that he is again forced into battle, that twice now do the Italians choose warfare and break a second treaty. Discord rises among the shaken citizens: some bid unbar the town and fling wide their gates to the Dardanians, and pull the king himself towards the ramparts; others bring arms and hasten to defend the walls: as when a shepherd tracks bees to their retreat in a sheltering rock, and fills it with stinging smoke, they within run uneasily up and down their waxen fortress, and hum louder in rising wrath; the black pungent cloud rolls through their dwelling, and a blind murmur echoes within the rock as the smoke issues to the empty air.

This fortune likewise befell the despairing Latins, this woe shook the whole city to her base. The queen espies from her roof the enemy's approach, the walls scaled and firebrands flying on the houses; and nowhere Rutulian ranks, none of Turnus' columns to meet them; alas! she deems him destroyed in the shock of battle, and, distracted by sudden anguish, shrieks that she is the source of guilt, the spring of ill, and with many a mad utterance of frenzied grief rends her purple attire with dying hand, and ties from a lofty beam the ghastly noose of death. And when the unhappy Latin women knew this calamity, first her daughter Lavinia tears her flower-like tresses and roseate cheeks, and the frenzy spreads from her to the whole train around; the wide palace echoes to their wailing, and from it the sorrowful rumour spreads abroad throughout the town. All hearts sink; Latinus goes with torn raiment, in dismay at his wife's doom and his city's downfall, defiling his hoary hair with soilure of sprinkled dust.

Meanwhile on the skirts of the field Turnus chases scattered stragglers, ever slacker to battle, ever less and less exultant in his courser's victorious speed. The confused cry came to him borne in blind terror down the breeze, and his startled ears caught the echoing tumult and disastrous murmur of the town. 'Ah me! what agony shakes the ramparts? or what is this cry that fleets so loud from the distant town?' So speaks he, and distractedly checks the reins. And to him his sister, as changed into his charioteer Metiscus' likeness she swayed horses and chariot-reins, thus rejoined: 'This way, Turnus, let us pursue the brood of Troy, where victory opens her nearest way; there are others whose hands can protect their dwellings. Aeneas falls fiercer on the Italians, and closes in conflict; let our hand too deal pitiless death on his Teucrians. Neither in tale of dead nor in glory of battle shalt thou retire outdone.' Thereat Turnus: . . .

'Ah my sister, long ere now I knew thee, when first thine arts shattered the treaty, and thou didst mingle in the strife; and now thy godhead conceals itself in vain. But who has bidden thee descend from heaven to bear this sore travail? was it that thou mightest see thy hapless brother cruelly slain? for what am I doing, or what fortune yet gives promise of safety? Before my very eyes, calling aloud to me, I saw Murranus, than whom none other is left me more dear, sink huge to earth, borne down by as huge a wound. Hapless Ufens is fallen, not to see our shame; corpse and armour are in Teucrian hands. The destruction of their households, this was the one thing yet lacking; shall I suffer it? Shall my hand not refute Drances' jeers? shall I turn my back, and this land see Turnus a fugitive? Is Death all so bitter? Do you, O Shades, be gracious to me, since the will of heaven is estranged; to you shall I go down, a pure spirit and ignorant of your blame, never once unworthy of my mighty forefathers of old.'

Scarce had he spoken thus; lo! Saces, borne flying on his foaming horse through the thickest of the foe, an arrow-wound right in his face, darts, beseeching Turnus by his name. 'Turnus, in thee is our last safety; pity thy people. Aeneas thunders in arms, and threatens to overthrow and hurl to destruction the high Italian fortress; and already firebrands are flying on our roofs. On thee, on thee the Latins turn their gazing eyes; King Latinus himself mutters in doubt, whom he is to call his sons, to whom he shall incline in union. Moreover the queen, thy surest stay, has fallen by her own hand and in dismay fled the light. Alone in front of the gates Messapus and valiant Atinas sustain the battle-line. Round about them to right and left the armies stand locked and the iron field shivers with naked points; thou wheelest thy chariot on the sward alone.'

As the scene shifted before him Turnus froze in horror and stood in dumb gaze; together in his heart sweep the vast mingling tides of shame and maddened grief, and love stung to frenzy and resolved valour. So soon as the darkness cleared and light returned to his soul, he fiercely turned his blazing eyeballs towards the ramparts, and gazed back from his wheels on the great city. And lo! a spire of flame wreathing through the floors wavered up skyward and held a turret fast, a turret that he himself had reared of mortised planks and set on rollers and laid with high gangways. 'Now, O my sister, now fate prevails: cease to hinder; let us follow where deity and stern fortune call. I am resolved to face Aeneas, resolved to bear what bitterness there is in death; nor shalt thou longer see me shamed, sister of mine. Let me be mad, I pray thee, with this madness before the end.' He spoke, and leapt swiftly from his chariot to the field, and darting through weapons and through enemies, leaves his sorrowing sister, and bursts in rapid course amid their columns. And as when a rock rushes headlong from some mountain peak, torn away by the blast, or if the rushing rain washes it away, or the stealing years loosen its ancient hold; the reckless mountain mass goes sheer and impetuous, and leaps along the ground, hurling with it forests and herds and men; thus through the scattering columns Turnus rushes to the city walls, where the earth is wettest with bloodshed and the air sings with spears; and beckons with his hand, and thus begins aloud: 'Forbear now, O Rutulians, and you, Latins, stay your weapons. Whatsoever fortune is left is mine: I singly must expiate the treaty for you all, and make decision with the sword.' All drew aside and left him room.

But lord Aeneas, hearing Turnus' name, abandons the walls, abandons the fortress height, and in exultant joy flings aside all hindrance, breaks off all work, and clashes his armour terribly, vast as Athos, or as Eryx, or as the lord of Apennine when he roars with his tossing ilex woods and rears his snowy crest rejoicing into air. Now indeed Rutulians and Trojans and all Italy turned in emulous gaze, both they who held the high city, and they whose ram was battering the wall below, and took off the armour from their shoulders. Latinus himself stands in amaze at the mighty men, born in distant quarters of the world, met and making decision with the sword. And they, in the empty level field that cleared for them, darting swiftly forward, and hurling their spears from far, close in battle shock with clangour of brazen shields. Earth utters a moan; the sword-strokes fall thick and fast, chance and valour joining in one. And as in broad Sila or high on Taburnus, when two bulls rush to deadly battle forehead to forehead, the herdsmen retire in terror, all the cattle stand dumb in dismay, and the heifers murmur in doubt which shall be lord in the woodland, which the whole herd must follow; they violently deal many a mutual wound, and gore with their stubborn horns, bathing their necks and shoulders in abundant blood; all the woodland echoes back their bellowing with a moan: even thus Aeneas of Troy and the Daunian hero rush together shield to shield; the mighty crash fills the sky. Jupiter himself holds up the two scales in even balance, and lays in them the different fates of both, trying which shall pay forfeit of the strife, whose weight shall sink in death. Turnus darts out, thinking it secure, and rises with his whole reach of body on his uplifted sword; then strikes; Trojans and Latins cry out in alarm, and both armies strain their gaze. But the treacherous sword shivers, and in mid stroke deserts its eager lord. If flight aid him not now! He flies swifter than the wind, when once he descries a strange hilt in his weaponless hand. Rumour is that in his headlong haste, when mounting behind his yoked horses to begin the battle, he left his father's sword behind and caught up his charioteer Metiscus' weapon; and that served him long, while Teucrian stragglers turned their backs; when it met the divine Vulcanian armour, the mortal blade like brittle ice snapped in the stroke; the shards lie glittering upon the yellow sand. So in distracted flight Turnus darts afar over the plain, and now this way and now that crosses in wavering circles; for on all hands the Teucrians locked him in crowded ring, and the waste marsh on this side, on this the steep city ramparts hem him in.

Therewith Aeneas pursues, though ever and anon his knees, disabled by the arrow, hinder him and refuse to run; and foot hard on foot presses hotly on his hurrying enemy: as when a hunter courses with a fleet barking hound some stag caught in a river-loop or girt by the crimson-feathered toils, and he, in terror of the snares and the high river-bank darts forward and back in a thousand ways; but the keen Umbrian clings agape, and just catches at him, and as though he caught him snaps his jaws while the baffled teeth close on vacancy. Then indeed a cry goes up, and banks and pools answer round about, and all the sky echoes the din. He, even as he flies, chides all his Rutulians, calling each by name, and shrieks for the sword he knows. But Aeneas denounces death and instant doom if one of them draw nigh, and doubles their terror with threats of their city's destruction, and though wounded presses on. Five circles they cover at full speed and unwind as many, this way and that; for not light nor slight is the prize they seek, but Turnus' very lifeblood is at issue. Here there haply had stood a bitter-leaved wild olive, sacred to Faunus, a tree worshipped by mariners of old; on it, when rescued from the waves, they were wont to fix their gifts to the god of Laurentum and hang their votive raiment; but the Teucrians, unregarding, had cleared away the sacred stem, that they might meet on unimpeded lists. Here was lodged Aeneas' spear; hither borne by its own speed it was held fast stuck in the tough root. The Dardanian stooped over it, and would wrench away the steel, to follow with the weapon him whom he could not catch in running. Then indeed Turnus cries in frantic terror: 'Faunus, have pity, I beseech thee! and thou, most gracious Earth, keep thy hold on the steel, if I alway have kept your worship, and the Aeneadae contrariwise have profaned it in war.' He spoke, and called the god to aid in vows that fell not fruitless. For all Aeneas' strength, his long struggling and delay over the tough stem availed not to unclose the hard grip of the wood. While he strains and pulls hard, the Daunian goddess, changing once more into the charioteer Metiscus' likeness, runs forward and passes her brother his sword. But Venus, indignant that the Nymph might be so bold, drew nigh and wrenched away the spear where it stuck deep in the root. Erect in fresh courage and arms, he with his faithful sword, he towering fierce over his spear, they face one another panting in the battle shock.

Meanwhile the King of Heaven's omnipotence accosts Juno as she gazes on the battle from a sunlit cloud. 'What yet shall be the end, O wife? what remains at the last? Aeneas is claimed by Heaven as his country's god, thou thyself knowest and avowest to know, and is lifted by fate to the stars. With what device or in what hope hangest thou chill in cloudland? Was it well that a deity should be sullied by a mortal's wound? or that the lost sword—for what without thee could Juturna avail?—should be restored to Turnus and swell the force of the vanquished? Forbear now, I pray, and bend to our entreaties; let not all this pain devour thee in silence, and distress so often flood back on me from thy sweet lips. The end is come. Thou hast had power to hunt the Trojans on land or wave, to kindle accursed war, to put the house in mourning, and plunge the bridal in grief: further attempt I forbid thee.' Thus Jupiter began: thus the goddess, daughter of Saturn, returned with humbled aspect:

'Even because this thy will, great Jupiter, is known to me for thine, have I left, though loth, Turnus and earth; nor else wouldst thou see me now, alone on this skyey seat, enduring even past endurance; but girt in flame I were standing by their very lines, and dragging the Teucrians into the deadly battle. I counselled Juturna, I confess it, to succour her hapless brother, and for his life's sake favoured a greater daring; yet not the arrow-shot, not the bending of the bow, I swear by the merciless well-head of the Stygian spring, the single ordained dread of the gods in heaven. And now I retire, and leave the battle in loathing. This thing I beseech thee, that is bound by no fatal law, for Latium and for the majesty of thy kindred. When now they shall plight peace with prosperous marriages (be it so!), when now they shall join in laws and treaties, bid thou not the native Latins change their name of old, nor become Trojans and take the Teucrian name, or change their language, or alter their attire: let Latium be, let Alban kings endure through ages, let Italian valour be potent in the race of

Rome. Troy is fallen; let her and her name lie where they fell.'

To her smilingly the designer of men and things:

'Jove's own sister thou art, and second offspring of Saturn, such surge of wrath tosses within thy breast! But come, allay this madness so vainly stirred. I give thee thy will, and yield thee ungrudged victory. Ausonia shall keep her native speech and usage, and as her name is, it shall be. The Trojans shall sink incorporate with them; I will add their sacred law and ritual, and make all Latins and of a single speech. Hence shall spring a race of tempered Ausonian blood, whom thou shalt see outdo men and gods in duty; nor shall any nation so observe thy worship.' To this Juno assented, and in gladness withdrew her purpose; meanwhile she quits her cloud, and retires out of the sky.

This done, the Father revolves inly another counsel, and prepares to separate Juturna from her brother's arms. Twin monsters there are called the Awful Ones by name, whom with infernal Megaera the dead of night bore at one single birth, and wreathed them in like serpent coils, and clothed them in windy wings. They appear at Jove's throne and in the courts of the grim king, and quicken the terrors of wretched men whensoever the lord of heaven deals sicknesses and dreadful death, or sends terror of war upon guilty cities. One of these Jupiter sent swiftly down from the height of heaven, and bade her meet Juturna for an omen. She wings her way, and darts in a whirlwind to earth. Even as an arrow through a cloud darting from the string, which Parthian has poisoned with bitter gall, Parthian or Cydonian, and sped the immedicable shaft, leaps through the swift shadow whistling and unknown; so sprang and swept to earth the daughter of Night. When she espies the Ilian ranks and Turnus' columns, suddenly shrinking to the shape of a small bird that often sits late by night on tombs or ruinous roofs, and vexes the darkness with her cry, in such change of likeness the monster shrilly passes and repasses before Turnus' face, and her wings beat restlessly on his shield. A strange numbing terror unnerves his limbs, his hair thrills up, and the voice in his throat was choked. But when Juturna his hapless sister knew afar the whistling wings of the Fury, she unbinds and tears her tresses, with rent face and smitten bosom. 'How, O Turnus, can thine own sister help thee now? or what more is there if I break not under this? By what device may I lengthen out thy day? can I contend with this ominous thing? Now, now I quit the field. Dismay me not with your terrors, disastrous birds; I know these beating wings, and the sound of death, nor do I miss high-hearted Jove's haughty ordinance. Is this his repayment for my maidenhood? to what end was his gift of life for ever? why did I forfeit a mortal's lot? Could I but end all this pain now for good, and go with my unhappy brother side by side into the dark! Alas mine immortality! will aught of mine be sweet to me without thee, my brother? Ah, how may Earth yawn deep enough for me, and plunge my godhead deep in the world below!'

So spoke she, and wrapping her head in her grey vesture, the goddess moaning sore sank in the river depth.

But Aeneas presses on, brandishing his vast tree-like spear, and fiercely speaks thus: 'What more delay is there now? or why, Turnus, dost thou yet shrink away? Not in speed of foot, in grim arms, hand to hand, must be the conflict. Transform thyself as thou wilt, and collect what strength of courage or skill is thine; pray that thou mayest wing thy flight to the stars on high, or that sheltering earth may shut thee in.' The other, shaking his head: 'Thy fierce words dismay me not, insolent! the gods dismay me, and Jupiter's enmity.' And no more said, his eyes light on a vast stone, a stone ancient and vast that haply lay upon the plain, set for a landmark to divide contested fields: scarcely might twelve chosen men lift it on their shoulders, of such frame as now earth breeds mankind: then the hero caught it up with shaking hand and whirled it at the enemy, rising higher and quickening his speed. But he knows not his own self running nor going nor lifting his hands or moving the mighty stone; his knees totter, his blood freezes cold; the very stone he hurls, spinning through the empty void, neither wholly reached its distance nor carried its blow home. And as in sleep, when rest at night weighs down our tired eyes, we seem vainly to will to run eagerly on, and sink faint amidst our struggles; the tongue is powerless, the familiar strength fails the body, nor do words or utterance follow: so the awful goddess brings to naught all the valour of Turnus where he seeks a way. Shifting thoughts pass through his breast; he gazes on his Rutulians and on the city, and falters in terror, and shudders at the imminent death; neither sees he whither he may escape nor what force is his to meet the foe, and nowhere his chariot, nowhere his sister at the reins. As he wavers Aeneas poises the deadly weapon, and, marking his chance, hurls it in from afar with all his strength of body. Never with such a roar are stones hurled from some engine on ramparts, nor does the thunder burst in so loud a peal. Carrying grim death with it, the spear flies in fashion of some dark whirlwind, and opens the rim of the corslet and the utmost circles of the sevenfold shield. Right through the thigh it passes hurtling on; under the blow Turnus falls huge to earth with his leg doubled under him. The Rutulians start up with a groan, and all the hill echoes round about, and the width of high woodland returns their cry. Lifting up beseechingly his humbled eyes and suppliant hand: 'I have deserved it,' he says, 'nor do I ask for mercy; use thy fortune. If an unhappy parent's distress may at all touch thee, this I pray; even such a father was Anchises to thee; pity Daunus' old age, and restore to my kindred which thou wilt, me or my body bereft of day. Thou art conqueror, and the Ausonians have seen me stretch conquered hands. Lavinia is thine in marriage; press not hatred farther.'

Aeneas stood wrathful in arms, with rolling eyes, and lowered his hand; and now and now yet more the speech began to bend him to waver: when high on his shoulder appeared the sword-belt with the shining bosses that he knew, the luckless belt of the boy Pallas, whom Turnus had struck down with mastering wound, and wore on his shoulders the fatal ornament. The other, as his eyes drank in the plundered record of his fierce grief, kindles to fury, and cries terrible in anger:

'Mayest thou, clad in the spoils of my dearest, be snatched from me now? Pallas it is, Pallas who strikes the deathblow, and exacts vengeance in thy guilty blood.' So saying, he fiercely plunges the steel full in his breast. But his limbs grow slack and chill, and the life with a moan flies indignant into the dark.

THE ECLOGUES

ECLOGUE I.—TITYRUS

MELIBOEUS—TITYRUS

M.—Tityrus, thou where thou liest under the covert of spreading beech, broodest on thy slim pipe over the Muse of the woodland: we leave our native borders and pleasant fields; we fly our native land, while thou, Tityrus, at ease in the shade teachest the woods to echo fair Amaryllis.

T.—O Meliboeus, a god brought us this peace: for a god ever will he be to me: his altar a tender lamb from our sheepfolds shall often stain. He granted that my oxen might stray as thou descriest, and myself play what I would on the rustic reed.

M.—I envy not, I, rather I wonder, so is all the countryside being routed out. See, I myself wearily drive forth my she-goats; and this one, Tityrus, I just drag along: for here among the hazel thickets she has borne twins, the hope of the flock, and left them, alas! on the naked flints. Often, had a mind not infatuate been mine, I remember how lightning-scathed oaks presaged this woe of ours. But yet vouchsafe to us, Tityrus, who is this god of thine.

T.—The city they call Rome, O Meliboeus, I fancied in my foolishness like ours here, whither we shepherds are often wont to drive the tender weanlings of the sheep. Thus I knew the likeness of puppies to dogs, of kids to their mothers: thus would I compare great things with small. But she bears her head as high among all other cities as any cypress will do among trailing hedgerow shoots.

M.—And why might nothing less serve thee than seeing Rome?

T.—For freedom: she at last in spite of all turned her face upon a slothful servant, when now the beard was sprinkled with white that fell under the razor: in spite of all she turned her face and came after long delay, since Amaryllis holds us and Galatea has let us go. For I will confess it, while Galatea kept me, there was no hope of freedom, no thrift of savings: though many a victim went out from my pens, and rich cheese from my presses for the thankless town, never once did my hand come money-laden home.

M.—I wondered, Amaryllis, why thou calledst sadly on the gods, for whom thine apples were left hanging on the tree: Tityrus was away. The very pines, O Tityrus, the very springs and orchards here cried for thee.

T.—What was I to do? Neither might I free myself from service, nor elsewhere know gods so potent to help. Here I saw the prince, O Meliboeus, to whom yearly for twice six days the steam rises from our altars: here he gave present reply to my prayer: Pasture your oxen as of old, my children, rear your bulls.

M.—Happy in thine old age! so thy fields will remain thine, and ample enough for thee, although all the pastures be covered with bare stone or muddy rush of the fen. No strange fodder will try the breeding ewes, or touch of evil hurt them from any neighbour's flock. Happy in thine old age! here, amid familiar streams and holy springs thou wilt woo the coolness of the shade: here the hedge that ever keeps thy neighbour's boundary, where bees of Hybla feed their fill on the willow-blossom, shall often with light murmuring lull thee into sleep: here under the lofty rock shall rise the leaf-gatherer's song: nor all the while shall the hoarse wood-pigeons, thy delight, or the turtle on the elm's aëry top cease to moan.

T.—Therefore sooner shall light stags feed in the sky and the sea-channels leave the fishes naked on the beach; sooner, over-wandering both their boundaries, shall the exiled Parthian drink of Arar, or Germany of Tigris, than his countenance shall fade from our heart.

M.—But we! some shall pass hence to thirsty Africa, some reach Scythia and Oaxes' clay-laden torrent, and the Britons wholly sundered from all the world. Lo, shall I ever, long in time to come, again in my native borders marvel as I see my realm sunk to a poor cabin with turf-heaped roof behind a handful of corn? Shall a lawless soldier possess these trim fallows? a barbarian these cornfields? lo, to what wretched pass has civil discord brought us! lo, for whose profit we have sown our fields! Engraft thy pear trees now, Meliboeus, set thy vines arow! Go, my she-goats, go, once happy flock: never hereafter shall I, stretched in a green cave, see you afar hanging from the tufted rock: no songs shall I sing; not in my herding shall you, my she-goats, crop the flowering cytisus and bitter willows.

T.—Yet here for to-night thou mightst rest with me on green boughs: we have mellow apples and soft chestnuts, and curdled milk in abundance; and already afar the farm roofs smoke, and the shadows fall larger from the high hills.

ECLOGUE II.—ALEXIS

THE shepherd Corydon burned for fair Alexis, his master's darling, and found no hope: only among the thick shady-topped beeches he would continually come, and there alone utter in idle passion these artless words to the hills and woods.

O cruel Alexis, carest thou naught for my songs? hast no pity on us? thou wilt be my death at the last. Now even the cattle woo the shade and coolness, now even the green lizards hide in the thorn brakes; and Thestylis is bruising garlic and wild thyme, strong-smelling herbs for the mowers wearied with the fierce heat: but for all my company, as I trace thy footsteps, the copses ring with crickets jarring under the blazing sun. Was it not better to bear Amaryllis with all her sour displeasures and haughty scorns? or Menalcas, though he were dark, though thou wert white? O fair boy, trust not overmuch to colour; creamy privet-blossoms fall, dark hyacinths are gathered. I am scorned of thee, nor dost thou ask what I am, Alexis, how rich in flocks, how abounding in snowy milk. A thousand lambs of mine wander on Sicilian hills: fresh milk fails me not at midsummer nor in the frost. I sing as he was wont when he called his oxen home, Amphion of Dirce in Actaean Aracynthus. Neither am I so foul to view: of late I saw myself on the shore, when the sea stood in windless calm; I will not fear Daphnis in thy judgment, if the mirror cannot lie. Ah that thou wouldst but care to be with me in the rough country, to dwell in low cots, to shoot the deer, or drive a flock of kids to the green mallow bed. With me in the woods together thou shalt copy Pan in singing; Pan first taught to join with wax the row of reeds: Pan is guardian of the sheep and of the shepherds. Nor let it repent thee to run thy tender lip along the reeds: to know this same art what did Amyntas leave undone? I have a pipe joined of seven unequal hemlock-stalks, a gift that Damoetas once gave me, and said as he died: Now hath it thee for second master. Damoetas said it: stupid Amyntas was jealous. Furthermore two fawns, and in a perilous ravine I found them, with skin even yet white-dappled, drain a ewe's udders twice a day; and I keep them for thee. This long time Thestylis begs them to take away from me, and she shall, since our gifts are graceless in thine eyes. Come hither, O fair boy; for thee lo! the Nymphs bring baskets full of lilies; for thee the white Naiad plucks pale violets and poppy heads, and adds the narcissus and the fragrant anise-flower, and entwining them with casia and other sweet-scented herbs, spangles soft hyacinth-posies with yellow marigold. Myself will gather quinces with delicate silvery bloom, and the chestnuts that my Amaryllis loved, and waxen plums withal: this fruit likewise shall have his honour: and you will I pluck, O laurels, and thee, bordering myrtle, since so set you mingle your fragrant sweets. Thou art a country boor, O Corydon! nor does Alexis heed thy gifts: nor if the contest be of gifts may Iollas yield to thee. Alas, alas, what have I brought on my luckless head? I have loosed the tempest on my blossoms, woe's me, and the wild boars on my crystal springs. From whom fliest thou, ah infatuate? Gods likewise have dwelt in the woodland, and Paris of Dardania. Pallas may keep by herself the fortresses that she built: us before all else let the woodland satisfy. The grim lioness pursues the wolf, the wolf in turn the she-goat; the wanton she-goat pursues the flowering cytisus; as Corydon does thee, O Alexis, each drawn by his own delight. See, the bullocks return with the ploughs tilted from the yoke, and the sinking sun doubles the lengthening shadows: yet me love burns; for what bound may be set to love? Ah Corydon, Corydon, what madness has caught thee? thy vine hangs half unpruned on her leaf-laden elm. Nay but rather at least something of all that daily work needs, set thou to weave of osiers or soft rushes: if he disdains thee, thou wilt find another Alexis.

ECLOGUE III.—PALAEMON

MENALCAS—DAMOETAS—PALAEMON

M.—Tell me, Damoetas, who is the flock's master? **Meliboeus?**

D.—No, but Aegon: Aegon gave it of late to my keeping.

M.—Poor sheep, ever a luckless flock! while the master clings by Neaera and dreads lest she prefer me before him, this hireling shepherd milks the sheep twice an hour: the juice is stolen from the flock, the milk from the lambs.

D.—Yet remember to be more sparing in thy jeers at men. We know by whom thou, while the he-goats peered sideways —and in what shrine, though the easy Nymphs laughed.

M.—Then, I think, when they saw me slashing Micon's orchard and nursery vines with jealous hedgebill.

D.—Yes, or here by the old beeches, where thou brakest Daphnis' bow and reeds: for thou didst grieve, wicked Menalcas, when thou sawest them given to the boy, and it was death to thee if thou couldst not somehow have done him harm.

M.—What can the masters do, when the knaves make so free? Did I not see thee, villain, catching Damon's goat from ambush while the sheep-dog barked aloud? and when I cried: Where is he running off to now? Tityrus, gather the flock! thou didst hide behind the sedges.

D.—Was not he whom I conquered in singing to yield the goat that my tuneful pipe had won? If thou must be told, the goat was mine, as Damon himself confessed to me, but said he could not give it up.

M.—Thou him in singing? or hadst thou ever a waxenbound pipe? Wert not wont in the cross-roads, blockhead, to mangle a wretched tune on a grating straw?

D.—Wilt thou then we put to proof between us in turn

what each can do? I stake this heifer—lest haply thou draw back, she comes twice to the milking pail and withal feeds two calves from her udder—say thou what thou wilt stake with me in the strife.

M.—Of the flock I dare not stake aught with thee: for I have a father at home, and a wicked stepmother, and twice a day both count the flock, and one of them the kids. But, what thyself wilt confess far excels it, since be mad thou wilt—I will stake cups of beechwood, carved work of the divine Alcimedon, where a clinging vine raised by his light graver enfolds pale ivy with her scattered berries. In the middle are two figures, Conon, and who was that other whose compass marked out, on all the peopled globe, what seasons the reaper, what the bending ploughman should keep? nor yet have I put lip to them, but keep them laid by.

D.—And for us too Alcimedon made two cups, and wreathed the handles round with soft acanthus; and in the middle set Orpheus and the following woods: nor yet have I put lip to them, but keep them laid by. If thou lookest to the heifer in comparison, small praise is in the cups.

M.—Not to-day shalt thou escape me: I will come anywhere to thy challenge. Let one but hear us now—even he who approaches, lo! Palaemon. I will make thy voice henceforth cease from troubling.

D.—Nay come with what thou hast, there shall be no delay with me: nor do I shrink from any one: only, neighbour Palaemon, this is no small matter, lay it well to heart.

P.—Say on; since we are seated on soft grass, and now all the field, now all the tree is burgeoning, now the woodland is leafy, now is the fairest of the year. Begin, Damoetas: thou shalt follow on, Menalcas: you shall sing turn by turn as the Muses love.

D.—From Jove is the Muse's beginning: all things are full of Jove. He keeps the world: he gives ear to my songs.

M.—And me Phoebus loves: Phoebus' own gifts are ever by me. bays and the sweet flushed hyacinth.

D.—Galatea, playful maid, throws an apple at me, and runs to the willows, and desires that she first be seen.

M.—But my flame Amyntas comes to me unbidden: insomuch that now our dogs know not Delia better.

D.—Gifts are got for my love: for myself have marked the spot where the wood-pigeons have built aloft.

M.—What I could I have sent to the boy, ten golden apples plucked from the woodland tree; to-morrow I will send as many more.

D.—O the times and the words that Galatea has spoken to us! carry but a little thereof, ye winds, to the gods' ears.

M.—What boots it that thou scorn me not in thine heart, Amyntas, if while thou huntest the boar I am keeper of the nets?

D.—Send me my Phyllis: it is my birthday, O Iollas: when I shall make offering of a young heifer for the crops, come thyself.

M.—I love Phyllis before all women: for she wept at my going, and cried, My fair one, good-bye and a long good-bye, O Iollas.

D.—A sad thing is the wolf among the pens, rains on ripe cornfields, the winds in the trees, as Amaryllis' anger to us.

M.—A sweet thing is moisture to the crops, arbutus to weanling kids, the pliant willow to the breeding herd, as Amyntas alone to me.

D.—Pollio loves our Muse, rustic though she be: maids of Pierra, feed a heifer for your reader.

M.—Pollio himself too makes new songs: feed a bull, soon to strike with his horn and scatter the sand with his feet.

D.—Let him who loves thee, Pollio, come where thou too takest delight: let honey flow for him, and the rough briar yield him spice.

M.—Who hates not Bavius, let him love thy songs, O Maevius, and withal yoke foxes and milk he-goats.

D.—Gatherers of flowers and ground-strawberries, fly hence, O children, a cold snake lurks in the grass.

M.—Stay, my sheep, from too far advance: ill is it to trust the bank: the lordly ram even now dries his fleece.

D.—Tityrus, put back the grazing kids from the river: myself, when the time comes, will wash them all in the spring.

M.—Fold the sheep, children: if the heat steals the milk, as of late, vainly shall we squeeze the udders in our hands.

D.—Alas, alas, how lean is my bull among the juicy tares: the same love is death to herd and to herdsman.

M.—These assuredly (nor is love to blame) hardly keep their bones together: some evil eye is cast on my tender lambs.

D.—Tell in what lands (and thou shalt be to me as great Apollo) the open space of Sky is three yards and no more.

M.—Tell in what lands flowers are born engraven with names of kings, and have Phyllis for thine alone.

P.—Us it skills not to determine this strife between you: both thou and he are worthy of the heifer, and whosoever shrinks not from Love's sweetness shall not taste his bitterness. Shut off the rivulets now, my children: the meadows have drunk their fill.

ECLOGUE IV.—POLLIO

MUSES of Sicily, sing we a somewhat ampler strain: not all men's delight is in coppices and lowly tamarisks: if we sing of the woods, let them be woods worthy of a Consul.

Now is come the last age of the Cumaean prophecy: the great cycle of periods is born anew. Now returns the Maid, returns the reign of Saturn: now from high heaven a new generation comes down. Yet do thou at that boy's birth, in whom the iron race shall begin to cease, and the golden to arise over all the world, holy Lucina, be gracious; now thine own Apollo reigns. And in thy consulate, in thine, O Pollio, shall this glorious age enter, and the great months begin their march: under thy rule what traces of our guilt yet remain, vanishing shall free earth for ever from alarm. He shall grow in the life of gods, and shall see gods and heroes mingled, and himself be seen by them, and shall rule the world that his fathers' virtues have set at peace. But on thee, O boy, untilled shall Earth first pour childish gifts, wandering ivy-tendrils and foxglove, and colocasia mingled with the laughing acanthus: untended shall the she-goats bring home their milk-swoln udders, nor shall huge lions alarm the herds: unbidden thy cradle shall break into wooing blossom. The snake too shall die, and die the treacherous poison-plant: Assyrian spice shall grow all up and down. But when once thou shalt be able now to read the glories of heroes and thy father's deeds, and to know Virtue as she is, slowly the plain shall grow golden with the soft corn-spike, and the reddening grape trail from the wild briar, and hard oaks shall drip dew of honey. Nevertheless there shall linger some few traces of ancient wrong, to bid ships tempt the sea and towns be girt with walls and the earth cloven in furrows. Then shall a second Tiphys be, and a second Argo to sail with chosen heroes: new wars too shall arise, and again a mighty Achilles be sent to Troy. Thereafter, when now strengthening age hath wrought thee into man, the very voyager shall cease out of the sea, nor the sailing pine exchange her merchandise: all lands shall bear all things, the ground shall not suffer the mattock, nor the vine the pruning-hook; now likewise the strong ploughman shall loose his bulls from the yoke. Neither shall wool learn to counterfeit changing hues, but the ram in the meadow himself shall dye his fleece now with soft glowing sea-purple, now with yellow saffron; native scarlet shall clothe the lambs at their pasturage. Run even thus, O ages, said the harmonious Fates to their spindles, by the steadfast ordinance of doom. Draw nigh to thy high honours (even now will the time be come) O dear offspring of gods, mighty germ of Jove! Behold the world swaying her orbed mass, lands and spaces of sea and depth of sky; behold how all things rejoice in the age to come. Ah may the latter end of a long life then yet be mine, and such breath as shall suffice to tell thy deeds! Not Orpheus of Thrace nor Linus shall surpass me in song, though he have his mother and he his father to aid, Orpheus Calliope, Linus beautiful Apollo. If even Pan before his Arcady contend with me, even Pan before his Arcady shall declare himself conquered. Begin, O little boy, to know and smile upon thy mother, thy mother on whom ten months have brought weary longings. Begin, O little boy: of them who have not smiled on a parent, never was one honoured at a god's board or on a goddess' couch.

ECLOGUE V.—DAPHNIS

MENALCAS—MOPSUS

Me.—Why not, O Mopsus, since we are met so good a pair, thou to breathe in the slim reeds, I to utter the verses, sit down here among the mingled elms and hazels?

Mo.—Thou art the older: it is fit I should obey thee, Menalcas, whether where western breezes shift the flickering shadows or rather the cavern be our resting-place. See, how over the cavern the woodland wild vine scatters her thin clusters.

Me.—On our hills Amyntas alone contends with thee.

Mo.—What if he even contend to excel Phoebus in song?

Me.—Begin, O Mopsus, first, if thou hast aught of flames for Phyllis or praises of Alcon or flouts at Codrus. Begin: Tityrus will keep the grazing kids.

Mo.—Nay, the songs I have newly written down on green beech bark and marked the music between the lines, these will I essay: thou thereafter bid Amyntas enter the contest.

Me.—Even as the pliant osier yields to the grey olive, as the low scented reed to the crimson rose-plots, so far by our judgment Amyntas yields to thee.

Mo.—But cease thou further, O boy: we have reached the cavern.

Dead Daphnis cruelly slain the Nymphs wept; you, O hazels and rivers, were the Nymphs' witnesses; while clasping her son's wretched corse, his mother calls on gods and stars that pity not. None in those days, Daphnis, drove the pastured oxen to cool streams; no four-footed thing tasted the river nor touched the grassy sward. Daphnis, the wild hills and the woodlands repeat how even Punic lions bemoaned thy decease. Daphnis ordered the harnessing of Armenian tigresses to the car; Daphnis the processions of Bacchus' revellers and the soft leafage wound round their supple shafts. As the vine adorns her tree, as her grapes the vine; as bulls the herds, as corn the rich fields; so thou art all the ornament of thy people; since the Fates reft thee, Pales and Apollo themselves have left the country desolate. In the furrows where we often have bestowed the large barley, fruitless darnel and barren wild oats spring: instead of soft violet and shining narcissus rises the thistle and the thorn with his keen spines. Strew the ground with leaves, train shade over the springs, O shepherds: Daphnis bids such remembrance be done to him; and pile a mound, and over the mound add a verse: I am Daphnis the forester, known from here even to the heavens, keeper of a fair flock, myself more fair than they.

Me.—Such is thy song unto us, O divine poet, as sleep to the weary on the grass, as quenching of thirst in the heat from a gushing rivulet of sweet water. Nor on the reeds alone, but with voice too, thou equallest thy master: happy boy, thou shalt now be next to him. Yet we in turn will sing thee these songs of ours even as best we may, and raise thy Daphnis into the sky: we will ensky thy Daphnis, for us also Daphnis loved.

Mo.—And might aught be higher in our eyes than such a gift? Both the boy himself was worthy the singing, and these verses of thine Stimicon long since commended to us.

Me.—Clad in light, Daphnis marvels at Heaven's untrodden floor and sees the clouds and the stars beneath his feet. Therefore gay pleasure reigns in the forest and all the countryside, among Pan and the shepherds and the Dryad maidens. Neither does the wolf plot ambushes to the flock nor any hunting-nets ensnarement of the deer: gentle Daphnis loves peace. The unshorn mountains themselves cast echoes of gladness to the skies; the very rocks, the very copses now resound in song: A god, a god is he, O Menalcas. Ah be gracious and prosperous to thine own: see, four altars, two, lo! Daphnis, to thee, two for altars of offering to Phoebus: double cups frothing with fresh milk yearly, and two bowls of the fatness of the olive will I lay before thee; and above all making the banquet glad with much wine, before the hearth in the cold season, in harvest beneath the shade, I will pour from flagons the fresh nectar of Ariusian wine. Damoetas and Lyctian Aegon shall sing to me: Alphesiboeus shall mimic the leaping Satyrs. This shall ever be thine, both when we pay the Nymphs our accustomed vows and when we purify our fields. While the wild boar and the fish shall haunt mountain-ridge and river, while bees shall feed on thyme and grasshoppers on dew, ever shall thine honour, thy name and praise endure. As to the Wine-god and the Corn-goddess, so to thee shall the husbandmen make yearly vows; thou likewise shalt claim their payment.

Mo.—How, how may I repay the gift of such a song? for neither the whisper of the gathering South nor the wave breaking on the beach so delights me, nor streams that race down amid rocky dells.

Me.—First shall this brittle hemlock-pipe be our gift to thee: the pipe that taught us *Corydon burned for fair Alexis*, and withal *Who is the flock's master? Meliboeus?*

Mo.—But take thou the crook that, often as he besought it, Antigenes got not of me, and then he was worth loving, beautiful with ranged studs of brass, O Menalcas.

ECLOGUE VI.—SILENUS

First our Thalia deigned to dally with the verse of Syracuse, nor blushed to dwell in the woodland. When I was singing of kings and battles, the Cynthian twitched my ear and counselled me: A shepherd, Tityrus, should feed fat sheep but utter a slender song. Now will I—for thou wilt have many who long to utter thy praises, Varus, and to chronicle dreadful wars—brood on my slim pipe over the Muse of the country. Yet if one, if one there be to read this also for love of it, of thee, O Varus, our tamarisks, of thee all the forest shall sing; nor is any page dearer to Phoebus than that which writes in front of it Varus' name.

Proceed, maidens of Pieria. The boys Chromis and Mnasylos saw Silenus lying asleep in a cavern, his veins swollen as ever with the wine of yesterday: just apart lay the garlands slid from his head, and the heavy wine-jar hung by its worn handle. Falling on him, for often the old man had mocked them both with expectation of a song, they fetter him in his own garlands. Aegle joins company and reinforces their faint courage, Aegle fairest of the Naiads; and, now his eyes are open, stains his brow and temples with blood-red mulberries. He, laughing at their wiles, cries, Why tie these bonds? release me, boys: enough that you fancied you were so strong. Mark the songs you desire; for you songs, for her shall be another payment. And with that he begins. Then indeed thou mightest see Fauns and wild creatures sporting in measure, then massy oaks swaying their tops: nor so much does the Parnassian cliff rejoice in Phoebus nor so much Rhodope and Ismarus marvel at Orpheus.

For he sang how throughout the vast void were gathered together the seeds of earth and air and sea, and withal of fluid fire; how from these originals all the beginnings of things and the young orbed world itself grew together; then began to harden its floor and set ocean-bars to Nereus and gradually take shape in things: while now earth in amaze sees the new-born sun rise shining higher, and the rains fall as the clouds uplift; when the forests first begin to spring, and when live creatures roam thinly over the unknowing hills. Next he tells of the stones cast by Pyrrha, of the realm of Saturn, and the birds of Caucasus and the theft of Prometheus: thereto he adds how the sailors called on Hylas left at the fountain till Hylas! Hylas! echoed from all the shore: and consoles Pasiphaë (happy, had herds but never been!) with the love of her snowy steer. Ah hapless maiden, what frenzy hath hold of thee? Proetus' daughters filled the fields with counterfeited lowings, but yet none of them pursued such inhuman and shameful union, though her neck had shuddered as from the plough and she often had sought for horns on her smooth forehead. Ah hapless maiden, thou now wanderest on the hills: he, resting his snowy side on soft hyacinth blooms, under a back ilex munches the pale grass, or follows one among the vast herd. Bar, O Nymphs, Nymphs of Crete, bar now the forest glades, if haply that steer's wandering footprints may somewhere meet our eyes; peradventure he, either lured by green herbage or following the herbs, may come home on the cows' track to the yards of Gortyna. Then he sings of the maiden's marvel at the apples of the Hesperides: then enrings Phaethon's sisters with moss on bitter bark, and makes them spring tall in alder from the ground. Then he sings how as Gallus strayed by the streams of Permessus, one of the sisterhood led him to Aonian hills, and how before him all the choir of Phoebus rose up; how Linus the divine shepherd-singer, with blossoms and bitter parsley twined in his hair, spoke thus to him: These pipes, see, take them! the Muses give thee, the same they once gave the old man of Ascra; wherewith he was wont, singing, to draw down stubborn ash trees from the hills. On these be told by thee the birth of the Grynean forest, that there be no grove in which Apollo shall pride himself more. Why should I tell this tale either of Nisus' Scylla, whose after story is that girt with barking monsters round her white loins she harried the ships of Dulichium, and deep in her whirlpool, ah! tore their shivering crews with her sea-hounds? or of the changed limbs of Tereus; of that feast, that gift Philomela made ready for him; of her flight to desolate places, and of the wings on which she wretchedly hovered high in front of her home?

All that long ago happy Eurotas heard from brooding Phoebus and bade his laurels learn by heart, he sings: the smitten vales echo it to the sky: till bidding him gather the sheep to their cotes and tell their tale, the evening star came out in the unwilling heaven.

ECLOGUE VII.—MELIBOEUS

MELIBOEUS—CORYDON—THYRSIS

Lightly had Daphnis sate down beneath a whispering ilex, and Corydon and Thyrsis had driven their flocks together, Thyrsis his sheep, Corydon his milk-swoln she-goats; both in the blossom of age, both Arcadians, ready to sing and answer verse for verse. Hither, while I covered my delicate myrtles from the frost, my he-goat, lord of the flock, had wandered down: and I espy Daphnis: seeing me in turn, Quick, he cries, come hither, Meliboeus! thy goat and kids are safe; and, if thou canst take holiday, rest under the shade: hither come the bullocks unherded across the meadows to drink; here Mincius lines his green banks with a fringe of soft rushes, and the swarming bees murmur out of the holy oak.

What was I to do? I had no Alcippe, no Phyllis to shut in the weanling lambs at home; and Corydon against Thyrsis was a brave match. However, I put aside my business for their pleasure. So both began their contest, in alternate verses, since such the Muses willed them to remember. These Corydon, those Thyrsis uttered in his turn.

Co.—Nymphs of Libethrus, our delight, either grant me such a song as my Codrus' own: his come next to the verses Phoebus makes; or if we cannot all of us attain, this shrill pipe shall hang from your holy pine.

Th.—Shepherds of Arcady, deck with ivy your rising poet, that Codrus may burst his gall with envy; or, if he praise beyond my need, bind my brows with foxglove, lest an evil tongue harm the bard to be.

Co.—This bristling boar's head to thee, maid of Delos, and the branching antlers of a long-lived stag little Micon offers. If this thy grace abide, all in smooth marble thou shalt stand, the crimson buskin laced round thine ankles.

Th.—A bowl of milk and these cakes, O Priapus, yearly is enough for thee to claim; thou art keeper of a scanty garden.

Now we have fashioned thee in marble for the time: but do thou, if lambing-time fill up the flock, be there in gold.

Co.—Sea-Nymph Galatea, sweeter to me than thyme of Hybla, whiter than the swan, lovelier than pale ivy, so soon as the pastured bulls seek the yard again, if thou carest aught at all for thy Corydon, come!

Th.—Nay, but may I seem to thee bitterer than herbage of Sardinia, rougher than the spiky broom, more worthless than stranded seaweed, if to-day is not longer already to me than a whole year: go home from pasture, for very shame go, my cattle.

Co.—Mossed springs and grass softer than sleep, and green arbutus that covers you with thin shade, shielded the midsummer from the flock; now parching summer is coming, now the buds swell on the tough vine-shoot.

Th.—Here is the hearth and resinous billets; here the fire ever burns high and the doorposts are black with constant soot: here we care as much for the freezing North as the wolf for the flock's multitude, or rivers in flood for their banks.

Co.—Junipers and shaggy chestnuts tower up: under each tree lie strewn her fallen apples. All now smiles; but if fair Alexis be absent from the hills, thou wilt see even the rivers dry.

Th.--The field is parched, the dying grass thirsts in the distempered air; the wine-god denies the slopes the vine-tendrils' shade: at our Phyllis' coming all the woodland will be green, and heaven descend in glad and abundant showers.

Co.—Alcides takes most delight in the poplar, Iacchus in the vine, fair Venus in the myrtle, Phoebus in his own bay-tree: Phyllis loves hazels: while Phyllis loves them neither shall myrtle excel the hazels, nor Phoebus' bay.

Th.—The ash is most beautiful in the forest, the pine in the garden, the poplar by the river, the fir on the mountain heights: but if thou come back yet again to me, O fair Lycidas, the forest ash, the garden pine shall yield to thee.

These songs I remember, and how Thyrsis strove for victory in vain: henceforth Corydon, Corydon is ours.

ECLOGUE VIII.—THE SORCERESS

DAMON—ALPHESIBOEUS

The Muse of the shepherds Damon and Alphesiboeus, at whose strife the wondering heifer forgot the grass, at whose song the lynx stood breathless and the streams changed their current and were still, the Muse of Damon and Alphesiboeus we will tell.

Thou, my friend, whether thou climbest now great Timavus' rocks or dost skirt the coast of the Illyrian sea, ah shall ever the day come when I may tell of thy deeds? ah shall it come that I may blason over all the world thy strains that alone challenge the buskin of Sophocles? From thee I began; for thee will I end: take the songs that were essayed at thy commands, and let this ivy curl among the conqueror's laurel around thy brows.

The chill shadow of night had hardly retreated from the sky, when the dew on the tender grass is sweetest to the flock: Damon, leaning on his smooth olive-staff, thus began:

Rise, Morning Star, and herald in the gracious day, while, beguiled by Love's tyranny, I complain over Nisa the bride, and though it has availed me nothing that the gods were witnesses, yet in this utmost hour call on them as I die.

Begin with me, my flute, the verses of Maenalus. Maenalus ever keeps his vocal forest and talking pines: ever he hears the loves of shepherds, and Pan who of yore would not let the reeds lie idle.

Begin with me, my flute, the verses of Maenalus.

Mopsus gets Nisa: what may we lovers not look for? now will gryphons couple with horses, and in following time shy fallow deer come with the hounds to drink.

Begin with me, my flute, the verses of Maenalus.

Mopsus, cut fresh torches: for thee a wife is led home. Scatter nuts, O bridegroom: for thee the Evening Star leaves Oeta forlorn.

Begin with me, my flute, the verses of Maenalus.

O wedded to thy mate! while thou scornest all the world, and while my pipe and while my she-goats annoy thee, and my shaggy eyebrows and untrimmed beard, nor fanciest thou that any god cares for human things.

Begin with me, my flute, the verses of Maenalus.

In our orchard-close I saw thee, a little girl with her mother—I guided you both—gathering apples wet with dew: the next year after eleven had just received me: I could just reach the brittle branches from the ground. As I saw, how I perished, how the fatal craze swept me away!

Begin with me, my flute, the verses of Maenalus.

Now I know what Love is: on iron flints of Tmaros or Rhodope or the utmost Garamants is he born, no child of our kin or blood.

Begin with me, my flute, the verses of Maenalus.

Fierce Love taught the mother to dabble her hands with her children's blood: cruel thou too, O mother! Crueller the mother or the boy insatiate? insatiate the boy; cruel thou too, O mother!

Begin with me, my flute, the verses of Maenalus.

Now even let the wolf flee unchased before the sheep; let gnarled oaks bear apples of gold: let the alder flower into narcissus, and rich amber ooze from tamarisk bark: yes, let screech-owls vie with swans, let Tityrus be Orpheus, Orpheus in the forest, Arion among the dolphin shoals—

Begin with me, my flute, the verses of Maenalus.

Even let mid-ocean cover all. Farewell, O woodlands! from my watchtower aloft on the hill I will plunge headlong into the waves: keep thou this my last gift as I die.

Cease, O flute, cease now the verses of Maenalus.

Thus Damon: you, maidens of Pieria, tell of Alphesiboeus' reply: we cannot all do everything.

Fetch water forth, and twine the altars here with the soft fillet, and burn resinous twigs and male frankincense, that I may try by magic rites to turn my lover's sense from sanity: nothing is wanting now but the songs.

Draw from the city, my songs, draw Daphnis home.

Songs have might even to draw down the moon from heaven: with songs Circe transformed the crew of Ulysses: by singing the cold snake is burst asunder in the meadows.

Draw from the city, my songs, draw Daphnis home.

Threefold first I twine about thee these diverse triple-hued threads, and thrice round these altars I draw thine image: an odd number is god's delight.

Draw from the city, my songs, draw Daphnis home.

Tie the threefold colours in three knots, Amaryllis, tie them then: and say, 'I tie Venus' bands.'

Draw from the city, my songs, draw Daphnis home.

As this clay stiffens and as this wax softens in one and the selfsame fire, so let Daphnis do for love of me. Sprinkle barley-meal, and kindle the brittle bay-twigs with bitumen. Cruel Daphnis burns me: I burn this bay at Daphnis.

Draw from the city, my songs, draw Daphnis home.

So may Daphnis love, as when the heifer, weary with seeking the steer through woodland and high grove, sinks on the green sedge by a water brook, in misery, and recks not to retire before the falling night: so may love hold him, nor may I care to heal.

Draw from the city, my songs, draw Daphnis home.

This dress he wore of old the traitor left me, dear pledges of himself: which now I even in the doorway, O earth, commit to thee: for these pledges Daphnis is the debt.

Draw from the city, my songs, draw Daphnis home.

These herbs, and these poisons gathered in Pontus, Moeris himself gave me; in Pontus they grow thickest. By their might I have often seen Moeris become a wolf and plunge into the forest, often seen him call up souls from their deep graves, and transplant the harvests to where they were not sown.

Draw from the city, my songs, draw Daphnis home.

Fetch ashes, Amaryllis, out of doors, and fling them across thy head into the running brook: and look not back. With these I will assail Daphnis: nothing cares he for gods, nothing for songs.

Draw from the city, my songs, draw Daphnis home.

See! the embers on the altar have caught with a flickering flame, themselves, of their own accord, while I delay to fetch them. Be it for good! something there is for sure; and Hylax barks in the doorway. May we believe? or do lovers fashion dreams of their own?

Forbear: from the city, forbear now, my songs, Daphnis comes.

ECLOGUE IX.—MOERIS

LYCIDAS—MOERIS

L.—Whither footest thou, Moeris? leads thy way townward?

M.—O Lycidas, we live to have come to this, what we never feared, that an intruder in our little fields should say, These are mine; hence with you, old freeholders! Now crushed and sorrowing, since all goes with Fortune's wheel, these kids (small joy may he have thereof!) we are sending to him.

L.—Surely I had heard that, where the hills begin to retire and lower their ridge in a soft slope, even to the waterside and the old beeches that now moulder atop, your Menalcas had saved all the land by his songs.

M.—You had; and so rumour ran. But songs of ours, Lycidas, have no more power among warring arms than Chaonian doves, as they say, when the eagle comes. Had not a raven from the hollow ilex on my left forewarned me to cut short my young suit as best I could, neither thy Moeris nor Menalcas himself were alive and here.

L.—Alas! can such wickedness come over any one? alas for thee and our comfort in thee, Menalcas, so nearly lost to us! Who would sing the nymphs? who strew the ground with blossoming plants, or train green shade over the springs? or those songs I caught of late from thee on thy way to our darling Amaryllis: Tityrus, while I return, (short is the way,) feed the she-goats; and drive them full-fed to drink, Tityrus; and amid the work, take heed of crossing the he-goat; he strikes with his horn.

M.—Nay these rather, which yet unfinished he sang to Varus: Varus, thy name, if but our Mantua survive, Mantua, ah too near a neighbour to unhappy Cremona, singing swans shall bear aloft to the stars.

L.—So may thy swarms shun yews of Corsica, so may

cytisus pasture swell the udders of thy kine, begin with what thou hast. Me also the maidens of Pieria have made a poet: I also have songs: even me the shepherds call a singer; but I believe them not. For, I think, I utter as yet nothing worthy of Varius or of Cinna, a cackling goose among these swans of song.

M.—So I do, Lycidas, and am thinking over silently with myself if I may avail to remember; and it is no mean song:

Come hither, O Galatea: what sport is among the waves? Here spring glows, here round the streams the ground breaks into many a flower; here the silver-white poplar leans over the cavern and trailing vines weave a covert of shade. Come hither; leave the mad billows to beat on the shore.

L.—How of what I once heard thee singing alone under the clear night? I remember the notes, had I the words sure:

Daphnis, why gaze upward on the ancient risings of the signs? lo the star of Caesar, Dione's child, has advanced, the star whereunder fields should rejoice in corn and the grape gather colour on sunny hills. Engraft thy pear-trees, Daphnis; thy children's children shall pluck their fruit.

M.—Time wastes all things, the mind too: often I remember how in boyhood I outwore long sunlit days in singing: now I have forgotten so many a song: Moeris is losing his voice too; wolves have caught first sight of Moeris; but yet Menalcas will repeat them to thee oft enough.

L.—Thy talking prolongs our desire: and now, see, all the mere is smooth and still, and all the windy murmur of the breeze, look, is sunk away. Just from this point is half our road, for Bianor's tomb begins to show: here, where rustics strip the thick-leaved sprays, here, Moeris, let us sing; here set down thy kids; for all that, we shall reach the town. Or if we fear lest night ere then gather to rain, we may go singing all the way; so the road wearies the less: that we may go singing, I will lighten thee of this bundle.

M.—Cease thou further, O boy, and let us do our present business: when he is come himself, we will sing his songs better then.

ECLOGUE X.—GALLUS

THIS last labour, Arethusa, grant to me: verses must be sung for my Gallus, few, yet such as Lycoris' self may read: who would deny verses to Gallus? So, when thou slidest under Sicilian waters, may bitter Doris not mingle her wave with thine. Begin; let us tell of Gallus' weary loves, while the flat-nosed she-goats crop the tender bushes. We sing not to deaf ears; the forests repeat all.

What woods or what lawns held you, Naiad girls, while Gallus pined in love's tyranny? for not on Parnassus, for not on Pindus' slopes did you linger, nor by Aonian Aganippe. Him even laurels, even tamarisks wept: him, as he lay beneath a lonely cliff, even Maenalus with his crown of pines wept, and the rocks of chill Lycaeus. The sheep too stand round; nor are they ashamed of us, nor be thou ashamed of thy flock, O divine poet: even fair Adonis pastured sheep by the river. Came too the keeper of the sheep: slow-pacing came the swineherds: dripping from the winter acorns Menalcas came. All ask, Whence this love of thine? Apollo came: Gallus, why this madness? he said: thy love Lycoris amid the snows and amid the rough camp has followed another. Came too Silvanus with rustic bravery on his head, shaking his blossomed fennels and large lilies. Pan god of Arcady came, whom our eyes have seen, red with blood-stained elderberries and vermilion. Shall there be a limit? he said: Love recks not aught of this. Neither is cruel Love satiated with tears, nor the grasses with the rills, nor bees with cytisus, nor she-goats with leafage. But sadly he: Yet you will be singing, O Arcadians, to your hills of this: alone Arcadians are skilled to sing. Ah how softly then may my ashes rest, if your pipe once may tell of my loves. And would God I had been one of you, and yours been the flock I kept or the ripe grapes of my vintage! surely Phyllis, were it so, or Amyntas, or whosoever were my passion (what then, if Amyntas be swarthy? violets too are dark and dark are hyacinths) would lie with me among the osiers beneath a trailing vine: Phyllis would pluck me coronals, Amyntas would sing. Here are chill springs, here soft meadows, O Lycoris: here the woodland: here with wasting time I too at thy side would waste away. Now a mad passion holds thee down among the hard War-god's arms, encircled by weapons and confronting foes. Thou, far from home (let me not quite believe it!) alone, without me, ah cruel, lookest on Alpine snows and the frosts of the Rhine. Ah may the frosts not hurt thee! Ah may the rough ice not cut thy delicate feet! I will be gone, and the songs I fashioned in Chalcidian verse I will set to the Sicilian shepherd's reed: resolved in the woods among the wild beasts' dens, to embrace endurance, and to cut my loves on the tender trees; with their growth you, O loves, will grow. Meanwhile I will range Maenalus amid the rout of Nymphs, or hunt the keen wild boar; no rigour of cold shall forbid me to encircle Parthenian glades with my hounds. Even now I think I pass among rocks and echoing groves, and delight to speed the Cydonian arrows from a Parthian bow: as if this could be healing of our madness, or that God could learn to soften at mortal griefs! Now neither Hamadryads once more nor songs themselves delight us: once more, O forests, yourselves retire. Him toils of ours cannot change; neither if in the mid-frosts we drink of Hebrus and abide the rainy winter among Sithonian snows; nor if while the dying bark scorches on the lofty elm, we guide Aethiopian sheep beneath the tropic. Love conquers all: let us too yield to Love.

This shall suffice, goddesses of Pieria, that your poet has sung while he sate and wove a basket of slim mallow shoots: you will make this precious for Gallus: for Gallus, love of whom grows in me as fast every hour as the green alder shoots up when spring is young. Let us arise; the shade is wont to be heavy on singers: the juniper shade is heavy: shade too hurts the corn. Go home full-fed, the Evening Star comes, go, my she-goats.

THE GEORGICS

THE GEORGICS
BOOK FIRST

WHAT makes the cornfields glad; beneath what star it befits to upturn the ground, Maecenas, and clasp the vine to her elm; the tending of oxen and the charge of the keeper of a flock; and all the skill of thrifty bees; of this will I begin to sing. You, O bright splendours of the world, who lead on the rolling year through heaven; Liber and gracious Ceres, if by your gift Earth exchanged Chaonian acorns for the swelling ear, and tempered her draughts of Achelous with the discovered grape; and you, O Fauns, guardian presences of the country, trip it together, Fauns and Dryad girls; of your gifts I sing. And thou, Neptune, at whose mighty trident-stroke Earth first bore the neighing steed; and thou, O forester, whose three hundred snow-white bullocks crop the rich Cean brakes; even thou, leaving thy native woodland and thy Lycean lawns, Pan of Tegea, shepherd of the flock, so thou love thy Maenalus, be gracious and come; and Minerva inventress of the olive, and thou, boy teacher of the crooked plough, and Silvanus carrying thy slim cypress uprooted; gods and goddesses all who keep the fields in your care, or who feed the fresh plants from no sown seed, or who send down on the crops plentiful rain from heaven; and thou, whatsoever place thou art soon to hold in the gods' consistory, whether thou wilt look on cities and have earth in keeping, and the vast world receive thee as fosterer of harvests and sovereign of seasons, and wreathe thy brows with thy mother's myrtle; or whether thou come as god of the infinite sea, and thy deity only be adored of sailors, to thee utmost Thule be tributary, thy hand Tethys purchase for her daughter with dower of all her waves; or whether thou set thyself as a new sign among the lingering months, where space opens between Erigone and the following Claws, while before thee the blazing Scorpion draws in his arms, and retreats from more than the allotted space of heaven; whatso thou wilt be—for neither does hell hope thy reign, nor may so dread a desire of reigning ever be thine, though Greece be enrapt in her Elysian plains, and Proserpine care not to follow the mother who calls her back: grant a fair passage, and favour my bold endeavour, and with me pitying the country folk who know not of the way, advance, and even now learn to be called on in prayer.

In early spring, when chilly moisture trickles from the hoar hills and the crumbling clod thaws in the west wind, even then would I have the bull begin to groan over the deep-driven plough and the share glitter with polish of the furrow. That field at last replies to the greedy farmer's prayers, which has twice felt the sun, twice the frost; that bursts his granaries with overflowing harvests.

And ere yet our iron cleaves the unknown plain, be our care first to learn the winds, and the sky's shifting mood, and the ground's native nurture and dress, and what each quarter will bear and what each will reject. Here corn, there grapes come more prosperously; yonder the tree drops her seedlings, and unbidden grasses kindle into green. Seest thou not how Tmolus sends scent of saffron, India ivory, the soft Sabaeans their spice; but the naked Chalybes steel, and Pontus the castor drug, Epirus mares for Elean palms? From of old Nature laid such laws upon certain regions, an everlasting covenant, what time Deucalion of old cast on the unpeopled globe those stones whence the hard race of man was born. Come therefore, from the first months of the year straightway let the strong bulls upturn the rich floor of earth, and the full strength of summer suns bake the flat clods to dust. But if the land be not fertile, it will serve to ridge it by shallow furrows hard on Arcturus' rising; there, lest weeds choke the corn's luxuriance; here, lest scant moisture leave a barren waste of sand.

In turn likewise shalt thou let the stubbles lie fallow, and the idle field crust over unstirred; or else there under changed skies sow golden spelt, where before thou hadst reaped the pea with wealth of rattling pods, or the tiny vetch crop, or the brittle stalks and rustling underwood of the bitter lupin. For the field is drained by flax-harvest and wheat-harvest, drained by the slumber-steeped poppy of Lethe, but yet rotation lightens the labour; only scorn not to soak the dry soil with fattening dung, nor to scatter grimy ashes over the exhausted lands. Thus too the fields find rest in change of crop; nor meanwhile are thanks lost on unploughed land. Often likewise it is well to burn barren fields and consume the light stubble in crackling flame: whether that earth thence conceives secret strength and sustenance, or all her evil is melted away and her useless moisture sweats out in the fire; or that the heat opens more of these ducts and blind pores that carry her juices to the fresh herbage; or rather hardens and binds her gaping veins against fine rain or the fierce sun's mastery or the frostbite of the searching North.

Great service withal he does the fields who breaks their dull clods with the mattock and drags osier hurdles over them, nor from high Olympus does golden Ceres regard him in vain; or he who, raising ridges along the furrowed plain, again turns his plough to break them across, and labours earth incessantly and makes the fields own his sway.

Pray for dripping midsummers and clear winters, O husbandmen; from winter dust the spelt grows strongest, and the field is glad; never does Mysia triumph in such pride of tillage, or Gargarus himself wonder at his harvests. Why tell of him, who, when the seed is cast, follows close over the field and breaks down the lumps of sticky soil? then guides over the crops chasing runlets from the river; and when the blade is dying on the scorched and feverous field, look! on the brow of the slope he lures the wave from her channel; the falling wave wakens a hoarse chatter among the smooth pebbles, and gushes cool over the parched fields. Why of him, who, lest the stalk sink prone under the heavy ear, grazes down the rankness of the cornfield in the tender blade, when the crop first levels the furrow? or who gathers and drains away the moisture of the marsh with porous gravel, above all if in the doubtful months the floods go out on the river, covering all the broad flats with mud, and leave pools steaming with warm moisture in the hollows.

Nor yet, though labours of men and oxen have so wrought in turning the soil, are the villain goose and Strymonian crane and the bitter-fibred succory unavailing to injure, or the shade to harm. Our Lord himself willed the way of tillage to be hard, and long ago set art to stir the fields, sharpening the wits of man with care, nor suffered his realm to slumber in heavy torpor. Before Jove no tillers made the fields subject; not even might the plain be parted by landmark or boundary line; men gathered to a common store, and unaided and unasked earth bore all things in a fuller plenty. He it was who gave the black snake his venom, and bade wolves ravin and the sea be tossed, who shook the honey from the leaves and took fire away, and stopped the brooks that ran wandering with wine: that so practice and pondering might slowly forge out many an art, might seek the corn-blade in the furrow and strike hidden fire from the veins of flint. Then first rivers felt the hollowed alder, then the sailor gave the stars their number and name, Pleiads and Hyades and the bright Lycaonian Bear. Then was invented the snare to catch game and the treacherous lime-twig, and the ring of dogs round the wide forest-lawn; and even now one whips the wide stream and searches the pool with his casting-net, and another draws his lines dripping from the sea. Then rigid iron and the blade of the shrill saw came—for they of old split wood in clefts with wedges—then arts many in sort; nothing but yielded to unrelenting toil and the hard pressure of poverty. Ceres first instructed mortals to upturn earth with iron, when now acorns and arbute-berries were failing from the sacred forest, and Dodona denied them sustenance. Soon the labour of the cornfield too increased; vile mildew must devour the stalk and the thistle lift over the field his lazy spears: the crop dwindles, a rough forest of clivers and burs advances, and fruitless darnel and barren wild-oats reign over the shining tilth. Nay, except thou wilt harass the weeds with ceaseless mattock, and frighten off the birds with clamour, and thy pruning-hook lop the darkening rustic shades and thy prayers call down the rain, ah! all in vain wilt thou eye the garner pile of another, and allay thine own hunger from the shaken oak in the woodland.

Likewise must be told what are the weapons of the hardy countryfolk, without which can be neither sowing nor springing of harvests: the share first, and the heavy strength of the curved plough, and the slow rolling wagons of our Lady of Eleusis, sledges and harrows and the weary weight of the mattock; withal the slight wicker ware of Celeus, arbutus hurdles, and Iacchus' mystical winnowing-fan. All these thou wilt heedfully provide and lay up long in store, if the divine country keeps her due honour in thine eyes. Early the forest elm is bowed by main force to bend into a share-beam, and takes the shape of the curving plough; to the stock of it are fitted the long eight-foot pole, the two mould-boards, and the double back of the share-head; and the light lime is cut to season for the yoke, and the tall beech for the plough-tail that is to turn the carriage from above and behind, and oak battens are hung over the fire for the smoke to search them through.

I can repeat to thee many a counsel of them of old, if thou shrink not back nor weary to learn of lowly cares. Above all must the threshing-floor be levelled with the ponderous roller, and wrought by hand and cemented with clinging potter's clay, that it may not gather weeds nor crack in the reign of dust, and be playground withal for manifold destroyers. Often the tiny mouse builds his house and makes his granaries underground, or the eyeless mole scoops his cell; and in chinks is found the toad, and all the swarming vermin that are bred in earth; and the weevil, and the ant that fears a destitute old age, plunder the great pile of spelt.

Look thou likewise, when the walnut in the woodland attires herself in wealth of blossom, and bends with scented boughs; if her fruit exceed, the corn will keep pace with it, and abundant threshing come with abundant heat; but if her shade overflow in luxuriance of leaf, vainly will the chaff-laden straw be beaten on the winnowing-floor.

In truth I have seen many a sower steep his seeds and wash them beforehand in black olive-lees, that the fruit in the treacherous pod might be larger and soften quickly even over a little fire: I have seen them, though long chosen and toilsomely approved, still fall off unless the strong hand of man picked the largest year by year: so it is fated that all things run to the worse and fall dropping backwards; even as one who with strain of oarage urges a skiff up stream, if once he slacken his arms, the prone river current sweeps him headlong down.

Likewise must we no less regard the star of Arcturus and the days of the Kids and the gleaming Serpent, than they who sailing homeward over windswept seas adventure the Pontic and the straits by Abydus' oyster-beds. When the Scales make daylight and sleep equal in hours and just halve the globe between light and shadow, set your bulls at work, O men! sow the barley-fields, right into the showery skirts of frost-bound mid-winter: no less is it time to cover in earth the flax-plant and the corn-poppy, and to urge on the belated ploughs while the dry soil allows it, while the clouds hang aloft. In spring beans are sown; then the crumbling furrows receive thee likewise, clover of Media, and the yearly care of the millet crop approaches; when the milkwhite Bull with gilded horns opens the year, and the setting Dogstar retires backwards. But if for wheaten harvest or strong spelt thou wilt work thy ground, and the corn-ear alone is thy desire, first let the Atlantides be at their morning setting and the blazing star of the Cretan Crown sink away, ere thou yield their debt of seed to the furrows, or ere thou hasten to intrust the year's hope to an unwilling earth. Many begin before the setting of Maia; but a harvest of empty stalks mocks their expectation. If indeed thou wilt sow the vetch or the common kidney-bean, nor despite the care of the Pelusiac lentil, the setting Bear-warden will send thee no uncertain sign; begin, and carry thy sowing on to the mid-frost.

To this end the golden sun rules an orbit measured out in certain divisions through the twelvefold star-girdle of the world. Five zones are placed in heaven; whereof one ever reddens in the blazing sun and ever is parched by his fire; and round it right and left sweep the utmost two, bleak, stiff in ice and dark with showers; two between these and the central zone are granted by grace of the gods to weary mortals, and through both a path is drawn where the slant procession of the signs may turn. The world, rising steeply towards Scythia and the Rhipean fortresses, sinks sloping to Libya and the south. This pole of ours is ever uplifted; but the other black Styx and the deep world of ghosts see underneath their feet. Here the enormous Serpent glides forth, wreathing his coils in fashion of a river around and between the two Bears, the Bears that dare not dip under the Ocean floor: there, one saith, either dead night is soundless, and the gloom thickens in night's perpetual pall, or dawn returns from us and leads back the day; and when dayspring touches us with his panting horses' breath, there crimson Hesperus kindles his lamp at evenfall. Hence can we foreknow the changeful sky's seasons, hence the day of harvest and the time of sowing, and when it befits to drive our oars through the treacherous sparkling sea, when to launch armed fleets, or in due season lay low the woodland pine.

Neither in vain do we mark the signs in their dawning and decease, and the four seasons that make equal division of the year. Whensoever chilly rain keeps the husbandman indoors, many a thing, which must else be hurried through in clear weather afterward, may be done at leisure; the ploughman beats out the stubborn point of his blunted share; one hollows troughs out of the tree; one marks the stamp on the flock or the numbers on the grain-sacks; others sharpen stakes and forked poles, and sort Amerian bands for the trailing vine. Now let the basket be lightly woven of briar-rods, now parch corn over the fire and pound it in the stone. Nay, and even on holydays some works are right and lawful; no scruple forbids to guide forth the rivulet, to fence off the cornfield, to set snares for birds, to burn brambles, and to plunge the bleating flock in the healthful stream: often the driver loads his slow-paced donkey's sides with oil or cheap apples, and returning, carries a dressed mill-stone or a lump of black pitch back with him from the town.

The moon's self ordains the days in their several order to be diverse in luck of labour. Shun the fifth, birthday of pale Orcus and the Eumenides; on it earth bore that accursed brood, Coeus and Iapetus and fell Typhoeus, and the brothers that leagued to pluck down heaven. Thrice they essayed to plant Ossa on Pelion, ay, and roll up leafy Olympus upon Ossa: thrice our Lord smote asunder the piled mountains with his thunderbolt. The seventeenth is lucky for setting the vine, for catching and breaking oxen, for stringing loops in the loom: the ninth favours runaways, but thwarts the thief.

Many a thing even makes better way in the chill of night, or when at sundawn earth is dewy under the orient star. By night the light stubbles, by night the parched meadows are better mown; clinging moisture fails not through the night. And one I know keeps awake late by the winter firelight, and points torchwood with sharp steel: meanwhile, lightening her long toil with song, the wife runs her ringing comb through the web, or boils down the sweet liquid must over the fire and skims with leaves the wave of the bubbling copper. But ruddy corn is cut in noon-day heat, and in noon-day heat the parched grain is trodden on the threshing-floor.

Strip to plough, strip to sow; winter is the farmer's holiday, and the husbandmen feast on their stores all through the frozen time, and spread the banquet among themselves in mirthful round. Merry winter bids the guest and lightens the heart; even as when laden keels at last touch their haven, and the rejoicing mariners hang garlands on the stern. But then nevertheless is the season to strip acorns from the oak and berries of the laurel, the olive and the blood-red myrtle: then to set snares for the crane and nets for the stag, and to hunt the long-eared hare: then to strike down the fallow-deer with the whirling stroke of the hempen Balearic sling, while snow lies deep, while ice blocks the rivers.

Why tell of autumnal storms and stars, and when now the day is briefer and the summer softer, what watches men must keep? or when showerful spring pours down, when the spiky harvest even now ripples on the plains, and when the green blade swells with her milky grain? Often have I seen, when the husbandman was marching in his reapers to the golden fields and just cutting the slim-stalked barley, how all the winds, clashing in battle, would tear right from the roots and fling high whole breadths of heavy corn; in so black a gust would the storm sweep light blade and flying straw away. Often likewise the waters of heaven descend in infinite armies, and clouds charged from the deep thicken into foul weather black with thundershowers: the sky pours sheer down and washes away the glad crops and labours of the oxen with flooding rain; ditches fill, and river channels swell roaring, and the narrow seas seethe and smoke. Our Lord himself in the midnight of the storm-clouds wields the flashing bolts in his right hand: at their shock ancient Earth trembles, wild beasts slink away, and mortal hearts throughout the nations bow low in terror: he hurls down his flaming shaft on Athos or Rhodope or the Ceraunian heights; the south winds blow fiercer and the rain streams drenching down, and the rushing wind wails over forest and shore.

Fearing this, regard thou heaven in his months and seasons, whither the chill star of Saturn withdraws, to what circles in the sky the Cyllenian wanderer turns his fire. Above all, worship thou the gods, and bring great Ceres her yearly offerings, doing sacrifice on the springing grass close on the verge of dying winter, when now spring skies are clear. Then lambs are fat, and then wines mellowest, then sleep is sweet where the shade thickens on the hill. To Ceres let all thy rustic folk do service; to her wash thou the honeycomb with milk and soft wine, and for luck let the victim thrice encircle the springing crops and all the band of thy fellows keep it joyful company, and loudly call Ceres into the homestead: neither let any lay sickle to the ripe ears till in Ceres' praise, his brows wreathed with twisted oak, he move in rude dances and chant her hymn.

And these things that we might avail to learn by sure tokens, the heats and the rains and the winds that bring cold weather, our Lord himself hath ordained what the moon in her month should foreshadow, at what sign the south wind should drop, what husbandmen should often mark and keep their cattle nearer the farmyard. Straightway when gales are gathering, either the seaways begin to shudder and heave, and a dry roaring to be heard on the mountain heights, or the far-echoing beaches to stir, and a rustling swell through the woodland. Even in that hour the rude surge spares not the curving hull, when gulls fly swiftly back from mid ocean and press screaming shoreward, or when sea-coot play on dry land, and the heron leaves his home in the marshes and soars high above the mist. Often likewise when a gale is toward wilt thou see shooting stars glide down the sky, and through the darkness of night long trails of flame glimmer in their track: often light chaff and fallen leaves flutter in air, or floating feathers dance on the water's surface. But when it lightens from the fierce northern regions, and when Eurus and Zephyrus thunder through their hall, the whole countryside is afloat with brimming ditches, and every mariner at sea furls his soaking sails. Never is rain on us unwarned: either as it gathers in the valley bottoms the crane soars high in flight before it; or the heifer gazing up into the sky snuffs the breeze with wide-opened nostril, or the shrill swallow darts circling about the pond, and the frogs in the mire intone their old complaint. Often likewise the ant carries forth her eggs from her secret chambers along her narrow trodden path, and a vast rainbow drinks, and leaving their feeding-ground in long column armies of rooks crowd with flapping wings. Then seafowl many in sort, and birds that search the fresh pools round the Asian meadows of Cayster, eagerly splash showers of spray over their shoulders, and thou mayest see them now ducking in the channels, now running up into the waves, and wantoning in their bath with vain desire. Then the villain raven calls full-voiced for rain, and stalks along the dry sand in solitary state. Nor even to girls who ply their spinning nightlong is the storm unknown, while they see the oil sputter, and spongy mould gather on the blazing lamp.

And even thus sunlight after rain and cloudless clearness mayest thou foresee and know by sure tokens. For then neither is the keen edge of the starlight dulled to view, nor does the moon rise flushed by her brother's rays, nor are thin woolly fleeces borne across the sky; neither do kingfishers beloved of Thetis spread their plumage to the sun's warmth upon the shore, nor unclean swine remember to shake out their litter and toss it with their snout. But the mists gather lower down and settle on the flats, and, constant to sunset, the night-owl from the roof-top keeps vainly calling through the dark. Aloft in the liquid sky Nisus is in sight and Scylla pays the debt of that purple hair: wheresoever her pinions cleave the thin air in flight, lo, hostile, fierce, loud-swooping down the wind, Nisus is upon her; where Nisus mounts into the wind, her hurrying pinions cleave the thin air in flight. Therewithal rooks repeat three or four times a clear thin-throated cry, and often where they sit aloft, happy in some strange unwonted delight, chatter together among the leaves, glad when rains are over to look to their little brood and darling nests once again; not, to my thinking, that their instinct is divine or their dower of fate a larger foresight into nature: but when the weather veers about and the saturated air shifts, and under dripping skies of the south what was rare but now condenses and what was dense expands, their temper changes its fashion, and other motions stir within their breasts than stirred while the clouds drove on before the wind; hence the birds make such chorus in the fields, and the cattle are glad, and the rooks caw in exultation.

If indeed thou wilt regard the hastening sun and the moon's ordered sequences, never will an hour of the morrow deceive thee, nor wilt thou be taken in the wiles of a cloudless night. When the moon first gathers her returning fires, if she clasp a dark mist in her dim crescent, drenching rain will be in store for husbandman and seafarer; but if a maiden flush suffuse her face, wind is coming: wind always flushes the gold of the moon: while if at her fourth rising (for that is surest of warrant) she travel through the sky with clear sharp-cut horns, both that whole day and those that shall dawn after it till the month be done will be rainless and windless, and sailors preserved will pay their vows on the shore to Glaucus and Panope and Melicertes son of Ino.

The sun likewise, both in his arising and when he sinks into the waves, will issue signs; most sure are the signs that attend the sun, yielded with morning or at the ascending of the stars. When at dayspring he is dappled with spots and sunk in a mist, and his orbed centre retires, mistrust thou of showers; for a gale is bearing hard from seaward, ill-ominous for trees and crops and herds. Either when towards daybreak spreading shafts struggle out between thick clouds, or when Dawn springs pale from Tithonus' saffron bed, alas! weak defence will the vine-tendril be then to the mellow cluster, so heavily the rough hail dances rattling on the roofs. This likewise, when he has run his race and is now sinking from the sky, will be of yet more service to remember; for often we see shifting colours fluctuate on his face; green presages rain, flame-colour east winds; but if spots begin to mingle with fiery red, then wilt thou see all a single riot of wind and storm-clouds; not on such a night at any persuasion would I voyage through the deep or part moorings from land. But if his circle be bright alike when he brings the day and buries the day he brought, vain will be thy terror of rain-clouds, and thou shalt discern the forests weaving in a clear wind from the north.

Lastly, what burden evenfall carries, whence the wind chases clear the clouds, what the dripping South broods over, the sun will signify to thee; who shall dare to call the sun untrue? He likewise often warns of the imminence of dim alarms, of treachery and the gathering of hidden wars; he likewise had pity on Rome at Caesar's decease, when he veiled his shining face in dim rusty red, and an evil age dreaded eternal night. Yet at that season earth too and the plains of sea, and unclean dogs and ominous birds gave presage. How often did we see Etna flooding the Cyclopean fields with the torrent bursting from her furnaces, and rolling forth balls of flame and molten rocks! Germany heard the clash of armour fill the sky; the Alps quaked with unwonted shocks. Moreover a voice was heard of many among silent groves, crying aloud, and phantoms pallid in wonderful wise were seen when night was dim; and cattle spoke, a monstrous thing: rivers stop and earth yawns; and ivory sheds tears of mourning and bronzes sweat in the temples. Eridanus, king of rivers, whirled whole forests away in the wash of his raging eddies, and swept herds and stalls together all across the plains. Neither at that same time did boding filaments ever cease to show themselves in disastrous victims, or blood to ooze from wells, and high cities to echo night-long with howling of wolves. Never elsewhere did more lightnings fall from clear skies, or ghastly comets so often blaze. Therefore a second time Philippi saw Roman lines meet in shock of equal arms, and our lords forbade not that Emathia and the broad plains of Haemus should twice be fattened with our blood. Surely a time too shall come when in those borders the husbandman, as his crooked plough labours the soil, will find spears eaten away with scaling rust, or strike on empty helms with his heavy mattock, and marvel at mighty bones dug up from their tombs. Gods of our fathers, of our country, and thou Romulus, and Vesta, mother who keepest Tuscan Tiber and the Roman Palatine, forbid not at least that this our prince may succour a ruined world! Long enough already has our life-blood recompensed Laomedon's perjury at Troy; long already the heavenly palace, O Caesar, grudges thee to us, and murmurs that thou shouldst care for human triumphs, where right and wrong are confounded, where all these wars cover the world, where wickedness is so manifold and the plough's meed of honour is gone; the fields thicken with weeds, for the tillers are marched away, and bent sickles are forged into the stiff swordblade: here the Euphrates, there Germany heaves with war; neighbouring cities rush into arms, one against another over broken laws: the merciless War-God rages through all the world: even as when chariots bursting from their barriers swerve out on the course, and, vainly tugging at the curb, the driver is swept on by his horses, and the car hearkens not to the rein.

BOOK SECOND

Thus far of tillage of the fields and stars in the sky: now of thee, Bacchus, will I sing, and with thee no less of woodland copses and the slowly waxing olive growth. Hither, lord of the winepress; here all is full of thy bounties, for thee the field flowers, heavy with tendrils of autumn, and the brimming vintage foams; come hither, lord of the winepress, by my side pluck off thy buskins and dye thy bared ankles in the new wine.

First of all, Nature is manifold in the birth of trees. For some with no human urging come at their own will and spread wide by plain and winding river, like the soft osier and tough broom, the poplar, and pale willow-beds with their silvery leafage; and some rise from seed they drop, like the towering chestnuts, and Jove's winter-oak, lordliest of leafage in the woodland, and those oaks that Greece holds oracular. Others, like the elm and cherry, multiply from the root in serried undergrowth; and the tiny bay-tree on Parnassus springs beneath her mother's vast shade. These ways are of Nature's ancient gift; in these wear their green all the tribes of forest and underwood and sacred grove.

Others there are, which experience has found out for itself on the way. One tears suckers from their mother's tender stem and sets them in trenches; one plunges in the soil stocks and cross-cleft billets and sharpened stakes from the core: and some forest trees await the layer's pinned arch and slips alive in their parent earth: others need a root in nowise, and the pruner doubts not to commit the topmost twigs to earth's keeping. Nay, and from the dry wood of her sawn trunk, wonderful to tell! the olive pushes forth a root. And often we see the boughs of one turn lightly into another's, and the changed pear-tree bear her grafted apples, and plums redden on the stony cornel.

Wherefore come, O husbandmen, learn the proper training of each after their kinds, and soften the wild fruits by your nurture, nor let earth lie idle: good it is to plant Ismarus thick with vines and clothe mighty Taburnus in olive. And be thou nigh, to fulfil at my side the task begun, Maecenas our honour, by just due the chiefest sharer in our fame, and give thy flying sails to the spacious sea. I ask not to embrace it all in these my verses; no, though I had an hundred tongues and an hundred mouths, and my voice were iron: come, and skirt close by the shore's edge. The earth is in hand: I will not keep thee here in mazes and long-drawn preludes of fabulous song.

Plants that rise unbidden into the borders of day are unfruitful indeed, but lusty and strong of growth, for native force is in the soil. Yet even these, if one graft them or transplant them into trenched mould, will outgrow their savagery, and under ceaseless training will soon follow thy call to whatsoever ways thou wilt. Even the barren sucker that springs from the stem's foot will do likewise, if set in rank over a clean plot; now the mother's deep-foliaged boughs overshadow it, and steal the produce of its growth, and stifle its fruitfulness. Once more, the tree that rises from shed seed is slow in coming, and will yield shade to thy children's children on a later day; apples dwindle, forgetting their former savour, and ragged clusters hang for birds to plunder from the vine.

Truth to say, on all must labour be lavished, and all be forced into the furrow and tamed at a great price. But olive-trees answer better in truncheons, vines in layers, myrtles of Paphos in the solid wood; and from slips are born the hardwood hazel and the mighty ash, and the shady tree of Hercules' garland, and the acorns of our lord of Chaonia; in like wise is born the tall palm and the fir that shall look on the perils of the sea: while by grafting the rough arbutus yields the walnut, and barren planes carry sturdy apple-boughs, chestnuts a beech-crop; and the mountain-ash silvers with white pear-blossom, and swine crush acorns beneath the elm.

Nor is there one single way of grafting and of budding. For where the buds push out from amid the bark and burst their delicate sheaths, there, just on the knot, a narrow slit is made; in it they imbed the shoot of an alien tree, and teach it to grow into the wet sapwood. Or again, smooth trunks are cleft open and a way driven deep by wedges into the core, then grafts of the fruit-tree let in; nor long time, and the tree climbs skyward in breadth of prosperous boughs, and marvels in strange leafage and fruits not her own.

Furthermore, not single in kind are either strong elms or willow and lotus, or cypresses of Ida; nor in a single likeness is born the fat olive, the ball and the spindle-shaped, and the pausian with bitter berry, nor apples in Alcinous' orchards; nor does the same twig bear Crustumian and Syrian pears and the heavy wardens. Not the same is the vintage that trails from trees of ours, and that which Lesbos gathers from the branch of Methymna: there are Thasian and there are pale Mareotic vines, these meet for a rich, those for a lighter soil; and the Psithian more serviceable for raisin-wine, and the thin Lagean that in her day will trip the feet and tie the tongue, and the purple and the earlier grape; and in what verse may I tell of thee, O Rhaetian? yet not even so vie thou with Falernian vaults. Likewise there are Aminaean vines, theirs the soundest wine of all, for which the Tmolian and even the royal Phanaean make room; and the lesser Argitis, that none other may rival whether in abundant flow or in lasting through length of years. Let me not pass thee by, O Rhodian, well-beloved of gods and festal boards, and Bumastus with thy swelling clusters. But there is no tale of the manifold kinds or of the names they bear, nor truly were the tale worth reckoning out; whoso will know it, let him choose to learn likewise how many grains of sand eddy in the west wind on the plain of Libya, or to count, when the violent East sweeps down upon the ships, how many waves come shoreward across Ionian seas.

Nor indeed can all soils bear all things. By riversides willows grow, and alders in thick swamps, barren mountain-ashes on rocky hills; on the seashore myrtle thickets flourish best; and the god of the vine loves open slopes as yew trees do the freezing north. Look too, where the ends of the earth obey men's tillage, on the Arabian dwellings of the East and the painted Gelonian; so diverse are the native lands of trees. Alone India bears black ebony, alone the Sabaeans have their rod of spice. Why should I rehearse to thee the scented wood that drips with balm, and the clusters of the evergreen thorn? why those Aethiopian forests silvered with a soft fleece, or how Chinese comb off leaves their delicate down? or the groves which India wears nearing Ocean in the world's utmost recesses, where no arrow-shot can ever win through air up to the tree-top; and truly these tribes are not slack when they handle the quiver. Media bears the sour juices and lingering savour of the citron, than which naught is more sovereign, if ever a cruel step-mother has drugged the cup with mingled herbs and baleful charms, to arrive for succour and expel the black poison from the limbs. The tree is large, and most like a laurel to view, and were a laurel but for the difference of wide-wafted fragrance; the leaves drop not in any wind, the flower clings close as may be; with it the Medes anoint their faces and perfume their breath, and cure the pantings of old age.

But neither those Median forests where earth is richest, nor fair Ganges and Hermus turbid with gold, may vie with the praise of Italy; not Bactra nor Ind, or all Panchaia with her wealth of spicy sands. This land of ours no bulls with fire-breathing nostrils have upturned where the monstrous dragon's teeth were sown, no harvest of men has bristled up with helms and serried spears; but heavy cornfields and Massic juice of wine fill it all, olives and shining herds hold it in keeping. Hence the war-horse issues stately on the plain; hence thy white flocks, Clitumnus, and the lordly victim bull, often bathed in thy holy stream, lead on Roman triumphs to the gods' temples. Here is perpetual spring and summer in months not her own; twice the cattle breed, twice the apple tree yields her service. But the raging tigress is not there or the fierce lion-brood, nor does monkshood deceive the wretched gatherer, nor the scaly serpent dart in huge coils over the ground or gather so long a train of spires. Add thereto all her illustrious cities and the labours wrought in her, all her towns piled high by men's hands on their sheer rocks, and her rivers that glide beneath immemorial walls. Or shall I tell of the seas that wash above her and below? or her great lakes, thee, lordly Larius, and thee, Benacus, heaving with billows and roar as of the sea? or tell of her harbours, of the barriers set upon the Lucrine and the thunder of the indignant sea where the Julian wave echoes afar in the tideway, and the Tyrrhene surge pours into the channels of Avernus? She it is likewise who unlocks from her veins streams of silver and ore of brass, and flows with abundant gold: she who rears a valiant race of men, the Marsian and the Sabellian stock, the Ligurian trained in hardship and the Volscian spearmen; she the Decii, the Marii, and the mighty Camilli, the seed of Scipio stern in war, and thee, princely Caesar, who even now victorious in Asia's utmost borders does keep aloof the unwarlike Indian from the towers of Rome. Hail, mighty mother of harvests, O land of Saturn, mighty of men: for thee I tread among the glories and arts of old, and dare to unseal these holy springs, making the song of Ascra echo through the Roman towns.

Now, for a space, of the tempers of the fields, the strength of each, and the colour, and the native power of fruit-bearing. First, stubborn soils and ungracious hills, fields of lean marl and pebbly brushwood, welcome the long-lived olive groves of Pallas; for sign thereof, in this same region the oleaster springs abundant, and strews the fields with her wild berries. But fat land glad with sweet moisture, and flats thick with herbage and bounteous in richness, such as many a time we may descry in the cup of a mountain valley (for hither streams trickle from the cliff-tops and draw down their rich mud), and the southern upland that feeds the fern, hateful to crooked ploughs; this one day will yield thee vines excelling in strength and flowing with wealth of wine, this is fertile of the grape, this of such juice as we pour in offering from cups of gold, when the sleek Etruscan blows his ivory flute by the altars and we offer the steaming entrails on bulged platters. But he whose desire is rather the keeping of cattle and calves, or the breed of sheep or she-goats that strip the plantations, let him seek the lawns and distances of rich Tarentum, or such a plain as unhappy Mantua lost, where snow-white swans feed in the weedy river: not clear springs nor grass will fail the flocks, and how much soever the cattle crop through the long days, as much the chilly dew of a brief night will restore. Land that is black and rich under the share's pressure, and crumbling-soiled (for this it is that we imitate by ploughing) is always the best for corn: from no other harvest floor shalt thou discern the slow oxen bring thy wagons oftener home: or where the angry ploughman has carted the forest-trees away, and levelled the copses that lay idle many a year, and rooted clean out the birds' ancient homes; they spring skyward from their abandoned nests, but the tangled field gleams behind the driven share. For in truth the starved gravel of the hill-country scarce serves the bees with dwarf spurge and rosemary; and scaling tufa and chalk tunnelled by black-scaled snakes call no other land their like to furnish dainty food and yield winding retreats for serpents. Such land as exhales thin mist and flitting smoke, and drinks in and drains away the wet at will, such as is evergreen in clothing of native grass, and mars not iron with a scurf of salt rust, this will garland thine elms with laughing vines, this is fruitful of oil, this wilt thou prove in tillage gracious to the flock and yielding under the crooked share. Such is the tilth of wealthy Capua and the coast that borders the Vesuvian ridge, and where Clanius encroaches on desolate Acerrae.

Now I will tell in what wise thou mayest know each from each. If thou must know whether it be loose or compact beyond the wont (since the one is good for corn, the other for Bacchus, for the corn-goddess where more compact, where loosest for the wine-god), first shalt thou choose a spot by eye, and bid a pit be sunk deep in the solid ground, and again replace in it all the soil, and level the earth atop with thy feet. If earth is lacking, loose will be the plot and fitter for flocks and gracious vines; but if it refuses to return whence it came, and soil is over when the trenches are full, that land is solid; look for sticky clods and lumpy ridges, and furrow the ground with thy strongest oxen. Salt land moreover, and sour so-called—unfruitful for corn it is and no ploughing softens it, nor does the grape keep her race nor orchard-fruits their name therein—will offer such proof as this: pluck thou down from the smoky rafters close-plaited wicker-baskets and strainers of wine-presses; herein let that evil soil and sweet spring-water be filled and trodden; all the water will be squeezed out, yes, and large drops trickle through the wicker-work; but the savour will give plain token, and its bitterness felt will writhe the taster's displeased face. Again, what land is fat we learn briefly in this wise: when tossed from hand to hand it never crumbles, but grows sticky like pitch on the fingers in the handling. Wet ground nurtures a taller herbage, and the native growth is ranker than is right. Ah, may mine be not thus over-fertile, nor show itself too lusty in the early blade! Heavy soil betrays itself without words by weight, light likewise; thine eyes will at first glance know the black, and the several colour of each. But to search out cruel cold is difficult: only that sometimes pitch-pines and baleful yews are there, or the dark ivy spreads her creepers.

Which things regarded, remember long time first to bake thy land in the sun and cleave the broad hillsides with thy trenches, first to lay bare the upturned clods to the North, ere thou plant in the glad stock of the vine. Fields of crumbling soil are the best; for that winds and icy frosts provide, and the sturdy delver that shakes and stirs the acres. But men who will let nothing escape their vigilance seek out beforehand a bed where the seedling tree may have her early training, like to that whither thereafter it shall be borne and set in the row, lest a sudden change of mother estrange the plant. Nay, and they score on the bark the quarters of the sky, to replace in each as it stood the face whereon it bore the ardours of the South, the back it turned towards the Pole; so strong is the habit of infancy.

Whether hill or flat be the better for thy vine-setting, inquire beforehand. If thou wilt rule thy plots in a rich plain, plant thickly; thickly set, the vine is no less bounteous in bearing; but if on the sloping soil of knolls or on couchant hills, give the ranks larger room; yet no less let every alley where the trees are set be drawn square and true to line: as often in pomp of war, when a legion deploys in long line of cohorts and draws up from column on the open plain, and the ranks are straightened and all the earth surges wide with sparkle of brass, nor yet do they close in grim conflict, but the War-god wanders wavering amid their arms. Let equal space of passage be measured every way; not merely that the view may regale a vacant mind, but since none otherwise will earth supply equal strength to all, nor clear space be left for the outstretching boughs.

Haply too thou mayest inquire of the cuttings for thy trenches. The vine I would dare to intrust to ever so slender a furrow: the tree is sunk deeper and right into the earth; the winter-oak beyond all, who, as high as her top scales the air skyward, strikes at root as deep to hell: therefore not storms nor blasts nor rains uproot her; she abides unstirred, and outlives many children's children, and sees roll by her many generations of men; and stretching wide to right and left her strong boughs and arms, uprears the mass of her own enfolding shade.

Neither let thy vineyards slope to the setting sun; neither plant hazel among the vines; neither cut the uppermost vine-switches, or tear away the uppermost shoots from the tree (such is their love of earth); neither plant among them stems of wild olive: for often heedless shepherds drop a spark, which hiding stealthily at first under the resinous bark, fastens on the core, and, darting out among the high sprays, roars loudly skyward; thence pursues its way, and reigns victorious over bough and summit, and wraps all the woodland in flame, and, thickening, streams into the sky in a cloud of pitch-black gloom: above all if a storm falls prone on the forest and the wind fans and spreads the fire. Where this is, the trees have no force left at root, nor can they recover when cut away, nor grow green again from under earth as before; the barren and bitter-leaved oleaster only is left.

Nor let any counsellor how wise soever persuade thee to stir the earth when stiffened under the breath of the North. Then winter keeps the country ice-bound, nor though the seed be scattered lets the frozen root fasten in the ground. Best is the setting of vineyards when with the flush of spring comes that snow-white bird abhorred of long snakes, or hard on the first frost of autumn, when the fiery horses of the sun yet touch not winter, and even now summer passes away. Spring aids woodland leaf and forest tree; in spring earth yearns and cries for the life-giving seed. Then the lord omnipotent of Sky descends in fruitful showers into the lap of his laughing consort, and mingling with her mighty body nourishes all her fruits in might. Then pathless copses ring with warbling birds, and at the appointed days the herds renew their loves; the bountiful land breaks into birth, and the fields unbosom to wavering breezes of the West: everywhere delicate moisture overflows, and the grasses dare in safety to trust themselves to spring suns, nor does the vine-tendril fear gathering gales or sleet driven down the sky by the blustering North, but thrusts forth her buds and uncurls all her leaves. None other to my thinking were the days that shone at the first dawn of the rising world, none other the course they kept; spring was then, spring reigned on the broad earth, and the east wind held back his wintry blasts, when the first-born beasts drank the daylight, and the earthen brood of men reared their head on the firm fields, and the wild creatures were let loose in the forests and the stars in heaven. Neither might things so delicate endure this their toil, except such space of calm passed between the cold and the heat, and earth were cradled by an indulgent sky.

For the rest, what plantations soever thou wilt set over thy fields, scatter fatting dung, and hide it heedfully deep in earth; dig in porous stone or rough shells, for through them rains will trickle and thin vapour ascend, and the plants take courage; and before now have some been found who would load them down with a stone or the weight of a massy tile, this their defence against streaming rains, this when the dogstar brings the heat and the fields gape in cracks for thirst.

The seedlings set, it remains again and again to bank the earth up to the stalks, and swing the stiff hoe, or to work the soil beneath the ploughshare's pressure and wheel thy straining oxen between the vineyard-rows: therewithal to fit together light reeds and shafts of peeled rods, and ashen stakes and strong crutches, in whose strength they may learn to climb, and scorn the winds, and climb from story to story high up the elm.

And while the earlier youth of the fresh foliage grows towards maturity, spare their tenderness; and while the glad shoot springs upward and mounts unchecked into the blue, not yet should it feel the edge of the pruning-knife, but the leaves be broken off and thinned with bent fingers. Thereafter, when now they have shot up and their strong stems enringed the elm, then strip their tresses, then lop their arms; till then they shrink under the steel; then at last keep imperious rule and check the trailing branches.

Likewise must hurdles be woven and all the flock fenced in, specially while the leaf is tender and innocent of toil; since besides rude storms and the tyrant sun, buffaloes from the thickets and restless roe-deer make it their playground, sheep and hungry heifers their pasture. Not so deadly to it is the stiffening chill of hoar-frost, or the whole weight of summer brooding on the parched crags, as the flocks with the poison of their hard teeth, and the indented scar left on the bitten stem. For none other crime is the goat slain to Bacchus on all our altars while the antique plays advance upon the stage, since Theseus' people ordained prizes for inventions among the villages and clustering hamlets, and joyfully amid their cups danced on oiled wine-skins in the soft meadows. And Ausonian settlers likewise, the race sent forth from Troy, disport with rude verses and careless jest, and put on frowning masks of hollow cork, and call on thee, O Bacchus, in joyous song, and to thee hang swinging amulets from the lofty pine. Thus all their vines ripen with abundant increase, and teem in hollow dells and deep lawns and wheresoever the god turns his goodly head. Therefore meetly shall we recite Bacchus' due honour in ancestral hymns, and bear cakes and platters, and led by the horn the victim goat shall stand by the altar, and the fat flesh roast on spits of hazelwood.

Likewise is there that other labour of vine-dressing, which nothing is ever enough to satisfy; for year by year must all the soil thrice and again be loosened, and the mattock everlastingly turned to break the clod, must all the orchard be lightened of his leaf. The circling toil of the husbandman returns even as the year rolls back on itself along the familiar track. And now what time the vineyard sheds her lingering leaves and the icy North scatters the tresses of the forest, even then the active farmer reaches his care into the coming year, and presses on to lop the bared vine and trim it into shape with the crooked tooth of Saturn. Be first to dig the ground, first to wheel away and burn the prunings, and first to carry the vine-poles indoors; be last to gather the vintage. Twice the shade thickens on thy vines, twice weeds clothe the field with thick entanglements; both make hard work; praise great estates, farm a little one. And therewithal the rough shoots of broom are cut in the woodland, and the river-reed on the banks, and the wild osier-bed gives work to keep. Now the vines are tied, now the shrubberies lay by the pruning-knife, now the last vine-dresser sings over his finished plots; yet must the soil be broken and the dust stirred, and the lord of the sky be dreaded for the grapes even as they ripen.

Contrariwise olives grow all untended; they look not for the sickle-shaped knife or the stiff hoe, when once they have struck root on the field and borne the weather: earth herself, when laid open by the crooked fang, yields sap in sufficience and heavy crops following the ploughshare: so shalt thou nurture the fat olive dear to Peace.

Orchard-trees likewise, so soon as they feel strength in their stem and possess their full vigour, climb fast skyward of their own force and needing no aid of ours: no less withal the whole woodland grows heavy with increase, and the untilled haunts of birds flush with blood-red berries; the cytisus is mown, the high forest yields store of firewood, and nightlong the fires are fed and scatter their radiance; and do men doubt to plant and lavish their care? Why should I keep by larger trees? the osier and the low broom, even they yield leafage to the herd or shade to the herdsman, and hedge the crops and pasture the honey-bee. And fain would I gaze on Cytorus billowy with boxwood, or groves of Narycian pine; fain see fields that owe no debt to the mattock nor to any mortal care. Even fruitless forests on a Caucasian summit, which angry east winds perpetually shatter and toss, yield produce after their kind, yield profit of timber, pines for ships, cedar and cypress for dwellings; from one the countryfolk turn spokes for wheels, from one fashion drumheads for wagons and curving keels of ships; withies grow thick on osiers, leaves on elms, but strong spear-shafts on the myrtle and the cornel trusty in battle; the Ituraean yew is bent into bows; therewithal smooth lime and polished boxwood take shape under the lathe or are hollowed out by the sharp chisel; and therewithal the light alder, sent down the Po, swims on the bubbling wave; and therewithal the bees hide their swarms in the hollow bark or the core of a mouldering ilex. What have Bacchus' gifts bestowed of equal renown? Bacchus gives cause for blame likewise; he it was who laid the mad Centaurs low in death, Rhoetus and Pholus, and Hylaeus as he aimed that great flagon at the Lapithae.

Ah too fortunate the husbandmen, did they know their own felicity! on whom far from the clash of arms Earth their most just mistress lavishes from the soil a plenteous sustenance. Though no high proud-portalled house pours forth the vast tide of morning visitors that fill her halls; though they feed no gaze on doors inlaid with lovely tortoise-shell or raiment tricked out with gold or bronzes of Ephyre; though the fleece's whiteness is not stained with Assyrian dye nor the clear olive-oil spoiled for use with cinnamon; but careless quiet and life ignorant of disappointment, wealthy in manifold riches, but the peace of broad lands, caverns and living lakes, and cool pleasures and the lowing of oxen and soft slumbers beneath the tree fail not there; there are the glades and covers of game, and youth hardy in toil and trained to simplicity, divine worship and reverend age; among them Justice set her last footprints as she passed away from earth.

Me indeed first and before all things may the sweet Muses, whose priest I am and whose great love hath smitten me, take to themselves and show me the pathways of the sky, the stars, and the diverse eclipses of the sun and the moon's travails; whence is the earthquake; by what force the seas swell high over their burst barriers and sink back into themselves again; why winter suns so hasten to dip in Ocean, or what hindrance keeps back the lingering nights. But if I may not so attain to this side of nature for the clog of chilly blood about my heart, may the country and the streams that water the valleys content me, and lost to fame let me love stream and woodland. Ah, where the plains spread by Spercheus, and Laconian girls revel on Taygetus! ah for one to lay me in Haemus' cool dells and cover me in immeasurable shade of boughs! Happy he who hath availed to know the causes of things, and hath laid all fears and immitigable Fate and the roar of hungry Acheron under his feet; yet he no less is blessed, who knows the gods of the country, Pan and old Silvanus and the Nymphs' sisterhood. Him fasces of the people or purple of kings sway not, not maddening discord among treacherous brethren, nor the Dacian swarming down from the leagued Danube, not the Roman state or realms destined to decay; nor may pity of the poor or envy of the rich cost him a pang. What fruits the boughs, what the gracious fields bear of their own free will, these he gathers, and sees not the iron of justice or the mad forum and the archives of the people. Others vex blind seaways with their oars, or rush upon the sword, pierce the courts and chambers of kings; one aims destruction at the city and her wretched homes, that he may drink from gems and sleep on Tyrian scarlet; another heaps up wealth and broods over buried gold; one hangs rapt in amaze before the Rostra; one the applause of populace and senate re-echoing again over the theatre carries open-mouthed away: joyfully they steep themselves in blood of their brethren, and exchange for exile the dear thresholds of their homes, and seek a country spread under an alien sun. The husbandman sunders the soil with curving plough; from this is the labour of his year, from this the sustenance of his native land and his little grandchildren, of his herds of oxen and his faithful bullocks; and unceasingly the year lavishes fruit or young of the flock or sheaf of the corn-blade, and loads the furrow and overflows the granary with increase. Winter is come; the Sicyonian berry is crushed in the olive-presses, the swine come home sleek from their acorns, the woodland yields her arbute-clusters, and autumn drops his manifold fruitage, and high up the mellow vintage ripens on the sunny rock. Meanwhile sweet children cling round his kisses, the home abides in sacred purity, the kine droop their milky udders, and on the shining grass fat kids wrestle with confronting horns. Himself keeps holiday, and stretched on the sward where the fire is in the midmost and the company wreathe the wine-bowl, calls on thee, god of the winepress, in libation, and marks an elm for contests of the flying javelin among the keepers of the flock, or they strip their hardy limbs for the rustic wrestling-match. This life the ancient Sabines kept long ago, this Remus and his brother; even thus Etruria waxed mighty, ay, and Rome grew fairest of the world and ringed her sevenfold fortresses with a single wall. Yes, before the sceptre of that Cretan king, before a guilty race slew oxen for the banquet, this life golden Saturn led on earth; nor yet withal had they heard war-trumpets blown, nor yet the hard anvil clink under the sword.

But we have crossed a boundless breadth of plain, and now is time to loosen the necks of our steaming horses.

BOOK THIRD

THEE also, mighty Pales, and thee will we sing, O renowned shepherd of Amphrysus, and you, Lycaean woods and rivers. All else that might have held idle minds fast in song is staled by usage now: who knows not cruel Eurystheus or accursed Busiris' altars? to whom is untold the boy Hylas, and Latona in Delos, and Hippodame, or the hero of the ivory shoulder, the keen horseman Pelops? A path must be adventured where I too may rise from earth and fly triumphing on the lips of men. First will I lead home with me, if life but last, the Muses from their Aonian hill; first, my Mantua, bring thee back the palms of Idume, and build a shrine of marble on the green meadow by the waterside, where broad Mincius wanders in slow windings, and borders his banks with delicate reed. In the midst shall Caesar be my temple's habitant: to him will I, splendid in Tyrian scarlet, drive in triumph by the river an hundred chariots fourfold-yoked; for me all Greece, leaving Alpheus and the groves of Molorchus, shall contend in the foot-race or with the raw hide boxing-glove. Myself, chapleted with stripped leaves of olive, I will bear offerings: even now is it good to lead the fitly ordered processions to the shrines and see the oxen sacrificed, or the stage opening as the scenes swing round, and the inwoven Britons rising on the crimson curtains. On the doors I will fashion in gold and solid ivory the tribes of the Ganges in battle and Quirinus' conquering arms, and here Nile surging in war with swollen flood, and columns rising decked with the bronze of ships; and beside them, vanquished Asian cities and Niphates driven in rout, and the Parthian confident in flight and in his arrows shot backward, and the double trophy torn in fight from a diverse foe, and the nations twice triumphed over from either shore. There too shall stand breathing images in Parian stone, the brood of Assaracus and the names of the nation of Jove's descent, and Tros their ancestor, and the Cynthian founder of Troy: and wretched Envy shall fear the Furies and Cocytus' relentless river, the twisted serpents of Ixion, the awful wheel and the stone that never may scale the steep. Meanwhile follow we the woodland ways and fresh lawns of the wood-nymphs; thine, Maecenas, are no light commands. Without thee my spirit never springs aloft; lo, up! break off dull delay! with ringing cries Cithaeron summons, and Taygetus with his hounds and Epidaurus trainer of steeds, and the call echoes back redoubled from the applauding woods. Yet soon will I gird myself to tell of Caesar's fiery battles, and carry his name's renown through as many years as separate Caesar from Tithonus' primal birth.

Whoso either breeds horses for the wondered prize of Olympian palm, or strong bullocks for the plough, let his foremost choice be of the mothers of the herd. The best cow is ugly-shapen; her head coarse, her neck of the largest, with dewlaps hanging down from chin to leg; and to her length of flank there is no limit; large of limb and of foot, and with shaggy ears under inward-curving horns. Nor would I quarrel with one marked with spots of white, or one reluctant to the yoke and sometimes hasty with her horn, and almost like a bull to view, and tall all her length, with a tail that sweeps her footprints below her as she moves. The age for just marriage and travail of birth ceases before the tenth, begins after the fourth year. Beyond these, she is neither fit for breeding nor strong for the plough; between them, while the lusty youth of thy flock endures, let loose the males, put thy herds early to breeding, and generation by generation keep up the succession of thy stock. In this poor mortal life the fairest day is ever the first to fly; sickness and melancholy age advance, and toil and hard death's pitilessness sweep us away. Ever will there be some stock that thou wouldst exchange: then ever replace them, and that thou miss not the lost, be beforehand in selecting the young of the herd year by year.

Even in like wise must the breed of horses too be chosen:

only do thou, on such as thou purposest to nurture for the hope of the race, lavish from infancy onward thy foremost pains. From the first a well-bred foal in the fields lifts a higher pace and plants a lighter limb; he dares to advance in front and to try the threatening torrent, and trust the unknown bridge, and starts not at vain noises: his are a high crest and fine head, a short belly and fleshy back, and a breast rippling in proud slopes of muscle. Bays and greys are proper, the worst coloured are white and dun. Moreover, if haply armour clashes near, he may not stand still, he pricks his ears and quivers in all his limbs, and rolls from his nostrils a gathered volume of fiery breath. His mane is thick, and when flung up falls back on the right shoulder: a double ridge runs between his loins, and his hoof of solid horn prints the sod with heavy clatter. Such was that Cyllarus who obeyed Amyclean Pollux' rein, and the two-yoked steeds of Mars chronicled of Grecian poets, and mighty Achilles' team: such too tireless Saturn's self when, shaking the horse-mane free over his neck at his consort's coming, he filled high Pelion with his shrill neighing as he fled.

Even him, when failing either from weight of sickness or dulness of growing years, house out of sight and be not overtender with the faults of age. Age is cold to love, and vainly drags on the ungrateful task, and when the battle is come, as it were a fire blazing without strength among stubble, he rages to no avail. Therefore spirit and youth thou wilt mark beyond all; then his other merits, his parents' breeding, and his own grief at defeat and exultation in victory. Seest thou not when in headlong contest chariots shoot into the racecourse and pour streaming from the barrier, when the young drivers' hopes are at height, and throbbing fear drains their riotous hearts? they ply the curling lash and stoop loose over the rein; the glowing axle flies fiercely on; and now they sink, and now rising high they seem to bound through empty air and mount into the wind: no slackening nor stay; the sand rises in a yellow cloud, and they are wetted by the foam and breath of the pursuers; so great is desire of honour, so great their care for victory. First Erichthonius dared to yoke four steeds to the chariot and stand triumphant rushing above the wheels; the Pelethronian Lapithae mounted on horseback and bequeathed the bridle and the ring, and taught the armed rider to spurn the sod and gather his feet proudly in the canter. For both the task is alike, alike the trainer searches out one in his prime, hot of spirit and fleet of pace, how often soever another have driven the flying foe in rout, and boast Epirus or valiant Mycenae for his country, and trace his line from Neptune's own ancestry.

Which things regarded, they are busier as the time draws near, and lavish all their care to fill out with firm fat him whom they have chosen leader and named bridegroom of the herd; and mow flowering grass and supply river-water and corn, lest he fail of mastery in the delicious toil, and ill-fed fathers have their record in weakling sons. The brood mares moreover they purposely starve into leanness, and when the foreknown pleasure stirs them first to union, deny them the boughs and fence them from the fountain, and often shake them with galloping and tire them in the sun, while the threshing-floor groans daily under the corn-flail, and while the empty chaff flutters to the freshening west wind. This they do, that the fruitful field be not dulled for use and the sluggish furrows choked by overabundant ease, but thirstily swallow the seed and hide it deeper within.

Again the care of the sires begins to drop and of the dams to follow in turn. When the breeding mares wander at the months' fulfilment, let no one allow them to draw heavy wagon-yokes, nor clear the road at a leap and dart over the meadows in violent speed or swim in rushing rivers. On clear lawns they feed them and beside brimming streams, where moss grows and the grass is greenest on the bank, by sheltering caves and jutting shadow of cliffs. About the groves of Silarus and Alburnus evergreen with ilex there swarms a fly whose Roman name is asilus, oestrus the Greeks render it in their speech, fierce, shrill of note, that scatters whole herds distracted through the forest: their bellowings madden the shaken air and the woods and the parched Tanager's bank. With this plague Juno of old wreaked the terrors of her wrath and counselled woe on the heifer-daughter of Inachus: this likewise, for it attacks more fiercely in the burning noons, thou shalt ward off from the breeding flock, and pasture thy herds when the sun is newly risen or the stars usher in the night.

After birth all the care passes to the calves in turn; and immediately they brand the name and mark of race on such as they choose to rear for stock-breeding, or to keep sacred for the altar, or to cleave the soil and upturn the broken clods of the ridgy meadow. The rest of the herd are at pasture on the grassy green; such as thou wilt shape to pursuit and profit of husbandry, instruct while yet ungrown, and set on the road of training while their minds are light in youth and their age flexible. And first tie round their shoulders loose rings of light osier: next, when the free neck is grown used to bondage, yoke matched bullocks in pairs by these same collars, and make them keep step each with each; and now let empty carts be often drawn by them along the ground and score a light track on the dust: thereafter may the beechen axle creak to the strain of a weighty load, and the brazen shaft pull the harnessed wheels. Meanwhile for their unbroken youth thou shalt cut not grass alone nor thin willow-leaves and marsh sedge, but the corn sown by thine hand; nor shall the mother cows after ancient use fill the snowy milking-pails, but spend all their udders on their darling children.

But if thy desire be rather towards wars and fiery squadrons, or to roll charioted by Pisa's Alphean streams and urge the flying team in the grove of Jupiter, the charger's first task is to look on warriors in pride of arms and endure the bugle note, and stand the scream of the dragging wheel and hear the rattle of harness in the stall; then more and more to rejoice in a kind word of praise from the trainer and love the sound when his neck is patted. And venturing this even when just weaned from his mother, again in turn let him yield his mouth to the soft halter, while weak and yet unsteady and yet ignorant in youth. But when three summers are past and the fourth is added, presently he may begin to pace the ring and mark time with clattering footfall, and bend his legs in alternating curves, and take the look of work; then, then let him race against the gale, and flying over open spaces, as though free from the rein, hardly lay his foot-prints on the soil's surface: even as, when the gathered North wind swoops down from Hyberborean borders and scatters the wintry and waterless clouds of Scythia, the deep cornfields and floating plains shiver in light gusts, and the forest tops utter a cry and the long waves race to the beach; he wings his way, sweeping field and flood in his level flight. Hence shall he either sweat towards Elean goals over long spaces of the course with mouth spurting bloody foam, or his supple neck better bear on the Belgic car. Then at last when now they are broken, let their body fill out with coarse mash; for before breaking their pride will swell high, and they will refuse when taken in hand to endure the tough lash and obey the cruel curb.

But no diligence more confirms their strength than to keep love and the stings of blind passion aloof, whether profit of oxen or of horses be more to our mind. And therefore they banish the bull far into lonely pasturage, behind a mountain barrier and across broad streams, or keep him shut indoors by the rich farmyard; for the female gradually wastes his strength and consumes him in gazing and allows him not to remember woodland or meadow; yes and often her sweet allurements drive her proud lovers to let their horns decide the rivalry. On broad Sila gazes the shapely heifer: they join in violent battle and alternate the frequent wound; dark blood bathes their bodies and their crashing horns strain in confronting pressure, while forest and far-stretching sky echo back. Nor will the warriors herd together; but the conquered retires, and keeps exile afar in strange regions, making many a moan over his disgrace and the haughty conqueror's blows and his love's loss unavenged; and gazing on the stall he quits his ancestral realm. Therefore with all diligence he trains his strength and lies tireless on an unstrewn couch among flinty rocks, feeding on prickly leaves and sharp rushes; and tries himself, and learns to throw his rage into his horns by butting at a tree trunk, and buffets the winds with blows, and scatters the sand in rehearsal of battle. Thereafter, in gathered might and strength renewed, he advances his standard and rushes headlong on his forgetful foe: as a billow beginning to whiten in mid ocean gathers a lengthening curve from the deep, and as rolling landward it thunders over the rocks and falls in very mountain mass, while the wave boils up eddying from the bottom and hurls the black shingle high up the beach.

Yes all on earth, the race of man and beast, the tribes of the sea, cattle and coloured birds break into fury and fire; in all love is the same. At none other season does the lioness forgetful of her whelps range fiercer on the plains, nor the clumsy bear deal so many a death and such widespread devastation through the forests. Then the wild boar is fierce, then the tigress most fell: ah, ill is it then to stray in the solitary Libyan land! Seest thou not the shudder that thrills the whole body of the horse, if only the familiar scent is wafted on the gale? and now neither reins nor cruel whips of men, not cliffs or caverned rocks delay him, nor barring rivers that unseat and whirl away mountains with their wave. The great Sabellian boar charges with whetted tusks, tramples the earth before him and chafes his flanks on a tree, and on this side and that hardens his shoulders against wounds. What of the youth, through whose frame unrelenting love darts his mastering fire? late in the blind night he swims the straits vexed by stormy gusts, and over him thunders the mighty gate of heaven, and the seas dash echoing on the crags; nor can his wretched parents call him back, nor the maiden left with cruel death for her doom. What of Bacchus' dappled lynxes, and the fierce tribe of wolves and hounds? what of the battles fought by unwarlike deer? Doubtless before all the madness of mares is eminent, and Venus' very self inspired them on the day when that Potnian chariot-team champed the limbs of Glaucus in their jaws. Across Gargarus and across the roaring Ascanius love leads them; they scale the mountain and swim the river. And all at once when their inward longing kindles into flame, (in spring the rather, since in spring their vital heat returns,) they all wheel and stand facing the West on rocky heights, and snuff the light breezes, and often without bodily union, wind-impregned, wonderful to tell, over crag and cliff and deep-sunken vale they scatter in flight not to thy springs, O East, nor to the rising of the sun, but towards the north and northwest winds, or whence the South issues wrapped in gloom and saddens heaven with his chilly rains. Then that clammy fluid, rightly named hippomanes in shepherds' language, oozes from their groin: the hippomanes that wicked stepmothers often gather, and mingle with herbs and baleful spells.

But time fleets meanwhile, fleets beyond recovery, while in loving enthralment we pass on and on. Enough now of cattle: half of our charge is left, the herding of fleecy flocks and rough she-goats. Here is work; hence look for praise, sturdy tillers of the soil. Nor am I of doubtful mind how hard it is to win all this in words, and crown things so slight with honour. But in fond desire I am rapt over Parnassus' lonely steeps, fain to pass along the hill where the trace of no earlier wheel winds down the soft slope to Castaly.

Now, august Pales, now must sound an ampler tone. In the beginning I ordain that sheep crop their fodder in the soft pens while leafy summer lingers on his return, and that the hard ground be strewn beneath them with abundant straw and trusses of fern, lest chill frost hurt the tender flock, and bring mange or rotting feet. Thence I pass on and order for the goats store of arbute-sprays and supply of fresh river-water, and wind-sheltered pens turned to the mid-day and facing the winter sun, even when chill Aquarius is now setting shower-ful upon the verge of the dying year. Them too must we guard with no lighter carefulness: nor will the profit be less, how great a price soever be exchanged for Milesian fleeces steeped in Tyrian crimsons: from them is a more numerous breed, from them wealth of abundant milk; the fuller the pails have foamed from their drained udders, the richer will drip the stream when the teats are squeezed anew. And no less withal men shear the beards and silvered chins of the Cinyphian he-goat, and his hairy bristles, for service of the camp and sail-cloth for hapless seafarers. Their pasture indeed is on Lycaean wood and hill-top, rough briars and brushwood clinging to the steep; and unherded they return heedfully home, leading their young, and hardly lift their heavy udders through the doorway. Therefore with all diligence, as their need of human care is the less, wilt thou guard them from frost and snowy winds, and cheerfully deal them sustenance and fodder of boughs, and keep thine hay-lofts unlocked all mid-winter. But indeed when western breezes call, and glad summer sends forth either flock into lawn and mead, with the glimmer of the morning star let us haste to the chilly countryside while morning is fresh and the grass frosty-white, and the dew on the tender herbage sweetest to the cattle. Thereafter, when the fourth hour in heaven has gathered thirst and the note of the shrill tree-crickets pierces the copses, by wells or by deep pools I will bid the flocks drink the wave that runs in troughs of ilex; but in the noonday heats seek some shady dell, where Jove's great oak, massy and old, stretches his giant boughs, or where, dark with many an ilex, broods the sacred shadow of the grove: then once more offer them the thin runlets and feed them once more about set of sun, when cool evening allays the air and now the dewy moonlight revives the lawns, and the kingfisher is loud on the shore and the warbler in the thickets.

Why pursue to thee in verse the shepherds of Libya, why their pastures and the scattered roofs of the huts that are their home? Often daylong and nightlong and the whole month unbroken the flock goes grazing for lonely leagues without a dwelling; so wide stretches the plain. The African herdsman carries with him all his wealth, his house and household god, his weapons and Amyclaean dog and Cretan quiver; even as the valiant Roman in his ancestral arms, when he speeds his march beneath a cruel burden, and the column halts and the camp is pitched beside the surprised foe.

But not so where the tribes of Scythia border the Maeotic wave and the yellow Danube rolls thick with sand, or where outstretched Rhodope runs back under the mid pole. There they keep their herds shut in stall, and no grass shows on the plain or leaf on the tree; but earth lies featureless in mounded snow and deep fields of ice that rise to seven fathoms, under eternal winter and eternal breath of icy north-west winds. Nor ever does the sun pierce that pallid gloom, neither when he rides his horses up the steep of sky nor when he slakes his headlong chariot in Ocean's ruddy floor. Sudden ice-flakes gather on the running stream, and even now the water bears iron-tired wheels on its back, and gives broad wagons the harbourage it gave to ships before. Brass vessels burst continually, and clothes stiffen on the body, and liquid wine is cut with hatchets; whole pools turn into solid ice, and the rough icicle congeals on the shaggy beard. Meanwhile all the air is a single drift of snow: the cattle die, the broad-backed oxen stand in a frosty shroud, and the deer huddle in troops, benumbed by the fresh masses that their antler tips barely outreach. On them men slip not the hounds, hunt them not with any nets or the terror of crimson-feathered toils; but while they vainly push against the breasting hill, slay them steel in hand and cut them down deep-braying and with merry clamour carry them home. Themselves in caverns deep sunken under earth they fleet their careless leisure, and roll to the hearth oak from the wood-pile and whole elms to feed the fire. Here they pass the night in games, and with beer and bitter meaths joyously counterfeit draughts of the vine. Such is the wild race of men that lies under the seven stars of the utmost North, buffeted by Rhipaean gales and wrapped in the tawny fur of beasts.

If wool-growing be thy care, first keep far from brushwood, from bur and briar; shun rank pasturage; and choose from the beginning a white and soft-fleeced flock. The ram moreover, be he else silvery as may be, if only his tongue is black under the moist palate, reject thou, or he will darken the lamb's fleeces with dusky spots, and choose another from the flock that fills the meadow. With such snowy wool for dower, if belief be deigned, Pan the god of Arcady ensnared thee, O

Moon, in his treachery, when he called thee into the depth of woodland and thou didst not scorn his call.

But whoso sets his heart on milk, let him with his own hand carry store of lucerne and lotus, and salted grass to the pens: so they desire water the more, and the more swell their udders, and give back in the milk an undertaste of salt. Many too take the new-born kids from their mothers, and fix iron-spiked muzzles on their baby mouths. What they milk at dayspring or in the daylight hours, they let curdle at night; what at gathering dusk and with the setting sun, they pack off in frails at dawn and the shepherd trudges to the town; or sprinkle it sparingly with salt and store it up for winter.

Neither be the care of thy dogs the last-deferred; but feed together on fattening whey the puppies of the fleet Spartan and the keen Molossian: never in their guard shalt thou dread thief by night in thy pens or inroad of wolves or restless Iberians behind thee; often likewise wilt thou urge the chase of the shy wild ass, and course hare or fallow deer with thy hounds, often rout the boar startled with their baying from his woodland wallowing-pool, and high among the hills drive the lordly stag with shouts into thy nets.

Learn also to burn scented cedar in the stalls, and clear out noisome scaled snakes with fumes of gum. Often under sheds long unmoved the dangerous viper lurks and shrinks fearfully out of the daylight; or that sore plague of oxen, wont to glide under the shadow of the roof and dart his venom at the flock, the snake lodges in the ground. Snatch up sticks and stones, O shepherd, and as he rises threatening and puffs out his hissing throat, strike him down! and now he hides his head deep in fearful flight, while his coiling body and the last folds of his tail unwind, and he slowly trails the utmost curve of his rings. Likewise there is that malign serpent of Calabrian lawns that rolls along with uplifted breast, scaly-backed and marked with large spots down the length of his belly; who while streams yet gush from their fountain-heads, and while earth is wet with moist spring and southern rains, lives in ponds and housing on river banks, there greedily fills his black gorge with fish and chattering frogs; after the marsh is burnt up and the earth cracks in the blazing sun, he darts out over the dry land and rages in the fields, rolling his fiery eyes, exasperate in thirst and frantic with heat. May I not then be tempted to take soft sleep beneath the sky, or lie along the grass on the forest ridge, when fresh from his cast slough and glittering in youth he glides forth stately in the sunlight, leaving his young or his eggs at home, and his mouth flickers with triple-forked tongue.

Likewise will I instruct thee of diseases in their sources and signs. Rotting mange attacks sheep when icy rains and the hoar frost of rough mid-winter sink deep in their live flesh, or when, after shearing, the sweat clots unwashed and tangled brairs cut their body. Therefore the keepers bathe all the flock in fresh running water, and the ram is plunged in the pool and sent floating down stream with drenched fleece: or they smear the shorn bodies with bitter olive-lees, and mingle scum of silver and virgin sulphur, pitch of Ida and wax ointment, and squills and strong-smelling hellebore and black asphalt. Yet no device helps the trouble more, than when one can cut away the festering surface with steel; the sore is fed into life by concealment while the shepherd refuses to lay healing hands to the wound and sits idly praying to his gods for better fortune. Nay, and when raging pains run deep in the bleating people and parching fever preys on their limbs, it is found of service to allay the burning heat and strike a vein where it throbs with blood between the hoofs: as is the wonted manner of Bisaltae, or of the fierce Gelonian in retreat to Rhodope and Getan solitudes, whose drink is milk curdled with blood of mares. If from far thou seest one passing oftener into the languid shade, or more listlessly cropping the tops of grass and following behind the rest, or lying down in midpasture of the meadow and retiring alone before deepening night, straightway check the evil with thy knife ere the terrible infection spread through the heedless multitude. Not so heavy comes the rush of rain when a squall sweeps over the sea as diseases multiply in the flock: neither do ailments seize them singly, but whole summer-pastures at a stroke, the flock and the flock's hope together, and all the race root and branch; as any may know who sees even now so long afterward, by soaring Alps and Noric hill-forts and fields of Iapydian Timavus, the deserted pastoral realm and far-stretching lawns left desolate.

Here once the air sickened and a woful season came, that kindling with the gathered heat of autumn dealt death on all the tribes of cattle and wild beasts, and poisoned the rotting pools and putrid fodder. Nor was the march of death straightforward: but when fiery thirst coursing in all the veins had shrunk the aching limbs, again the watery humours flooded out and all the bones dissolving under the disease melted into them piecemeal. Often amid divine sacrifice the victim standing by the altar, while the snowy-ribboned fillet of wool was being twined about it, fell dying among the tardy ministrants. Or had the priestly steel slain in time, no flame rises from those filaments when laid upon the altar, nor can the soothsayer return counsel or reply: hardly is the knife at the throat stained by the blood or the sand's surface darkened by the thin gore. Next calves lie dying all over the luxuriant grass, and yield up their sweet life by the full manger: next madness comes on the kindly dogs, and a hard rattling cough and choking swelling of the throat on the sickened swine. Joyless in his exercises and heedless of the grass the victor steed pines, and turns away from the fountain, and beats the earth with impatient foot: his ears droop, and by them sweat comes and goes, and that cold and betokening death: his skin is dry and hard when stroked, and resists the touch. Such are the signs that for the first days foreshadow the end; but as the sickness begins to advance and gather violence, then indeed their eyes burn and their breath is fetched deep, heavy with broken moans, their flanks below heave with long-drawn sobs, black blood oozes from their nostrils, and their throat is blocked by their rough and swollen tongue. It helped to thrust in a horn and pour down it juice of the winepress; that seemed the one restorative for the dying: in short space the very cure was fatal; reviving they maddened in fever, and even in mortal weakness (the gods send better things to the righteous and that bewilderment on our foes!) they tore and mangled their own limbs with naked teeth. And lo, smoking under the iron share the bull drops down, spurts from his mouth mingled blood and foam, and heaves a last groan: sadly the ploughman advancing unyokes the bullock mourning his brother's death and leaves the plough stuck fast in mid-furrow. Not shades of stately groves, not soft meadows can stir his sense, not the river that curls brighter than amber over his rocks to seek the plain; but his deep flanks relax, his dull eyes are weighed down in stupor, and his neck sinks drooping heavily to earth. What avails his toil or services? what that his ploughshare has upturned the ponderous clods? And yet no Massic bounty of the vine, no crowding banquets have done harm to these; they feed on leaves and simple pasture of grass, their cups are clear springs and racing rivers, nor does care break their healthful sleep. Then as never before they say that in that countryside oxen were to seek for Juno's rites, and chariots were drawn by ill-matched buffaloes to the high votive shrines. Therefore they wearily furrow earth with mattocks, and cover in the seed-corn with their own nails, and with straining necks drag their creaking wagons over the hill heights. No more does the wolf prowl in ambush round the sheepfolds nor pace nightlong nigh the flocks; a fiercer care makes him tame. Shy fallow deer and timid stags now stray among the dogs and about the houses. Nay the brood of the infinite sea and all the tribe of swimming creatures lie on the verge of the strand like shipwrecked corpses in the wash of the wave, and seals take unwonted refuge in the river: and in the vain defence of her winding recesses the viper perishes, and the snake with scales stiffened in dismay: to the very birds the air is cruel, and they drop, leaving their life high under the clouds. Furthermore, no change of food is now aught of avail, and arts are sought but for harm; Chiron son of Phillyra and Amythaonian Melampus give up their mastery. Loosed into daylight from Stygian gloom wan Tisiphone maddens, and drives plague and panic before her, and day by day towers insatiate with higher uplifted head; river and parched bank and couchant hill echo with incessant lowings and bleating of flocks. And now she deals destruction in battalions, and heaps the very folds with carcases rotting in foul decay, till men learn to cover them with earth and hide them out of sight in pits. For neither might the hides be used nor can any one dissolve or consume the flesh in water or flame: not even can they shear the fleeces, eaten through by corruption of the pestilence, nor set hand to the rotten web: nay, even if any had braved so abhorred a garment burning pustules and foul-smelling sweat overran his limbs, and in no long space of delay thereafter the fatal fire devoured his infected frame.

BOOK FOURTH

NEXT will I advance to heaven-born honey, the gift of air, (let this likewise, Maecenas, share thy regard,) and tell thee of the wondrous show of a tiny state, of high-hearted princes, and a whole nation's ordered works and ways, tribes and battles. Slight is the field of labour; but not slight the glory, if but thwarting deities allow, and Apollo listen to prayer.

First of all a home must be sought for bees, and a post where neither winds may have entry—for winds hinder them carrying their forage home—nor sheep and butting kids tread down the flowers, or the straying heifer brush the dew from the meadow and trample the springing grass. Likewise let the bright scale-backed lizard be far from their rich folds, and the birds that come with the bee-eater, and the swallow, her breast marked with those blood-stained hands: for they spread universal havoc, and carry off the bees on the wing, dainty morsels for their fierce nestlings. But let clear springs be nigh, and ponds green with moss, and a thread of rill fleeting through the grass; and let a palm or tall wild-olive overshadow the entrance, that when the new kings shall lead forth their earliest swarms in the sweet springtime, and the young brood disport unprisoned from the comb, the bordering bank may woo them to cool retreat, and the tree meet and stay them in her leafy shelter. Amid the water, whether it stagnate or run, cast large stones and willow-boughs crosswise, that they may have many a bridge to stand on and spread their wings to the summer sun if haply a shower overtake them or a gust of wind plunge them in the watery realm. All round green casia and far-fragrant wild thyme and wealth of heavy-scented savory should bloom, and violet beds drink the channelled spring. Let thy hives moreover, whether they be stitched of hollow bark or woven from pliant osier, have narrow doorways; for the honey freezes in winter cold, and again melts and wastes in the heat. Extreme of either the bees dread alike; nor in vain do they eagerly plaster with wax the draughty chinks in the roof and stop up the rims with pollen of flowers, and for this very service gather and store their gum, stickier than bird-lime or pitch from Phrygian Ida. Often likewise, if the tale is true, they keep house in recesses scooped out underground, or are found deep in hollow sandstone or the cavern of a mouldering tree. Yet do thou smear smooth clay warmly round about their creviced chambers, and spread on the top a thin coat of leaves. Neither suffer the yew too near their house, neither burn crab-shells to redness in the fire, neither trust them where a marsh is deep or by a strong smell of mire, or where encircling rocks echo to a stroke and fling back the phantom of a call.

For the rest, when the golden sun has driven winter routed underground and flung wide the sky in summer light, forthwith they range over lawn and wood, and harvest the shining blossoms and sip lightly of the streams; then glad with some strange delight, they nurture their brood in the nest, then deftly forge the fresh wax and mould the clammy honey. Then, as looking up thou seest their armies swarming skyward from the hives and floating through the clear summer air, and wonderest at their dim cloud trailing in the wind, mark! ever they steer for sweet water and leafy shelter. Here sprinkle the odours ordained, crushed balm and lowly tufts of honeywort, and make a tinkling round about and clash the cymbals of our Lady; themselves will settle on the scented seat, themselves in their wonted way creep into the inmost covert of their nest.

But further, if they are gone forth to battle—for often high swelling discord rises between two kings, and at once and afar thou mayest foreknow the raging of the multitude and the hearts beating fast for war; for a note as of the hoarse brass of our Mars chides the lingerers and a cry is heard that mimics broken trumpet-blasts:—then they muster hurriedly together with vibrating wings, and whet their stings on their beaks and brace their arms, and crowd in mingled mass round their king and close up to the royal tent, and with loud cries challenge the enemy. So when they find the spring sky rainless and their field open, they sally from the gates; high in air the armies clash and the din swells; gathering they cluster in a great ball and come tumbling down, thick as hailstones through the air or the rain of acorns from the shaken ilex. The monarchs move splendid-winged amid the ranks, and mighty passions stir in their tiny breasts, stubborn to the last not to retreat, till weight of the conqueror forces these or those to turn backward in flying rout. These stormy passions and these mighty conflicts will be lulled to rest by a handful of scattered dust.

But when thou hast recalled both leaders from the battle-field, do to death him who seems inferior, that he be not a waste and harm; let the better reign in a clear court. One will be ablaze with spots of embossed gold; for there are two kinds, this the better, fair of feature and splendid in flashing scales; the other, rough-coated and sluggish, crawls meanly with his breadth of belly. As the two kings in aspect so are their subjects shapen; for some are rough and dirty, even as a traveller when he issues from deep dust and spits from his mouth the gritty soil, all athirst; others shine and sparkle in splendour, and their bodies blaze with evenly marked drops of gold. These are the choicer breeds; from their combs at the ordained season of the skies thou shalt squeeze sweet honey, and yet less sweet than crystal-clear, to soften the harsh taste of wine.

But when the swarms fly aimlessly at play in the sky, and despise their combs and leave their house to grow cold, thou shalt stop their light-minded and idle game. Nor is it much work to stop; tear off the wings of the kings; while they linger, not a bee will dare to set out on their aëry way or move standard from the camp. Let garden plots woo them with fragrance of their yellow flowers, and the watchman of thieves and birds, Hellespontic Priapus, keep them in guard with his hook of willow. Himself should the keeper of such plant about their houses broad belts of thyme and laurels brought from the hill heights; himself wear his hand hard with work, himself bed the soil with fruitful shoots and water them with kindly showers.

And truly, but that already nearing my task's final limit I furl my sails and hasten to turn my prow to land, perchance I might also sing of the care and keeping that deck the rich garden mould, and of the Paestan rosebeds with their double blossoming, and how the endive rejoices in drinking the rill and the banks are green with parsley, and how the curved gourd swells bellying along the grass, nor had kept silence of the late-flowering narcissus or the shoot of the curled acanthus and pale ivy-sprays and the myrtles that love the shore. For I remember how beneath the towered fortress of Oebalia, where dark Galaesus moistens his golden cornfields, I saw an old man of Corycus, who owned some few acres of waste land, a field neither rich for grazing nor favourable to the flock nor apt for the vineyard; yet he, setting thinly sown garden-stuff among the brushwood, with borders of white lilies and vervain and the seeded poppy, equalled in his content the wealth of kings; and returning home when night was late, would heap his table with unbought dainties. The first roses of spring, the first apples of autumn he would gather; and when even yet the frost of bitter winter cleft the rocks and laid an icy curb on the running waters, already he plucked the soft-tressed hyacinth, chiding the late-lingering summer and the west wind's delay. So likewise was he the first for whom the bees' brood overflowed in swarming multitudes, and the frothing honey drained from the squeezed combs; lime trees were his, and wealth of pine; and as many apples as had arrayed his orchard-tree in the fresh blossom, so many it carried ripe at autumn. He too transplanted into rows full-grown elms and the hard-wood pear, and the blackthorn with sloes already upon it, and the plane already yielding shade to the drinker. But this for my part, debarred by jealous limits, I pass by and leave to be told by others after me.

Now come, I will set forth the gifts wherewith Jove himself

has dowered bees at birth, their wages when, following the musical cries and tinkling brasses of the Curetes, they fed the king of heaven in that low cave of Crete. Alone they have community of children and shelter of a confederate city, and spend their life under majesty of law; alone they know a native country and established gods of the household, and, mindful of winter's coming, they ply their summer task and lay up their gatherings in a common store. For some are diligent to provide food, and labour in the fields by ordinance of the league; others within their fortified houses lay the combs' first foundations with tear of narcissus and sticky resin of bark, and hang thereon the clinging waxen walls: some guide forth the grown brood, their nation's hope; others press down the pure virgin honey and brim the cells with liquid sweets. To certain of them falls the lot of guard at the gates, and in turn they keep watch on showers and cloudy skies, or take the loads of the incomers, or in ranked array keep the drones, that idle gang, aloof from the folds: the work is all aswarm, and fragrance breathes from the thyme-scented honey. And even as when the Cyclopean forgers of the thunder hurry on the ductile ore, some make the wind come and go in bellows of bull-hide, some dip the hissing brass in the trough; Etna groans under their anvils' pressure, as alternating they lift their arms mightily in time, and turn the iron about in the grip of their tongs: even so, if small things may be compared with great, are our Attic bees urged on each in her proper duty by inborn love of possession. The aged have the town in charge, and the walling of the combs and the shaping of the curious chambers; but the younger return weary when night grows late, their thighs laden with thyme, and pasture all abroad on arbutus and grey willow, on casia and the crimsoned crocus, and the rich lime-blossom and the rust-red hyacinth. For all is one rest from toil, work-time for all is one. With morning they stream out of their gates; nowhere a lingerer; alike again, when evening warns them at last to quit their meadow pasture, then they seek their home, then they refresh their bodies; murmuring, they hum around the edges of the doorway. Thereafter, when now they are quiet in their cells, silence deepens with night, and kindly slumber overspreads their tired limbs. Nor indeed when rain threatens do they withdraw very far from their folds, or trust the sky when east winds are on their way; but fetch water in shelter close round their city walls, and essay short sallies, and often lift pebbles, as boats take in ballast when they rock in the tossing surge, and poise themselves so among the bodiless clouds.

This custom approved of bees may truly waken thy wonder, that they neither delight in bodily union, nor melt away in languor of love, or bear their young by birth-throes; but straight from the leaves, from the scented herbage gather their children in their mouths, themselves keep up the succession of king and tiny citizens, and fashion anew their halls and waxen realm. Often moreover in wandering they crush their wings against flinty rocks and freely yield their life beneath the burden; such is their love of flowers and their pride in honey-making. Therefore although their own life be brief and soon taken to its rest—since to the seventh summer it lasts and no further—yet the race abides immortal, and through many years the Fortune of their house stands, and their ancestors are counted to the third and fourth generation.

Furthermore not Egypt and mighty Lydia, not the Parthian peoples or the Mede by Hydaspes so adore their king. Their king safe, all are of one mind; he lost, they break allegiance, plunder the honey-cells themselves have built, and break open the plaited combs. He is guardian of their labours; him they regard, and all gather round in murmuring throng and encompass him in their swarms; and often lift him on their shoulders and shield him in war with their bodies, and seek through wounds a glorious death.

Noting this and led by these instances, certain have claimed for bees a share of some divine intelligence and a draught of the springs of heaven. For God, they say, extends through all lands and spaces of sea and depths of sky; from him flocks and herds and men and all the race of wild creatures, each at birth, draw the slender stream of life; to him thereafter all things as surely return, and are dissolved into him again; nor is there place for death; but living they flit to their starry mansions and rise to a heaven above.

If ever thou wilt unseal their imperial dwellings and the stored honey in their treasuries, first sprinkle thyself and wash thy mouth with a draught of water and hold forth searching smoke in thine hand. Twice men gather the heavy foison in two seasons of harvest: so soon as Taygete the Pleiad shows forth her august face upon the world, and spurns with her foot the recoiling ocean streams; or again when retreating before the star of the rainy Fish she sinks from a glooming sky into the wintry waves. They are furious beyond measure, and when attacked breathe venom in their bite and fastening on the veins leave their buried stings behind and lay down their lives in the wound. But if dreading a hard winter thou wilt spare future provision and compassionate their broken spirit and shattered estate, yet to fumigate with thyme and cut away the empty cells who could hesitate? for often unnoticed the eft nibbles at the combs, and beetles build their nests and hide out of the light, and the drone, sitting idle at another's board, or the fierce hornet joins battle with overpowering arms, or moths, an ill-omened tribe, or the spider hated of Minerva spreads her loose web in the doorway. The lower they are brought, the more eagerly will all press on to repair the ruin of their fallen race, and will fill their galleries and build their woven granaries of blossoms.

If indeed, since to bees also life brings such mischances as ours, they droop under sore bodily ailment;—and this thou wilt readily know by no uncertain signs: straightway their colour changes in sickness; they lose their looks and grow thin and haggard, and carry out of doors the bodies of their dead and lead the gloomy funeral train; and either hang clutching by their feet at the doorway, or shut their house and idle within, spiritless with hunger and benumbed by a cramping chill. Then a deeper hum is heard, and they murmur in long-drawn tone, like the cold south wind sighing in the forest, like the hissing waves of a restless ebbing sea, like the fierce fire roaring behind the furnace doors. Hereat I will counsel thee to burn scented gum and drip honey in through pipes of reed, calling with uninvited urgency the tired creatures to their familiar food. It will be well to mingle withal juice of pounded galls, and dry rose leaves, or wine boiled thick over a strong fire, or raisin-clusters from the Psithian vine, and Attic thyme and strong-smelling centaury. Likewise there is a meadow-flower named amellus by husbandmen, a plant easily found by the seeker, for it lifts from a single stalk a dense growth of shoots; golden the flower, but the petals that cluster thickly round it are dark violet shot with crimson; often the gods' altars are decked with its woven wreaths; it tastes bitter in the mouth; shepherds gather it in the cropped valley grass and beside the winding streams of Mella. Boil the roots of this in fragrant wine and set it in basketfuls for food by the doorway.

But for one whom the whole breed shall fail of a sudden, and he have nothing left to renew the race in a fresh family, it is time to unfold further the famed invention of the Arcadian keeper, and in what wise often ere now bees have been born from the putrefying blood of a slain bullock. More fully will I discover all the tale and trace it from its earliest source. For where the favoured race of Macedonian Canopus dwell by the still broad overflow of Nile and ride round their own farms in painted boats, and where the quivered Persian land presses nigh and the rushing river that pours straight down from the swarthy Indians parts into seven separate mouths and enriches green Egypt with its dark sand, all the realm builds on this art a certain remedy. First a small room is chosen, straitened down just to serve for this; they confine it by a narrow tiled roof and cramped walls, and towards the four winds add four windows with slanting lights. Then is sought a calf of two years old with horns already curving from his forehead; his double nostrils and breathing mouth are stopped up, spite of all his struggling, and he is beaten to death and the flesh pounded to pulp through the unbroken skin. Thus they leave him shut close, laying under his sides broken boughs and thyme, and fresh sprays of casia. This is done when west winds first ruffle the waters, ere yet the meadows flush with fresh colours, ere yet the chattering swallow hang her nest from the rafters. Meanwhile the humours heat and ferment in the soft bones, and creatures wonderfully fashioned may be seen, at first limbless, but soon they stir with rustling wings, and more and more drink in the delicate air: until like a shower bursting from summer clouds they swarm forth, or like arrows from the quivering bowstring when light Parthian skirmishers advance to battle.

Who, O Muses, who wrought for us this miraculous art? Whence did this strange experience enter the paths of men?

The shepherd Aristaeus fled from Peneian Tempe, his bees lost, they say, by sickness and scarcity, and stood sad by the holy spring of the river-head, and with many a complaint called thus upon her who bore him. Mother, Cyrene mother, who dwellest here deep beneath the flood, why hast thou borne me in the gods' illustrious line—if indeed my father is he whom thou sayest, Apollo of Thymbra—to be the scorn of doom? or whither is thy love for me swept away? why didst thou bid me aspire to heaven? Lo, even this mere pride of my mortal life, so hardly wrought out by infinite endeavour in skilful tendance of harvest and flock, this, and thou art my mother, I see depart. Nay come, and with thine own hand uproot my fruitful orchards, carry destroying fire into the folds and kill the harvests, wither the cornfields and wield the strong axe upon the vines, if thou art grown so weary of my praise.

But from her chamber in the river depth the mother heard his cry. Around her the Nymphs carded Milesian fleeces stained with rich sea-dyes, Drymo and Xantho, Ligea and Phyllodoce, their bright tresses falling loose over their snowy necks; and Cydippe and golden-haired Lycorias, the one a maiden, the other even then knowing the first throes of travail; and Clio and Beroë her sister, both daughters of Ocean, both decked with gold, both girt with dappled skins; and Ephyre and Opis and Asian Deïopea, and fleet Arethusa, her arrows at last laid by. And among them Clymene was telling of Vulcan's fruitless care, and the wiles of Mars and the stolen sweetness, and recounting from Chaos downward the myriad loves of the gods. And while amid the witchery of her song the soft spun wool curls off their distaffs, again Aristaeus' lament thrilled his mother's ears, and all were motionless on their crystal chairs; but before the rest of the sisterhood Arethusa glanced forth, lifting her golden head above the wave, and cried from afar: O not vainly startled by so heavy a moan, Cyrene sister, he thine own, thy chiefest care, mourning Aristaeus stands in tears by Peneus' ancestral wave, and calls thee cruel and names thy name. To her the mother, stricken in soul with fresh alarm, Lead him, quick, lead him to us; he, she cries, may unforbidden tread the threshold of gods. With that she bids the deep streams retire, leaving a broad path for his steps to enter in. But round him the mountain-wave stood curving and clasped him in its mighty fold, and sped him beneath the river. And now marvelling at his mother's home and watery realm, cavern-locked pools and roaring forests, he passed on, and, stunned by the vast whirl of waters, gazed on all the great floods of distant regions rolling under earth, Phasis and Lycus, and the spring head whence breaks forth high Enipeus' source, whence the lord of Tiber and whence the streams of Anio, and Hypanis roaring over his rocks, and Mysian Caïcus and, with the twin gilded horns on his bull's forehead, Eridanus, than whom no other river flows fiercer out through his rich tilth into the shining sea. After they entered the chamber with its hanging roof of rock, and Cyrene heard her son's idle tale of tears, her sisters duly pour clear spring-water on his hands and bring towels with close-cut fleece: others pile the banquet on the board and array the brimming cups; flame of Panchaean spice swells from the altars, and his mother cries, Take up a flagon of Maeonian wine; let us pour libation to Oceanus. Herself therewithal offers prayer to Oceanus father of all things and to the

Nymphs' sisterhood who have an hundred forests, an hundred floods in their keeping: thrice she pours clear nectar over the blazing altar-fire, thrice the flame flared up anew to the crown of the roof. And strengthening his courage by this omen, she thus begins:

In the Carpathian sea-gulf dwells a soothsayer, blue Proteus, whose chariot yoked with fishes and twy-footed coursers spans the mighty ocean plain. He now visits again Emathia's borders and his birthplace of Pallene; to him we Nymphs do worship, and aged Nereus our lord; for he has the seer's knowledge of all things that are or that have been or that draw nigh to their coming: this by grace of Neptune, whose monstrous flocks and ugly seals he herds under the gulf. Him, my son, must thou first enfetter, that he may fully unfold the source of the sickness, and give prosperous issue. For without force he will give counsel in nowise, nor wilt thou bend him by entreaties; with sheer force and fetters must thou tie thy prisoner; around them his wiles at last will break unavailing. Myself will lead thee, when the sun has kindled the heat of noon, when the grass is athirst and the shade now grows more grateful to the flock, to the old man's covert, his retreat from the weary waves, that while he lies asleep thou mayest lightly assail him. But when thou shalt hold him caught and fettered in thine hands, even then the form and visage of manifold wild beasts shall cheat thee; for in a moment he will turn to a bristly boar or a black tiger, a scaly serpent and tawny-necked lioness, or will roar shrill in flame and so slip out of the fetters, or will melt into thin water and be gone. But the more he changes into endless shapes, the more do thou, my son, strain tight the grasp of his fetters, until his body change again into the likeness thou sawest when his eyes drooped and his sleep began.

So says she and sprinkles abroad liquid scent of ambrosia, anointing with it all the body of her son: but his ranged curls breathed a sweet fragrance, and supple strength grew in his limbs. There is a vast cave in the hollowed mountain side, where countless waves are driven before the gale and break among the deep recesses: of old a sure anchorage for mariners caught by storm: within it Proteus takes shelter behind the barrier of a mighty rock. Here the Nymph places her son in hiding away from the light, and herself stands apart dim in a mist. Now fierce Sirius blazed from the sky, scorching the thirsty Indian, and the fiery sun had swept to his mid arch: the grass was parched, and in hollow river-beds, dry-mouthed, the heated mud baked in his rays; when Proteus advanced from the waves to seek his familiar cavern; around him the wet tribes of the mighty deep gambolling splashed wide the briny spray. His seals stretch themselves asleep here and there along the shore; he, as some guardian of a hill-fold when evening leads the calves homeward from pasture and the wolves rouse as they hear the bleating of the lambs, takes his seat on a rock among them and tells their tale. And upon him Aristaeus, as his chance offers, hardly allowing the ancient to settle his weary limbs, darts with a loud cry and slips the shackles over him as he lies. He in return, not unmindful of his cunning, transforms himself into things manifold and marvellous, fire and dreadful wild beast and flowing river. But when none of his magic finds him escape, he returns foiled into his own shape and at length speaks with human visage: Ah, who bade thee, most venturous youth, draw nigh our home? or what wouldst thou? he cries. But he: Thou knowest, O Proteus, thyself knowest: nor canst thou at all delude me. But cease to struggle. Following divine commands we are come, to seek here oracular counsel for a worn estate. So far he spoke: thereat the soothsayer at last violently rolled the glassy orbs of his flaming eyes, and gnashing his teeth heavily thus gave voice to fate:

Not save by wrath of deity art thou plagued: great is the crime thou dost expiate. This punishment, less than deserved, wretched Orpheus calls forth upon thee—unless Fate oppose —in mad grief for his wife torn away. She indeed, flying headlong before thee through the river, saw not her death upon her in the deep grass before her girlish feet, where that monstrous snake guarded the bank. But the band of her

Dryad playmates filled the mountain summits with their cries: Rhodopeïan fortresses wept, and Pangaean heights and Rhesus' martial land, Getae and Hebrus, and Actian Orithyia. He, soothing his love-sickness on his hollow shell, sang of thee, O sweet wife, of thee alone on the solitary shore, of thee at dayspring, of thee at the death of day. Even that gorge of Taenarus, the high gateway of Dis, and the grove that glooms in horror of darkness he entered, and drew nigh the ghostly people and their awful king, and the hearts that know not to melt at human supplications. But startled by his song from the deep sunken realm of Erebus thin shadows rose and phantoms of the lost to light, millionfold as birds shelter in the leaves when evenfall or wintry rain drives them from the hill; matrons and men and bodies of high-hearted heroes whose life was done, boys and unwedded girls and young men laid on the pyre before their parents' eyes: whom all round the black slime and ugly reeds of Cocytus and the sluggish wave of the unlovely pool enfetter, and Styx severs with the barrier of her ninefold flood. Nay, the very halls of death and Hell's recesses were amazed, and the Furies with livid serpents twined in their tresses; Cerberus held his triple jaws agape, and Ixion's whirling wheel hung motionless on the wind. And now his returning feet had outsped every peril, and his regained Eurydice was issuing to upper air, following at his back—for thus had Proserpine ordained—when a sudden madness seized the unwary lover, surely to be forgiven, if Death knew forgiveness. He stopped; his own Eurydice was just on the edge of daylight; forgetful, alas! and impassioned he looked round on her. There all his toil was spilt and the treaty broken with that merciless monarch; and thrice a thunder pealed over the pools of Avernus. Who, woe's me! she cries, hath destroyed me, and thee with me, Orpheus? what frenzy is this? Lo, again the cruel fates call me backward, and sleep hides my swimming eyes. And now goodbye: I pass away wrapped in a great darkness, and helplessly stretching towards thee the hands that, alas! are not thine. She spoke and suddenly out of his eyes, like vapour melting in the thin air, fled into the distance, neither saw him more as he vainly grasped at the shadows and fain would say many a word; nor did the gatekeeper of Orcus suffer him again to cross that barring pool. What could he do? or whither turn now his wife was twice torn away? how stir Death with weeping, what deities with his cry? and she even now floated cold in the Stygian bark. Seven whole months unbroken they say he wept alone beneath an aëry rock by Strymon's solitary wave, and poured forth all his tale under the freezing stars, soothing tigresses and moving oaks with song: even as the nightingale mourning under the poplar shade moans her lost brood whom the cruel ploughman has marked and torn unfledged from the nest: but she weeps nightlong, and seated on the bough renews her pitiable song and fills the region round with her mournful complaint. Never did love nor ever a bridal stir his spirit: alone he ranged Hyperborean icefields and snowy Tanaïs and Rhipaean plains that never unloose their frosts, murmuring over his lost Eurydice and the vain gifts of Dis: till slighted by such tribute, Ciconian matrons, amid divine sacrifice and Bacchic revels by night, rent him asunder and scattered him wide over the land. Even then, when torn from the marble neck his head went rolling down the mid-eddies of Oeagrian Hebrus, the very voice and chill tongue cried Eurydice! ah poor Eurydice! as their life ebbed away: Eurydice! the banks re-echoed all down the stream.

Thus Proteus, and sprang with a bound into the sea depths, and where he sprang the wave spun eddying in foam. But not so Cyrene: for she accosted him in words of cheer:

O my son, thou mayest dismiss the care that saddens thy soul. This is all the source of the sickness; this why the Nymphs with whom she wheeled the dance in depth of groves have dealt destruction on thy poor bees. Do thou humbly seek their favour with gifts outstretched, and worship the gracious maidens of the lawn: for to thy prayers they will yield pardon and relent from wrath. But first I will tell thee duly what is the way of supplication. Choose out four noble bulls of stately girth that now graze the heights of green

Lycaeus, and as many heifers whose neck no yoke has touched; for these rear four altars by the lofty shrines of the goddesses and let the devoted blood trickle from their throats, and leave the bodies of the oxen alone in the leafy copse. Thereafter, when the ninth dawn brightens to her birth, thou shalt send Lethean poppies for funeral gifts to Orpheus, and adore appeased Eurydice with a slain heifer-calf, and sacrifice a black ewe and again seek the grove.

Delaying not, forthwith he fulfils his mother's counsels. He comes to the shrines; he bids the ordained altars rise: four noble bulls of stately girth he leads up, and as many heifers whose neck knows not the yoke; thereafter, when the ninth dawn had risen to her birth, he sends funeral gifts to Orpheus and again seeks the grove. Here indeed they descry a portent sudden and strange to tell; bees humming among the dissolving flesh of the carcases and swarming forth from the rent sides of the oxen, and trailing in endless clouds, till now they stream together on the tree-top and hang clustering from the pliant boughs.

Thus I sang of the tending of fields and flocks and trees, while great Caesar hurled war's lightnings by high Euphrates and gave statutes among the nations in welcome supremacy, and scaled the path to heaven. Even in that season I Virgil, nurtured in sweet Parthenope, went in the flowery ways of lowly Quiet: I who once played with shepherd's songs, and in youth's hardihood sang thee, O Tityrus, under the covert of spreading beech.

873
V51m

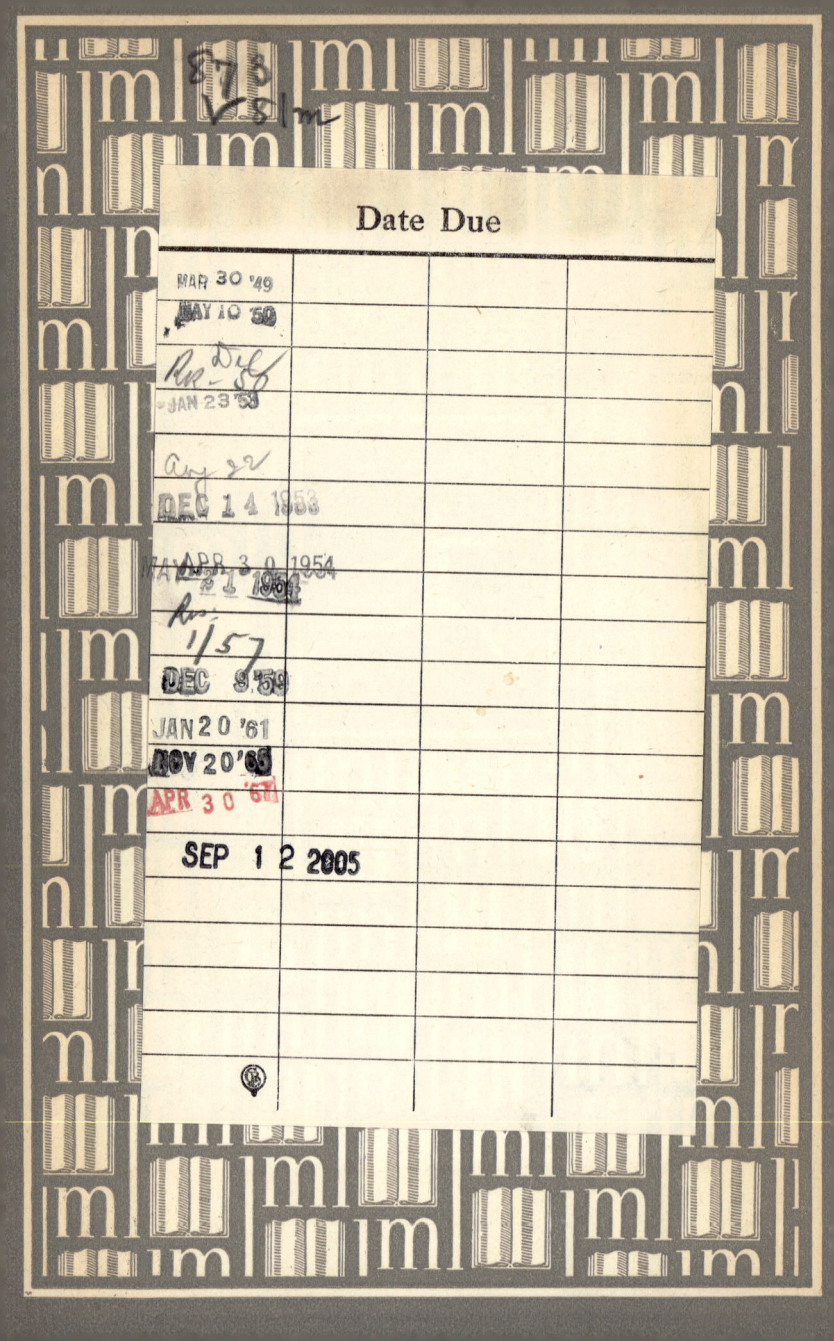

Date Due

MAR 30 '49			
MAY 10 '50			
Ret Def			
JAN 23 '53			
Aug 22			
DEC 14 1953			
APR 30 1954			
#1 1954			
Ret. 1/57			
DEC 9 '59			
JAN 20 '61			
NOV 20 '65			
APR 30 '67			
SEP 1 2 2005			